PLAYING DETECTIVE WITH FAMILY LORE

Plugging the holes in a family history unintentionally tells the saga of Jews in a microcosm

Daniella Weiss Ashkenazy

ISBN: 978-965-7041-16-1 (paperback)
ISBN: 978-965-7041-17-8 (ebook)

Cover design: Avi Katz

Publishing services provided by JewishSelfPublishing. The author acts as the publisher and is solely responsible for the content of this book, which does not necessarily reflect the opinions of JewishSelfPublishing.

www.jewishselfpublishing.com
info@jewishselfpublishing.com
(800) 613-9430

The author can be contacted at daniella@playingdetective.com.
www.playingdetective.com

Contents

Preface

As a professional journalist who spent decades (since 1986) writing news analysis, social and political commentary, major feature stories and personal satire and humor columns, writing a family memoir wasn't even on my radar.

My dad (known to most as Gil, Gibby and at times Gilbert) felt his life was not only filled and fulfilling as an individual but also reflected the 'miracle' of a unique generation, a reason to celebrate — not to mourn. His passing in 1998 indeed turned into a celebration, a gathering of the tribe where people who hadn't seen one another in 30 years were reunited. They came from places near and far, filling Temple Sinai in Washington, DC to the gills. Hundreds and hundreds of people. Everyone wanted to say something in his memory. Obviously, this was impossible, so I promised to put together a modest booklet (this is an Israeli custom) where anyone who wanted to could have a say. Some of these sentiments — from then and now — and words spoken at other important occasions are included, as promised, within a special section of parting words, tributes and reminiscences at the back of the book in Chapter VI, just before the Appendix.

Gil Weiss, 1915–1998

Initially, the main thrust of this volume was unwittingly written by Gil Weiss himself, transforming the focus from a memorial pamphlet to one special person into a memorabilia 'album' of the family as a whole. But that version underwent a second and unexpected metamorphosis, fleshed-out by hours of taped interviews with my mother Pearl stashed on a shelf in my office, containing not just family lore and recollections but also insights about the times. The tapes were only transcribed 16 years after Gil's death and a year or more after Pearl's. Between 2016 and 2018 the contents of this 'project', worked on in spurts, over more than 13 years, underwent a third metamorphosis — augmented, illuminated and expanded by countless hours of Internet sleuthing about the family, often cross-referencing personal events with historical events which expanded the manuscript into a full-length book. But it first took form due to the Memorabilia.

~

They say there is a Collector Gene that runs in some families. We Weisses definitely carry it. Gil Weiss saved everything, as I discovered sifting through the Weiss 'open stacks' filing system that filled the house in Potomac, Maryland covering counters and countless other flat surfaces with piles of papers, including the dining room table (except at Passover and other special occasions). This task took three weeks and filled an industrial size dumpster[1] with (among other things) a dozen used motors — stripped for the most part from old washing machine casings in case someone ever needed an old motor and 15 years of mat board catalogs. (Admittedly, I saved the most recent, for one never knows when one will need a mat board catalog.)

---

1. When he realized his days were numbered, less than 36 hours before he died, Gil spent hours and hours telling us 'where things were' — grandson Ben taking notes on a tiny Palm Pilot (there were no laptops). He told us not only where important papers were (think bank accounts to insurance policies, check books, billing receipts, passports and...the deeds to their burial plots). This included where the main water shutoff and fuse box were hiding behind piles of other stuff in the basement — even ensuring we'd know where his beloved and priceless black walnut in the rough was stashed, a piece of wood Gil had been aging for decades — fearing it would be thrown out. While sitting *shivah*, Pearl had confided in me: "Either 'someone' will have to go through all this stuff (by golly, your Dad truly thought he'd live forever!) — or I'll have no choice but to walk out the front door, lock the house and never come back..." Thus, my son Asaf and I embarked on putting the house in order as a mercy mission for Pearl.

Weiss 'Open Stacks' System

But among the genuine junk and the Good Junk (please note the distinction) both of which were tossed — the latter recorded for posterity in a section in Chapter V under the title The Holy of Holies — there was a gold mine of really neat stuff that in its quirky *ad hoc* way captured part of the essence of the family. Thus, the working title for this work for 18 years was *The Spice of Weiss.*

As a result, the first draft of this memoir took form based on prints and digital colored photos taken in 1998 at the house in Potomac, Maryland of bulk items, scans of weird souvenirs slated for the dumpster, a handful of vintage black-and-white photos and genuine documents/memorabilia archived for posterity in half a dozen modest size cardboard boxes — taken by Pearl to Leisure World. It was there, in 2003, at Pearl's new digs in her three-bedroom apartment in an independent living retirement community in Silver Spring, after the sale of the house in Potomac, Maryland, that I first opened the archived boxes that had waited patiently for five years on the upper shelf of the front office closet on Democracy Lane, and then on the upper shelf of the library/office in Leisure World. Several weeks of this month-long annual visit in 2003 was dedicated exclusively to transforming the contents into a coherent whole, in writing.

It was a fascinating joint project both my mother and I attacked with relish. Pearl watched the manuscript take form before her eyes ("Mom, you won't believe what I just found out!"), listening to what I wrote each day, sometimes filling in the blanks. Her elation when I discovered where her father came from in Europe (Jaroslaw, noted on her mother's marriage certificate, among Gil's Miscellaneous). How floored Pearl was when I found her mother and her two aunts in Ellis Island's online archive of passenger manifests, showing Nana had *not* exaggerated when she said she was "only a little girl" when she sailed for America — unescorted and orphaned, with two smaller siblings in tow. Laughing together after I walked into the living room to hand her a *third* marriage certificate to Gibby saying, eyes twinkling: "Mom, is there something you forgot to tell us???" Both Pearl and I had a jolly good time.

However, after reading the full manuscript several years later (after she moved to Minnesota in February 2007) Pearl seemed to lose interest in the project when asked repeatedly every year to review the manuscript for factual errors (and how could it be otherwise, for spelling errors?) on my annual visits between 2009 and 2013.

It was only when I returned to this work-in-progress in 2014 after her death — armed with the time needed to embark on transcribing hours and hours of interviews audiotaped over the years between 1997 and 2009 — that it dawned on me that Gil's Memorabilia had unwittingly relegated Pearl to second fiddle,[2] an accessory to the family's history.

---

2. It was definitely out of character for Pearl to play second fiddle: The women in the Weiss-Silverman-Jaffe-Summers 'Quartet' (their best friends) — all strong, confident, accomplished and knowledgeable — were the real kingpins in the power matrix. As someone once quipped: The men decided the national budget and whether NASA would go to the moon (actually none of the men were politically inclined), while the women decided where the families would celebrate holidays, when the couples would go out — to which restaurant, what

Was that why she lost interest? Gil may have told his story through the things he saved; Pearl's medium was language...and the tapes, it turned out, were chock full of priceless information, anecdotes and insights, not only giving depth and color to the section Pearl — The Ultimate Mentor, but also changing the entire narrative. Excerpts from the tapes, transcribed in fits and starts between 2014 and 2016, came to enhance other chapters about the family's roots, Pearl and Gil's formative years and other junctures in their lives — transforming the second draft, where Pearl's voice took center stage, ringing out loud and clear, alongside Gil's incredible Memorabilia. And in the last push to take this work off my literary bucket list, in 2018 and 2019 statistical data of births, marriages and deaths dating as far back as 1877 (!) — now digitized and growing constantly, and accessible to anyone anywhere seeking their family roots — revolutionized the chapter on family roots and in a sense brought the dead to life.

This, however, didn't diminish at all the magic of 67 years of Miscellaneous that Gil had accumulated that set this project in motion back in 1998.

~

The *oldest* item found in 1998 among the Memorabilia unearthed in the Shop[3] at the bottom of the pile of things 'waiting to be framed' was a 1931 certificate of merit from Camp Marshall Field — a camp for kids from poor neighborhoods — where Gil at age sixteen had learned that he could run.

Camp Marshall Field was situated on the North Shore of Long Island in Eaton's Neck. It operated between 1924 and 1938 on land provided by the wife of department store chain baron Marshall Field to "provide underprivileged boys a taste of country life" and give them "a summer respite from the heat and noise of the city".[4] Why in the

---

play they would see and where they would go on vacation, often together.

3. Gil's woodworking shop — in Silver Spring (1955–1975) and in Potomac (1975–1998).

4. From a profile of Camp Marshall Field in a local periodical: Bob Little,

CAMP MARSHALL FIELD

This is to certify that

Gilbert Weiss

has satisfactorily passed the requirements
for the

Senior

Emblem Test
and is
thereby entitled to wear the

CAMP MARSHALL FIELD EMBLEM

Gilbert Weiss
Pres. C. M. F. Assn.

Camp Director

Camp Marshall Field Certificate of Merit

world had Gil saved this stenciled piece of paper for close to 70 years? The answer was hiding in an audiotape my sister Wendy had made with the folks in 1997:

> Gil: [...] Friends of the family — gentile friends — were going to this camp...which costed a dollar a day. So they arranged for us — Bernie and I — to go to camp. [...] We had wonderful [athletics] coaches [who] taught us how to swim, and play all the sports — including track. I found out I had legs that could move.
>
> Pearl: Actually, his camp experience was a turning point in his life.
>
> Gil: Up to that point I was a poor student and then suddenly it gave me initiative and I became an A student, [a member of] the honor society and the high school track team.

From that transformational encounter at Camp Marshall Field, Gil never stood still, but he still left a zillion projects waiting to be done and certainly no time to attack the granddaddy of them all — that thankless task of weeding out the real Memorabilia from that four-letter word: the mess.

Gibby running—age 16

In the course of reclaiming the house, I ran into numerous copies of my father's famous "To-Do" lists. Those yellow legal pads always had two things prioritized as #7 or #8 in urgency...after small jobs like "door lock adjustment"

"The Old Camp Grounds", *Village Connection*, June 2012, 26, https://issuu.com/villageconnection/docs/june2012.

The famous yellow 'To-Do' lists

or "Nicole wedding present" and big jobs like "varnish deck and family room steps" or "repaint front main door" and minor tasks like "file dental and eye refunds" (which consisted of tossing all the new medical papers into the top drawer of the file cabinet in the front office 'til tax time). To-Do lists included activities that marked changes of the seasons like "plant Glad bulbs" in spring, or "check window calking" in the fall. There were even "to do" listings on the To-Do list, such as "check list of 'to do' things for Val [the handyman–DA]".

The famous yellow 'To-Do' lists

Two jobs were never crossed off, carried forward from list-to-list and year-to-year like the Passover promise *Next Year in Jerusalem*: "office mess!" and "clean up shop mess". This explains why although Gil had promised to do a major spring cleaning before the 1975 move from Silver Spring to the house on Democracy Lane in Potomac, the mover ended up going *back* to Woodland Drive for a second run because all

Gil's favorite comic strip — found taped to the wall in the Shop

the stuff in the basement wouldn't fit in the van! A coupon for One Spring Cleaning that I gave Gil on his 80th birthday in 1995 was never cashed in, either. Tossing out even some of the Good Junk would have killed him.

The sheer volume of Miscellaneous by 1998 was daunting. But some of the mementos, large and small, were a freeze-frame that reflected the tempo and the times for an entire generation. Among the things 'waiting to be framed' was a signed etching of an airplane sent as a Christmas gift by the Fairchild Corporation—*still in its original 1948 envelope*—now worth about $250 in galleries (yes, I checked). The stuff worth saving slowly began to emerge: The personal letters, the vintage photos and the certificates, and some amazing period pieces—from ivory handle single-edge razors to a giant Lay's Potato Chip can, the family's Second World War ration books and Gil's metal air-raid warden helmet, and even a red clothbound membership card in the Clothing Workers Union (that belonged to Nana's second husband Dave Lefkowitz), whose color was not coincidental, with the radical trade union's constitution printed inside in Yiddish.

Items worth saving ranged from Nana's February 1937 naturalization papers as an American citizen[5] to personal family nostalgia like the mimeographed announcement flier of the Weiss family's March

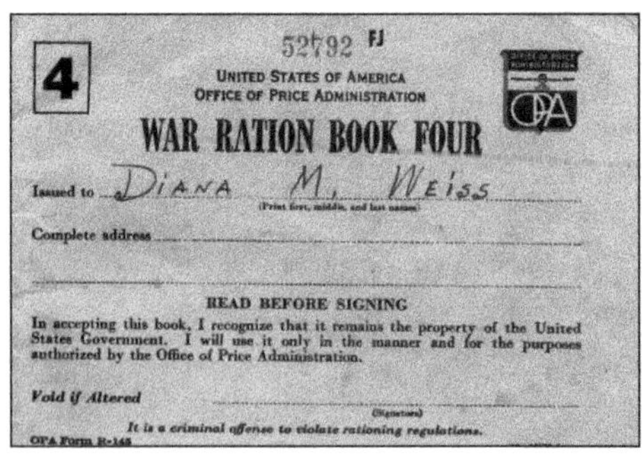
4

52792 FJ

United States of America
Office of Price Administration

OPA

WAR RATION BOOK FOUR

Issued to Diana M. Weiss
(Print first, middle, and last names)

Complete address

READ BEFORE SIGNING

In accepting this book, I recognize that it remains the property of the United States Government. I will use it only in the manner and for the purposes authorized by the Office of Price Administration.

Void if Altered
(Signature)

It is a criminal offense to violate rationing regulations.

OPA Form R-145

Left: WWII ration book
Right: Ivory-handle razors

5. Pearl's mother (Nana) arrived in the United States in 1902 but only took out American citizenship three-and-a-half decades later in 1937, after Pearl discovered, as an adult, that her mother 'hadn't bothered to do so'. She only

1955 move to Maryland from Washington, DC. The first is an exquisite document with calligraphy and border ornamentation identical to a crisp new $2 bill. The second is a stencil drawing of Gil carrying a saw,

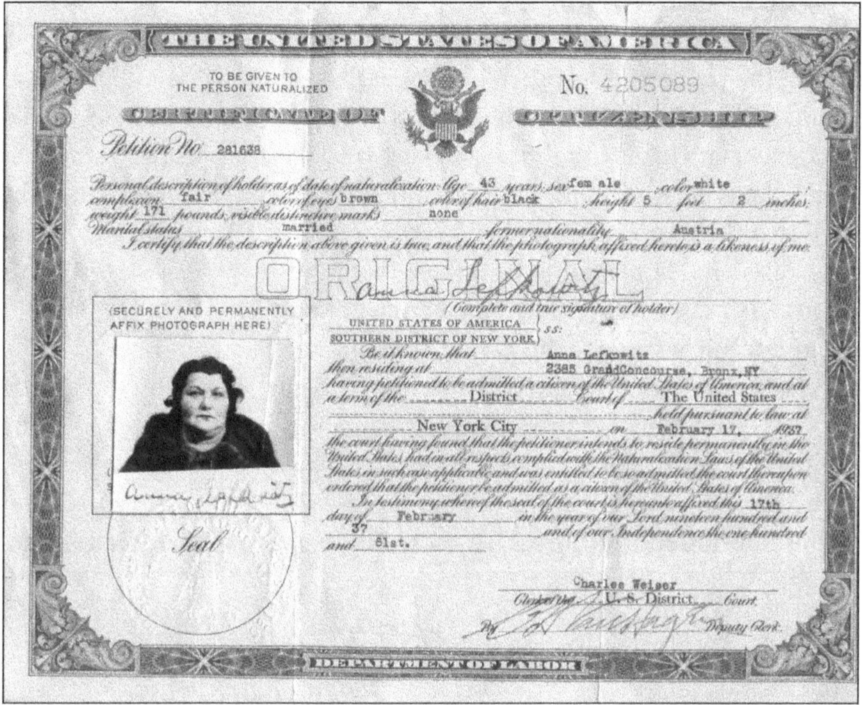
THE UNITED STATES OF AMERICA

TO BE GIVEN TO THE PERSON NATURALIZED

No. 4205089

CERTIFICATE OF CITIZENSHIP

Petition No. 281638

Personal description of holder as of date of naturalization: Age 43 years; sex female, color white, complexion fair, color of eyes brown, color of hair black, height 5 feet 2 inches; weight 171 pounds; visible distinctive marks none
Marital status married, former nationality Austria

I certify that the description above given is true, and that the photograph affixed hereto is a likeness of me.

ORIGINAL

(Complete and true signature of holder)

(SECURELY AND PERMANENTLY AFFIX PHOTOGRAPH HERE)

UNITED STATES OF AMERICA
SOUTHERN DISTRICT OF NEW YORK } SS:

Be it known that Anna Lefkowitz then residing at 2385 GrandConcourse, Bronx, NY having petitioned to be admitted a citizen of the United States of America, and at a term of the District Court of The United States held pursuant to law at New York City on February 17, 1937 the court having found that the petitioner intends to reside permanently in the United States, had in all respects complied with the Naturalization Laws of the United States in such case applicable, and was entitled to be so admitted, the court thereupon ordered that the petitioner be admitted as a citizen of the United States of America.

In testimony whereof the seal of the court is hereunto affixed this 17th day of February in the year of our Lord nineteen hundred and 37 and of our Independence the one hundred and 61st.

Seal

Charles Weiser
Clerk of the U.S. District Court.
By Deputy Clerk.

DEPARTMENT OF LABOR

Nana's citizenship papers

---

changed her status from Austrian resident alien to American citizen *after* Hitler came to power and only a year before the *Anschluss*—the annexation of Austria to Nazi Germany in March 1938. After hours of searching online archives, it seemed fairly common that people decades in the United States—having more urgent issues like putting food on the table, had remained resident aliens even after they were eligible to apply for citizenship after five years in America. (Romanian Jews were an exception.) While there was no explicit educational requirement in American naturalization law, officially potential citizens had to demonstrate they understood the Constitution, the duties of a citizen and basic American history, but how this was determined was at the discretion of the presiding judge and the 'test' was oral—short and informal. Such 'knowledge about America' was taught in citizenship classes in the evening.

Pearl with a book, Nana with a broom, Wendy dreaming of romance and Yours Truly (Daniella—then called Diana) in cowboy boots and packing a pair of pistols.

Some documents unearthed were a total mystery—such as a receipt for a liquor license for Max's Delicatessen on 14th Street and Q listing the proprietor as Pearl Weiss. Pearl was renowned to be a cheap drunk who got flushed on one glass of wine, the last person one could imagine as a Retail Liquor Dealer. It turns out that just as Nana, her other daughter Ruth and her son-in-law Dan were about to close the deal to buy this grocery store and move to DC in 1944 from New York, they discovered one had to be a Washington resident for a year to get a license to sell wine and beer—a significant part of the business. Thus, Pearl became a front—the owner of their store on paper.

In this post-*shivah* mercy mission for Pearl, the contents of two offices, one furnace/storeroom and the Shop including seven filing cabinets (one filled with carefully filed sales slips, warranties and instruction manuals for every appliance, large and small, they had ever owned) were reduced from five rooms to five or six small cartons and

1955 move to Silver Spring

shoeboxes. The Shop[6] and the storeroom were no longer a fire hazard, but what had begun solely as a *mitzvah* had become an archeological expedition. About the time I placed on the 'save pile' a red white 'n' blue 1940s flyer entitled *AIR RAID SIGNALS: WHAT YOU MUST DO when you hear an "alert" a "seek shelter" or an "all clear"* it suddenly dawned on me: Among Gil's stuff—the endless papers, honorary plaques from the Navy to the NAACP,[7] the clearly labeled cigar boxes of Good Junk, the jerry-rigged gadgets he concocted and other piquant items saved

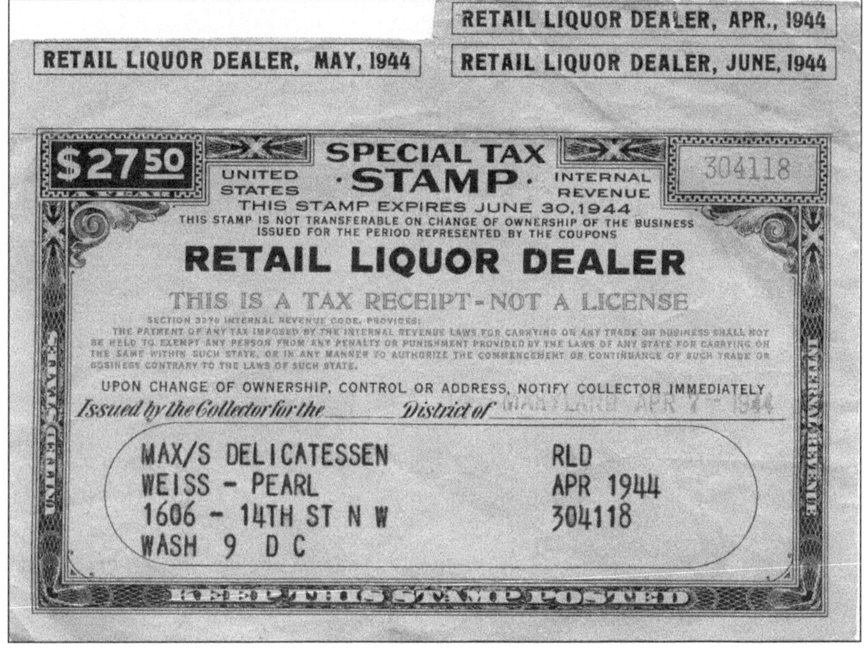

RETAIL LIQUOR DEALER, APR., 1944
RETAIL LIQUOR DEALER, MAY, 1944
RETAIL LIQUOR DEALER, JUNE, 1944

$27.50 A YEAR

UNITED STATES · SPECIAL TAX STAMP · INTERNAL REVENUE

304118

THIS STAMP EXPIRES JUNE 30, 1944

THIS STAMP IS NOT TRANSFERABLE ON CHANGE OF OWNERSHIP OF THE BUSINESS ISSUED FOR THE PERIOD REPRESENTED BY THE COUPONS

RETAIL LIQUOR DEALER

THIS IS A TAX RECEIPT - NOT A LICENSE

SECTION 3270 INTERNAL REVENUE CODE, PROVIDES:
THE PAYMENT OF ANY TAX IMPOSED BY THE INTERNAL REVENUE LAWS FOR CARRYING ON ANY TRADE OR BUSINESS SHALL NOT BE HELD TO EXEMPT ANY PERSON FROM ANY PENALTY OR PUNISHMENT PROVIDED BY THE LAWS OF ANY STATE FOR CARRYING ON THE SAME WITHIN SUCH STATE, OR IN ANY MANNER TO AUTHORIZE THE COMMENCEMENT OR CONTINUANCE OF SUCH TRADE OR BUSINESS CONTRARY TO THE LAWS OF SUCH STATE.

UPON CHANGE OF OWNERSHIP, CONTROL OR ADDRESS, NOTIFY COLLECTOR IMMEDIATELY

Issued by the Collector for the ______ *District of* MARYLAND APR 7 1944

MAX/S DELICATESSEN
WEISS - PEARL
1606 - 14TH ST N W
WASH 9 D C

RLD
APR 1944
304118

KEEP THIS STAMP POSTED

Pearl's liquor license

6. I had hoped the industrial quality power tools (the table saw, the lathe, the drill press), the work benches (his and mine) and other equipment could be passed on as a package deal where the Shop could be donated for a good cause in his memory—such as a workshop for youth-at-risk. I even wrote a detailed proposal of possibilities. Despite friend Bernie Wassertzug's efforts, there were no takers, and the tools were sold to hobbyists or given away, except for my Craftsman power jigsaw which Wendy took to Minneapolis with my blessings.

7. The National Association for the Advancement of Colored People, of which Gil became a member as a sign of support for its goals.

CD

Remember These

AIR RAID SIGNALS

WHAT YOU MUST DO

When You Hear:—

BLUE SIGNAL— One continuous blast on the horns or sirens

If at night, all homes, buildings, and street lights black out. Pedestrians may continue to walk. Vehicles may continue to move at normal city speed in day time, but not to exceed fifteen miles an hour with depressed beam headlights (normal city headlights) at night. Civilian Defense workers go to their posts. Be on the alert and ready for the RED SIGNAL.

RED SIGNAL A series of short blasts on the horns or a rising and falling wail on the sirens

If at night, homes, buildings, and street lights remain blacked out. Day or night, all vehicles, except authorized emergency vehicles pull to the nearest curb and stop. If at night, extinguish all car lights. Occupants of vehicles and pedestrians must get off the street and seek shelter. Civilian Defense workers are at their posts.

BLUE SIGNAL One continuous blast on the horns or sirens same as first blue signal

A BLUE SIGNAL always follows a RED SIGNAL. If at night, homes, buildings, and street lights remain blacked out. Pedestrians and vehicles may move on the streets, vehicles at normal city speed if in day time but at FIFTEEN MILES AN HOUR and with depressed beam headlights if at night. Civilian Defense workers remain at their posts. Be on the alert! The enemy may return. There may be a second RED SIGNAL.

ALL CLEAR— One short blast not to exceed 15 seconds on the horns or sirens.

Radio announcement. Street lights turned on.

IMPORTANT: Keep this for ready reference. It may save you a penalty for violating the blackout regulations.

H. C. Whitehurst, Director
Department of Civilian Defense
District of Columbia

Left: The basement—before and after

Right: WWII air raid instructions

for posterity—was not only a composite portrait of Gil Weiss himself but also one of 'Gibby and Pearly',[8] one of the whole family...and even

8. How should Pearly be spelled? The 'ie' diminutive suffix (think, Ruth/Ruthie) was a natural choice, but was pushed aside by 'i' being more authentic: Pearl's paternal grandparents in the Jewish community's registry in Jaroslaw Poland

perhaps a generation, maybe two, even extending to the third[9] with a firm bond of love and friendship epitomized by a fax[10] from grandson Asaf declaring: "Saba,[11] love you, even on the other side of the world".

Thus, the idea of this booklet-turned-book was born. It justly opens with an eclectic, albeit far from systematic and far from comprehensive but certainly representative, sample of family Memorabilia...*not* to be confused with an orderly rendition of lifetime achievements and other pursuits one always finds in conventional memoirs and family history projects, including this one. Hopefully, these 'thumbprints', focusing for the most part on the 1930s, 1940s and 1950s, will not only let readers savor or re-savor the special people Gil and Pearl Weiss were, but also in their own haphazard fashion reflect the quantum leap their generation of American Jews made as second-generation Americans[12] who went from poverty in an era of gaslighting and tenement life, to comfortable middle class living in the space age and the computer revolution. From times when a Jew could not get a job as an engineer, to a time when all the chairpersons of the Federal Reserve since 1987 to this day have been Jews.[13]

Researching the family's roots in Europe unexpectedly revealed a complex saga that dovetails the triumphs and tragedies of two centuries of Jewish life in American *and* Eastern Europe in a microcosm, while

---

reads — Jonas Schwarzer and *Perli* (no 'a'). Waldman and Pearl's brother was called Joni. So, why was 'y' chosen? Because Gibby and Pearly were inseparable.

9. Four generations if we count Nana.

10. That magical instant communications device that replaced waiting for fourteen-day-old letters from 6,000 miles away, once we convinced our father to get a fax machine after Gil *returned* the one Wendy and I got him for his 80th birthday to the store (!) (under the mistaken impression that you needed to know how to type to use one).

11. Granddad in Hebrew.

12. The term used by demographers for American-born children of foreign-born parents.

13. Nevertheless, in recent decades, antisemitism has resurged on both sides of the Atlantic. See discussion in Chapter V in the closing passages of the section Jewish in the 1950s.

providing the broader context of the family's actions. Such a wide canvas—from the port city of Nikolayev in the Pale of Settlement to the Romanian city of Jassy in Moldavia, from the tiny *shtetl* of Radekhiv in Galicia to the market town of Jaroslaw—makes the work significant not only for the descendants of the one particular family whose story set this project in motion and holds the work together. In its final state, the book is a touchstone, relevant also for the eighty percent of American Jews who trace their ancestry back to Eastern Europe.

Furthermore, while it's not exactly *Researching Your Family Roots for Dummies*, as I read the final manuscript for the last time, I realized the structure—a rollercoaster ride with readers in the back seat—shares not only *where* I mined data, but also *how* to piece together fragments of seemingly unconnected information using the logic of a detective (without hiding the dead ends and faulty premises and other traps encountered along the way). Thus, this memoir is likely to find a ready audience among novice genealogists who are not even Jewish. This revelation led me to drop the working title all these years, chosen for a modest family memoir when I began this project back in 2003—*The Spice of Weiss a Quirky Family Memoir of Memorabilia and Recollections*, to a far more appropriate title that befits the finished product: *Playing Detective with Family Lore: Plugging the holes in a family history unintentionally tells the saga of Jews in a microcosm.*

~

When I began what I thought was the last revision of this family saga in late 2018, I faced a dilemma: I felt like I was back in elementary school when my mom was called in as a substitute teacher in my classroom for the day: Was I supposed to call her 'Mommy' or 'Mrs. Weiss'?!

In a similar predicament, I vacillated how to address my parents in this memoir, finally settling on 'Pearl' and 'Gil'. In a family history largely written from my perspective, admittedly, it sounds a bit weird as their daughter to say 'Pearl said this' or 'Gil did that' instead of 'Mom said this' or 'Dad did this', but then again—it is thus that they are remembered by most of the potential readers of this memoir who knew them (and certainly by any other readers and subsequent generations that seek their roots).

To set the record straight: No, my sister Wendy and I *never* called our parents by their first names[14] and readers should not in any way interpret this as a dog whistle signifying lack of closeness in the relationship sometimes employed in memoirs where parents and children have been emotionally distanced or had a very troublesome relationship. On rare occasions, in certain sections I've employed 'the folks', 'our parents' and at times 'my father' or 'my mother' when it seemed nothing else would work.

Pearl's mother Nana — an integral part of the family and an incredible figure in her own right — was easy: Nana remained Nana.[15]

For those who would like to view the black-and-white photographs in this book in full color, they will be viewable on the book website www.playingdetective.com.

Note to the Grammar Police: Although the spelling in this memoir is American English, in most cases it uses European punctuation which is more abbreviated than American punctuation.

Daniella Weiss Ashkenazy
Kfar Warburg, Israel
Fall 2020

---

14. My husband Rafi, who grew up in a *HaShomer HaTza'ir* kibbutz was raised to call his parents by their first names (Aviva and Aronchik) not Mom or Dad — part of the kibbutz rearing practices that sought to create a New Jew, including breaking the loaded emotional bond of Jewish parenthood deemed 'unhealthy' by the founding generation. Even as an adult, I never once heard Rafi address them as *Ima* or *Abba*, but he literally *ordered* his mother that she be called '*Savta*' (grandma) by her grandkids (and not 'Aviva' as she wished) although my mother-in-law never really felt comfortable with this appellation and oft spoke of herself in the third person to our kids as toddlers — 'Come here to Aviva...'

15. Some of the relatives called Pearl's mother Anna (née Reiter) Schwarzer, then Lefkowitz. Or 'Aunt Annie'. But for most relatives and friends, as well as her grandchildren and great-grandchildren and even caregivers in her declining years, she was 'Nana'. In excerpts from the tapes, Pearl often talks of 'Momma' — quoted verbatim.

Chapter I

Missing Links to Family Roots

It was only vaguely known where the family came from in Europe: Somewhere in Russia. Somewhere in the Austro-Hungarian Empire. Somewhere in Romania. A key missing detail was preserved in a letter from Gil's mother, Hannah Weiss, stapled to an FBI security clearance form draft, another scribbled on a piece of paper in a pile of raw data of a family tree stuffed in a manila envelope with a GEDCOM CD. Other key facts were found in a forgotten photocopy of Nana's marriage certificate to Michael Schwarzer (always spelled *without* a 't') and the amazing searchable Ellis Island online database of ship passenger manifests. A decade later — First World War draft cards, birth, marriage and death certificates[1] and even registries of births, deaths and marriages from Poland and business directories from Galicia and Romania and other European sources were online. Genealogy websites were backed up by countless nights of online research collecting-reading scanned handwritten raw census data that provided the rest. And there were days and days devoted to reading relevant passages in popular and scholarly works about the places the family lived, to understand their lives and the times.

1. Marriage licenses in particular are a short cut to finding a previous generation. The names of the newlyweds' parents *are not cited online*, but are in the *original* document. One can email the New York Historical Records Department at familyhistory@records.nyc.gov with a name and certificate number and they will send a pdf (for free!) of the original handwritten document. Other cities seem to ask for a service fee. For example, Pearl didn't know her step-grandmother's name — she had only called her 'grandmother' in Yiddish; it was recorded on Nana's half-brother's 1927 marriage license (Benjamin Reiter to Irene Gass) archived in the New York City Marriage Records 1829–1940 on the Familysearch.org website.

Yes, this section took on a life of its own, far beyond what I first intended in length or focus, not to mention time investment — as the manuscript unintentionally was transformed into a social and political history — with the virtual camera lens jumping back and forth between the personal and broader context. Furthermore, on one level, Pearl and Gil Weiss seem to epitomize the mainstreaming of second-generation Jews of immigrant parents, but as I found the perspective broadening as I dug deeper into the lives of *their* parents and grandparents, time and time again, I was amazed how individual family members — their lives and their decisions — oft seemed to epitomize *in micro* the experiences and the fate *in macro* of this or that East European Diaspora community, or Eastern European Jewry as a whole.

The Reiter-Schwarzer Side

Nana's Life in Radekhiv (Galicia, Poland)

Pearl's mother, Nana (Gmendel/Annie Reiter) was born in Radekhiv or Radziechov[2] (pronounced Rad-ah-CHUV) — a small *shtetl* in the eastern part of Galicia, in the western Ukraine, 72 km (42 miles)

---

2. While the four orphans' place of origin in census data only says Galicia, their brother Josel who arrived several years after his three sisters is listed on the passenger list as originating in Radekhiv — the town Pearl remembers her mother saying she came from. Other spellings for the record: ראדז׳ייחוב [Heb] Radekhiv [Ukr], Radziechów [Pol], Radzichov and ראדעכעוו [Yid], Radekhov [Rus], Radechov, Radechiv, Radikhiv, Radikhov, Radzekhuv, Radzhekhuv. (It *may* also have been called Radoshkovichi or Radoszkowice.) To confuse things, there are *four* places listed in Wikipedia with identical or near-identical names: Radziechów in Lower Silesia (southwest Poland); Radekhiv (in Polish: Radziechów), a village near Liuboml in the northwest of the Ukraine, and the small city Rzhyshchiv, 62 km (38.5 miles) southeast of Kiev — all three alongside the town of Radekhiv (Polish: Radziechów), now a small 'city' in the Lviv Region of Ukraine — apparently Nana's birthplace. There is a small museum, the "Historical and Cultural Museum of Radekhiv Region", at https://www.karpaty.info/en/uk/lv/rd/radekhiv/museums/history/. The community Memorial Book (*Sefer Zikaron*) is very detailed. The full volume in Hebrew is "*Sefer Zikaron Lekehillot Radekhiv Lopatyn Vehasevivah*" by Getzel Kressel,

Two views of the Radekhiv marketplace, 1900

from Lviv/Lvov (a major Jewish center). Today, both are on the Russian (Ukrainian) side of the border, and are not part of Poland.[3]

Back when the Reiters lived in Radekhiv — as a result of the partition of Poland[4] in 1772 — the *shtetl* and the region as a whole (Galicia) became part of Austria. In short, when Nana was born, Radekhiv was part of the Austro-Hungarian Empire, and she always told the story how "I remember how Emperor Franz Josef once passed through our town when I was a little girl". Between 1919-1939 (Nana and her three siblings were already in America) Radekhiv was part of eastern Poland, but in

---

1976, Dorot Jewish Division, The New York Public Library. "Radekhiv" New York Public Library Digital Collections at http://digitalcollections.nypl.org/items/71177aa0-7b6d-0133-868c-00505686a51c. For a partial English translation, see Sara Ecker Feuerstein, "In Radekhov before the Holocaust", https://www.jewishgen.org/Yizkor/Radekhov/rad072.html/.

3. Various GPS coordinates are given by different sources about Radekhiv/Radziechov: 50°17' N, 24°39' E (Jewishgen.org) 50.28018 24.63975 (Radekhov Museum) 50.2824° N / 24.6353° E, 50°16'56" N / 24°38'7" E (Radziechów in Virtual Shtetl). There is also 50°55' N, 25°16' E / 50°16′58″N 24°38′15″E (Radekhiv Wikipedia, which may be one of the 'other Radekhivs').

4. Between the 1772 division of Poland and the present, although Poland had its own geographic integrity, distinct culture and language — it was only briefly an independent country (in the relevant period) between 1919-1939, before Eastern Poland was swallowed up by powerful neighbors.

1939 — after the invasion of Poland by Germany and Russia, the Lvov region became part of the USSR (absorbed by the Ukrainian Soviet Socialist Republic) — the upshot of the infamous Molotov-Ribbentrop Non-Aggression Pact between Nazi Germany and Stalinist Russia to gobble up Poland between them. The Lvov region remains part of the Ukraine[5] to this day.

The *shtetl* was the dominant pattern of Jewish settlement for over 600 years among Ashkenazi Jews in Eastern Europe. What were *shtetls* exactly? The name is a Yiddish diminutive for *shtot* designating a 'large town' or a 'city' that refers to a relatively small type of community found throughout Eastern Europe: A *shtetl* was not an agricultural village, rather, it was a market town that was predominantly Jewish — numerically and culturally — with a minority (up to half the population) being ethnic Polish or Ukrainian neighbors with whom relations varied from amicable to tense to hostile, even lethal, from town-to-town and time-to-time. The *shtetls* served their surrounding agricultural hinterland. One needs to keep in mind that the pattern of settlement in Europe (and in Israel, incidentally) is different from the American model of isolated family homesteads with the nearest village or town serving as a service center for farmers. In Eastern European peasant farmers live together in hamlets and villages called *dorfs*. Outlying fields surrounded this cluster of domiciles, while a neighboring town (*shtetl*) served as a service center and marketing hub.

There were an estimated two thousand *shtetls* in Poland prior to the Holocaust.[6] In the late 19th century — on the cusp of the great exodus

---

5. While today it is not politically correct to say "the Ukraine" in order to signify Ukraine is now a sovereign country, "the Ukraine" is used in this work as a *geographical* region — like 'the Great Plains' (a region that historically was controlled by different governements at different times). Identity politics is irrelevant in this context.

6. For an opener–and eye-opener, the following article separates mythical *Fiddler on the Roof* images from reality: See Joellyn Zollman, "What Were Shtetls: Clearing Up Myths about these Eastern European Villages where Jews Lived", https://www.myjewishlearning.com/article/shtetl-in-jewish-history-and-memory/. The following profile explains how Jewish life was organized in a typical *shtetl* (community institutions and how they operated) with vintage photos,

of Russian Jewry that began after the Kishinev Pogrom in 1903[7] that set in motion the migration of two million East European Jews westward–three-quarters of the Jewish population in the Pale of Settlement[8] lived in *shtetls*. Some demographers say half these Jews actually lived in larger towns, not tiny market towns like Radekhiv. At the same time, there was a clear trend in Jewish life towards urbanization and modernization and in 1897 half a million Jews lived in cities. Ten percent of the Jewish population resided in three cities–Warsaw, Odessa and Lodz.

As for Nana's birthplace, Radekhiv was still more or less in the boondocks — 72 km (45 miles) from Lvov, although a Galician train network was built from the late 1870s to the early 1900s with a lot of local stops. Historically, Lvov was a hotbed of Belz Hassidim. It was a large town that was urban by standards of the times (44,250 inhabitants in 1900). Poles owned most of the land, and Jews owned most of the shops and inns. The only item of historical importance I could find regarding Radekhiv — indeed a small *shtetl* by any yardstick — is that some of the first members of the Third Aliyah (1919–1923) came from the town. Among these Jews who immigrated to Mandatory Palestine after the First World War (all told, there were some 40,000 persons in this wave, who increased the Jewish population in the country to about 90,000) most were young socialist pioneers who played a pivotal role in shaping the course of modern Zionism. In addition,

---

see Chaya Mindel Way, "What Is a Shtetl? The Jewish Town", https://www.chabad.org/library/article_cdo/aid/3025072/jewish/What-Is-a-Shtetl-The-Jewish-Town.htm. For some vintage footage see https://www.youtube.com/watch?v=5uQu_C6kO6A. On food insecurity in impoverished *shtetls*, see Paul Glasser, "What Did Poor Jews in the *Shtetl* Eat?" https://forward.com/yiddish/378007/what-did-poor-jews-in-the-shtetl-eat/. For a portrait of life in one particular *shtetl* — Bransk in Poland, near the Russian border, today, void of any Jews, see Mariann Marzynski's two-part PBS documentary "Shtetl", 1996, https://vimeo.com/129440101 and https://vimeo.com/130762012.

7. See discussion of the Kishinev Pogrom in the section on Nikolayev.

8. The area where Jews were allowed to reside in Czarist Russia. For more about the demographics, see Joshua Rothenberg, "Demythologizing the *Shtetl*", *Midstream* 27 (March 1981): 25-31, http://faculty.history.umd.edu/BCooperman/NewCity/Shtetl.html.

a not-very-well-known, troubled but talented Yiddish author named Lamed Shapiro was born in Radekhiv.[9]

Radekhiv began as a 'private town'[10] established — as was the custom in Poland — to provide services, manpower and income to one of the estates of Galician Polish nobleman Count Stanislaw Badeni[11] whose estate overlooked the hamlet and dominated the economy from the 16th to 19th centuries and even at the beginning of the 20th. Scattered ruins of Badeni's castle in Radekhiv (the dynasty had many residences) can be found to this day on a low rise above the town.

During Nana's childhood, 1897 archival data show there were 1,519 Jews in the town — approximately 59 percent of the overall population; most of the gentiles were ethnic Ukrainians. The most vivid and complete description of the town in the late 19th century was compiled by the Centre for the Heritage of Polish Jewry which described economic life in Radekhiv:

---

9. Ironically, all the biographers cite Lamed Shapiro's birthplace as sound-alike Rzhyshchiv near Kiev while the 1900 circa photo with an arrow pointing to "Lamed Shapiro's house" scribbled in Yiddish, is Radekhiv near Lvov, 400 km. from Kiev... Shapiro was a talented but largely forgotten Yiddish-American journalist and fiction writer who today could have made a fortune in the horror movie genre with his short stories rife with lurid scenes of violence. To read one of his best-known short stories, "The Cross", see Lamed Shapiro, *The Cross and Other Jewish Stories* (New Haven and London: Yale University Press, 2007), 3-18, https://tikvahfund.org/wp-content/uploads/2018/05/Lamed_Shapiro-The_Cross-1.pdf.

10. One could say that in some respects these 'private towns' were the Polish form of 'company towns' established by coal barons in America — without script and company stores...

11. About this noble family, see "Badeni", on Revolvy.com website, https://www.revolvy.com/page/Badeni. For a 1908 vintage photo of the Count's former castle, see "Radziechów" on Fotopolska.eu website https://fotopolska.eu/Radziechow/b35647,Zamek.html?f=958123-foto. Count Stanislaw Badeni's estate at Radekhiv was among his largest according to Polishroots.com: 2,952 *morgas* [half a hectare or 1.25 acres per *morgas*–DA] divided into a large and a smaller estate, that included 1,008 *morgas* under cultivation, 57 meadows and gardens, 266 pasture plots and 992 woodlots. Only a few ruins remain.

> The first Jews in Radekhiv engaged in leasing, running inns/taverns and commerce (exporting agricultural products from surrounding estates, importing spices, wines, industrial products and crafts). In the second half of the 19th century, the number of Jewish tailors, furriers, and hatters spread, but the majority continued to engage in petty commerce and peddling in nearby villages. [...] In the center of the town was a brewery[12] owned by Badeni that he leased to the local Jews. At the end of the 19th century a Jewish-owned sawmill was established which employed Jewish workers. The wages of these workers were low (about 2 crowns for a day's work from dawn to dusk). [...] Jews also served as agents and overseers for the Count.[13]

Like every Jewish community no matter how small, Radekhiv had all the institutions necessary for Jewish life — from a ritual bath (*mikvah*) to elementary education (*heder*) to a burial society (*hevrah kadishah*), but in the second half of the 19th century, it also boasted the presence of a famous *tefillin*-maker,[14] Rabbi Shlomo-Elimelech Bedner, whose handwritten scrolls for *mezuzahs* and *tefillin* were prized by Hassidim throughout Galicia. According to some sources, most of the town's Jews were Mitnagdim — a somber ultra-Orthodox stream of Judaism (a lifestyle that had been the Jewish norm for centuries). The Mitnagdim (literally 'opponents') opposed Hassidism which argued Jewish life and religious practices needed more room for spontaneity, joy and celebration.[15]

---

12. For a photo of the old beer brewery in Radekhiv (2006), see *Wikipedia*, s.v. "Radekhiv", https://en.wikipedia.org/wiki/Radekhiv#/media/File:Radekhiv5.JPG.

13. For this detailed history of Radekhiv (in Hebrew, use Google translate to read) see the Center for Jewish Heritage in Poland, https://moreshet.pl/he/node/498.

14. For the role of *tefillin* (phylacteries) in Jewish religious practice, see *Wikipedia*, s.v. "Tefillin", https://en.wikipedia.org/wiki/Tefillin.

15. The Mitnagdim rejected the singing and dancing (and at times, drinking

However the Polish Jewry heritage site suggests even in Radekhiv with only 1,519 Jews including children, things were far more diversified, upholding the age-old axiom "two Jews–three opinions" and reflecting the classic joke of "Why does every Jewish community have three synagogues?"[16] Thus, at the close of the 19th century, during the period of Nana's childhood, two Hassidic *kollelim* (singular *kollel*, probably each with only a handful of scholars) were established in Radekhiv: one loyal to the Belz dynasty, the other followers of the Husiatyn-Rizhin dynasty.[17] A *kollel* was a 'cluster' of Talmudic scholars whose student body, unlike the Talmudic academy (*yeshivah*), was comprised of married men who received monthly living stipends for exclusively devoting themselves to Torah study, but most of the town's Jews — like Nana's grandfather — were busy eking out a living. Nana's father Jacob Reiter's simple and deep piety — he even interpreted photos as 'graven images'[18] — was perhaps extreme, but on the whole, attitudes and practices that in today's parlance would be labeled ultra-Orthodox were commonplace in small villages where almost every Jewish household was Orthodox. But since both Hassidim and Mitnagdim

---

to excess) as a path to spirituality that typified Hassidic communities — viewed by some leaders as dangerously reminiscent of past false messianic movements due to the supernatural powers oft attributed to this or that Hassidic rabbi or sage, "seen as posing a threat to the scholarly rabbinical leadership of the major Jewish communities". On the Mitnagdim, see Allan Nadler, *The YIVO Encyclopedia of Jews in Eastern Europe*, s.v. "Misnagdim", http://www.yivoencyclopedia.org/article.aspx/Misnagdim.

16. The third being the one where neither of the rival members of the first two synagogues would set foot...

17. The terms 'dynasty' and 'court' reflected the regal style in which some of the heads of these Hassidic sects lived. See, for example, a description of the Husiatyn Rebbe's home between the world wars — a residence that could rival the great houses of English gentry or Polish nobility... And rivalry between 'courts' were exceedingly acrimonious, though no one imprisoned rivals in the tower or cut off their heads. See *Wikipedia*, s.v. "Hasidic dynasty", https://en.wikipedia.org/wiki/Husiatyn_(Hasidic_dynasty).

18. See Pearl's description of his refusal to have his picture taken, in the next section — Life on the Lower East Side on page 32.

both opposed modernism[19] his behavior makes it hard to know for sure which stream the Reiter family belonged to.

Nevertheless, I would take — pardon the expression — a 'leap of faith' and argue that there are signs the Reiters were Mitnagdim. Nana described (in stories she told us) the somber almost terrifying atmosphere she remembers as a child in her father's household, adding 'she was sure if she would turn on a light on Shabbos, God would come down from Heaven and strike her dead on the spot'. Furthermore — somewhat of a dead giveaway — I never once heard Nana hum a Hassidic *nigun* (tune).[20] Understanding why this behavior is important requires a bit of context: The *Shulchan Aruch*, that codified Jewish Law, written by Josef Karo in 1563, said that 'as a sign of mourning for the destruction of the Temple, Jews should refrain from singing or playing musical instruments' — and a somber musicless atmosphere characterized Jewish life until the advent of Hassidism in the 1770s.[21] It was only in 'defense' that the Mitnagdim began slowly and grudgingly to develop their own limited musical vocabulary — so different in tone from Hassidic music that even a novice can hear the differences in the 'voice'.[22]

19. The battle — fought tooth and nail in the first half of the 19th century (when the worldview of both Jacob and his father Josef were shaped) — subsided with the appearance of a common enemy in the mid-19th century: the Jewish Enlightenment or *Haskalah* that called for a secular curriculum alongside a traditional Jewish education a trend both Hassidim and Mitnagdim opposed as an existential peril to Judaism as they understood it.

20. My mother-in-law Aviva's second husband — author Yehoshua Bar-Yosef — was totally non-observant and a die-in-the-wool atheist from early adulthood, having turned his back on his Hungarian Hassidic *haredi* upbringing in Mea Shearim. Nevertheless, despite his loss of faith, he continued to 'bim-bum' Hassidic melodies so deeply engrained in the psyche, to his dying day. See *Wikipedia*, s.v. "Yehoshua Bar-Yosef", https://en.wikipedia.org/wiki/Yehoshua_Bar-Yosef. Nana *did* enjoy listening to Theodor Bikel records of Yiddish folk music.

21. For a short discussion on the role of music in Hassidic thought, see Yaakov Mazor, *The YIVO Encyclopedia of Jews in Eastern Europe*, s.v. "Hasidism Music", http://www.yivoencyclopedia.org/article.aspx/Hasidism/Music.

22. The music of the Mitnagdim (sometimes called the 'Lithuanian stream'

Furthermore, music among the Mitnagdim was approved only in very limited circumstances and the somber ambience of the Reiter household almost shouts 'Mitnagdim'.

To return to Nana's childhood in Radekhiv, sudden tragedy would have ramifications in a myriad of ways on the course Nana's life would take — both good and bad: Her name at birth was Gmendel Reiter.[23] Her mother Rosa Zand/Sahn[24] died suddenly in her sleep, leaving four orphans. Their father had gone to America several years earlier after the youngest was born...or after she was conceived (Yetta, born circa 1898[25]), to pave the way to bring his family over. According to family oral history, when Jacob Reiter heard his wife had died, he remarried.[26] As Pearl described the circumstances:

---

since the hub of opposition to Hassidism was in Lithuania) is solemn and anguished, definitely not upbeat. See, for example, “ניגונים 4.11.16 - מוסיקה של מתנגדים ל"ע”, posted by JLM FM radio, www.mixcloud.com/jlmfm/41116-ניגונים. Compare with typical Hassidic tunes: “The Hassidic Niggun as Sung by the Hassidim” posted by the Jewish Music Research Centre, https://open.spotify.com/album/3YWVUzoiRzAHpfFsT29xot.

23. It was entered in the database this way, but looks like 'Gemeindel' on the microfilm of the handwritten ship manifest.

24. The spelling varies from Sand to Zand, to Sahn and a dozen other possibilities, thus, Martin Sahn (Kyla and Thea's father) and their Aunt Miriam Sahn were first cousins through Nana's mother Rosa.

25. On her 1920 marriage certificate to Saul Cantor it says 1899 but this is likely a mistake (she was four when she came in 1902). Yetta had, at some point, taken the first name Pearl (although known as Aunt Yetta to the Weisses) and is registered in subsequent documentarian (citizenship, social security records and so forth) as Pearl Cantor.

26. To Rosa Raubfogel. While it may be pure coincidence, there were Raubvogels in Radekhiv (spelled with a 'v' as on Jacob's second marriage certificate, but with an 'f' in census data). Was stepmother Rose Raubfogel also from the town, or was she a relative of someone from Radekhiv who told Jacob, 'I want to introduce you to my cousin who is also widowed'? This was very common. See Yaakov Shmuel Weissman, “My Father's House”, in the Radekhiv Memorial Book (*Sefer Yizkor*), https://www.jewishgen.org/yizkor/Radekhov/rad033.html#Page62.

> My [maternal] grandmother died during the night. They all slept in one big bed, and my mother got up in the morning and she felt her mother [...] and her mother was dead. She told me this story a lot, so I believe this must have been very accurate. She went for help. [...] Her father was in America. A lot of them — the head of the family — would go to America, would live very frugally to make enough money for a ticket for their family. My grandmother's sister — I think she was a sister but was definitely a female relative — sent tickets for them. She figured now that his wife was dead, he (Jacob Reiter) would forget about the children. This happened often with immigrants. They would find another woman and forget about the first family and started another family. She was afraid this would happen and didn't want it to happen to the children [and she apparently pressured to bring them over and sent the tickets].

There isn't a lot of information about the children in the interim, but it is known that there was a grandfather in Radekhiv. Nana said while she was taking care of her younger sisters, their older brother Josel was "teaching little children to read".[27] Despite his young age — at most ten years old[28] — this is plausible since in a memoir

27. Boys in Eastern European communities, even the smallest *shtetl*, began school at age three or four in a one-room schoolhouse or *heder* (literally a 'room') with a strict teacher called a *melamed* (tutor) where they were taught to read and daily Jewish religious rituals. For a description of a *heder*, see Mordechai Zalkin, *The YIVO Encyclopedia of Jews in Eastern Europe*, s.v. "Heder", http://www.yivoencyclopedia.org/article.aspx/Heder. It is noteworthy that all Jewish boys, no matter how poor, were literate while most of their gentile peers in these small *shtetls* were illiterate — a reflection of contrasts in worldviews — the value of education and whether literacy was an essential skill (for reading holy texts) in their respective cultures.

28. There are discrepancies about Josel-Joe's age discussed in note 45. He may have been 'helping the *melamed*' after his mother's death, as early as age seven to ten to help put food on the table. Nana recalled time and again how poor they were.

about the Radekhiv[29] *heder* in the community's memorial book, the author recalled that the teacher had a number of 'assistants'—young children who knew how to read, who helped the little children memorize the texts.

Pearl recalled talks with her mother about Nana's childhood:

> There were these four kids wandering around with no one to really take care of them. My mother was like their mother in this little *shtetl*. She used to tell me how she had to go down to the river to wash the sheets, and the gentiles in the town were very nice to her. They would see her with these big sheets and she was a little kid and they would help her to wring them out. [...] She used to tell me that her grandfather had a saloon, and he would let her stand behind the counter on a box and serve customers. But really, nobody was taking care of them.

Who was this grandfather? No one even knew his name...but in March 2019 when the City of New York sent me (literally within hours) a scanned copy of Jacob Reiter's second marriage certificate with the woman who would become Nana's stepmother when she and her sisters arrived in America—there on the yellowing tag board card were the names of the parents of Nana's father Jacob, miraculously taking the family tree back another generation[30]: Joseph Reiter and Rebecca Goldberg.[31]

In a 1975 taped interview, Nana had described her grandfather Joseph Reiter:

---

29. The *Sefer Yizkor* [Memorial Book] is devoted primarily to the town prior to and during the Holocaust. There are a few pieces about life in Radekhiv in earlier times that note this.

30. Seven generations (!)—making Josef Reiter my great-great-grandfather, and my grandchildren's great-great-great-great-grandfather.

31. Was Pearl's sister Ruth (Rebecca in the 1910 Census) named after Nana's grandmother Rebecca or her mother Rosa-Rebecca...or both?

> When I was a little tot, he used to teach me to give change to customers. He had a beer saloon. I also remember that people [the Ukrainian gentiles in the town] bought tickets to buy beer on Saturdays since Jews won't handle money on Shabbos.[32]

Joseph Reiter's 'saloon' was one of 23,269 taverns in Galicia — which were literally part of the landscape at the end of the 19th century — an 'inheritance' from a unique 300-year-long economic order in Poland: In 1496 the royal monopoly on production and sale of alcohol was transferred to the gentry; subsequently, under what are called propination laws (Latin for "to treat" or "pour out"), this lucrative perk included not only a monopoly on manufacturing alcoholic beverages in a nobleman's vicinity but also *coercing* bonded peasants to buy the alcohol in quantity (mainly cheap potato vodka) or to provide the equivalent revenue in *corvée* labor to this landowner, making drinking a no-brainer. Scholars say this unique Polish enterprise both helped keep the peasantry docile in a stupor and fueled epidemic alcoholism. Nobles who established private towns often built their own local breweries as Count Stanislaw Badeni had done. And since nobility such as Badeni owned and leased out all the real estate — residential and commercial — they could generate income by leasing out taverns with 'propination rights' to townspeople. It is claimed that landowners' income accrued from propination rights often exceeded that from agriculture. While forced alcohol purchase was abolished in 1889 in Galicia, not surprisingly high alcohol consumption continued. Most of the tavern lessees in the late 19th century and into the 20th (and earlier) were Jews like Nana's

---

32. It's unclear how this worked. Either Josef Reiter had a gentile who ran the tavern on Saturdays or Jacob Reiter was forced by the terms of the lease from Count Badeni who owned all the real estate in town, to open his saloon on Saturdays out of economic necessity and therefore sold tickets in advance in order not to break the Sabbath. (A common practice, for decades. For example, in years past, the Israel Museum in Jerusalem as a public institution was expected to honor the Sabbath by operating on a similar footing: The ticket counter was closed on the Sabbath, but exhibitions were open for those who bought tickets in advance...)

grandfather and his 'saloon'.[33]

Although in 1920 a fire destroyed many of Radekhiv's original wooden houses (including its large wooden mid-18th century Polish-style synagogue), the town's "Stone Synagogue" — currently an auto garage — is slated to be renovated as a 'tourist attraction'.[34] Miraculously, despite this, the main street of Radekhiv remains to this day almost untouched by time. Although there are no Jews left[35] — the same second-story balconies of former Jewish homes facing the marketplace that one can see in the 1900 vintage photograph still exist! And the doorposts bear empty niches testifying to where *mezuzahs* once were placed — remnants documented by photographer-documenter Christian Herrmann who visited Radekhiv in 2017.[36] Today this row of houses is mainly homes, but originally the ground floor was a shop, in the basement was a warehouse and the top floor was a family home. Did one of these homes facing the marketplace square house Grandfather Reiter's saloon? Who's to know?

How many years transpired between their mother's death and the

---

33. See Anrdriy Dorosh, "Propination Laws and Alcohol Consumption in Galicia", 4 March 2019, https://forgottengalicia.com/propination-laws-and-alcohol-consumption-in-galicia/.

34. This is a phenomenon throughout Europe — including renovating a gutted Bulgarian synagogue to the tune of $5 million by municipal authorities in the hopes of attracting Jewish 'heritage tourism'. See note 65 for more on this strategy of attracting Jewish tourists, which is particularly widespread in Poland, after 90 percent of the Jews were exterminated in the Holocaust. There are about 7,000 Jews in all of Poland — most in Warsaw and Krakow, but lots of empty restored synagogues without Jews...

35. There were 2,008 Jews in Radekhiv in 1941 when Hitler invaded the Soviet Union. Radekhiv's Jews were sent to Bełżec extermination camp near Lublin and those who fled were hunted down by the Nazis and the Jews' Ukrainian neighbors. When Radekhiv was liberated by the Red Army in July 1944, only a few Jews remained alive — and they left.

36. See the photos of Radekhiv by Christian Herrmann, "I Have Nothing to Say, Just to Show: Traces of a Genocide", Museum of the Jewish People at Beit Hatfutsot, 4 October 2018, https://www.bh.org.il/blog-items/nothing-say-just-show-traces-genocide//.

year Rosa Zand's kin pressured to reunite the Reiter kids with their father in America? There is little to go on, but it seems evident from oral history and the data, that it was at least a couple of years until the kids arrived in America. It may have been two, and Pearl believes (though it is only a guess) that it was three years. But it may have been five!

The 'elasticity' of dates on vintage documents is notorious, thus initially I discounted the date in the 1910 US Census where Jacob Reiter reported he arrived in America in 1896...assuming it was a clerical error. Or even messy penmanship, scribbling a '6' instead of an '8'. The fact is, census data *is* rife with errors and discrepancies from census-to-census, and even Pearl's birth year 1916 is erroneously entered as 1917 in one census.[37] But not in the above case... Only in June 2019, while sorting the raw material in piles — Weiss-Ehrlich-Reiter-Schwarzer — to box all the data printouts and scholarly articles for posterity, I noticed the witness on the citizenship application of Rosa Zand/Sahn's brother Harris Sahn (Thea Sahn's grandfather) was a Morris Sahn. Out of curiosity, I took a break to search for him on Familysearch.org. In a roundabout way, the results *may* have solved this enigma of when Nana's mother died.

This kind of sleuthing into family lore oft boils down to noticing a tiny fact that may be significant: Morris (born in 1865-1869 on different documents) was clearly Harris' brother (born 1868) although a Morris was never mentioned in the scant family oral narratives. The clincher was Morris' second marriage on 23 January 1897 to Enny/Annie Silverman which cites his parents' names — taking Nana's *maternal* ancestors back another generation. His father's name (Nana's maternal grandfather) was listed as Getzel Sahn. But the surprise was *his* mother's name: Gmendel Mantel! Likewise, Morris' 23 December 1931 death certificate spelled her name "Gwendel" Mentel. Gmendel, an exceedingly rare name, was *Nana*'s birth name, thus clearly Nana

37. The information was provided by the head of the household to census-takers, without any supporting documents and there was no comparison of data from decade-to-decade. Not only was age often estimated; it appears that dates were also 'adjusted' for convenience sake — for example, to make oneself older (when getting married, for example). Moreover, there are gross errors — to the extent that in the 1910 census, *all* the children in Jacob Reiter's household appear as 'Reiters' including the two Raubfogel kids, Rae and Joe.

Radekhiv marketplace, 1900 and today

was named in memory of her maternal grandmother — Gmendel/Gwendel (née Martel) Sahn — Rosa Zand/Sahn's mother. I couldn't help but recall how Nana told us repeatedly when we were kids that when she wanted to Americanize her name "people suggested Gwendolyn, but I said it was 'too fancy', so I chose the name Anna". Digging deeper for additional clues, the handwritten original of the 1900 Census shows eight of Morris Sahn's nine offspring; his seventh child, named Rosey Sahn, was born in May 1897. In other words, *assuming* Rosey Sahn was named after her father Morris' sister, Nana's mother died in her sleep in early 1897. So the 1910 Census could be correct! Indeed, subsequently, Jacob's naturalization papers that I found after 'discovering' Morris, confirmed this, stating Nana's father (whose address on Essex Street on the Lower East Side was identical to Jacob and Rosie Reiter's in the 1910 and 1915 New York censuses) had arrived in New York from Hamburg on 10 October 1896. An exact date. This was eight months before his brother named his daughter Rosey in May 1897, and just short of five years before the three girls arrived in America in July 1902.

It sounds incredible, but could it be that the Reiter kids had "been wandering around this *shtetl*" (as Pearl put it) for *five years* until they were sent tickets and arrived in America in the summer of 1902? That's what it would seem.

Only Yetta's age on the ship manifest (there were no birth certificate in those days) is off and begs the question whether Rosa Zand/Sahn died when Yetta was still either an infant or a young toddler when her father Jacob Reiter had only been in America for a short time and was in no position to send for his orphaned children. If this is the case, Nana's youngest sister Yetta/Pearl would have been at least five — not four when she arrived at Ellis Island (conceived before late September 1896 when her father left for America, and born *before* May 1897). Alas, indicative of just how difficult it is to pin down actual ages even based on census data, in the 1910 Census Yetta Reiter (who by then was living with her sister and brother-in-law "Mike Schwarzer") was said to be 16 years old (which would mean she was born in 1894) and would make her eight when she arrived in America...not four or five. In the 1940 Census, Yetta said she was three when she came (born in 1899)...

Keep in mind, when queried about her age Nana only knew "we were three little girls" on the boat; she didn't know how old she was, in what year (according to the Gregorian calendar) she was born, not to mention an exact day of birth. The date 2 April was chosen at random by Pearl when she registered her mother to receive a belated Social Security number, giving her estimated birth year as 1889 (they figured she had to be at least 11 years old to have 'taken care of her sisters on the boat' when they arrived in 1902 as she said). In fact, she was nine.

A bit of context: According to the *Encyclopedia Judaica*, the marking of birthdays was not a Jewish custom. Furthermore, for generations, to call attention to a good thing—including a certain child was viewed as 'tempting the evil eye'—undue attention that had to be 'cancelled out' by immediately saying '*kinahora*' (*keyn eyn hara* in Yiddish or *bli eyn ha-ra* in Hebrew): 'without the evil eye". Chabad sources add that other than a boy's third birthday when a male child received his first haircut, the fifth birthday when he began the formal study of Torah and the child's bar mitzvah at age thirteen, among traditional Jews birthdays passed without ceremony.

As for exact dates, the year was not marked...and certainly not according to the Christian Gregorian calendar, and at best one knew 'I was born just before Hanukah' or I was born 'during Sukkot' although community records were more precise (with the full date according to the Hebrew calendar).

I found no familiar first names on Ancestry.org in the index of *Galicia, Ukraine, Births, Marriages, and Deaths 1789–1905* when keying-in 'Reiter' in the Zloczow and Kamionka sub-districts of the Lemberg/Lvov administrative region to which Radekhiv belonged in the latter half of the 19th century under Austrian rule. In the absence of a Radekhiv registry, we'll never know for sure how many years elapsed. Digging further into Austrian records would require hiring a genealogist in Europe.

What's for sure, the New York Marriage Index 1866–1937 testifies that Jacob Reiter only remarried in America on 10 March 1902.[38]

---

38. This marriage certificate initially eluded me in umpteen searches because his new wife's name was spelled Rosa Rabvogel instead of Raubfogel.

Date of Marriage.	March 10th 1902
Groom's Full Name.	Jacob Reiter
Residence.	85 Gerry St.
Age.	38
Color.	White
Single or Widowed.	Widowed
Birthplace.	Austria
Father's Name.	Joseph Reiter
Mother's Maiden Name.	Rebecka Goldberg
Number of Groom's Marriage.	Second
Bride's Full Name.	Rose Reiter
Residence.	85 Gerry St.
Age.	31
Color.	White
Single or Widowed.	Widowed
Birthplace.	Galitzia
Maiden Name, if a Widow.	Rose Rabvogel
Father's Name.	Joseph Rabvogel
Mother's Maiden Name.	Fanny Berg
Number of Bride's Marriage.	First
Name of Person performing Ceremony.	Rev. Joseph Gottschalk
Official Station.	[illegible]
Residence.	86 Graham Ave
Date of Record.	

Jacob Reiter's second marriage certificate

Discovery of the date calls into question how accurate the family version of events is. Did Jacob Reiter "remarry to start a new family having forgotten about his previous family, as many men did"? Or did he marry the widow Rose Raubfogel because he would soon — within a few short months — have three or four small children on his doorstep while he was fully occupied eking out a living dawn-to-dusk as a peddler with a pushcart? Marriages of convenience were very common. But the proximity of dates of his marriage and the children's arrival tells a slightly different story than the family's oral narrative, although Rosa Zand/Sahn's brothers Harris and Morris and their wives may indeed have pressured and even helped to bring the orphaned children over.

Be what may, lack of data leaves a five-year 'window' of possibilities as to when the children were orphaned, particularly considering nine-year-old Nana described her father meeting them at Ellis Island, noting that the younger children — said to be ages six and four, didn't recognize their father, suggesting he'd been absent a *number* of years if Nana's sisters didn't recognize him. She told the interviewer on tape:

> [When we arrived] our father met us [came to fetch us]. I pointed him out to my younger sisters saying 'that's Papa'... He was very tall [Jacob Reiter was only 5'7" but Nana was, after all, only about nine years old — DA] and had a nice long beard. And he came to us.

No matter how many years had gone by, what is known for sure is that in mid-1902[39] the four orphans were sent for — the ship manifest noting their passage had been paid by their father and that he would

Searching, in some cases, is a balancing act in setting filters between 'sound alike's, which bring up hundreds to thousands of 'possibles', while 'exactly as spelled' brings up manageable quantities of data to plow through but may overlook the right record.

39. Polish records show 28,000 Jews departed from Poland between 1890–1904; 64 percent (18,000) from five Polish provinces on the right bank of the Vistula — that is, in Galicia (the poorest part of Poland) where Radekhiv is situated.

Furst Bismarck, circa 1899–1902

fetch them, giving his street address.[40] As mentioned above, when the three girls were met at Ellis Island by Jacob Reiter, he was already remarried to Rose Raubfogel, a widow with two children of her own. The three little girls, registered in the ship manifest as Gmendel (Anna) age nine, Chane (Hannah) age six and Itte (Yetta)[41] age four, had traveled steerage from Hamburg on 9 July 1902 on the *Furst Bismarck* — a ten-day voyage, along with another 700 third-class (steerage) immigrants among the ship's 1,292 passengers. Nana described the voyage 73 years later, as she remembered it:

> We got to the ship with 'marks' — that is, we were marked that 'these children have to be taken care of by a nurse'

---

40. Irrespective of when or why Jacob remarried, family oral history held it was Rosa Zand's kin, the Sahns in America (said to be "a sister or a sister-in-law") who insisted the four orphans be brought to their father in America. See also note 45 for details.

41. I had searched the Ellis Island archive repeatedly for a 'Yetta' and a 'Hannah' with various spellings, without success. Only when I systematically scrolled down through *all the Reiters in the Ellis Island online archive* (!) did I find them — and only because I spotted the Yiddish-Hebrew pronunciation for Hannah and Yetta: Chane and Itte.

> [the shipping company nurse, on board]. The nurse came from the ship, took all we three little girls down to steerage and we reached America. We were all sick — very sick on the seven-day voyage. We couldn't see anything from steerage, and we didn't see other people. The nurse came, she brought us food, but we couldn't eat — we were seasick.

Conditions in steerage were horrific according to a 1908 congressional investigatory commission (after in 1907 slight improvement on paper in the "minimum passenger space" had been enacted, but not enforced). The report charged "disgusting, demoralizing" and "revolting" conditions generally prevailed in transatlantic steerage.[42] A 1911 report of the Immigration Commission to President William Taft fills in the gaps about conditions in steerage — where immigrants were 'accommodated' below deck on the same level as the food galleys, engine rooms and the steamship's steering mechanisms — thus, the term 'steerage'. Packed in between regular first- and second-class passengers in the upper decks and the heavy cargo assigned to the lower decks as a ballast for the stability of the vessel — steerage passengers were little more than what one observer dubbed "self-loading freight". The Immigration Commission's report was graphic:

> [...] The only provisions for eating are frequently shelves or benches along the sides or in the passages of sleeping compartments. [...] Toilets and washrooms are completely inadequate [...] The ventilation is almost always inadequate, and the air soon becomes foul. The unattended vomit of the seasick, the odors of not too clean bodies, the reek of food and the awful stench of the nearby toilet rooms make the atmosphere of the steerage such that it is a marvel that human flesh can endure it... Most immigrants lie in their berths for most of the voyage, in a stupor caused by the

42. Drew Keeling, "Oceanic Travel Conditions and American Immigration: 1890–1914", (Munich: MPRA, 2013), https://mpra.ub.uni-muenchen.de/47850/1/MPRA_paper_47850.pdf.

> foul air. The food often repels them. [...] It is almost impossible to keep personally clean. All of these conditions are naturally aggravated by the crowding.[43]

Pearl added some additional details of Nana's crossing in a tape, from stories her mother told her time and again (stories Nana also told us, her grandchildren, when we were young):

> She went up and would talk to people above — they may not have been first-class passengers but they weren't in steerage and were in a better situation than she was, asking 'could they please get her oranges' and they went and got her oranges [that helped with seasickness]. When they landed, my grandfather was there. They notified him somehow that his kids were coming.

According to Ellis Island's permanent exhibit, immigration authorities sent postcards to the 'recipients' of such unescorted children, and they came to pick up the kids with this 'claim ticket'. In the meantime, unaccompanied minors were kept in a special holding area on Ellis Island — sometimes for days, sometimes for weeks — until someone came to claim them. In an Ellis Island video clip about the holding area, an elderly woman who had been one such child recalled regarding these 'marks' Nana spoke of: "We had to wear these tags [on the ship and at Ellis Island] that made us look like marked-down merchandise in Macy's Bargain Basement". (Don't miss

Unescorted children,
Ellis Island Museum exhibit

43. Cited in "The Immigrant Journey", OhRanger.com, http://www.ohranger.com/ellis-island/immigration-journey.

the award-winning documentary *Island of Hope — Island of Tears* about the crossing, traveling steerage to America!)[44]

Between 1881–1914 some 350,000 Jews left Galicia — the poorest part of Poland, seeking a better future, the majority going to North America, others migrating to Central Europe, and still others heading for South America or Palestine.

~

If all four children were sent for, why did only the three girls arrive in America?

Tragically, their eldest[45] brother Joe (Josel) Reiter was turned back at the dock in Hamburg due to an "eye ailment" according to family

---

44. Charles Guggenheim, National Park Service, "Island of Hope — Island of Tears", YouTube video, 28 minutes, 1989, https://www.youtube.com/watch?v=u-4wzVuXPznk. History buffs will also enjoy reading Vincent Cannato, *American Passage: The History of Ellis Island* (New York: HarperCollins, 2009) for more details on the 'immigration experience'.

45. Was Joe the eldest of the four orphans? There are multiple discrepancies in age: Nana said Josel was older than she, and had been assisting the *melamed* or tutor in the *heder* in Radekhiv where three- to five-year-old boys went to school in the *shtetl*. If Joe was older than Nana, he would have been at least ten years old in 1902 (born in 1892) *if* Nana's age is correct on the passenger list... The 1910 Census — when he was already living with his father in America — says Joe was eleven when he arrived in 1906, and 15 (born in 1895) at the time of the 1910 Census... However, the *Kronprinz Wilhelm* ship manifest says passenger #15 Josel Reiter was nine when he sailed for America from Bremen in June 1906 (that is, born 1897)... Whether Joe was nine or eleven or fourteen when he boarded the ship to America, there are two women from Radekhiv (spelled Radziechów on the document — the Polish spelling) on the same page of the passenger list: One (#9 on the manifest) was a married 26-year-old passenger named Keile Moyhel who was being met by her husband Moses. (Although Kyla is an unusual name, in fact, it turns out Keile Moyhel was *not* a close relative...According to Thea, her sister Kyla [née Sahn] Volter was named after her father Martin Sahn's *mother* whose name is given as Kate in census data.) This paternal grandmother Kyla/Kate is believed to be the relative of Rosa Zand — who in fact was 'only' a sister-in-law, not a

oral history. Probably he had or was suspected of having trachoma.

Trachoma is an infectious bacterial disease found mainly, but not only, among children. In the first stage, it causes "itchy, watery, and painful eyes". Thus, initially, it looks quite similar to benign forms of conjunctivitis or "pink eye" before the telltale signs of trachoma (granulation of the inner surface of the upper eyelid) appear in the second stage.[46] Medical diagnoses in Europe and America were made within seconds by public health officials on the lookout for trachoma, and not surprisingly, there were incorrect diagnoses.[47] In 1897 trachoma had become the first disease classified as 'a dangerous contagious disease'

---

sister — who pressured to bring the children over. Also on the same boat with Josel Reiter was *another* 26-year-old passenger (#26 on the manifest) from Radekhiv–Dwojre Grim who was single and being met by her father. She *could* have been 'keeping an eye on Josel' to some extent. Yet, her presence could also be mere coincidence. As for Josel's age, there are many lapses in Nana's memory on the tape she made at age 88. But her niece Evelyn (Yetta's daughter) also told me in 2018 that Joe was the oldest, and in the tapes, Pearl lists Joe first when numerating the Reiter children.

46. Medical historian and pediatrician Howard Markel writes: "There were few effective means of treatment that would ameliorate the disease and make [Eastern European Jews with trachoma] eligible to immigrate to the United States". Markel describes in detail the daily treatment involved in curing even early stage trachoma — costly, painful and lengthy, taking months. Would such a poor family as the Reiters in a small *shtetl* have had the access to or the means to pay for such treatment? Had Josel endured such an ordeal prior to arriving in 1906, wouldn't this episode and the miracle of 'getting through' Ellis Island have been part of the family's oral history (or was it buried due to the stigma associated with the disease)? For the summary, see Howard Markel, "'The Eyes Have It': Trachoma, the Perception of Disease, the United States Public Health Service, and the American Jewish Immigration Experience, 1897-1924", *Bulletin of the History of Medicine* 74, no. 3 (2000): 525–60, http://dx.doi.org/10.1353/bhm.2000.0137/.

47. See, for example, P.J. Imperato and G.H. Imperato, "The Medical Exclusion of an Immigrant to the United States of America in the Early Twentieth Century. The Case of Cristina Imparato", *Journal of Community Health* 33, no. 4 (2008): 225–240, http://dx.doi.org/10.1007/s10900-008-9088-6/. The middle-aged Italian woman was deported within three days.

that would be grounds for denial of entry to the United States, and Public Health Service officers began performing medical inspections on all immigrants arriving in the United States examining their eyelids with a buttonhook for signs of the disease. Trachoma was not only contagious; it was a primary cause of blindness due to scarring of the cornea if left to progress untreated. By the outset of the 20th century other "loathsome and contagious diseases" as they were called (serious and trivial) had been added as grounds for rejection by American immigration officials and medical examiners (from tuberculosis and ringworm to 'feeblemindedness' or physical deformities).[48]

Shipping lines had passengers like Joe Reiter screened at the port of departure since those turned back at Ellis Island were returned to Europe at the shipping company's expense and the companies also had to pay for the cost of their detention at Ellis Island until deported (or during their treatment). It is estimated that half those detained and barred on medical grounds at Ellis Island had trachoma. The number of 'rejects' arriving at American ports dropped rather dramatically after 1903 following the passage of an amendment to immigration laws that imposed a $100 fine (raised to $200 in 1907) for every passenger afflicted "with a loathsome or with a dangerous contagious disease... [that] might have been detected by means of a competent medical examination at the time of foreign embarkation".

There were no refunds for unused tickets, so Joe was left behind while the three little girls sailed for America in 1902. Scholars say those

---

48. In fact, there were Boards of Special Inquiry at Ellis Island that reviewed every case where immigrants were detained on either financial grounds or medical grounds. Aside from those with contagious diseases, the two categories were often linked — viewing a weak physique grounds for "likely to become a public charge" — ranging from a man with a hernia who might not find work or a six-year-old minor who couldn't walk due to polio. Many persons flagged by medical personnel were admitted by the Boards' immigration officials who were not physicians. On the workings of the medical examiners and the Boards, see Elizabeth Yue, "Medical Inspection of Immigrants at Ellis Island, 1891-1924", *Bulletin of the New York Academy of Medicine* 56, no. 5 (1980): 488–510, https://www.ncbi.nlm.nih.gov/pmc/articles/PMC1805119/pdf/bullny/.

who were rejected on medical grounds were sent home and advised to "try again once they had been cured".

The Ellis Island Foundation stresses with pride that only one percent of the immigrants who arrived at Ellis Island between 1892 and 1924 were turned away. There is no mention that most 'candidates for rejection' after 1897 were turned back in Europe at the German border where they underwent a medical examination by physicians employed by the shipping company — oft followed by quarantine for a short period, then a second medical examination just before boarding at German ports. Such 'undesirable émigrés' never reached Ellis Island. For the year Joe Reiter was reunited with his family in June 1906, four years after his sisters left Europe, the United States Public Health Service claimed that "in the fiscal year ending in June 1906, 29,600 people with trachoma had been prevented from leaving foreign ports".[49] There were countless others who were not permitted to board on other grounds — medical or socioeconomic.

Medical historian Dvora Dwork says that according to a contemporary article in *Scribner's Magazine* published in 1901 "most of those detained by the physicians at Ellis Island for trachoma were Jews".[50] The journalist's full eyewitness account regarding those detained for further scrutiny and questioned by a Board of Inquiry is riveting.[51] Sholem

---

49. Kathleen Yu, "Naturalizing a 'Foreign Menace': Trachoma, the Geography of Disease, and Public Health in America, 1897-1938", Yale University, *History of Science, Medicine, and Public Health*, 3 April 2017, https://hshm.yale.edu/sites/default/files/files/Yu%2C%20Kathleen%20-%20Senior%20essay.pdf.

50. Tuberculosis, trachoma, and *tinea capitis* (ringworm) — dubbed TTT, were not only detrimental to health, they were "a key factor delaying Jewish immigration". Therefore in 1921 a special mass TTT eradication program was embarked on by OZE — founded in 1912 in St. Petersburg to enhance health among East European Jews and allow Jewish families, including those in Poland, to emigrate. See Shifra Shvarts et al., "The Mass Campaign to Eradicate Ringworm Among the Jewish Community in Eastern Europe, 1921–1938", *American Journal of Public Health* 103, no. 4 (2013): e56–e66, http://dx.doi.org/10.2105/AJPH.2012.301020/. This was, however, *after* Joe arrived in America.

51. Dwork (see note 52) citing Arthur Henry, "Among the Immigrants",

Aleichem captured the same heartbreaking moment of those pulled aside before boarding while still in Europe, in a short story the Yiddish writer published in February 1917 entitled "Off for the Golden Land":

> The time comes to go on board the ship. People tell them that they should take a walk to the doctor. So they go to the doctor. The doctor examines them and finds they are all hale and hearty and can go to America, but she, that is Goldele, cannot go, because she has trachomas on her eyes. At first her family did not understand. Only later did they realize it. That meant that they could all go to America but she, Goldele, would have to remain here in Antwerp. So there began a wailing, a weeping, a moaning. Three times her mamma fainted. Her papa wanted to stay here, but he couldn't. All the ship tickets would be lost. So they had to go off to America and leave her, Goldele, here until the trachomas would go away from her eyes...[52]

Schribner's, 29 (1901): 302. *Schribner's* was a reputable and prestigious American periodical that up to 1939 competed with *Harper's Monthly* and *The Atlantic Monthly*. The original piece can be accessed at https://babel.hathitrust.org/cgi/pt?id=mdp.39015030597127;view=1up;seq=8. Choose page 302 (pp. 301-311).

52. Deborah Dwork, "Health Conditions of Immigrant Jews on the Lower East Side of New York: 1880-1914", *Medical History* 25, no. 1 (1981): 1–40, https://doi.org/10.1017/S0025727300034086/. American consuls in the ports reported émigrés rejected by doctors weren't informed of such by physicians; they were sent back to their lodgings with a special 'red slip' of paper that indicted the individual would not be allowed to board, leaving it to the proprietor to break the news to the family, thus avoiding tearful scenes that could spark pandemonium on the docks. See Henry W. Diederich, "Immigration Archives — Inspection of Immigrants at Bremen–Norddeutscher Lloyd (1903): A Letter from Mr. Diederich to Mr. Peirce", Gjenvick-Gjønvik Archives, https://www.gjenvick.com/Immigration/Medical-Mental-Inspection-OfImmigrants/1903-InspectionOfImmigrantsAtBremen-NorddeutscherLloyd.html and O. W. Hellmrich, "Inspection of Emigrants by the Hamburg America Line (1903): Mr. Hellmrich to Mr. Peirce", Gjenvick-Gjønvik Archives, https://www.gjenvick.com/Immigration/Inspection/.

Life on the Lower East Side circa 1900

Jacob Reiter and Rose Raubfogel's second marriage[53] following the deaths of their respective spouses and prior to the arrival of the three orphaned Reiter girls in America, led to the birth of a string of offspring — four half-brothers and half-sisters[54] in addition to the four Reiter children born in Europe. Ties among the eight children were warm and very strong, like those of full siblings[55] — but relations between Nana and her two sisters, and their stepmother Rose Raubfogel after they landed on her doorstep, were far from rosy. Pearl said:

> My mother used to tell me stories about the only grandmother I knew [Rose Raubfogel/Reiter — DA] — how mean she was to them.
>
> She probably figured they would never come when she married my grandfather. [...] A sister of my [biological] grandmother Rosa Zand 'brought them over' and pretty much deposited them on my grandfather's doorstep, in this

53. Actually, this was Jacob Reiter's *third* marriage: According to Pearl, Jacob Reiter was married for ten years in Europe to a woman who was "barren" (whom he divorced, in accordance to Jewish Law) before marrying Nana's mother Rosa Zand. Unfortunately, there is no online town registry of births marriages and deaths in Radekhiv from the turn of the century to examine (newly digitized records are being added all the time). Most remaining Jews perished in the Holocaust and according to the International Jewish Cemetery Project (Under Ukraine, see "Radekhov" at https://iajgscemetery.org/eastern-europe/ukraine/radekhov) little remains of Radekhiv's unmarked and untended Jewish cemetery save pieces of broken headstones, some dating back to the 18th century. The site is now a municipal dump, some of the plots currently being used by residents as kitchen gardens.

54. The four additional Reiter children (Jossie/Josephine, Ben, Estelle and Frank) were very close to the 'original' four Reiter children (Joe, Nana, Hannah and Yetta).

55. The youngest — Frank Reiter — had a twin who died immediately after birth. Pearl recalled in one of the tapes: "Frank was rather sickly. My grandmother was rather old by this time, and didn't have much milk...so my mother [Nana was already married — DA] who was still nursing Ruth (Pearl's older sister born in 1908] *nursed Uncle Frank* [her half-brother].

> tenement house. They were very poor, so you can imagine the reaction: 'Oh God, three more mouths to feed!' She was not nice to them, although the stepmother never touched my mother who was the 'guardian' of her two sisters.
>
> The stepmother and her daughter Rae took things out on the youngest — Yetta, whom they used to pinch. Both were mean-spirited and [Nana] used to tell stories how the stepmother would go out and buy ribbons for Rae's hair and let them wear shoelaces.

In the meantime, brother Joe Reiter had been sent back to Radekhiv after being barred at the boat. Several years passed. Then out of the blue, Nana insisted that her mother had 'come to her in a dream' and her mother had told Nana that she must 'save her brother' left in Europe. Thus, at age eleven or twelve, Nana and Yetta worked all summer as chambermaids at a hotel in Lakewood, New Jersey to earn money to buy Josel a ticket. Pearl explained the circumstances:

> It sounds like something out of *Fiddler on the Roof* where they [Tevye] had this so-called dream where she [grandmother Tzeitel] says 'not to marry the butcher'? People took dreams very seriously. [...] She told Aunt Hannah — 'someway we have to earn money to bring Joe over because Momma came to me in this dream' [...] So they went to Lakewood and worked as chambermaids... Then the guy didn't pay them, the owner of the place. And the two of them were sitting in the bus terminal crying, and believe it or not, a Catholic priest came over and asked why they were crying, and he went and got the money from this bastard owner who was gypping them out of their summer wages and put them on a bus back to New York.

The cost of a 'budget-rate' steerage ticket — $34 — was equal to a month's wages for an unskilled laborer, but after 1900 a passport (an extra expense in addition to travel to the port of departure) was also required.[56]

Nana's father Jacob Leiser Reiter made his living — such as it was — selling tomatoes off of a pushcart on Pitt Street on the Lower East Side.[57] Nana recalled those days:

> My father was working — going to the market at three in the morning to pick up the fruit and bring it to sell to make a living. [...] When I complained to my father about how mean my stepmother was, he would say to me '*Mine zis kint*, [My little girl] I can't do anything else.' He worked day and night to support a family like that. It was hard, because [while] everything was cheap, we didn't make the money to cover [expenses].

Pearl also recalled her grandfather's pushcart, decades later:

> When Frank was in high school — Grandpa was already getting pretty old but he still had the pushcart and still had to make a living. Every morning, before going to school, Frank [the youngest of the Reiter children] would go with Grandpa to some kind of warehouse where they kept the

---

56. Pearl said they wanted to "buy Josel a more expensive second-class ticket, because such passengers were not scrutinized as thoroughly as those traveling steerage" (actually immigration officials were aware of this tactic) but nevertheless Joe Reiter was found in Ellis Island records so, he apparently went steerage... Indeed, first- and second-class passengers were processed by immigration officials who came on board when the boat docked in Manhattan and such passengers got off in Manhattan. Those in steerage got off the ship and were herded *en masse* to a barge headed for Ellis Island (along with some second-class foreign citizens sent for more scrutiny). The ticket price is cited in Drew Keeling, "Oceanic Travel Conditions and American Immigration: 1890s–1914" (see note 42).

57. For fleeting vintage footage of the pushcarts that lined the streets, see "Take a Ride Through the Turn-of-the-Century Lower East Side", Bowery Boogie, 0:41, 31 January 2014, https://www.boweryboogie.com/2014/01/take-ride-turn-century-lower-east-side-video/.

> pushcarts overnight, and he would push it to the place where his father 'stationed' himself on Pitt Street. I don't know if they had licenses or what but he always had the same spot, so he probably paid the city for this spot at the curb. And after school Frank would take the pushcart back to the shed. For me a big treat was to go by my grandfather's pushcart on Pitt Street and the first thing he would say to me was 'Pearly, do you want a tomato?' and he would pick me a very nice tomato. And I'd say 'Only if it's with salt...' So he would go into the grocery and get some salt. For me it was an afterschool treat. A whole tomato.
>
> [...] In retrospect, I still can't figure out how he made a living selling only tomatoes... He probably *didn't* make much of a living, but there was always food in his house.

Deeply religious, Jacob Reiter only had his picture taken twice — for his citizenship papers, apparently in November 1915 at age 55, and when his first great-grandchild Wendy was born in June 1941 when he was between 77-81 years of age:[58]

> He didn't allow anyone to take his picture, because it was a 'graven image', but he was so proud that he had his picture taken with Wendy — his first great-granddaughter. What he said was 'by [Wendy] being born and he living to see it, that was his entrance card to heaven' so he let us take a picture. I don't know by what logic, but we were happy we got a good picture of him.

---

58. Jacob Reiter's age in the first photo for his 1915 citizenship application is stated as 55 (and therefore he would be 81 in the second photo). His earlier 2nd marriage license states he was 38 in 1902, and therefore the first photo for naturalization would have been taken when he was four years younger — 51, making him 77 in the second 1941 photo. As already noted, his marriage to Rose Raubfogel led to two additional minors instantly 'entering the family' so to speak: Rae and Joe Raubfogel from his new wife's previous marriage — both born in Europe. Tragically, Joe would die at age 23 in the 1918 Spanish influenza pandemic.

Jacob Reiter, Nana's father

Nana recalled life on the Lower East Side as a kid, at the outset of the 20th century:[59]

> We lived in three rooms on the second floor on Ritz Street in New York. We were three children, and my stepmother's two made us five — with a sixth on the way. People [boarders — DA] slept on chairs, slept on a couch. People slept on the floor — so we could make ends meet. That was the kind of life we had. That lasted until I was about 11 years old. In the meantime two more children were

59. For vintage photos and a reconstructed tenement house — visit the Tenement Museum on the Lower East Side at https://www.tenement.org/ and read my 10 July 2010 feature article "Immigration Commemoration" in the *Jerusalem Post* weekend magazine, written after reading *American Passage* and interviewing the author Vincent Cannato, then visiting Ellis Island and the Tenement Museum, https://www.jpost.com/Travel/Travel-News/Immigration-commemoration.

> born, so we got a four-room apartment...but three more boarders too, so we could pay the rent. People slept one on top of another — here in America, not in Europe. The boarders came [to America] and looked for a room. We served supper and a place to sleep and there was more money coming in.

An 1890–1893 survey revealed boarders paid ten cents a night to sleep, and extra for a meal. A full seven percent of the population on the Lower East Side was boarders — not only a source of income to pay the rent for families in the tenements, such packed sleeping arrangements were also a source of emotional stress and strain on family life. With or without boarders, a 1908 census of 250 families on the Lower East Side taken at the time by the philanthropist Baron de Hirsch found 50 percent slept three or four per room, and 25 percent with five or more per room. Nana's description was typical of the times.[60]

Anna Reiter (Nana) never had the opportunity for even a grade school education. She was only six or seven when her mother died and was immediately pressed into service as a surrogate mother for her younger siblings and never went to school. Nana arrived in the United States at age nine, but after one year, her stepmother pulled her out of public school[61] and thrust her into the same role — taking care of her younger siblings, and Nana only learned to read as an adult (using her industry, gutsiness and 'survival skills' to prevail):

> [...] My stepmother went [to the school] and told them she was moving to Rochester, New York — that she has

---

60. Data cited in Dwork, "Health Conditions of Immigrant Jews on the Lower East Side of New York 1880-1914" (see note 52).

61. Not only was she still learning English when she entered school. *The New York Times* reported in 1895 that population density on the Lower East Side was as crowded as Bombay and by the time Nana arrived in 1902, congestion was even worse. Due to the acute shortage of public schools on the Lower East Side, kids only attended half-day sessions during the one year that Nana went to school. Cited in Dwork, "Health Conditions of Immigrant Jews on the Lower East Side of New York 1880–1914" (see note 52).

> brothers there. She made-believe she was going in order to get transfer papers to the new school, then took me out of school and put me in the house with four little children that I should take care of them. [...] She wanted me out of school [in a way that the authorities and the truant officers wouldn't look for her — DA] in order to send me to work.

In one tape Pearl recalls:

> My step-grandmother was a terrific cook — always baking and cooking, and that's how my mother learned to cook so well. But as a stepmother she was terrible. My mother would say 'you know Cinderella's stepmother? She was *good* compared to mine'.
>
> But the crazy thing is, as an adult, when Nana was married and had kids of her own, she maintained a relationship with her and I remember Mama going to take care of [her stepmother] when [Rose Raubfogel/Reiter] had cancer.

Already at age eleven or twelve — after a year or two as fulltime nanny and helper in her stepmother's house, Nana went out to work, finding employment in a sweatshop making artificial flowers — the reason she would write she was a "florist" on her marriage certificate and would tell the 1915 New York census-taker the same when asked her occupation. Nana recalled her first paying job:

> A friend was working at *Flowers and Feathers* on Broadway and 3rd Street, and I went to work there. And the boss used to come in and say 'little Anna, get under the table' and all the other people covered me [*sic* hid me] with their feet when the inspector came to see that they don't have children working there. But he hired me because I was a good worker.
>
> [...] I had to be there at 8:00 AM and we worked until 6:00 PM. [...] I used to bring home work [piece work, from her employer — DA]. Mr. Winstein my boss put a box of things together and I knew how to manage, so I came home

> and I put out two tables together and put all the children to work. Each child did something else. And I was the boss. The boxes of raw material that I took home were bigger than me. He gave me the curlers and the tools and all the children had to do was put the flowers together. I taught them to do it.
>
> I worked and gave in the money [to my stepmother]. And I had a whip over my stepmother — that if she would hit my sisters, she wouldn't get my money. That was my whip.

Taking work home in the evening after a grueling workday, to help make ends meet, was typical of the times. Moreover, it was widespread that tenement apartments served not only as homes for the occupants but also doubled as workplaces. Thus, a good portion of the needle trade was carried out in apartments that in the daytime functioned as workshops for assembling precut garments, farmed out as 'piecework' by sub-contractors or sweatshop owners.

❧ *Anna Reiter and Michael Schwarzer*

On 22 March 1908, at the age of 15.5[62] Anna Reiter married Michael

---

62. The 1908 marriage certificate says Annie was 19 — but this is apparently a fabrication. According to Ellis Island records, when she arrived in America in 1902, she was nine (thus, born in 1892/3) and married at age 15½–16. She always said she was 12 years younger than Michael, making him 28 when they tied the knot but Michael apparently knocked a few years off his age while courting her... Polish records I discovered later record Michael as born in 1877 — that is, Michael was actually 31 when he married 16-year-old Annie (and indeed was 41 when he registered for the draft...and died five weeks later!). Nana always celebrated her birthday as if she was born in 1889; however, this date 2 April 1889, as already noted, was an *arbitrary date* (the exact year they arrived — 1902 — was not yet known)...*but Nana was actually nine, not twelve* when they sailed for America. In, other words, Nana was apparently born in 1893, and was not 97 when she died in October 1986, she was probably 94 or closer to 95 years old.

Schwarzer[63] (who was 31 years old, although he said he was 27). Michael, whose birth name was Menashe, came from Jaroslaw — a port city on the San River in southeast Poland. Like Radekhiv, Jaroslaw was also part of the Austro-Hungarian Empire at the time.[64] In 1897 — when Michael would have been 20 years old and may already have left or was about to leave — Jaroslaw had a Jewish population of 5,701 out of a total population of 11,660 (about half of the residents).

What kind of place was Jaroslaw? It had a lengthy history of keeping Jews out, or at least at arm's length... Although Jaroslaw[65] traces its

63. All Pearl knew about her father was that he died when she was two, and that her father had a wealthy half-brother in the silk importing business who lived Uptown, with whom the family had almost no contact after her father died. She had encountered them only twice, and she didn't even remember their names — only that there was this one "nice cousin" — Louie/Lee Schwarzer (whom I never found in online archives...nor in inquires with the Other Schwarzers; see The 'Other Schwarzers' in the Appendix).

64. GPS: 50°01'N / 22°41'E. Galicia — where both Jaroslaw and Radekhiv are situated, was restored to Poland in 1919, but today the two are part of Ukraine.

65. Information about Jaroslaw was gathered from a host of sources, the main ones including: Ohad Levi-Zaloscer (translator), "Jaroslaw", translated from "*Pinkas Hekehillot Polin*", in *Encyclopedia of Jewish Communities, Poland*, Vol. III (Jerusalem: Yad Vashem, 213-220), https://kehilalinks.jewishgen.org/jaroslaw/jaroslawhistory1.html; Association of the Jewish Historical Institute of Poland, https://www.polin.pl/pl; Israel Halperin, "Virtual Jewish World: Jaroslaw Poland", https://www.jewishvirtuallibrary.org/jaroslaw-poland; Yitzhak Alprovitz (ed.), *Sefer Jaroslaw* [Jaroslav Book] (Tel Aviv: Association for Those Originating from Jaroslaw, 1978), 23, (Hebrew), https://digitalcollections.nypl.org/items/aa74e940-79b1-0133-6e8a-00505686d14e/book#page/28/mode/1up. Among the detailed history of Jews in Jaroslaw, an 11-page pamphlet (which sometimes glosses over uncomfortable details, diplomatically speaking of the "disadvantageous legal status of Jews" in lieu of citing consecutive edicts of expulsions, and calling participants in a 1869 pogrom a "crowd" rather than a 'mob' or 'assailants') was collected and published by the Foundation for the Preservation of Jewish Heritage in Poland. Ironically, the Foundation's prime objective is to bolster the Polish economy by developing "profiled tourism based on Jewish cultural heritage" that includes touring southeast Poland, marketing-branding it as "the Chassidic Route" (by Jews and gentiles) with

history back to the 14th century, a substantial Jewish community only took root in the 16th and 17th centuries due to a ban in the mid-15th to mid-17th centuries on Jews in any numbers — three households were 'too much'. The ban, called *de non tolerandis Judaeis* edict[66] was not singular to Jaroslaw, but it led to expulsions from time-to-time when the number of 'exceptions' was perceived as threatening by local burghers. Nevertheless, the Jewish community continued to grow[67] despite uncertainty; the threat of expulsion hung over the community throughout the 18th century since the *de non tolerandis Judaeis* remained in the law code until 1797, although it was no longer enforced.[68]

Despite such stumbling blocks, Jaroslaw was a great commercial hub, attractive to Jews. Such status largely emanated from Jaroslaw's strategic geographic and economic importance for the movement of grain from the San to the Dnieper rivers. In the 16th and 17th centuries, great fairs were held in the town three times a year — purported to be the largest in Europe. According to the Jaroslaw Municipality, the biggest of the three was held in August — a four-week affair that drew merchants not only from Europe but also from the Middle East who traded among other things in wheat, textiles, leather, metal products,

---

millions being poured into restoration of empty synagogues as tourist attractions. The Chassidic Route's itinerary covers a string of 20 towns in the Jaroslaw area (remains of synagogues and cemeteries) that have a rich Jewish heritage...but no living Jews. See Foundation for the Preservation of Jewish Heritage in Poland, "Jaroslaw — The Chassidic Route", 2008, https://fodz.pl/download/szlak_chasydzki_jaroslaw_EN.pdf.

66. The 1571 decree prohibited Jews to reside in more than two houses inside the town. When 'too many Jews' nevertheless managed to live in Jaroslaw *de facto*, the ban was renewed in 1687 — banishing them to the outskirts of the city.

67. According to the community's history in *Sefer Jaroslaw*, (see note 65), economic competition with gentile merchants caused periods of tension; in 1869 Jaroslaw even witnessed a ten-day pogrom in which houses of Jews were damaged and their shops plundered while authorities stood by, until an influential Jew got the local garrison to intervene.

68. See Cornelia Aust, *The Jewish Economic Elite: Making Modern Europe* (Bloomington, IN: Indiana University Press, 2018), 96.

jewelry, salt and spices. But the city's reputation was closely tied to the incredibly large livestock market—with some 40,000 oxen and 20,000 horses exchanging hands each year.[69] Jewish traders participated in the fair in large numbers and the Diaspora Museum described the Jewish character of this fair:

> The main one took place toward the fall, and Jewish traders took a prominent part. In business such as the sale of oxen, for which Jaroslaw was a market center, Jews were the main dealers. The fairs were the origin of Jaroslaw's importance in the history of Polish Jewry. Jewish communal leaders undertook to supervise the security of Jewish merchants visiting Jaroslaw [...] and a toll was levied on each trader or wagon to defray the expenses entailed. [...] It was a regular custom, as at every fair, that a place was set aside as a [temporary] synagogue to pray there every day.[70]

The traders were so numerous that according to the *responsa* of Rabbi Meir of Lublin they even borrowed a Torah scroll from an established nearby Jewish community in Przemysl to read the Torah on Saturdays. But Jaroslaw was not open to Jews actually setting up shop for good... Despite being unwelcome, by the 17th century Jews had become a permanent fixture. In 1640 a group of Jews built the town's first synagogue and established a Jewish cemetery on the outskirts of Jaroslaw in 1699. But it was only in 1738 that the Jewish community coalesced around a critical mass of 100 families.

Due to its role as the site of a major fair in the fall, Jaroslaw had the privilege of also serving as the venue for a very important and unique Jewish institution in Poland: the Council of Four Lands[71] that operated

69. For a short article about Jaroslaw's fair tradition, see "Trade and Fairs in Jarosław", Jarosław Tourist Guide, http://turystyka.jaroslaw.pl/en/artykul/2/trade-and-fairs-in-jaroslaw.

70. For further information about Jaroslaw see "Jaroslaw", The Museum of the Jewish People at Beit Hatfutsot, https://dbs.bh.org.il/place/jaroslaw.

71. For a discussion of the Council or Four Lands (*Vaad Arba Aratzot* in

from the second half of the 16th century up to 1764.[72] The Council's self-governing machinery was not designed to emancipate the Jews with enhanced autonomy, it was designed by the sovereign to streamline tax collection.[73] Yet in doing so, the Council was given jurisdiction by the government as the central body of Jewish authority in Poland over spiritual interests and communal affairs. It usually met twice a year for several days, alternating between Jaroslaw and Lublin — in Lublin in the spring between Purim and Passover (March–April) and at the fair in Jaroslaw [Galicia] in the Hebrew months of Av or Elul (August). Attending were representatives from each of the major Jewish communities in Poland. These scholars and wise men not only decided spiritual matters and legislated-regulated issues of internal governance, they even held supreme court sessions (in Lublin), sitting as a court of appeal, and held the power "to issue injunctions and binding decisions and to impose penalties at their discretion" [...] including civil and criminal suits with jurisdiction over all the Jews in Poland.

The Jews of Jarosław traditionally worked as financers or money-lenders, and toll collectors, leaseholders of inns and mills, and a member of the Jewish community even leased and ran a ferry crossing over the San River. By 1811, Jews (2,377) made up a quarter of Jaroslaw's 9,007 residents. As the Jewish community expanded, by the beginning of the 18th century most Jewish breadwinners were smalltime craftsmen and artisans, such as tailors, shoemakers, locksmiths, jewelers and glaziers. The upper crust (relatively speaking) was merchants — including importers of goods such as leather and textiles from Danzig/Gdańsk on

---

Hebrew), see *Jewish Encyclopedia*, s.v. "Council of Four Lands", 1906, http://www.jewishencyclopedia.com/articles/14164-synod-of-four-countries.

72. In 1764 it was disbanded by the Polish parliament having become superfluous.

73. The Council of the Four Lands' interpretations of the law were based on Talmudic legislation which, like secular law codes, is very broad and detailed. (Readers need to keep in mind that the Babylonian Talmud, as a legal code that was discussed and interpreted and reinterpreted, is encyclopedic in length: In standard print it would run 6,200 pages with opinions of thousands of rabbis covering every possible aspect of life.)

the Baltic (the destination for the area's grain).[74] Wealthier elements served as grain brokers and exporters.[75] There were also quite a few professionals in Jarosław's Jewish community, mostly physicians.

Unearthing the 'Other Schwarzers'

How did the Schwarzers make a living in Europe? There were no Schwarzers noted among the movers and shakers in narratives of Jaroslaw's history, although many names were cited. The only possible occupational paper trail found was an E. Schwarzer listed in the 1891 *Galicia Business Directory* as a "manufactured ware handler" in the field of "textiles" listed in the town Stryj.[76] Both Stryj and Jaroslaw are located in the Lvov Region—Jaroslaw 116 km (72 miles) east of Lvov; Stryj 65 km (40 miles) south of Lvov—both within the Austro-Hungarian Empire until 1919. In seeking to 'connect the dots' I discovered that by 1873 the two market towns were connected to Lvov by train. Could this person E. Schwarzer possibly be Michael's half-brother Esriel? (At this point I had already 'found' Michael's half-brother, about whom Pearl knew nothing other than 'there was a brother'—a crazy search discussed elsewhere under the rubric, the Other Schwarzers.) The name Schwarzer without a 't' is relatively rare, however, I discounted this possibility at first because Esriel and his wife Dora arrived in America in August 1890.

It was only four months after finding the *Galicia Business Directory*

---

74. Danzig linked the economies of Western and Eastern Europe.

75. One source says a Jewish broker dominated the corn market.

76. According to Iwona Dakiniewicz, "The Galician Railroad", Forgotten Galicia, 11 October 2018, https://forgottengalicia.com/the-galician-railway/. Styj (also spelled Stry) had a strong Jewish community for centuries—so much so that in 1676, Jewish residents requested that the Polish Monarch John III Sobieski change the day of fairs in Stryj from Saturday to Tuesday because trade activity had begun to move from Polish to Jewish hands! In 1890 there were 16,520 residents in Stryj including 6,572 Jews who were well integrated in all aspects of life in the city. For more details, see Kamil Baranski, "Stryj Before The Year 1919" in *Zagonczycy Chliborobi, Chasydzi of The Past: The Story of Stanislawowsko-Kolomyjsko-Stryjska Lands* (London, 1988) (English excerpt from Polish), https://kehilalinks.jewishgen.org/stryy/stryj-history.html.

that I encountered Esriel's 1906 Declaration of Intent to become a naturalized American citizen — citizenship that automatically included his household, thus, his wife and four children — Max, Gussie, Nate and Lillian were listed. His wife's place of birth was also duly recorded but hard to decipher. I scrutinized the document. It looked like "Slu, Austria" (the 'S' was identical to the 'S' in Schwarzer) but there was no such place in the online gazettes of Jewish towns and *shtetls* on Jewishgen.org and Geshergalicia.org. Not even close. Sometimes the devil is in the details. I sent the document to my detail-oriented nephew Ben Bard in California. Would Ben see something I missed? The answer was — yes:

> In addition to the "S" being the same as in "Schwarzer", the third letter seems to be an "r" because it's almost identical to the "r" in "Austria". So it looks like "S" "--" "r" "--". I want the final letter(s) to be "ee" although it looks very much like the "u" in "Austria"... The fact that it says "Austria" is a clue that it's somewhere in Galicia, though. Here's a very long shot: It's "Stree" where the "t" never got crossed. (Even though all the other "t"s got big bold crosses...) The circled town in the attached map is "Stryj" which had many different spellings (e.g., Stri, Stry, Stryei), but is pronounced "Stree".

Systematically reexamining the document, I saw that this was not a one-time oversight. Towards the end of the document, the clerk registrar didn't bother to cross his 't's or dot his 'i's. In short, the hastily scrawled notation *was* "Stree"–possibly "Strie" since for his children's

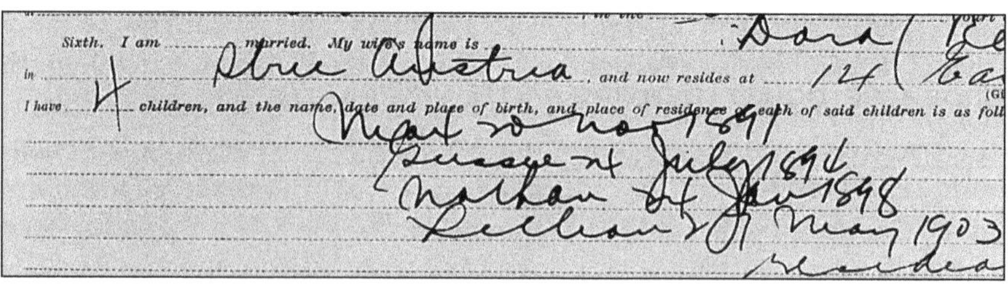
Sixth. I am married. My wife's name is Dora
in Stree Austria, and now resides at 124
I have 4 children, and the name, date and place of birth, and place of residence of each of said children is as foll[ows]
Max 20 Nov 1891
Gussie 24 July 1894
Nathan 24 Jan 1898
Lillian 27 May 1903

Deciphering Esriel's naturalization document

names that followed this notation at the bottom of the second page, the 't' in Nathan was not crossed with a flourish as earlier in the document and the 'i' in Gussie and Lillian also lacked a dot. It must have been a long day in circuit court...

So Dora had been born in Stryj! Actually, this exercise in penmanship was totally unconnected to the above search to shed light on the Schwarzers' occupations in Europe. It was part of an effort to pin-down whether Dora Schwarzer was of German-Jewish parentage (in one of the censuses she said she knew German, not just Yiddish) — something I felt was relevant in trying to decipher the loaded relationship between Dora and Nana after Michael's death (see The 'Other Schwarzers' in the Appendix).

It was only several hours later, as I was sharing the revelation that it was apparently Stryj with Mark Jacobson (a board member of the Gesher Galicia website who had graciously offered to help decipher/confirm the town name), that it suddenly dawned on me: Stryj! I know that name! I opened the final draft of the manuscript, hit Crl + F to search and keyed in the word "railroad"...and there it was. This couldn't be a mere coincidence. Not when E. Schwarzer in the *Galicia Business Directory* engaged in the same occupation — buying and selling lots of fabric — what in American parlance is labeled a 'textile jobber'... Esriel and his two eldest children ages 20 and 22 had listed in American censuses that their occupations were 'textile jobbers'. Clearly, the couple (who were married when they arrived in America) had been living in Stryj. The data for the 1891 *Directory* was surely collected in 1890 when they were still there (and the business in Stryj might have remained in the hands of Dora's family — the Rettichs) after the young couple left, but there are no subsequent business directories from Galicia.

Yes, members of the Schwarzer family were already textile brokers in Europe. Oral history and the paper trail support this. When they left for America in the summer of 1891 (Michael in Jaroslaw was 13 at the time), Esriel and Dora didn't go steerage where sleeping arrangements were gender-separated; records of their Atlantic crossing from Hamburg show they shared the same cabin, and the ship was a spanking new 'express' liner that would serve as a cruise ship in the Mediterranean during the winter months. There apparently were also relatives in France who were involved in silk, or at least textile import and export (see The 'Other Schwarzers' for details).

This listing in an 1891 primary source together with Dora's birthplace constitute boiler-plate evidence of the family's source of livelihood, but the French connection follows a pattern of 'kin in different cities' spread across the globe, interconnected in the same field of trade or commerce that has existed for hundreds if not thousands of years among Jews. Two sterling examples: One is well known, the Rothschild Family with a British branch, a French branch, an Austrian branch and a Naples branch. The other is less familiar: Among the contents of the famous *genizah* (sacred storeroom) of a Cairo synagogue[77] that spans a millennium beginning in the 9th century, alongside other sacred and secular documents is a mother lode of accounts, orders of payment, bookkeeping documents, private letters and business letters written in Judaeo-Arabic, Hebrew, Yiddish and Ladino which all use the Hebrew alphabet[78] — writings that testify to such family business webs. Families engaged in international trade who had familial networks of kin in other cities and other lands used to promote their commercial dealings are cited in a good number of studies of the *genizah*. The age-old Jewish joke about 'Export-Import-Rappaport' has more than a kernel of truth. Moreover, Jews, it turns out, have been silk importers (and traders in other textiles) since at least the late Middle Ages according to a host of *genizah* documents that discuss various types of silk and silk cloth, including two references in Hebrew to importing

---

77. For a peek at the fascinating source material in the Cairo *genizah*, see this truly piquant piece of research: Abraham David, "The Role of Egyptian Jews in Sixteenth-Century International Trade With Europe: A Chapter in Social-Economic Integration in the Middle East", in *'From a Sacred Source': Genizah Studies in Honour of Professor Stefan C. Reif* (Leiden: Brill, 2011), 99-126, https://www.academia.edu/13000286/.

78. Use of Hebrew letters — whether holy texts and *responsa* or a child's copybook when learning to read — meant such writings could not be trashed in the regular fashion; rather, such pages were put to rest in a 'sacred trash bin'. In Cairo, it consisted of a 'mail slit' near the ceiling in the synagogue, reachable only with a ladder. On the other side was a closed chamber where these papers accumulated for a thousand years.

meshi Florentine (Florence silk) and *bigdei meshi Florentine* (Florence silk apparel) to Cairo, while other sources provide evidence of Jewish imports from the Far East, as well.

In terms of religious ambience, the Jewish community in Jaroslaw boasted a renowned Talmudic center as well as adherents to Hassidic courts, the most dominant being followers of the Rokeach dynasty in Belz. The Jewish Enlightenment movement (*Haskalah*) that championed modernizing Jewish life[79] made limited inroads in Jaroslaw at the beginning. Eventually, in the mid-19th century, the efforts of a respected Jewish physician elected in 1845 to serve as chairperson or 'mayor' of the Jewish community (he would lead the community for 37 years, until 1883[80]) brought change — the tipping point being 1864 when Jaroslaw's Jews were split in a bitter quarrel over education between "those who wanted Hebrew and Judaic studies as the primary subjects and those who preferred German and secular subjects".[81] Subsequently, one hundred Jewish children enrolled in the General (i.e., public) schools taught in the German language, and by 1872, 300 Jewish children were attending such public schools — a state curriculum that the Jewish community supplemented by hiring a teacher in Jewish

79. A reformist movement in Jewish life led by Moses Mendelssohn that developed in Germany in the latter two-thirds of the 18th century that advocated optimal integration of the Jews into surrounding societies while continuing to safeguard Jewish continuity. The *Haskalah* called for a reform of traditional Jewish education to include general secular knowledge alongside Jewish studies to modernize Jewish economic life and thus improve the lot of the Jews — steps that included mastery of the vernacular and dropping external signs of Otherness in dress and custom. For a short overview of the Jewish Enlightenment — its roots and goals, see Louis Jacobs, "Haskalah, The Jewish Enlightenment" My Jewish Learning, https://www.myjewishlearning.com/article/haskalah/.

80. In fact, throughout most of its modern history between 1845 and 1905 the Jaroslaw Jewish community repeatedly elected physicians to head the community, rather than a leading merchant (*gvir* in Hebrew).

81. See Ohad Levi-Zaloscer, "Jaroslaw" (see note 65). And by the early 20th century there were a host of Zionist youth frameworks ranging from Mizrachi and Bnei Akiva and Betar to HaShomer HaTzair in Jaroslaw.

religious studies. But traditional Jewish frameworks (*talmud Torahs*) continued to flourish.

Such was the town from which Michael Schwarzer originated and where he apparently grew up, although the Jaroslaw Jewish community records show Michael-Menashe was born on the outskirts of Jaroslaw—in a village called Chlopice six km (four miles) from the town.[82] In 1880, when Michael was three, there were 4,474 Jews in Jaroslaw—40 percent of the overall population. Due to emigration, by 1901—about the time Menashe left Jaroslaw and well after his half-brother did so in 1890—the Jewish population had dropped back to 25 percent of Jaroslaw's 22,660 residents.[83]

~

When Michael was courting Annie Reiter six years after her arrival on the Lower East Side in 1902, their marriage was a 'package deal': Nana accepted his marriage proposal after Michael spied her in the corner grocery and asked to be introduced...provided that as newlyweds she and Michael would take care of her two younger sisters as part of the bargain. She was not about to leave them with her mean-spirited stepmother:

> At first, I left the older one [Hannah—DA] with my stepmother and only took the younger one [Yetta—DA] with me after my stepmother sent her to hang out diapers from her children and [in leaning out the window] she fell three flights down through the clothes lines. All she did was split her chin open. I took her to the doctor and she needed seven stitches [...] So, I took her home with me. Life was a struggle.

Three children were born to Anna and Michael: Ruth (Rebecca, December 1908), Joni (January 1912) and Pearl (July 1916). All were clearly

---

82. Pronounced CHO-pee-tzeh, GPS +48 16 622-24-22, https://en.wikipedia.org/wiki/Ch%C5%82opice/.

83. Based on Ohad Levi-Zaloscer, "Jaroslaw" (see note 65).

Joni Schwarzer, 1912–1916

named after the couple's deceased parents: Nana's mother Rosa, and Michael's parents — who according to Nana and Michael's marriage certificate and his death certificate were Jonas Schwarzer and Perli Waldman.[84]

In 1916 tragedy struck. Joni died[85] when he was just four months short of his fifth birthday. Pearl was a two-month-old infant. She recalled the brother she never knew:

84. Subsequently found in a Polish registry — with further information about family roots.

85. The date of death was found first, digitized, online. Only in December 2018 did I see the actual *certificate* of death with 'cause of death' signed by a physician, obtained from the New York Historical Records Department — a document that turned out to include unexpected details.

> There are only two pictures of Joni—no one had cameras in those days—one a tinted studio photo, the other taken on a pony.[86] The story that I got was that my sister came running upstairs to my mother and told her 'there is a man taking pictures. Let's get a picture of Joni'. And my mother came down and gave the man the money. People didn't take pictures in those days. We don't have any pictures of my father [...] and I don't have any pictures of my wedding [in March 1937] because it was just 'another expense' that could be skipped.

Michael, a successful gas lamp salesman, died two years later in the influenza ('Spanish flu') pandemic of 1918—together with his wife Annie's (Nana) stepbrother Joe Raubfogel who was only 23 when he died.[87] Pearl said on one of the tapes:

> Joe [Raubfogel] was a wonderful guy, but he got influenza at the same time as my father, and my mother went to take care of them [in the Lebanon Hospital in the Bronx—DA]. There weren't enough doctors or nurses. There was nothing. The doctors were falling like flies! It was very contagious and I don't know how my mother did that—considering she had two kids at home. I never managed to figure that out, but she did go, but, they both died nevertheless.

The only remaining memento of Michael, there being no photographs, is a cardboard-mounted photo from his catalog of wares of an arc lamp.

~ *Breathing Life into the Lives of Joni and Michael*

Pearl said she knew next to nothing about her brother and her father. She was two months old when her brother died. She was two years

86. From the same photo—one with the pony, one a close-up face portrait.

87. As children, Nana and Joe Raubfogel grew up in the same household after their parents (his mother, her father) married after the deaths of their respective spouses.

old when her father died. There had been two brief encounters with her father's half-brother and his family but she didn't have a clue who they were. Pearl said she was sorry she hadn't asked her sister — almost eight years her senior[88] — for more information about what she remembered, but when Ruth's sons Mike and David were queried in 2018, they were as clueless as their Aunt Pearl. Ruth had never talked about her brother or her father; perhaps it was too painful.

Michael Schwarzer, 1877–1918. A gas lamp fixture from his sales catalogue

Exactly when were they born? What were they like? When exactly had they died? Did anyone know where they were buried? There was very little to go on, however, as I sought in 2014 and 2016 to round up this project, recently digitized vital records paid off — filling in some of the blanks that gave Michael and Joni 'a life' of sorts.

The data retrieved could be summed up in a few sentences, but I believe the fascinating 'virtual road trips' taken in the wee hours of the night, digging through digitized archives going as far back as the 1870s, also have a place. While it is impossible to describe in words the feelings that washed over me as I uncovered this or that fragment confirming their existence, I hope making readers party to the 'ride' can be instructive for others — kin interested in digging further and perfect strangers investigating their genealogy, as more information is digitized, and more birth, marriage and death registries are translated from Romanian, Polish, Russian or Ukrainian that can shed light on the European chapter of family legacies.

I had already searched for Jonas, Jonie and Joni Schwarzer several years earlier with no results. It was as if Joni never existed and that

88. Pearl said in the tapes: "I made a great mistake not talking to my sister since she probably had a lot more to tell. I don't know why I didn't think of doing so. We spent plenty of time visiting her...and being bored with [listening to] her with her complaints and complaints..."

seemed incredibly sad. It was only after I realized that one 'John D. Schwarzer' in the 1915 New York Census was 'our Joni' that the pieces began to fall into place, almost by coincidence. Earlier, in searching all of the 'J Schwarzers' for something that would ring a bell, I had printed out a hard copy of one John D. Schwarzer as an 'improbable possible' since his parents were recorded as "Michael and Annie" and he was three years old in 1915, born in the Bronx in 1912. But, basically, I had given up. Months later, in the course of reading and proofing my transcript of Nana's 1975 taped interview that I had transcribed years earlier, I was dumbfounded to find Nana saying:

> I also had a son — between the births of my two girls. His name was Joni Schwarzer. He used to call himself 'John D' and I said–'No, darling, it's gotta be a Jewish name–*Yonaleh*'.[89]

My heart beating, I began to shuffle through a huge pile of printouts and other raw data and other source material covering the better part of my desk (the Weiss 'open-stacks' filing system...remember?) searching for the piece of paper that said "John D. Schwarzer". It had come from the Mormon's archives — Familysearch.org[90] — where I was able to access the details in the 1915 New York Census for free (and a host of other databases). With bated breath I keyed in 'John D. Schwarzer' and hit 'Enter': The scanned page in longhand confirmed I was on the right track: Four family members — Michael, Annie, Rebecca (Ruth) and John D. Schwarzer appeared on the same page 51, lines 8-11 — the year before Pearl was born (18 July 1916). The same Mormon archive

89. It was probably Michael who chose to put "John D. Schwarzer" down on Joni's birth certificate (which Nana couldn't read even if there was a hard copy in their possession). And it was definitely Michael who encouraged the kid to call himself John D....as if he was a Rockefeller, while his 'Jewish name' by which he was mostly called, was Joni (Yonah in Hebrew and Yiddish).

90. There are also subscription-based websites with more archival material such as Myheritage.com and Ancestry.com and Geshergalicia.org and professionals in Eastern Europe who will do research for a fee at Jewishfamilysearch.com who were not engaged.

led to Joni's birth certificate — showing he was born on 11 January 1912 and registered as John David Schwarzer.[91] Lots of immigrants chose super-duper American names for their children, but John D.? Joni's father Michael either had great expectations from his son or possessed a great sense of Jewish self-deprecating humor as a struggling immigrant to register his son as John David Schwarzer at birth and teach the kid to call himself John D...

It was already something like 2:00 AM when Ancestry.com's archive of vital documents brought up a death certificate for Joni showing he was just under five years old when he died on 21 September 1916.[92] All these years, he was thought by the family to have succumbed to spinal meningitis,[93] but this — it later turned out — was mistaken.

Ruth, Pearl and Joni's father Michael Schwarzer who died two years later of influenza was shown to have died on 26 October 1918.[94] There was a visceral sense of closure in subsequently finding a digitized death certificate under John Schwarzer and finding Joni had been buried in Mt. Zion Cemetery[95] on 22 September 1916 in the Jaraslauer Society section (such *landsmanshaft* organizations has reserved plots for those from the same town or city in Europe, in this case, families from Jaroslaw).[96]

What caused his death? In the 1975 taped interview Nana had said:

---

91. Clearly, first cousin David Platt was named after Ruth's dead brother, who (as already noted) was named after his grandfather Jonas David Schwarzer.

92. 24th of the Hebrew month of Elul 5676 would be Joni Schwarzer's *yahrtzeit* or the anniversary of Joni Schwarzer's death — seven days before *erev* [the eve of] Rosh Hashanah.

93. 'Thought' because that is what Nana (and Pearl) always said. But the full original certificate of death received three months after finding a digital record of when Joni died and where he was buried, said "acute poliomyelitis".

94. 20th of the Hebrew month of Heshvan 5679 would be his *yahrtzeit* or the anniversary of Michael Schwarzer's death — a month after the Sukkot festival.

95. See "The Faces of Mount Zion", Forgotten New York, 10 July 2004, http://forgotten-ny.com/2004/07/the-faces-of-mt-zion/.

96. The cemetery website indeed showed John Schwarzer in section 35R-2-722.

> ...I lost the boy—Joni, who got [spinal] meningitis, for which there was no cure then... He was a gorgeous child.

But in December 2018 when I asked Mt Zion Cemetery, on a hunch, whether they knew in what hospital Joni had died, it turned out this fact was strangely missing from their records, so on their advice, I fired off an email request to the New York Historical Records Department.

Why did it matter in which hospital he died? Sometimes this kind of sleuthing and cross-referencing to reconstruct family history conjers up images that can be true...or the figment of an overworked imagination. In my mind's eye, I wondered whether the sheer panic Nana experienced when Pearl almost hemorrhaged to death at age ten in Bronx Hospital (an incident described vividly elsewhere) was not 'further fueled' by Joni and Michael not only having died on her but having died in the *same* hospital for the indigent. It turned out Michael died in Bronx's Lebanon Hospital—not Bronx Hospital, and Joni had died at home in the Bronx. Nana's distraught state described by Pearl was genuine, but my conjecture of the circumstances had no basis in reality. But this tangent brought other surprises.

A scanned handwritten document arrived within hours as an attached pdf file. It showed Joni had died at home, stating in "Character of the place of death" that he had died in a Bronx "tenement". Below was the Cause of Death: "acute poliomyelitis" and Contributory Cause: "respiratory failure". Had Joni—who surely had been examined and cared for by a local pediatrician as soon as he fell ill[97] previously been thought to have spinal meningitis? Both polio and meningitis travel up the spinal cord and attack the central nervous system, and there was no autopsy, so we'll never know for sure. What we do know is it was a horrible way to die, as this little boy's chest muscles progressively got weaker and weaker and simply breathing became harder and harder until he became listless and lost consciousness from lack of sufficient oxygen and slipped into a coma.

Indeed, at the time Joni died, New York City was in the throes of a unique and particularly deadly polio epidemic noted in the professional

97. Doctors made house calls in those days—particularly pediatricians.

14 H—1915
1 PLACE OF DEATH
STATE OF NEW YORK
Department of Health of The City of New York
BUREAU OF RECORDS
CERTIFICATE OF DEATH

BOROUGH OF Bronx
No. 1360 Lyman Pl. St.
Character of premises, whether tenement, private, hotel, hospital or other place, etc. Tenement
Registered No. 5917
2 FULL NAME John David Schwarzer

3 SEX Male
4 COLOR OR RACE White
5 SINGLE, MARRIED, WIDOWED, OR DIVORCED (Write the word) Single
6 DATE OF BIRTH Jan (Month) 11 (Day), 1912 (Year)
7 AGE 4 yrs. 8 mos. 9 ds. If LESS than 1 day, ...hrs. or ...min.?
8 OCCUPATION
(a) Trade, profession, or particular kind of work None
(b) General nature of industry, business or establishment in which employed (or employer)
9 BIRTHPLACE (State or country) U.S.
(9 A) How long in U.S. (if of foreign birth) —
(9 B) How long resident in City of New York Life
10 NAME OF FATHER Michael Schwarzer
11 BIRTHPLACE OF FATHER (State or country) Austria
12 MAIDEN NAME OF MOTHER Annie Reiter
13 BIRTHPLACE OF MOTHER (State or country) Austria
14 Special INFORMATION required in deaths in hospitals and institutions and in deaths of non-residents and recent residents.
Former or usual residence

15 DATE OF DEATH Sep (Month) 21 (Day), 1916 (Year)

16 *I hereby certify that the foregoing particulars (Nos. 1 to 14 inclusive) are correct as near as the same can be ascertained, and I further certify that I attended the deceased from* Sep 15 1916 *to* Sep. 21 1916, *that I last saw* him *alive on the* 21 *day of* Sep. 1916, *that death occurred on the date stated above at* 10.30 A.M., *and that the chief and determining cause of death was:*
Acute Poliomyelitis
duration ... yrs. ... mos. 6 *days.*
That the contributory causes were:
Respiratory failure
That autopsy was performed and the findings were:
63

Witness my hand this ... day of ... 191
Signature A. J. Zuckerman *M. D.*
Address 1195 Boston Rd.

FILED SEP 21 1916
17 PLACE OF BURIAL Mt. Zion Cem.
DATE OF BURIAL Sept. 22 1916
18 UNDERTAKER Josef Schwartz
ADDRESS 50 Willett St

MARGIN RESERVED FOR BINDING
NO MUTILATED CERTIFICATE WILL BE RECEIVED

TO UNDERTAKERS.

1. No burial permit can be obtained without a proper certificate.
2. Certificates must be written throughout in black ink.
3. No certificate will be accepted which is **mutilated, illegible, inaccurate,** or any portion of which has been **erased, interlined, corrected or altered,** as all such changes impair its value as a public record.

I hereby certify that I have been employed as undertaker by Michael Schwarzer (NAME) the Father (RELATIONSHIP) of deceased. This statement is made to obtain a permit for the burial or cremation of the remains of deceased John David Schwarzer

Signature Josef Schwartz

Joni's death certificate

literature as "the most devastating epidemic in the history of poliomyelitis", widely quoted in medical literature saying its "extent and intensity was beyond all previous experience".[98] There was no effective treatment. Experimental serums and lumbar punctures were ineffective. Iron lungs only appeared in the 1940s. And eradication of polio with mass inoculation with the Salk vaccine only came 40 years later. It wasn't even known how polio spread; 72,000 cats were euthanized on the mistaken belief they were the carriers. Sick children were quarantined with red warning signs tacked to the front door, and treatment was limited to symptomatic remedies to reduce fever and pain.

The case-fatality rate was an unprecedented 25 percent![99] Moreover, 70 percent of the cases were among young children like Joni, under five years of age. Ninety percent were under age nine (those who had not been exposed to the previous 1907 epidemic). Tragically, it has been postulated that the deadly outbreak was sparked by the escape of a virulent laboratory strain of the poliovirus (through negligent handling of monkey spinal cord tissue) at the prestigious New York research lab — the Rockefeller Institute.[100] In New York City alone there were 8,900 cases of infantile paralysis and Joni was one of the 2,448 fatalities in the city in the space of a few months.

Back in November 2018 when I first called Mt. Zion, I was told they could check Joni's gravesite which I had found listed on Findagrave.com. I was told the chances were extremely slim that after 102 years anything remained, since most gravestones for children in those times were made of sandstone, not marble. Against all odds, several days later a digital photo arrived of a marble headstone. The Hebrew inscription read:

---

98. See this fascinating 2011 scientific article about this outbreak, H. V. Wyatt, "The 1916 New York City Epidemic of Poliomyelitis: Where did the Virus Come From?" *Open Vaccine Journal* 4 (2011): 13-17, https://benthamopen.com/contents/pdf/TOVACJ/TOVACJ-4-13.pdf. For a brief overview on how the city dealt with the emergency, see Dolan McGuire, *Responses to the 1916 Polio Epidemic in New York City*, https://tourbuilder.withgoogle.com/tour/ahJzfmd3ZWItdG91cmJ1aWxkZXJyEQsSBFRvdXIYgIDA8qTg-QoM.

99. The highest ever recorded.

100. "The 1916 New York City Epidemic of Poliomyelitis: Where did the Virus Come From" (see note 98).

פ"נ
הילד יונה דוד בר מנשה
נפטר כ"ג אלול תרע"ו
תנצב"ה[101]
OUR BELOVED CHILD
JONAS DAVE
SCHWARTZER
DIED SEPT 21, 1916
AGE 4 ¾ YEARS

Joni's gravestone

I told the sender how "touched and delighted" I was, thanking her profusely saying "with this photo, it's almost like you have given life to the dead".

~

To return to my digital research several years earlier: We knew next to nothing about Michael Schwarzer at that point. However, the 1915 New York Census showed Michael Schwarzer reporting he had come to America 16 years earlier (at age 22) — that is, in 1899 (the 1910 Census says 1900), but no Ellis Island record was found.

Familysearch.org brought up a copy of Michael Schwarzer's First World War Draft Registration from 12 September 1918 revealing another fragment of information: Michael's birth date — 18 August 1877. And not just that. It also noted that he was a 'declared alien' (he hadn't become an American citizen, but records show he had filed a preliminary Declaration of Intention to become an American citizen). The draft card stated he was married to Annie Schwarzer and lived in the

101. *Po nikvar ha-yeled Yonah David bar Menashe, niftar Kaf-Gimel Elul TARA"V TNTZB"H* (Here is buried the child Yonah David son of Menashe, died 23 Elul 5676, May his Soul be bound up in the bond of everlasting Life or RIP). Note: The misspelling — 'Schwartzer' not 'Schwarzer' — was apparently a glitch by the tombstone maker.

Bronx at 1272 Union Avenue. Nana's reminiscences from 1975 related that when they were newlyweds, Michael "sold gas light fixtures and fancy chandeliers — retail and wholesale" but by 1918 — ten years after they wed — Michael Schwarzer's draft registration says he was by then a "salesman of *electric* lamps" employed by Brilliant Light Works. Unfortunately, there are no picture IDs accompanying these vintage draft registrations (what I had hoped), but the card recorded that Michael had brown hair and brown eyes and was medium height and stout. This information, fragmentary and fractured as it might be, for me it was as if Michael Schwarzer had 'come to life' just a tiny little bit — something personal and tangible, beyond a page in a catalog.

Ironically and tragically, he registered for the draft six weeks before he died of the Spanish flu on 26 October 1918. During the epidemic, clinical signs usually appeared within days of exposure — a very short incubation period, and organ failure could follow within days or soon after. No, his trip down to the draft board was not the trigger, but the nature of his work as a salesman no doubt exposed him daily to crowds on public transportation and multiple customers. Michael was one of 20,608 deaths in New York City from the Spanish flu in the short space of two months, and one of an estimated 50 million persons who

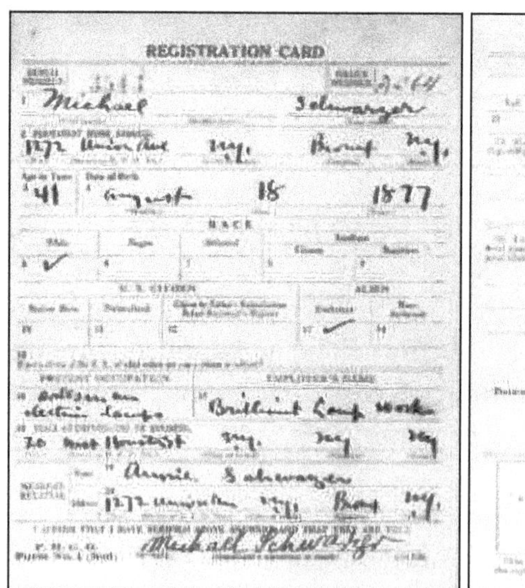

REGISTRATION CARD

Michael Schwarzer

1272 Union Ave N.Y. Bronx N.Y.

41 August 18 1877

salesman electric lamps Brilliant Lamp Works

Annie Schwarzer

1272 Union Ave N.Y. Bronx N.Y.

Michael Schwarzer

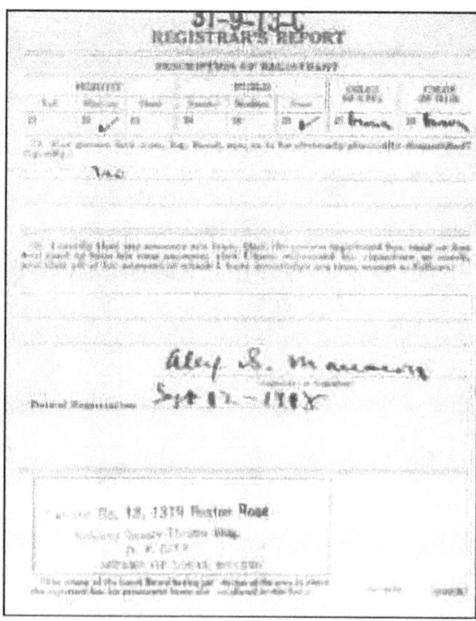

REGISTRAR'S REPORT

Sept 12 - 1918

M. Schwarzer draft registration

succumbed to the pandemic worldwide. The 1918 epidemic created an unprecedented W-shaped curve rather than the usual U-shaped curve of fatalities among young children and the elderly that the flu normally leaves in its wake. In other words, a disproportionate number of the mortalities were healthy young individuals, ages 20 to 40 years of age like Michael, an anomaly that is still shrouded in mystery and a source of speculation for epidemiologists and medical historians.[102]

An archive called the US Find a Grave Index 1600–Current revealed where Michael is buried: In Washington Cemetery in Brooklyn.[103] Staff found the 100-year-old gravestone. The inscription reads:

פ"נ

אבינו היקר

מנשה בר יונה דוד

הלוי

נפ' כ' חשון תרע"ט

תנצבה[104]

IN MEMORY OF
OUR
BELOVED FATHER
MICHAEL
SCHWARZER
DIED OCT. 26, 1918
AGE 41 YRS.

---

102. Jeffery K. Taubenberger and David M. Morens, "1918 Influenza: The Mother of All Pandemics", *Emerging Infectious Diseases* 12, no. 1 (2006), 15-22. https://dx.doi.org/10.3201/eid1201.050979/.

103. Located in the Washington Cemetery in the Anshe Jarislower [People of Jaroslaw] Congregation section, Cemetery 3, Row 2, Grave 1 NE.

104. Here lies our beloved father Menashe, son of Yonah David the Levite, died 20 Heshvan 5679, May His Soul be Bound Up in the Bond of Eternal Life (RIP).

The tombstone reveals that the Schwarzers were Levites—descendants of the tribe of Levi: Not only is his father noted to be a Levite in the Hebrew inscription; the tombstone is engraved with the symbol of the Levite line—a water pitcher.[105]

But there was more to be discovered elsewhere. As noted earlier, I had found out that Michael came from Jaroslaw, noted on his marriage certificate to Nana. Further sleuthing in the JRI Poland website (hosted by Jewishgen.com[106]) contains a partial registry of births, marriages and deaths beginning in 1877, kept by the Jewish community of Jaroslaw. That the translated material began in 1877 was a matter of pure luck. I knew that was the year of Michael's birth from his draft registration. When I clicked on the registry, Michael popped up on the second page! His birth was recorded as "Menasche Schwarzer"—Menasche being the Hebrew name he used in Europe that appears on Joni's tombstone and was mentioned by Nana in the audiotape she made 100 years later, in 1975.

Miraculously, the Jaroslaw Registry also allowed me to extract two more generations of Schwarzers. There was a Jonas Schwarzer born in 1836 who died in 1902 at the age of 66—who *apparently* is both Esriel's and Michael's father. The entry also reveals the names of this *Jonas'*

---

105. The water pitcher reflects the Levites' role in purification rituals on the Temple Mount. Furthermore, under Menashe's name in Hebrew, his father's name Yonah David is followed by the title ha-Levi. Had the family been observant in the Orthodox sense, Ruth and Pearl would have enjoyed the symbolic status of *bat Levi* (daughter of a Levite) but the Schwarzer's Levite status was not passed down to future generations: Had Joni lived, Pearl's brother would have been endowed with this special distinction in traditional Judaism and passed it on to his progeny. For a short video by the Jewish Genealogy Society of Long Island on symbols on Jewish tombstones, see: "7 Popular Symbols on Jewish Headstones", YouTube video, 3:35 minutes, 2015, https://www.youtube.com/watch?v=c7-acCXJIgE.

106. At http://www.jewishgen.org/. One must register for free first. Log in and go to https://www.jewishgen.org/databases/. Click on 'Poland'; click on Jewish Records Indexing (JRI), under 'Search' click on 'Search our Database', and under surname enter 'Schwarzer' and geographical region 'Lwów', and follow instructions to reach all the records.

parents — that is, Ruth and Pearl's great grandparents: Isak Nota Schwarzer and Bluma Weichholz — taking the family tree back another generation.

The Registry held another surprise: Michael had an unknown older sibling — a full brother named Abraham — born in 1874, who died at age three in 1877 — just before or just after Michael's birth. In other words, both Michael and his parents lost a son in early childhood: Abraham and Joni. And like Pearl who was two months old when Joni died, Michael had also lost a sibling when he was too small to remember — the same tragedy visited upon each successive generation, at least until the advent of antibiotics and other aspects of 20th-century medicine — explaining why these pharmaceuticals we take for granted were dubbed 'wonder drugs'. Indeed life was precarious, and second and even third marriages were all too common because a spouse could and did die in childbirth, or from cholera, from influenza or pneumonia, typhus, tuberculosis, scarlet fever, stepping on a nail or you-name-it — leading to a slew of half-brothers and half-sisters, stepparents and stepsiblings. One can't but notice the marked number of stillborn babies and infant mortalities in the index of *Galicia, Ukraine, Births, Marriages, and Deaths, 1789–1905* on the Ancestry.com website (i.e., of the historical province of Galicia in the Austrian empire). Even when one is cognizant of the difference between medicine today and medicine a century ago, the parallels and the capriciousness of life in times past are quite chilling.

Michael's gravestone

Are there more Schwarzers out there — aunts and uncles, nephews and cousins, even brothers or half-brothers born before 1877 we don't know about? There were dozens of Schwarzers (without a 't') in the Jaroslaw Registry of the Jewish Indexing database for Poland.[107] Keep in mind — the Jewish population of Jaroslaw was not large: 4,820 in 1890, 6,577 in 1921 according to Jewishgen.org. And there were even more Schwarzers in JRI Poland's compilation for Lvov and nearby communities like Jaroslaw that covers 1870–1901: Thirteen pages of Schwarzers! Undoubtedly, some are relations.

There was another sign: This half-brother of Pearl's father Michael — the 'silk Schwarzer' that Pearl mentioned with whom there was no contact? When I accessed the Polish archive, I already knew his name: Esriel. And as noted elsewhere there was a faint but visible paper trail to family in France. Thus, it is very likely there are other Schwarzer kin 'out there'. Yes, the patriarch of the 'silk Schwarzer' line — one Esriel Schwarzer — had been found, but relations with this branch of the family were complex and carried a residue of loaded 'emotional sediment'.

I had found Michael's half-brother's purely by chance. Aimlessly 'thumbing through' American census data of Schwarzers, curiosity got the best of me: 'Esriel' stood out as an odd name and I've always had a weak spot for the piquant. Who was this man who hadn't changed his super-duper Hebrew name to Eric or Erwin or Eddy after arriving in America? (Slowly scrolling off-screen to the right for clues, I found myself staring at a four-letter entry in the last column under "occupation". Silk. The feeling was paramount to cracking the Enigma Code thanks to a single crib.[108]

But once I established this Esriel had the same father as Michael Schwarzer, I vacillated whether to seek out living descendants of what

107. Jewish Records Indexing (JRI)–Poland, https://jri-poland.org/jriplweb.htm.

108. Cribs — a few words that should appear in an encrypted message that allow one to break the code.

I have labeled in this memoir 'the Other Schwarzers'. I was on the horns of a dilemma: Torn between curiosity and a desire to 'fill in the blanks' about the family, and loyalty to a painful chapter in the family history—allegiance to a narrative handed down to me about these Other Schwarzers. Echoing in my head was Nana's last words to her sister-in-law who, according to Nana, feared she'd become a burden: "You don't have to take care of me. I can take care of my own children!"

At one point in writing the first draft of this family saga, back in 2003, Pearl and I had googled "Schwarzer" and "silk" (she was curious). Yes, Pearl wanted to know more, but we came up with nothing. I decided to take this as a 'nod' of consent. Moreover, I was fueled by the hope these Schwarzers might have a photo of Michael since up until Michael's death, everyone agreed there was contact between Michael and his half-brother and Esriel's family, despite the age and economic gap (important facts that would subsequently be substantiated and fleshed-out in documentation).

What I discovered—the product of hours and hours digging through online archives—led to a fairly complete portrait of that branch of the Schwarzer tree culminating in an exchange of emails with living descendants along the way, and phone conversations with two (more or less contemporaries of mine)—none called Schwarzer incidentally. They shared with me some aspects of their own family's triumphs and *tzuros* (troubles). This information is *not* included in the body of *Playing Detective with Family Lore* for obvious reasons. It is placed in a special appendix titled The 'Other Schwarzers'. Fleshing out their story also led to a reexamination of the breakdown in communications that followed Michael's untimely death and what caused it.

Mostly, I was driven by the hope these hours spent tracing and tracking down and contacting living descendants of Esriel Schwarzer and his wife Dora would pay off, and *their* 'family archivist'—Dale Laszig or one of her cousins—could add more detail about Michael. About his family in Jaroslaw. Even by some small miracle, unearth a photo in their family photo albums, perhaps taken at a family *simhah* in New York with Michael in the frame...but to no avail.

We were left with the faceless cardboard gas lamp fixture from his catalog.

The Weiss-Ehrlich Side

The Benjamin Weiss Enigma

Benjamin Weiss[109] was born on 26 July 1890 in Nikolayev in Czarist Russia — today Mykolayiv (with an 'M') but in 1890 called Nikolayev[110] in Russian and Yiddish. Nikolayev is situated 70 km (45.5 miles) north of the Black Sea on a tributary of the Dnieper. In the late 19th century the city became the third largest foreign port in the Russian Empire after St. Petersburg and Odessa.[111] It had a Jewish population of approximately 20,100 persons in 1900 — 19.5 percent of the city's residents. Situated to the west of the Dnieper, Nikolayev was just inside the Pale of Settlement where Jews were legally allowed to reside in Imperial Russia between 1791 and 1917.[112]

What is known is that Benjamin Weiss immigrated to America at the age of 14 in December 1905,[113] so he told his family. Was there

---

109. The name Weiss can be found spelled as Wise, Wize, Weiz, Wiese, Weisz in English, and Veisz, Vies and Veys in English translations of Russian documents.

110. For an overview about the city, "Jewish History of Mykolayiv (Nikolayev), Kherson Gubernia", JewishGen KehilaLinks, https://kehilalinks.jewishgen.org/mykolayiv/history%20&%20geography.htm. For the record, there is a tiny *shtetl* in the Ukraine — memorialized in the Yiddish ditty called "In Shtetl Nikolaev". But Benjamin Weiss was apparently from the city Nikolayev, not this hamlet. To listen to the song, go to "Kapelye — In Shtetl Nikolaev", YouTube video, 3:13 minutes, 2010, https://www.youtube.com/watch?v=gw7L-9hQdXY and "In Shtetl Nikolaev", Framasphere, https://framasphere.org/posts/486944 (which also includes an English translation).

111. Nikolayev was a regional capital in the Southern Ukraine, on the Yuzhny Bug River (some sources say on the Buh River estuary), 35 km (22 miles) upstream from the point where the Yazhney Bug enters the Dnieper, east of Odessa. Today, Nikolayev is a city of half a million inhabitants, at GPS 46°58'N 32°00'E.

112. Between 1834 and 1860 the Jews were expelled from Nikolayev...

113. There are often discrepancies in the paper trail. Ben's age ranging from 1890 to 1891 from document to document — including his draft card, census to census and marriage certificate. Such primary sources need to be approached

Nikolayev, near Odessa

any connection between his departure and the widespread pogroms in mid-October 1905 that rocked Jewish life in Czarist Russia, including Nikolayev?[114] He never said anything, but during the 12-day rampage

---

with caution: Ben's October 1912 marriage certificate, for example, says he was 21 in October 1912 (actually 22) when he married supposedly 19-year-old Hannah (who was actually 16.5) Similar discrepancies appear in Michael Schwarzer's marriage certificate and elsewhere.

114. Could someone have made such a trip in such a short time? According to Tobias Brinkmann, "Jewish Migration", in European History Online (EGO), (Mainz: Institute of European History: 2010), http://www.ieg-ego.eu/brinkmannt-2010-en/, thanks to the development of the rail system, by 1900 travel time between a remote village in Central Europe to any place in North America "was a mere three weeks by train + steamship" (previously, months). Not only was Nikolayev a busy export port; the city was a short ferry ride from Odessa. Travel time is cited in Janet I. Wasserman, "The Journey from Eastern Europe to North America in 1900 & 1904", in *From Shtetl to Park Avenue: I Newton Kugelmass (1896–1979)*, (footnote 9), at https://www.

Top: Nikolayev shipyard, circa1900
Bottom: Downtown Nikolayev, 1900

throughout the Russian Empire 690 such pogroms occurred, in which "810 people were killed and 1,770 injured and 201,000 people suffered pecuniary loss to the amount of more than $30,000,000".[115] During the pogrom in Nikolayev "many Jewish families lost everything they owned, left without means of livelihood".[116] These events came on the heels of the particularly lethal 1903 Kishinev pogrom — a watershed event for Eastern European Jewry.[117] Most of the exodus after the 1905

---

jewishgen.org/Bessarabia/files/Emigration/JourneyFromEasternEuropeToNorthAmerica1900-1904.pdf.

115. Data cited in V. V. Obolensky-Ossinsky, "Emigration From and Immigration Into Russia", in *International Migrations, Volume II: Interpretations*, ed. Walter F. Willcox (Cambridge, MA: National Bureau of Economic Research, 1931), 521–80, https://www.nber.org/chapters/c5118. No full list of casualties in Nikolayev seems to exist, although there is a partial list extracted from the above-mentioned historiography of Nikolayev "1905 Mykolayiv/Nikolayev Pogrom", Jewish Gem's Genealogy: Mining for Your Elusive Ancestors, http://yourjewishgem.blogspot.com/2017/11/1905-mykolayivnikolayev-pogrom.html. More on damages in note 163. [...] can be accessed at this gate: "Collection: Vital Records — FHL Catalog Entry, Jewish, Nikolayev Town 1873-1920", Jewish Gen Ukraine SIG, https://www.jewishgen.org/ukraine/RES_collection.asp?id=1642. Individual microfilms by year for Nikolayev are archived at Familysearch, https://www.familysearch.org/search/catalog/1838584?availability=Family%20History%20Library; Births (Разводы) 1990-1993 Nikolayev: https://www.familysearch.org/search/film/007807331?cat=1838584; Deaths (Смерти). 1905 https://www.familysearch.org/search/film/007807328?cat=1838584; 1904 https://www.familysearch.org/search/film/007807328?cat=1838584; 1904 https://www.familysearch.org/search/film/007807328?cat=1838584; 1902 https://www.familysearch.org/search/film/007807328?cat=1838584. (See also note 149.)

116. Cited in a short history of the city "Mykolayiv, Kherson, Ukraine", JewishGen KehilaLinks, https://kehilalinks.jewishgen.org/mykolayiv/.

117. On Easter Sunday in Kishinev (the capital of the Bessarabia region, where a third of the population was Jewish), the Russian press, officials and priests instigated a pogrom by claiming Jews had used the blood of a murdered Christian child in baking Passover *matzah*. The Kishinev pogrom left 120 dead, 500 injured and 1,500 households in ruins, and was accompanied by widespread rape and other atrocities — an event that along with subsequent

pogroms — 44 percent of the Jewish émigrés — were from the south and southwestern areas of the Pale of Settlement (where Nikolayev is located). Between 1904 and 1908, immigration to the United States from Russia doubled compared to corresponding years towards the close of the 19th century.[118] All told, some 964,000 Russian Jews left Russia and poured into the United States between 1899–1913,[119] half in three short years following the 1903–1905 wave of pogroms...including Ben Weiss, whom Gil said was an orphan when he arrived in America.[120]

Grandma Hannah Weiss once told her granddaughter Toni (née Weiss) Robinson that Benjamin Weiss' mother was named Mary Kirech or Kurick (a family name also spelled Kerech, Corech and even Curyk). Indeed there are some 'Kurichs' in both Nikolayev and nearby Kherson that pop up when one keys in this surname on Jewishgen.org. I originally assumed that this was her maiden name and perhaps her first name wasn't Mary but Meri which could be short for Miriam or Muriel (Mary was a very 'goyish' name); but as time went on, other possibilities — each contradicting the others — emerged, leaving me juggling names and not just his mother's...including one suggestion that Mary's maiden name was Weiss and Ben's surname was Kurick... But I'll get to that later.

Gil and his mother both said that Ben Weiss' father was also called

---

pogroms in 1905 set in motion the departure of tens of thousands of Russian Jews for the West, and for Palestine. For a description of the Kishinev pogrom, see Steven J. Zipperstein, "Anatomy of a Pogrom", in *Pogrom: Kishinev and the Tilt of History* (New York: Liveright, 2018), https://www.tabletmag.com/jewish-arts-and-culture/257179/anatomy-of-a-pogrom.

118. From 673,000 émigrés between 1880 and 1900, to 1,346,000 between 1901 and 1914.

119. Data cited from Obolensky-Ossinsky, "Emigration From and Immigration Into Russia" (see note 115).

120. It is unclear when his brother Samuel arrived in America — but it seems likely it was *before* the First World War since he was in New York in 1917. It is highly unlikely Sam immigrated to the United States during the war years, as civilian traffic slowed to a trickle disrupted by the war and lack of passenger ships, and in 1918 was down to an all-time low of 110,618, from an average of nearly a million immigrants a year prior to the war.

Benjamin. Ashkenazi Jews don't normally name their children after living relatives, but there were a number of other possible explanations besides being orphaned before he was born. In short, in the beginning, we knew almost nothing and further details of Ben Weiss' extended family in America — if there was any — remained equally hazy. There were, however, vague recollections of an estranged brother named Sam Weiss somewhere in Connecticut. Pearl recalled:

> I never heard any stories about his parents or where he came from — except that he said that he came from Russia when I asked. This one brother once contacted us. When families got into feuds in those days it was usually over money. Someone asking for help from someone who was not forthcoming with the help — such as my mother and my father's [half-]brother...

In a last-ditch attempt to unravel the mystery, I set out in the fall of 2018 as this work took its final form, to search for this Sam. The online archives Findagrave.com showed only one Samuel Weiss[121] with a father named Benjamin in Hebrew on the tombstone — and he was buried in Hartford, Connecticut.[122] According to Hartford's 1940 census Samuel

---

121. I also searched for Weisses in Russia with various derivatives (Weissman, Weissblat, Weissbyne, etc.) but, once Samuel was found it was clear the family name was Weiss (or so I assumed). Vague talk that the original family name was perhaps Weissman or something like that seemed unlikely. Claims that Ellis Island officials misspelled family names or capriciously shortened names turns out to be a foundational myth of American Jewry! If names were Anglicized to 'invent new roots' upon arriving in America, *it was done by the immigrants themselves* who shortened Rogarshevsky to Rogers or changed Abrams to Abbott. Thus, Esriel became Eli and Menashe became Michael. There was no faceless official robbing them of their ethnicity... See Dara Horn, "The Myth of Ellis Island and Other Tales of Origin", *Azure Quarterly* 41 (2010), http://azure.org.il/article.php?id=544.

122. Sam Weiss died on 28 July 1963 and his father's name being Benjamin was noted both on the death certificate in English and on the headstone in Hebrew in Hartford, Connecticut. The Hartford Jewish Historical Society

was born in 1895,[123] but his signed First World War draft registration card[124] gives a full birth date: 24 May 1893. Sam Weiss and his wife Anna Kushner had one daughter — Minnie Weiss Helfand who died in 2004, but her obituary noted the names and location of two grandsons. In January 2019 I decided to cold call Minnie's son [Howard] Mark Helfand, who lives as fate would have it...in Potomac, Maryland.

Samuel's grandson turned out to be a retired scientist in climate modeling who worked for NASA in Greenbelt, Maryland...and had just started a second career in scientific editing.[125] Unfortunately, although he is the eldest of Sam's two grandchildren, Mark didn't know much about his grandfather. But, as we chatted, he suddenly remembered that his mother Minnie told him Samuel Weiss "arrived in America from Kiev, but he was born somewhere else, and had gone to Kiev after a series of bad pogroms in his hometown"(!)[126] strongly suggesting he might have been born in Nikolayev (I had not shared with him anything about the pogrom to this point). Was this mere coincidence? Samuel would have been 12 at the time of the 1905 pogrom in Nikolayev, a

---

told me Samuel was from Kiev — leading me to 'drop the chase' for several months. Other Sam Weisses in Connecticut were outside the age range or had the wrong father or mother or didn't originate in Russia. Only one remained a theoretical 'possible' but lacked identifying data: Reform congregations' ground-level 'plaques' in English only, in lieu of traditional Jewish tombstones (adopted in the name of graveyard aesthetics and rejection of assigning any importance to bloodlines or ancestry) don't have Hebrew inscriptions noting the father's name for men and mother's name for women for the deceased, always inscribed on traditional gravestones...a true loss as a crucial source (in fact often invaluable) for genealogists.

123. Census date is notoriously flawed. This is noted time and again in this chapter.

124. Only sought in January 2018.

125. We ended up talking at length about freelance editing.

126. There were also pogroms in Nikolayev in 1881 and 1899 in addition to the larger one in 1905 with five fatalities, and after both Benjamin and Samuel were in America, there was a fourth pogrom — the worst of them all — in 1919 in which 29 Jews were murdered, despite the efforts of a Jewish defense league established after the first pogrom.

Jewish community that Simon Wiesenthal noted was one of the worst hit communities in this particular antisemitic wave.[127] Was he sent to relatives in Kiev after being orphaned (whatever the circumstances) while his older brother Benjamin headed for America?[128] When exactly Samuel arrived in America is also unclear since neither he nor Pop Weiss (as we all called Ben Weiss) could be found in Ellis Island archives.[129] Mark said that his grandfather had departed for America

127. For example, Simon Wiesenthal's *Everyday Remembrance Day: A Chronicle of Jewish Martyrdom* (New York: Holt, 1987), 234, notes in a 19 October 1905 entry the wave of attacks on Jews throughout Russia "organized by the authorities, supported by the army, the Cossacks, the local police and hooligans lasting two to five days". He notes seven places by name including Nikolayev where "several Jews were killed".

128. It's possible. There are half a dozen people looking for links to the name Weiss from Kiev on Jewishgen.org. Could it be the family's roots are in Kiev?

129. There were countless ports of entry besides New York (Castle Gardens, then Ellis Island) from Boston and Philadelphia to Galveston, Texas and overland via Canada, and even via the Caribbean that are not in the Ellis Island archives. It only occurred to me in January 2019 that if Ben Weiss was 14 or 15 when he came to America and was an orphan, he would have had to lie about his age to avoid being detained in the Ellis Island holding area for children until a relative came to 'fetch' him or one of the Jewish immigration organizations would take him under their wing — 'sponsor him' — to ensure authorities he would not 'become a public charge'...if he had not been sponsored by his Philadelphia aunt whom I subsequently found — Aunt Safer). After Ben Weiss entered, the Immigration Act of 1907 declared that unescorted children under age 16 would be pulled aside and examined to determine "(1) that they are strong and healthy, (2) that while abroad they have not been the objects of public charity, (3) that they are going to close relatives who are able and willing to support and properly care for them, (4) that it is the intention of such relatives to send them to school until they are 16, and (5) that they will not be put at work unsuited to their years". Both boys could have lied about their ages to gain entrance to the United States. Source: Bureau of Immigration and Naturalization's "Immigration laws and regulations of 1 July 1907", https://archive.org/stream/cu31924021131101/cu31924021131101_djvu.txt. On the other hand, there *were* orphans whose entrance was organized by HAIS and other Jewish welfare organizations. For example, there is one source that says there are passenger lists of "Jewish orphans from Russia in

from Liverpool, but he doesn't know how long he was there or why he left from that port.

The fact is, according to historians, many passengers departing for America from Liverpool were 'transit migrants'[130] from throughout Europe, who preferred to travel by ship or overland to the UK, and embarked on their transatlantic voyage from UK ports — a shorter crossing with slightly better steerage 'accommodations'.[131] The trail — based on oral family history — only picks up in late 1917 when according to Mark, 25-year-old Samuel Weiss married Anna Kushner in New York, with daughter Minnie born the following year (21 May 1918).[132] Ben had married in mid-1912 and was already raising a family in Perth Amboy, New Jersey by this time. Samuel's First World War draft card shows that Samuel was still single and self-employed as a cabinetmaker in June 1917.[133] (Mark says in Hartford his grandfather was a peddler

1906" — apparently orphans from the pogroms — among Hamburg passenger lists, but I could not locate them online.

130. According to Keeling, "Oceanic Travel Conditions and American Immigration: 1890s–1914" (see note 42).

131. The price of tickets according to Drew Keeling remained the same for decades: Steerage from Hamburg, Bremen or Antwerp costed $34, and from Liverpool $25 at the time most of the family immigrated to America. Space per passenger improved between 1890 and 1915 on some routes, particularly northern ones (tied to improvement in the performance of steamships that lowered costs). The standard was an 'open berth' configuration with a hundred narrow metal cots per dormitory, while later some accommodation, while still in the belly of the boat and deplorable, were less cramped with more partitions — a dozen or so in a 'closed berth'. And more toilets.

132. Samuel Weiss' June 1917 draft registration stated he was still single. Daughter Minnie was born on 21 May 1918 in Hartford, Connecticut, thus it is likely Samuel Weiss and Anna Kushner got married between June and August 1917 (which also would have changed his draft status to having one dependent...). However, no records could be found: Unfortunately, the family doesn't have a copy of Sam's marriage certificate and none could be located online, a document that usually includes the names of the parents of the bride and groom.

133. A monograph in Russian (see note 137) notes that Nikolayev had a

selling fruit off the back of a pickup truck).

Suddenly 'out of the blue' so to speak, Mark asked me 'whether Pop Weiss had blue eyes like his father and himself' (explaining blue eyes run in his family). No, I replied, Benjamin Weiss' eyes were brown, but this revelation begged the question whether these were some of the genes where *I* got my blue eyes (i.e., not only from the Ehrlich gene pool via my blue-eyed grandmother Hannah).[134] On a hunch — it was now 2:00 AM — I sent Mark some vintage photos of Pop Weiss when he was a relatively young man, from among those archived in the *Playing Detective* portfolio on my computer. Mark's initial response was a bit guarded:

> It's quite possible that Ben and Sam were brothers. Judging from body type and the shape of the head, especially forehead and perhaps cheekbones. Not enough similarity to be certain, however.

The next morning I finally located the picture of Ben and Hannah Weiss as an elderly couple that I had searched for (i.e., It was hanging on the wall in our eating alcove among a photomontage of other photos...). Mark's grandfather or *zehde* in Yiddish, had died in 1963 when Mark was a young adult; (Ben passed more or less at the same time, in 1968 when we — his grandchildren — were also relatively young

---

state-run four-year Jewish elementary school supported by state funding and philanthropists, that paid "particular attention to training in 'manual labor'" — for which the school created "woodwork and turning and carving workshops". Perhaps somewhere there is a roster of pupils in Russian to see if a Sam Weiss studied woodworking there. In mid-1917 when he registered for the draft, Samuel was living at 132 Essex Street on the Lower East Side. Attempts to 'find him' in the 1915 New York state census failed to produce a Samuel Weiss of similar age and Russian origin. In mid-1917, as already noted, Benjamin and Hannah were already in New Jersey.

134. When I was a kid my grandmother Hannah Weiss repeatedly exclaimed with pride and joy (much to my consternation and discomfort) that with my blond hair and blue eyes I "looked like a little *shikseh*" (non-Jewish girl)...

adults).[135] Mark was floored by the faded photo of Pop Weiss just as I always remembered him:

> I just received your latest photograph---WOW! Seeing your grandfather at an age similar to how I remember my *Zehde* Weiss, I can only say they are brothers!!! They are not identical twins, but if I saw your grandfather walking down the street, I might be tempted to say, "Hi, *Zehde*".
>
> My *zehde* was never quite the dresser that your grandfather was, and they probably had different lifestyles, but I really think they were brothers.

Although no paper trail in Kiev and Nikolayev connecting the two directly has yet to be uncovered due to a language barrier,[136] there is additional circumstantial evidence: In the 1940 US Census Ben Weiss reported he had an 8th-grade education: Born in 1890/91, his schooldays ended or were already over in the fall of 1905. Samuel reported he had only a 5th-grade education: Born in 1893 his education came to an abrupt halt in late 1905. But how strong is this as a linkage? After all, most Eastern European Jewish boys finished their schooling in the 8th grade; that was the norm, and only a minority went on to high school

135. It seems almost a universal pattern: None of us asked questions as young adults, the questions with which I was now forced to grapple. At best, we possess a handful of anecdotal stories ('the oranges in steerage'). At this stage of life, most young adults are too self-absorbed to take an interest in their grandparents' lives...or their parents' for that matter. Luckily, in Pearl's case she lived long enough for me to take an interest in audiotaping her recollections and insights on my annual visits to DC and Minnesota — a true windfall in a project such as this.

136. Entries (1834–1917) in the scanned microfilm of births, weddings and deaths in Nikolayev, scrawled longhand in Russian and Hebrew, are said to contain registration of burial of the dead including names and nicknames, gender, age, information about cause of death (disease or circumstances how the person died) that might shed light on the fate of Benjamin and Samuel's parents. Unfortunately they are in Russian. The marriage and divorce registry is also detailed and orderly. See note 115 for links.

(gymnasia). Maybe Ben Weiss was leaving because he had finished school in mid-1905 (with or without a pogrom looming just after the start of the school year). Was I getting carried away?

Ben Weiss said in multiple documents including his draft card that he was from Nikolayev. These two facts strongly suggest the two brothers were together until the 1905 pogrom. As for the physical resemblance Mark found, their draft cards also show both men were identical in stature — Ben's card categorized him as 'short', Sam's gave his exact height: 5'6" — also relatively short. On the other hand, this was hardly unusual: According to a 1901 medical article, on the average, European Jews were 162.1 cm tall (5'4")–the shortest of all European peoples... Mark was convinced there was the striking resemblance between the two, but the family could not find a photo to send me. Both of us were thrilled by the discovery that we *might* be cousins. Mark promised to query his 99-year-old father in Hartford whether Arnold Halfand could shed light on his father-in-law's and his late wife's origins but his father's deteriorating health did not make this possible.

Alas, the core question remained unanswered and may never be fully known: What were the circumstances that led a 14 or 15-year-old boy to pick up and take off for America on his own, a month after a major pogrom in his hometown, and what became of his brother Samuel? Assuming Mark's grandfather *is* the lost brother, how did Samuel end up in Kiev, what happened to their parents and why weren't the two brothers closer? In hopes of gaining a partial answer, I went back to the Internet to delve deeper into events in October 1905 in Nikolayev.

Although they lived in a very large and very 'Russian' city, in terms of the city's demographic profile, the Jews in Nikolayev were fairly typical in many ways of Jews throughout the Pale — only more so: Only 13.4 percent of the gentile population in Russia in 1897 was urban while 50.5 percent of the Jews lived in cities (and most of the rest lived in genuine towns); 71.5 percent of the gentiles engaged in agriculture while 78.1 percent of the Jews engaged in commerce (mostly as middlemen) and industry (the latter, mostly simple craft workshops) — a source of ongoing economic tension.

A 100-page historiography in Russian published in 2009 about the

Nikolayev Jewish community was a breakthrough in the research — accessible thanks to Google translate... I hoped this minutely detailed monograph by a Nikolayev State University professor could shed light on the circumstances of how the lives of Benjamin and Samuel were apparently turned upside down in 1905. The work includes a profile of the city in the late 19th and early 20th centuries when the two brothers were growing up...focusing on events during, and impact of, the 1905 pogrom.[137] The research is based on archival material — from newspaper reports, Imperial Russia's 1897 census[138] and other statistical data, police reports, and material in the Jewish community's archive at the Nikolayev Society of Jewish Culture.[139]

Even at the outset of the 20th century Jews were absent from the city's skilled laborers in the shipyards, the military, construction and government administration (where Jews were barred from serving on city councils). But once the port was opened to foreign vessels in 1862 (not just serving as home to the Black Sea Fleet), and particularly after the establishment of a Grain Exchange in 1885 that replaced guilds that excluded Jews, Jewish businesspeople began to play a larger role in the movement of Ukrainian grain as grain brokers. There were even storage granaries in Nikolayev owned by Jews.[140] Nikolayev at the turn of the century was the third-largest export port in Russia and some Jews had even been previously involved for decades 'behind the scenes' financing shipbuilding. Coauthors Shchukin and Pavlyuk of this scholarly

137. Professor W. Shchukin and A. N. Pavlyuk, "Jewish Pogroms in Mikolayev", 2009, 62–152, http://litnik.org/images/Biblioteki/NasaBiblioteka/SchukinPavlyuk.pdf (Russian). The Jewish historical society — the Museum of Nicholas Society of Jewish Culture — may have more information on Nikolayev families.

138. The 1897 census was the first and only census carried out in the Russian Empire.

139. A Messenger query in English via the JCC's Facebook account at https://www.facebook.com/nikolaevjcc/ asking for some assistance remained unanswered.

140. Including one named Veysbeyn who was on the governing committee of the Grain Exchange — apparently not a relation.

tract say that as a community, Jews constituted a "fairly weighty and economically significant group of the population of Nikolayev in the 19th century"—particularly in the small-scale manufacturing realm: The majority of Jewish breadwinners were either craftsmen or artisans. The Russian Empire's 1897 census shows there were 17,974 Jews in the city—30 percent of whom engaged in handicrafts in small workshops with 16 to 18-hour workdays and rife with child labor as was the norm in those times. In Nikolayev, Jews constituted not only 50 percent of all the craftsmen in the city but also 50 percent of the artisans. Such craftsmen, as already noted, engaged for the most part in simple crafts (for example, 70 percent of the shoemakers and tailors were Jews). They often lived in "dire poverty" say the monograph's authors—tottering on the brink of ruin (reflected in police records that reveal 14 percent of the prostitutes in the city were local Jewish women).

The more financially stable artisans within the Jewish community ranged from carpenters and blacksmiths, to watchmakers, jewelers and distillers to mention a few. Thus, numerically, a significant portion of the Nikolayev community eked out a living with all the insecurity that entailed, while the stability and resilience of the Jewish community and its institutions rested heavily on the Jews among the city's merchant class and artisans and the local Jewish intelligentsia. Jews were prominent as shopkeepers (from stationery to haberdashery) and the wealthy included several major grain brokers and factory owners. These comfortable to wealthy Jews established and helped maintain the Jewish community's autonomous institutions—from ritual baths and synagogues[141] to a Jewish hospital, Jewish elementary schools (*Talmud Torahs*) and Jewish social services (care for orphans, widows, the sick, the indigent, etc.).[142]

---

141. There were two large synagogues (one 'German'–the Coral Synagogue influenced by the spirit of the Jewish *Haskalah* or Enlightenment), plus dozens of small *shuls*, and the population was a mixture of all streams of Judaism and all levels of religiosity and irreligiosity.

142. For example, according to Shchukin, among the Jewish merchants it was considered good form to donate money for free education (paying tuition for those in need).

Gil recalls further on in this work that his father "wouldn't have been caught dead in a synagogue" and was totally non-observant. Was this a reaction to a rigid Orthodox upbringing? Loss of faith triggered by loss of his parents? Exposure to revolutionary messages? Jewish secularization? Something else? Nikolayev, according to the above historiography was a very heterogenic mixture of strictly Orthodox Hassidic Jews[143] and somber Mitnagdim,[144] alongside Jews who ascribed to more liberal practices influenced by the Jewish Enlightenment. (The city's Coral Synagogue and its size[145] reflect their weight.) There were various rival fractions of the Zionist movement and their ideological rivals — the anti-Zionist socialist Bundists.

At the close of the 19th century Nikolayev had two large synagogues: the Old Synagogue — built in 1819 and dubbed 'the cobbler's synagogue' since the founders were Jewish shoemakers who made a living sewing shoes for Russian sailors, and the Coral Synagogue. In addition there were 14 smaller houses of prayer. The gradual secularization of Jewish life in Europe was evident in Nikolayev, as well. The government-appointed rabbi of Nikolayev from 1903–1906, Rabbi Yehuda Leib Wilensky (a former chemist and ardent Zionist), described the city of Nikolayev in his memoirs[146] as "goyish" saying "most of the Jews from the bottom to the intelligentsia, did not know the Hebrew language, especially not [Jewish] history" charging "even religious grain traders have agreed to make trading transactions on Saturdays, arguing income superseded the importance of respect for tradition". Moreover, the rabbi "noted with irritation and amazement the growing number of converts [to Christianity] among the Jewish intelligentsia

143. Menachem Mendel Schneerson — the seventh Lubavitcher Rebbe from Crown Heights, was born in 1902 in the city Nikolayev.

144. Literally 'Opponents' in Hebrew. Their practices and the milieu of Jewish life they followed had been the norm for generations; they opposed change, both modernism (the Jewish Enlightenment movement that sought to introduce secular subjects in Jewish education) and Hassidim (that sought to 'lighten up' Jewish life — stressing prayer and spiritual experiences over study).

145. See note 149 for a description.

146. According to Shchukin and Pavlyuk.

did not prevent them to participate actively in Jewish charitable and educational work in the community".

Thus, during Ben and Samuel's childhood at the close of the 19th century, as Charles Dickens said — "It was the best of times and the worst of times". Nikolayev, open to the West and relatively cosmopolitan, described in the historiography as a "multinational city" was the last place Jews expected pogroms. But it was precisely the presence and success of Jews in Nikolayev's bread-and-butter grain trade as brokers and exporters — a key role in the city's port economy, and the prominence of the Jewish merchant class (and some Jews' prominence in 'subversive' reformist circles), coupled with deep-seated antisemitism at all levels that set the Jews up as easy scapegoats for pogroms that killed two birds with one stone. An academic studying emigration from Russia described the underlying strategy behind the pogroms that began in 1881 and continued through the first two decades of the 20th century thus:

> The competition between Hebrews and non-Hebrews within the Pale was not the real cause of the pogroms. The real cause was the organized effort of conservatives to strengthen the old régime by stirring up ethnic hatred [deflecting anger towards the Jews — DA] and thus crushing the revolutionary tendencies of the Hebrews.[147]

Like a game of billiards, emigration was not the objective of the powers-that-be behind the pogroms (in fact, officials would note that the exit of Jews had a dampening effect on the city's economy). But the impact of the pogroms inadvertently became a tipping point for the Jewish exodus that followed.

It was the wealthiest segments of the community that were hardest hit in the 1905 pogrom that began in the center of Nikolayev and spread to other Jewish areas on the second, third and fourth day. However, the losses of the richer Jews radiated to affect the entire community,

147. Obolensky-Ossinsky, "Emigration From and Immigration Into Russia", 542–3. (See note 115.)

since those of means 'subsidized' the Jewish community's operations as a whole, including safety nets for the weakest elements. Among the establishments looted and demolished were many offices, at least three pharmacies, two soda water factories, the warehouses of Jewish grain dealers and two large Jewish manufacturers and dozens of smaller retail shops and businesses including 17 grocery stores on the first day alone, and dozens of Jewish homes.

The full impact of the pogrom is hard to access since only a small portion of the damage reports survive. Apparently, only five persons were killed (fatalities were much higher in other Jewish communities) and it does not appear that Ben and Samuel's parents were among the fatalities. The Jewish hospital, however, was already overwhelmed with walking wounded on the first day of the four-day rampage that began on 19 September. Some gentiles hid their Jewish neighbors, and many other Jews hid or fled. The sense of helplessness was reflected in events at the Jewish technical school hours after the pogrom began: "Rioters surrounded the technical school and began pounding on the windows and doors"; when police arrived, instead of dispersing the mob, they "arrested fifteen students accusing them of shooting into the crowd from the school windows".[148] Even at the height of looting, there was no real show of force by police to speak of, except symbolic attempts to restore order, until martial law was declared on 22 October with a 7:00 PM curfew and prohibition of any gathering of crowds — a measure only lifted on 27 October.

The reports of property damage that do exist speak of losses ranging from 300 to 1,200 rubles per report — including shops that were totally demolished. One merchant reported: "I worked for ten years with sweat and blood, and two hours demolished-looted [my business] to the extent that not a thread remains". Damage to the largest Jewish factory warehouse — a total loss — was extensive: 150,000 rubles lost to looting and arson and another 7,000 in cash.[149] Documentation,

---

148. After the 1903 Kishinev massacre, Jewish communities organized self-defense groups, but the local one in Nikolayev of mostly Zionist youth was only organized on the second day of the pogrom to try and keep the mobs at bay.

149. Indicative of the extent of the damage in monetary terms: construction

however, is fragmentary. It is not only that few written damage reports survived. Not all the damage was reported to authorities due to rumors in the Jewish community that the police had sent the rioters, fanning fear of retaliation should the victims submit complaints. Such fears were fanned by a libelous report filed by the Nikolayev Chief of Police claiming the Jews were responsible for the pogrom: That the trigger was a non-existent demonstration in the morning of 19 October of "10,000–13,000 Jews[150] [...] screaming and singing revolutionary songs with frenzy" demanding release of jailed revolutionaries, a mob that had clashed with a crowd of Russians carrying a portrait of Emperor Nicolas II and praying for his wellbeing [...] enraged by taunts [from the Jews], attacked beating them with sticks and fists". The Admiralty chimed-in with similar contrived allegations.

Such allegations fell on fertile soil, coming against the backdrop of unrest and demands throughout Russia for political reform (the 1905 Revolution[151]) in which Odessa and Nikolayev were among the hubs of ferment. Moreover, Jews, indeed, were hardly absent from such circles. Ironically, among the most prominent Jewish figures in revolutionary circles in Nikolayev that provided fertile soil for the canard was none other than Lev Davidovich Bronstein-Trotsky (!)[152] although

---

of a 600-seat synagogue in Nikolayev in 1880 — the Choral Synagogue — had costed 20,000 (twenty-thousand) rubles (13,000 rubles donated by wealthy members of the community). The Choral Synagogue, one of the most beautiful buildings in the city, had Moorish-style columns, stone floors and two rows of large compass windows. On the other hand, the damage from the most devastating pogrom of the times — the Kishinev pogrom in 1903 (with 48 fatalities, 495 wounded, 2,000 homeless among Kishinev's 50,000 Jews) was much higher: 2.5 million rubles in property damage.

150. Had this been true, this would be equivalent to the entire adult population of Nikolayev's Jewish community at the time participating in the 'demonstration': In 1906, 19,310 Jews, including children and elderly, lived there.

151. For an overview, see *Encyclopaedia Britannica*, s.v. "Russian Revolution of 1905", https://www.britannica.com/event/Russian-Revolution-of-1905.

152. In his autobiography (I read the relevant parts out of curiosity, and it is indeed fascinating) Trotsky says it was in Nikolayev, as a secondary school student, that he was radicalized (after several months in the city after being

the allegations about the trigger of the pogrom were a total fabrication. As for fear of retaliation if members of the community would report their losses: When the government-appointed head of the Jewish community in 1906 — Rabbi Yehuda Leib Nisan Wilensky — pressed for an investigation into the role of Russian authorities in instigating the 1905 pogrom in Nikolayev, Wilensky was arrested and expelled from the country, only returning to Russia from Berlin in 1911.[153]

A gauge of just how devastating the pogrom was, after steady growth of the Jewish population in the city over the course of a hundred years (both drawn by and contributing to the growth of trade and industry), the Jewish community witnessed an exodus of those who had lost their livelihoods and/or were rattled by events: "1906 was the first time the [Jewish] birth rate fell below the citywide rate, and to a certain extent can be attributed to the effect of the 1905 riots", says Professor Shchukin in the monograph. After the pogrom, it was not only Ben and Samuel who left Nikolayev, whatever the circumstances and motivations. The fact is, in the course of the twelve months between mid-1905 and mid-1906 some 200,000 (!) Jews emigrated from Russia–154,000 to America.[154]

---

kicked out of school in Odessa, saying: "I repudiated my assumption of conservatism and swung Leftward with such speed that it even frightened away some of my new friends"). In 1897 the 19-year-old Bronstein was arrested for involvement in organizing the South Russian Workers' Union (whose proletarian following was miniscule, and whose subversive activities were mainly circulated purple mimeographed 'underground writings'). Bronstein was arrested and held in Nikolayev, then in Odessa, tried in Moscow and sent to Siberia in 1902... See Trotsky's autobiography *My Life*, at https://www.marxists.org/archive/trotsky/1930/mylife/1930-lif.pdf.

153. According to *Encyclopedia Judaica*, 2nd ed., s.v. "Wilensky, Yehudah Leib Nisan", https://ketab3.files.wordpress.com/2014/11/encyclopaedia-judaica-v-21-wel-zy.pdf.

154. And 13,500 to Argentina, 7,000 to Canada, 3,500 to Palestine. This was a tsunami-like wave — 200,000 after the pogroms of 1905, considered the worst year for pogroms. (See H. H. Ben-Sasson, *A History of the Jewish People* (Cambridge, MA: Harvard University Press, 1976, cited in Shmuel Ettinger, "Jewish Emigration in the 19th century", https://www.myjewishlearning.com/article/jewish-emigration-in-the-19th-century/.) In September 1941, 22,467

The breakthrough...or what appeared to be a breakthrough in my search to unravel the enigma called Pop Weiss and his family came after I had given up the search for the circumstances that led to Ben and Sam being orphaned. Well, at least I had found Sam...or had I?

In March 2019 I was 'clearing my desk' — ready to send the finished manuscript to a professional editor for proofing[155] — when I opened a manila envelope with a small pack of Gil's raw data of 'who begot whom' that Toni had mailed to me in 2009 with the original digital tree software and tree file. I had never read it; after all, all the data had been digitized — right? Rifling through the jungle of schematics, telephone numbers, names and arrows, I came upon a single sheet of paper with the word "POP'S" encircled to the side. On the upper half was a schematic of several of Pop Weiss' relatives beginning with the mysterious Aunt Safer in the photo!

Who? What photograph?

In a family photo album kept by Gil's brother Bernie Weiss there was a vintage photo of an 'Aunt Safer' noting she was one of Pop Weiss' kin. Attempts to find out who she was led to dead ends — including a Sofie Safer of the same vintage who had immigrated to California from Russia who might have been a sister

Aunt Rose Safer from Philly
1860–1969

Jews and Communists functionaries (Yad Vashem says 5,000–8,000 Jews) were murdered in the Jewish cemetery and mass executions in ravines surround the city of Nikolayev by Einsatzgruppen (a special SS unit commanded by Otto Ohlendorf — the same unit which was at Babi Yar). See "Nikolayev", The Untold Stories: The Murder Sites of the Jews in the Occupied Territories of the Former USSR, https://www.yadvashem.org/untoldstories/database/index.asp?cid=601.

155. Even professional writers need someone with a fresh perspective — a 'second pair of eyes' to not only pick up typos and unify punctuation, but also spot occasional hazy wording or flaws in logic...or Hebrew syntax...or else I would be out of a job.

but wasn't. It wasn't even clear if the photo had been taken in Russia or America although my gut feeling was that the checked plaid shirt under the very 'Russian' shawl was a dead giveaway that it was taken in America. Suddenly I remembered that Pearl had mentioned in the tapes visiting the relatives in Philly at the height of the Depression — arriving unannounced. Pearl mentioned some of the first names of 'the relatives' but never said whether they were Ehrlichs or Weisses or both:

> Pop Weiss would suddenly say on a Sunday (he normally opened the tire and battery store half-days on Sunday) "I want to go visit the relatives" and Gil would call me up and say "Pop wants to go to Philadelphia". We would all pile into the car and go to Philadelphia. And I'd say "Aren't you gonna call them that we're coming?"[156] And he'd say "No"... Maybe *nobody* was going anywhere at the height of the Depression. And we would drive all the way from New York to Philadelphia — a couple of hours. [...] The next thing you know — they would be calling out the back door to the sister who lived on the other side of the fence. These were little tiny townhouses, and the back yards faced one another. All of a sudden so-and-so's mother would yell across to whoever it was — "Ben and his family are here!"[157] and they would spread the word and people would come [...] I don't know where the food came from — whether they brought food or someone stopped and picked up food, but suddenly the table was covered with food and we all ate and visited with them and then we would go back to New York.

---

156. Whenever Pearl reminisced with dialogue from those days, she'd lapse back into a quasi-New York accent that she had to work so hard to get rid of in the 1930s in order to qualify to teach in New York!

157. It seems significant that they said "Ben's family" — not "Hannah's family". Yes, the devil is in the details, and recognizing the significance of the seemingly insignificant.

Benjamin Weiss, 1933

I went back to census data at Familysearch.org and Ancestry.org and limited my search filters to Philly. Aunt Safer turned out to be Rose Safer (born 1860) subsequently found in Philadelphia in the 1910 Census with three of her four children jotted down on Gil's sheet of paper — Hannah,[158] Lena[159] and Dora Safer.[160] Arrows connected the names of eight grandchildren (whom, unfortunately, 'disappeared' leaving nary a trace). Nathan and Rose Safer had both come to America in 1891. There is no sign of Ben in the 1910 census but Aunt Safer's presence — both in America and in Ben's photo album — begs the question: Had Uncle Nathan and Aunt Safer been the magnet for him heading for America in 1905 knowing there were close relations there? And had Aunt Rose and Uncle Nathan facilitated Ben Weiss — orphaned and a minor — gaining entry to the United States (taking responsibility he would not become a welfare case)?

This was only part of the rollercoaster ride this scrap of paper contained. After I studied the schematic of Pop Weiss' relatives at the top — scribbled longhand requiring some deciphering, I looked down at something else scribbled at the bottom of the page and my jaw literally dropped when I deciphered the short notation:

---

158. Americanized to Annie.

159. Who married someone named Weissner, just to add some spice.

160. The fourth — Cecelia ('Celia' born 1886) was apparently already living elsewhere with her husband Beitchman and she and her five kids left a paper trail — from census data to a 1974 obituary–but these offspring of Aunt Safer, contemporaries of Pearl, are all dead while the living offspring couldn't be found.

Pop came from Padorynia or Pedolya Gebernia Ukraine. Kerech name of father—died or killed. Pop's mother died also and mother's name—Weiss. He was raised by mother's mother (grandma)—so took name of Weiss.

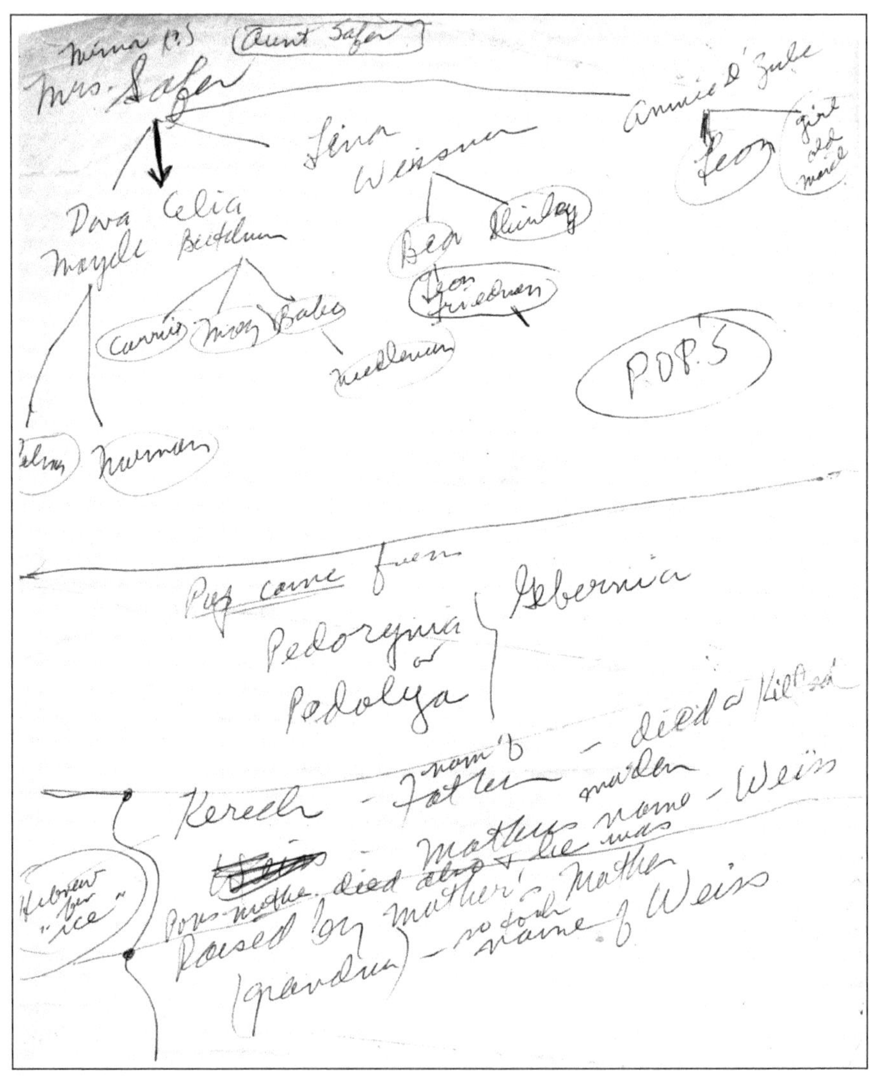

Was Benjamin a Weiss, a Kerech, or a Safer?

Yikes! Yes, there is such a place 'Pedolya'—the Podolia Gebernia (Province)—a frontier region of the Russian Empire in the southwestern Ukraine (northwest of Nikolayev). Podolia was a sparsely populated part of the Ukrainian plains southeast of Kiev that according to the Ukraine Jewish Heritage website Jewua.org had approximately 100 small *shtetls* with at least a thousand Jews according to the 1897 Russian census (only 17 of them much larger Jewish towns). In the mid-19th century the Russian government had encouraged agricultural settlement among Jews, a tradeoff for exemption from forced conscription, but Jews were only 12 percent of the population of the Podolia region in 1897.

As for the 'bombshell' about family names: There was no indication on the yellowing sheet of paper who told Gil this, or when. Ben Weiss died in 1968, Hannah Weiss in 1983, Nathan Safer in 1913 and Rose Safer in 1969, and Ben's first cousin and oldest 'contemporary' Celia (born in Russia) in 1974. No doubt Celia's siblings all died before Gil embarked in earnest on his 'tree project' in 1992, thus most probably it was one of the younger Philly relatives whose names are jotted down at the top of the same piece of paper who related this to Gil second- or

Podolia Province, 1917

third-hand. *Gil never mentioned this to anyone.* He never pursued this tidbit. But there it was among the raw data. Undated. Unattributed. It turned everything I thought I knew on its head.

If this is true (I got a lot of misinformation from relatives passed on as oral history in the course of rooting out family history, tidbits that the sources swore was the Gospel Truth...), where would this version take us? Ashkenazi Jews name children after dead relatives, particularly their parents and grandparents. Does this suggest Benjamin Kerech was killed or died while his wife Mary Weiss was pregnant and she named the infant Ben after his father? Where does Samuel Weiss from Hartford, Connecticut, born three years later in 1893, fit into this new picture? He doesn't.

Perhaps there is an unfound piece of the puzzle that would connect Sam Weiss from Connecticut with Pop Weiss (for example, Sam's parents' names which would have been listed on his marriage certificate to Anna Kushner that Mark never found). If the story of being raised by his maternal grandmother is correct, was there something that happened to this grandmother in 1905 that she couldn't continue to care for Ben and Sam, leading Benjamin Weiss to take off for America and for 12-year-old Samuel to be sent to unnamed relatives in Kiev? What are the chances there was *another* Sam Weiss in Connecticut who had escaped my sleuthing who was *older* than Pop Weiss and had a father named Benjamin? I rechecked and found nothing, however, the information for one or two Sam Weisses remained fragmentary and inconclusive. Lastly...and this sounds like a bit much: If Pop Weiss was twice orphaned, could Ben Weiss have taken his father's first name Ben when he himself was already a young man — to perpetuate *his* memory, having already adopted his mother's maiden name — to perpetuate *her* memory?

If this wasn't enough to leave me baffled, while searching for Aunt Safer in the data, I finally found Benjamin and Hannah Weiss' elusive 21 July 1912 marriage certificate — registered under the names Benny Weiss and Anna Ehrlich as they struggled to be 'more American'. Rather than confirming this note among the family tree data... their marriage certificate only added to the confusion! The parents of Gil's mother Hannah were duly noted: Father's Name: 'Harry' (further

Americanized from Harris), Mother's Maiden Name: Tuttelman. But Pop Weiss' parents said — hold your hats: 'Benjamin' and...'Mary Safer'!

So his mother's name really was Mary! And his father's name was really Weiss. Was this true, or had Pop Weiss simply not wanted to 'call the bears from the forest' as we say in Hebrew, and have to give an explanation why he didn't carry his father's last name? So, did he let it slide and 'switched his parents' surnames'? Or was this primary document — straight from the horse's mouth so to speak — on Ben's own marriage certificate in 1912, the final word? That in fact he 'was a Weiss' — even if he very well may have been raised by a grandmother, knowing he had an aunt and uncle in America — his deceased mother's close kin in Philadelphia. In other words, Aunt Rose Safer in the photo was the wife of Nathan Safer, Mary Safer's brother and Aunt Rose Safer was Mary's sister-in-law. If so, who the blazes were the 'Kerechs' that Gil jotted down as his father's surname on that slip of paper? I felt like Alice in Wonderland; things were becoming 'curiouser and curiouser'. Alas, one enigma closed, and a host of other questions remained open.

However, sifting through census data in pursuit of Pop Weiss' Philadelphia kin did solve one question: The photo of the elderly but energetic Aunt Safer, with milk bottles on a shelf behind the counter, was clearly taken in the grocery store of Ben Weiss' Aunt Safer's daughter Cecelia. Celia (née Safer), as she was called, was a first cousin and contemporary of Ben Weiss; she was several years his senior and born in 1886 in Russia and came to the United States in 1901. According to the 1910 and 1940 censuses her husband Jacob Beitchman — a cousin of Rose according to her obituary, whom 'Cellie' married in 1907 — owned a grocery store! That's where all the food probably came from when Pop Weiss decided to drop in on his relatives in Philly — unannounced, with a car-full of kin... At least one small mystery has been solved. As for Ben Weiss' name — we'll never know for sure if it was Weiss. Or Shafer. Or Kerech. Or something else. The answer would require hiring a professional genealogist who knows Russian and Ukrainian.

The Ehrlich Clan: Jassy-London-America

Grandma Hannah Weiss was born as Hannah Ehrlich on 25 December 1897 in Jassy (Iasi), Romania, a city in Moldavia west of Kishinev.

Fannie Ehrlich

She was part of a huge family,[161] one of eight children — six born in Europe, two in America. Besides Hannah, there were five more girls (Sophie, Shirley, Pearl, Betty and Annie) and two boys (Isador and Avram).

Her mother Fannie Ehrlich was not born in Jassy in 1864; rather, she came from Belz,[162] a provincial administrative center of the Republic of Poland — three kilometers from the Ukrainian-Polish border. Belz was one of the oldest towns in the western Ukraine, first mentioned as a fortified town in 1031. A wooden synagogue[163] was built in 1587 by a few dozen Jewish families, but a Jewish community only coalesced in the mid-17th century. In the second decade of the 18th century, Belz became the center of the Bełz Hassidic movement — a major force in the stream of Orthodox observance that sought to stem both modernization and secularization (including Zionism) though strict adherence to Orthodoxy. Belz practices and traditions attracted adherents, especially in Jewish communities in Galicia and Hungary. To this day, the Belzers remains one of the largest Hassidic sects in Judaism. Although a tiny town, from the mid-19th century onwards Belz boasted a large and imposing fortress-style

161. We know Gil's grandparents Harris and Fannie had eight living offspring, but in a 1992 draft of a letter to Ehrlichs across the USA, Gil said his Aunt Shirley (Hannah Weiss' sister) had told Gil his grandmother had 18 (!) children (remember, there was no effective form of birth control in those times) including three sets of twins that did not survive and an eldest named Avraham who did not survive (which leaves three unaccounted for pregnancies or three 'unaccounted for infants').

162. For a detailed profile of Belz (GPS 50°23' N, 24°01' E, the home of the Rokeach rabbinical dynasty) with many vintage photos, see Bozhena Zakaliuzna and Anatoliy Kerzhner, "Belz - guidebook", Shtetl Routes, http://shtetl-routes.eu/en/belz-putvnik/.

163. Destroyed in a large 1806 fire, along with a large part of 'wooden Belz'.

Belz, circa 1930

synagogue, dedicated in 1848, with seating for 5,000 men. Between 1880 and 1920 the town only had 1,880 to 2,104 Jewish residents (50.7 to 51.7 percent of the total population), but Belz drew hordes of visiting Jews from outside the town—much like Crown Heights did for followers and admirers of the Lubavitcher Rebbe.[164] A visitor recalled the milieu in his memoirs:

> My visit to the Belzer Rebbe was remarkably special. I came by train to Belz on the eve of the holiday of Shavuot. The train was completely packed with Jews. [...] We arrived in Belz in the afternoon [...] thousands of Jews came from out of town to visit the Rebbe, even from Hungary and Russia. I went to the synagogue for the evening prayer. There was no place to sit. There were thousands of Jews standing,

164. The same 'Edifice Complex' (strange in that the Rokeach rabbinical leadership—renowned as healers and 'wonderworkers' as well as Torah scholars—had an ascetic streak) exists to this day. The Belz Great Synagogue in Jerusalem, completed in 2000, is "an enlarged copy of the original (destroyed by the Nazis) with a main sanctuary that seats 10,000 (yes, ten thousand) worshipers and boasts an 18-ton, 12-meter-high ark that can hold 70 Torah scrolls" (cited as the largest Torah ark in the world in *Guinness Book of Records*). To view the two edifices, see "The Prince's Town", in Zakaliuzna and Kerzhner, "Belz - guidebook" (see note 162).

Belz Great Synagogue, circa 1905

> crowding and swaying during prayer like sheaves of grain in the wind.[165]

Nothing is known about Fannie's family, except her maiden name — Tuttelman — which was found on the New York City marriage certificates of her son Isador and daughter Hannah Weiss, as well. All that remains is a vintage studio photo from when Fannie and Harris arrived in America in 1905.

All that is known about the ancestors of Hannah's father is that Harris Ehrlich's father was named Mann Ehrlich — probably a shorted version of the name Mannas or Emanuel/'Manny' (but it could also be the tail-end of Hy*man* or Her*mann*[166] or even a 'misconstrued'

165. Dr. Arthur Ruppin (at age 27), who subsequently would become a key Zionist leader, recalling a 1903 visit to Belz in his autobiography, Arthur Ruppin, "A Visit to Belz in the Year 1903", in *The Chapters of My Life* (Vol. 1), excerpt in English translation, https://www.jewishgen.org/yizkor/belz/bel157.html.

166. Jacob ('Jake') Ehrlich named a son Hermann (Hyman after it was Americanized); Isador named a son Henry in 1913. While there is no way to link

Abra*ham*).[167] Harris (Ehrlich) was born in 1860[168] — one of four children: two boys Asher (Usher in Yiddish, Americanized to Harris and in some places Harry) and Jacob (Americanized to 'Jake') and two girls Rivka (Rebecca) and Hannah.

Harris Ehrlich

Harris was not born in Jassy; rather, he was born in Falesht/Faleschti[169] where his father Mann came from. Falesht was a tiny town in Bessarabia about 20 km (12.4 miles) southwest of Belz, the reason he was listed as a Russian subject (throwing me off the paper trail for a while since all these Ehrlichs — his and Jake's — put their origins in census data as 'Russia'). Falesht is situated close to the

this — there is no Falesht cemetery registry — Jewishgen.com's Worldwide Burial Registry for Moldavia brings up a Mattas Her*man* Ehrlich in the *Men's Register 1915–1943* who died on 4 September 1927 who is buried in the Jassy Jewish Cemetery (7 Elul 5687) Class: 7B Class F Row: 4 No. 22...if anyone visits Jassy and wants to check it out.

167. Strangely, in a Yad Vashem Testimony Page filled out by a member of the Israeli branch of the Ehrlichs — Hannah Tova's son-in-law (Yetta Sacomsky's husband Israel Zilberman) says the names of Hannah Tova's parents were "Abraham and Sara". Sometimes Jews use the names of the progenitors of the Jewish People 'Abraham and Sara' when they don't know the real names. Then again, Herman's Hebrew name could indeed have been Abraham...

168. Others sources say 1866.

169. Also spelled Făleşti/Făleşti/Faleshty. For some recent photos of the hamlet and the Jewish cemetery taken in 2016 by Christian Herrmann, "First Black and Whites from the Recent Trip to Bessarabia", https://vanishedworld.wordpress.com/tag/falesti-faleshty/. One should not confuse Filesht (sometimes called Faleshti) with the Romanian oil refining center Ploiesti, 56 km (35 miles) north of Bucharest.

Russian-Romanian border — only 30-something km (18.6 miles) northwest of Jassy in Romania. The Diaspora Museum says that because the town of Falesht was close to the border where Jews were forbidden to reside according to an edict by the Czar, "Jews were frequently expelled from the town on the grounds that they were living there illegally".[170] It is likely that Mann Ehrlich relocated to nearby Jassy across the Russian-Romanian border in one such expulsion, 'sometime' (one should interpret this broadly) before Hannah Ehrlich was born in Jassy in December 1897.

It is hard to know if Hannah's older siblings were born in Falesht or Jassy and how much of their childhood was spent in Jassy. The fact is, the whereabouts of Harris and Jake's sisters revealed in Holocaust victim documentation, show the family moved around within a relatively small geographical area: Harris was apparently born in Falesht, since his younger sister Hannah Tova[171] [misspelled in Gil's records as Hannah Tuba] was also born there 13 years later (in 1873). But after Hannah Tova married a *landsman* from Falesht (Mordechai Sacomsky born 1892) — the couple had a son Avraham (born 1892) whose vitals were recorded among those who perished in the Holocaust and the document says he was also born in Falesht.[172] When Avraham grew up, this son of Hannah Tova (née Ehrlich) Sacomsky lived prior to the Second World War in Bivolari — a village only 45 km (28 miles) north of Jassy, and halfway to Falesht which is northeast of Bivolari.[173]

---

170. Today there are no Jews in Filesht (the town's remaining Jews were decimated in the Holocaust). In the old Jewish cemetery, the remains of 400 tombstones exist — some dating back to the 19th century — but most are so weathered or broken that it is impossible to read the inscriptions. See Yefim Kogan, "The Old Jewish Cemetery of Fălești (Faleshty)", https://www.jewishgen.org/bessarabia/files/cemetery/falesti/FalestiOldCemetery.pdf.

171. After he married, Hannah Tova's son Avram Sacomski lived in Bivolari as well.

172. He was Hannah Weiss' first cousin.

173. Details of his life and death were extracted from three different Testimony Pages submitted to Yad Vashem by different members of the family for Avraham Secomsky and one for his mother Hannah Tova Secomsky.

During the Second World War Abraham was in Jassy, where the family had been forcibly deported,[174] and it is there in Jassy that Avraham met his death.[175] The whereabouts of his Aunt Rivka's family is not known for sure but some of her children fled eastward into Russia over time.[176]

With such a pattern (the Wandering Jew label wasn't just an epithet, relocation due to marriage, edicts or economic opportunity were common), there was clearly a strong connection with Jassy even for those Ehrlich kin living elsewhere in the vicinity, but it is hard to know how many of the four Ehrlich offspring — Harris, Jake, Hannah Tova and Rivka — were raised at least in part in Jassy. All we know is sometime in the late 18th century Harris and Fannie Ehrlich were in Jassy where Hannah Ehrlich was born. What makes it hard to determine is the fact that Yiddish was their first language, spoken by the family in the home — not Russian or Romanian (and thus it is listed as mother tongue on American census data). Furthermore, acquiring Romanian citizenship even for those born in Jassy was blocked for Jews[177] thus Mann and his family

---

174. The Jews in Moldavia — if they weren't murdered outright, sent to forced labor camps or dispatched directly to concentration camps — were clustered in hubs, large and small (including Falesht at one point for surrounding villages). A large percentage was ultimately concentrated in Jassy (where a 'special census' of men — their ages and occupations, was drawn up in 1941) to streamline 'treatment' of the Jewish Problem.

175. Arrested in the 1941 pogrom in which a third of Jassy's Jews were liquidated, he was taken to the police station and never heard from again. Either he was shot with many other Jewish men, or put on the Jassy 'death train' of locked boxcars in the height of the summer, designed to slowly kill all the occupants. For a description of this little-known atrocity, see "The Iasi Death Train, Romania, 1941", https://isurvived.org/2Postings/Iasi_death_train.html.

176. Hannah Tova — who was the 68-year-old widow of Mordechai Socumsky who had died in 1932 — perished in the Holocaust (possibly together with her daughter Rivka) in one of the Transnistria death marches in 1941. Apparently her daughters Bessie and Yenta (born 1903, called 'Initka') and several granddaughters from her daughter Rivka, managed to flee eastward before Germany overran this part of Romania.

177. Only Christians were eligible for citizenship, and even later when this

remained Russian subjects with resident alien status in Romania, which explains why Hannah's brother Isador told US census-takers in 1930 that he was 'from Russia': Even if Isador was born in Jassy in Romania in 1888 as well as Hannah, he remained a Russian subject.

~

Downtown Jassy, circa 1900

Jassy[178] (Iasi in Romanian spelling) in contrast to Falesht, was a genuine city that had a Jewish population of almost 40,000 in 1899[179] — half the overall population of Jassy.[180] Jews had lived in Jassy since the 16th century; in the 18th-century Moldavian leaders granted special charters to attract Jews and encourage them to develop commerce because the area was a 'frontier area' — both under-populated and underdeveloped.

One description of life at the beginning of the 19th century paints

---

changed, acquisition of citizenship by Jews was near impossible — discussed elsewhere in detail.

178. Called Yosh in Yiddish and Yas in Hebrew. For vintage pictures of Jassy circa 1900, see "Iasi 1900", YouTube video, 8:16 minutes, 2007, https://www.youtube.com/watch?v=drtVsOqPV8o. For an overview of the history of Jews in Jassy, see Lucian-Zeev Herşcovici, *The YIVO Encyclopedia of Jews in Eastern Europe*, s.v. "Iaşi", http://www.yivoencyclopedia.org/article.aspx/Iasi, and Itic Svart-Kara, *Contributions to the History of Jews in Iaşi* (excerpts translated into English from Romanian), (Bucharest: Editura Hasefer, 1977), https://www.jewishgen.org/yizkor/iasi/Iasi.html#TOC and https://www.jewishgen.org/yizkor/iasi/ias007.html#Page13\ which also gives a good overview of the Jews' role in economic modernization and the status of *sudits* or foreign subjects (i.e., resident aliens) such as the Jews.

179. For comparison's sake, in 1897 there were 4,518 Jews living in Falesht out of a total population of 6,672.

180. By 1910 the number of Jews had dropped to 35,000.

Jassy's Jewish population as very diverse — from lower-class craftsmen to Jewish merchants in tobacco, cotton, iron goods, rice, copper, and salt to manufacturers of spirits, paper and gun power to mention a few. There were wealthy free professionals, as well. The profile further explained:

> In the late nineteenth century, Jews were active in small industry and crafts, local and international trade, finance, and liberal and intellectual professions (they were doctors, teachers, writers, journalists, bookshop keepers, editors, public servants, and musicians). They also contributed to the setting up of steam mills and mechanical workshops, as well as to organizing freight.[181]

While there was a dominant Hassidic element in the Jewish community (alongside a Reform community from the mid-19th century), Jews were not concentrated in singularly Jewish neighborhoods — except for the poor. Most spread out among the general population even residing on the main drag — the equivalent of living on Riverside Drive in Upper Manhattan or Rothschild Boulevard in Tel Aviv. Yiddish culture was vibrant — and it was in Jassy that the first Yiddish language newspaper was founded (1855) and the world's first professional Yiddish theatre (1876) was formed. Another claim to fame: It was in Jassy that poet Naphtali Herz Imber penned the words to what became Israel's national anthem — *Hatikvah*. Yet, despite this rosy picture of a relatively cosmopolitan Jewish community in the mid-18th century, Hannah Ehrlich was taken as a baby to London in the closing years of the 1890s.

In the UK, Harris Ehrlich and his family most probably lived in the London neighborhoods where most Jews resided at the close of the 19th, and outset of the 20th, century — in the East End,[182] the British

181. Herşcovici, "Iasi" (see note 178). YIVO says that in 1890–1892, there were 3,048 Jewish artisans and 3,404 Jewish merchants. By 1909, 77 percent of the craftsmen in Jassy were Jews, but Jews were also active in banking, both domestic and international.

182. Descriptions and statistical data about the East End at the turn of the

capital's equivalent of the Lower East Side.[183] (No paper trail was found.) According to one history, in the 1880s and 1890s the majority of Jews arrived by steamer from Hamburg, and these vessels docked at a wharf facing the East End. Immigrants often literally 'settled where they got off the boat'. The East End was also an undesirable neighborhood and therefore a low-rent district of London and consequently affordable to immigrants.

As already noted, only a small minority of Jews debarking in the UK weren't 'in transit' with their sights set on reaching America. According to one profile of the East End's Jewish history "many of them staying in London for a few weeks or even several years before crossing the Atlantic". Indeed, if between 1870 and 1914 two million Eastern European Jews immigrated to America, only 120,000 chose to make the UK their permanent home in the corresponding period. But the East End, like the Lower East Side, was poor and overcrowded, filled with substandard housing and what the English called 'sweating dens'—sweatshops with 14 to 20-hour workdays.[184] Different students

---

century are based on input from a host of sources, including: Laura Vaughan, "A Study of the Spatial Characteristics of the Jews in London 1695 & 1895", MA thesis, University College of London, 1994, https://discovery.ucl.ac.uk/id/eprint/659/1/Vaughan_1994.pdf; Nathan Friedenberg, "The End of the Jewish East End: Jewish Migration Patterns in a Metropolis", http://www.academia.edu/9866755/The_End_of_the_Jewish_East_End; Steven Burstin, "London's Lower East Side", *The New York Jewish Week*, 1 December 2011, https://jewishweek.timesofisrael.com/londons-lower-east-side/, and Richard Jones, "Eastern European Jews Arrive", https://www.jack-the-ripper.org/jewish-east-end.htm, among others.

183. For some vintage footage of Jewish life on London's East End circa 1900, see Martin Koddenberg, "Jewish East End", YouTube video, 7:11 minutes, 2014, https://www.youtube.com/watch?v=5YNZhjMqINM&t=30s and the Huntley Film Archives footage "East End of London in the 1900's", YouTube video, 1:03 minutes, 2013, https://www.youtube.com/watch?v=Ldcw8XEqYv8.

184. For history buffs, there is a priceless English archive of some period publications that provides a first-hand 'unfiltered' look at the temper of the times—prevailing conditions, attitudes towards Jews and more: "Jewish settlement in the late 19th century" in the Warwick University Archives, https://warwick.ac.uk/services/library/mrc/studying/docs/racism/jewish/.

of the period estimate that the Jewish population in East London was in the vicinity of 35,000 in 1880 and 50,000 in 1890, and swelled to 120,000 in 1910 — with most working in the needle trade, shoe manufacturing or cabinetmaking.[185]

The East End was also attractive to Eastern European Jews fleeing persecution because word had spread among Eastern European Jewry that it had a host of Jewish social and welfare institutions already established in the mid-19th century by earlier Jewish newcomers from elsewhere (brethren mainly from the Netherlands and Germany). The most renowned was the East End's Jews' Free School for penniless immigrant children. In 1900, it became the largest elementary school in both the UK and all of Europe (!) with an enrollment of 4,250 pupils.

Some context is called for, however. The average Englishman was not exactly thrilled by the influx of Jews from Eastern Europe that began in 1881. Reflecting the mood, major news media such as the weekly British magazine of culture and politics, *The Spectator*, branded the Jewish influx a case of "wholesale pauperism", while in 1887 the influential pro-Tory London evening newspaper *St. James Gazette* published a 1,500-word unsigned article saying Jews in the Whitechapel and Spitalfields neighborhoods raised "social, economic, moral, and political questions" described as:

> [...] the presence in East London of a colony of 30,000 to 40,000 aliens, steeped to the lips in every form of moral and physical degradation [...] exacting to the utmost the privileges that the law confers on Englishmen [...]

The article charged "the presence of such a colony constitutes a very serious social and economic evil".[186] Gentile society was convinced that the infamous 1888 serial killer Jack the Ripper who stalked his victims

185. In 1892, of 2,240 laborers, 62 percent were in the garment industry or shoe and boot makers.

186. For the full piece, see "Jewish East London", *St. James Gazette*, 4 April 1887, https://cdm21047.contentdm.oclc.org/digital/collection/tav/id/5204.

in East London was surely one of these 'Polish Jews'.[187]

The small established community of Anglo Jewry didn't exactly welcome such Jewish brethren with open arms either, fearing such overwhelmingly poor, religiously observant, Yiddish-speaking Jews (dubbed *Ostjuden* by German Jews) would stoke antisemitism by their Otherness and endanger the status of such 'civilized' Jews as tolerable-good Jews... In mid-1890 the *Jewish Chronicle* editorialized:

> Anyone with eyes to see must know that there are limits to the receptive capacity of this country. Already we have a large immigrant body camped down East, which is a rock of offence to many Gentiles, and taxes the resources of our community to exhaustion point. Is there not a danger of raising an outcry [...] against Jewish refugees from whatever land they may hail?[188]

Every 'greenie' (the British term for greenhorn) underwent interrogation before receiving any assistance from the Board of Guardians for the Jewish Poor. One scholar says the most desperate and destitute

187. Regarding Jack the Ripper, see https://www.jack-the-ripper.org/. For the Jewish perspective, see Richard Jones, "The Whitechapel Murders and the Jewish Community", https://www.jack-the-ripper.org/jewish-history.htm, and slanted depictions of the East End in scholarly and popular discussions in Heidi Kaufman, "1800–1900: Inside and Outside the Nineteenth-Century East End", *BRANCH: Britain, Representation and Nineteenth-Century History*, January 2016, http://www.branchcollective.org/?ps_articles=heidi-kaufman-1800-1900-inside-and-outside-the-nineteenth-century-east-end. In 2014 a claim was made that the murderer was a schizophrenic Polish Jew, based on DNA analysis of a contaminated piece of forensic evidence by an expert in historic DNA, but the findings — published in the sensationalist *Daily Mail* and a popular book, Russel Edwards, *Naming Jack The Ripper* (London: Sidgwick and Jackson, 2014) rather than a scholarly journal — have been roundly contested for flaws and lack of peer review.

188. David Cesarani and Irving Jacobs, *The Jewish Chronicle and Anglo-Jewry, 1841–1991* (Cambridge: Cambridge University Press, 1994), 74. Excerpts on Google Books.

(some of those leaving Romania in 1899–1900 were literally traveling *by foot* to Bremen to sail for England or America) were not just turned down for relief:

> As groups of bedraggled and desperate refugees congregated on street corners and besieged the Board of Guardians, the Jewish organizations adopted a ruthless policy of repatriating as many as possible.[189]

Thus, it should come as no surprise that the established Jewish community didn't protest the passage of Great Britain's Alien Act of 1905 that sought to stem the flow. According to one scholar, as early as 1882 the Board of Guardians of the Jewish Poor established by well-to-do West End Jews:

> [...] was taking advertising space in the Jewish press in Russia and Romania warning potential immigrants that if they came to England they would face great hardships and that the Board would give them no relief in the first six months of their residence.[190]

Nevertheless, there were minimal emergency safety nets that including a huge hostel-like shelter for people 'just off the boat' and a soup kitchen that fed up to 2,200 mouths per day on site. By 1905, the soup kitchen was providing food for over 1,600 families (about 8000 individuals). Some historians argue that such services on the East End were established in part to 'hide' such Jewish brethren from the eyes of the gentiles—viewed both as a source of shame and fuel for the antisemites who were not lacking in British society.[191] As for monetary assistance

189. Ibid., 74.

190. Laurie Magnus, *The Jewish Board of Guardians and the Men Who Made It, 1859–1909.* (London: The Jewish Board of Guardians, 1909), 91-92.

191. Phillip Carstairs, "Soup and Reform: Improving the Poor and Reforming Immigrants through Soup Kitchens 1870–1910" citing "Soup Kitchen for the Jewish Poor", (1889a). General Committee, Minutes, Annual Accounts,

from the Board of Guardians of the Jewish Poor:

> Between 1900 and 1910 it made 26,479 loans to the East End's Jews, averaging £7.00 per loan. The loans were interest free and repayable at six pence in the pound per week. They were made to people who wished to set up as independent traders or as their own masters.[192]

Such seed capital was roundly criticized even by relatively sympathetic English reformers. One wrote with exasperation that:

> [...] though the accusation of wholesale pauperism brought against the Jewish community cannot be maintained [*sic*, is unsubstantiated], there is doubtless, from the standpoint of industrial health, a grave objection to the form of relief administered by the Jewish Board of Guardians. Money lent or given for trade purposes fosters the artificial multiplication of small masters, and is one of the direct causes of the sweating system.[193]

Between 1890 and 1902 somewhere between 5,000 and 8,000 Jews from Eastern Europe arrived annually in London — including the Ehrlichs who, while not among the destitute masses, hardly encountered a 'welcoming' mood in London.

What was their life like? How did they make a living? Besides learning English while in London, did Harris or his two sons attend any of the 489 institutions specializing in training craftsmen and tradesmen that existed on the East End in 1900? None of the younger Ehrlich

---

1872–1889: ACC/2942/002, Metropolitan Archives, London.

192. See "Eastern European Jews Arrive", https://www.jack-the-ripper.org/jewish-east-end.htm and "The Whitechapel Murders and the Jewish Community", https://www.jack-the-ripper.org/jewish-history.htm.

193. Published in 1889 by Beatrice Potter (AKA Webb), "East London", in Charles Booth, *Labour and Life of the People*, 7, https://cdm21047.contentdm.oclc.org/digital/collection/tav/id/5175.

children appear on the rosters of the Jews' Free School[194] and years later Isador told American census takers he had a 5th-grade education — in short, when they left Romania his formal education came to an end. The one thing we do know is that Harris Ehrlich's seven to eight-year-sojourn in the UK with his family was the source of Hannah's slight cockney accent and her claim to having been "a little English lass" before she came to America in 1905 at the age of eight. It is also clear that they did not arrive penniless in America though it is anyone's guess how Harris made a livelihood — perhaps initially as a tailor, but no one really knows.

What prompted Harris (and later, Jake Ehrlich) to leave Romania?[195]

194. To appreciate just how extensive archival material is becoming: Believe it or not, a full searchable roster of 20,000 students who attended the Jews' Free School has been compiled, https://www.jewishgen.org/databases/UK/JFS/index.html.

195. Clarification: There are signs that Jake may have spent a period in Kishinev while his brother Harris was in England. Moe, born in 1898, told the 1920 census he was from 'Kishneff'. Moreover, I found Jake and four of his family...as well as his nephew Isador and his wife Ada interred in the Kishnever Congregation section of the Mount Hebron Cemetery in Flushing, New York ('Ehrlichs' buried there between 1947 and 1985). Keep in mind however: *Landsmanshaft* organizations were formed by people from the same town, *shtetl*, or region of Eastern Europe and served both social and economic needs — including 'I can get it for you wholesale' — when it came to burial plots! There were at least 3,000 *landsmanshafts* in New York alone, many of which bought burial plots 'wholesale' in a given cemetery; using a *landsmanschaft* organization's burial society services was much cheaper than buying an individual burial plot so many availed themselves of the service offered even if they were not from a particular town. For more on *landsmanshafts*, see the New York Genealogical Society's burial society FAQs, https://jgsny.org/searchable-databases/burial-society-databases/burial-society-faq, and *landsmanshaftn* at https://jgsny.org/searchable-databases/indexes-to-jewish-organizations/yivo-landsmanshaftn-collection. More about the role of these societies is found in Daniel Soyer, "Landsmanshaft Culture and Immigrant

A profile of Romanian Jewry in the 1901–1902 edition of the *American Jewish Yearbook*[196] (further fleshed out by more recent academic studies) reflects the darker side of Romanian Jewish life — the milieu in the decade or two before Harris and Fannie Ehrlich picked up and left for London towards the close of the 18th century.

Romania was characterized by a special brand of institutionalized antisemitism.[197] On paper, the 1878 Congress of Berlin[198] promised equality to all inhabitants of Romania, but in fact, Romanian independence that had been granted under the international treaty only fanned nationalism and xenophobia. Romania did not intend to honor this proviso to Romanian independence. While following independence Jews were supposed to be enfranchised, in practice all but a handful[199] were left as resident aliens without any avenue to become naturalized citizens.

This was paralleled by a host of anti-Jewish laws and regulations from 1880 onward designed to expel Jews from villages and towns by stripping them of their livelihoods, not only prohibiting them to farm but now also prohibiting them from providing services in rural areas. Elsewhere (i.e., in the cities), severe quotas were then enacted on the

---

Identities", in *Jewish Immigrant Associations and American Identity in New York 1880–1939* (Detroit: Wayne State University Press, 2018), 349–80.

196. Dr. E. Schwarzfeld, "The Jews of Roumania from the Earliest Times to the Present Day", in the *American Jewish Year Book 1901–1902*, ed. Cyrus Adler (Philadelphia: The Jewish Publication Society of America, 1901), 11-62, http://www.ajcarchives.org/AJC_DATA/Files/1901_1902_3_SpecialArticles.pdf#page=11.

197. Ironically, there are only a few thousand Jews today (most in Bucharest) compared to 750,000 before the Holocaust; nevertheless, a 2015 survey conducted by the Elie Wiesel National Institute for Holocaust Studies in Romania found nearly a quarter of Romanian survey respondents said their country should have no Jewish residents — 11 percent described Jews as "a problem for Romania" and 22 percent said they would like them "only as tourists".

198. The Congress of Berlin (13 June–13 July 1878) was a summit following the Russo-Turkish War of 1877–78 which liberated the Balkan states (Greece, Serbia, Romania and Montenegro) from Ottoman rule.

199. According to one source, 887 soldiers who had fought in the 1877 war between Turkey and Romania.

number of Jews in every aspect of economic life and socioeconomic organization — from managerial positions to rank-and-file employees even in a Jewish-owned (!) enterprise — as well as outright bans on Jews engaging in countless occupations (just one example, employment by the railways in any capacity) by reserving such position for Romanian citizens only — which the Jews weren't and couldn't become. Many of the laws were cloaked in Catch-22 provisos. For example, Jews were not barred *per se* from being lawyers, but they could not plead cases before tribunals and courts of appeal because only members of the bar were eligible to do so...and *that* privilege was reserved, of course, for Romanian citizens only. Just how draconian these regulations were is capsulated in the following passage — published in 1902 in the *American Jewish Yearbook* — that describes the discrimination in the medical professions:

> At most, the Jew may be engaged as country physician, provided he gives up his place the moment a Roumanian physician claims it. Jews are accepted at hospitals as externs and as interns only in default of Roumanians. In competitive examinations, they are put into the lowest class, no matter if they obtain the best marks. Jewish pharmacists may neither acquire nor manage pharmacies, and pharmacies may employ Jewish apprentices only if they already have one Roumanian apprentice. Jews may not be received as free patients in hospitals, except in case of sickness at once serious and urgent, and as pay patients only so many may be taken in as can be accommodated in ten per cent of all the beds, provided, of course, that no Christian aliens are applicants for these places reserved for aliens. The same regulation obtains [*sic* applies] in the private hospitals [...] After all the above, it is superfluous to add that the Jews are not admitted to the medical service in the army, and contrary to law, Jewish physicians are forbidden to conduct [*sic* manage] asylums for the insane.

Anti-Jewish laws also limited access to education. However, beginning in 1893, Jews were allowed to enroll in state schools without special quotas; subsequently, "the primary and secondary schools were literally overrun" with Jewish enrollees and by 1891 Jewish children constituted 39 percent of all pupils in the public-school system... To remedy the 'problem', in 1893 the regime made primary school free for Romanian citizens, while resident aliens (in essence, all the Jews[200]) had to pay a tuition fee, and were accepted only if places were still available. In 1898, the same tactic was employed to exclude Jews from secondary schools and higher education. In 1899 such non-citizens were barred from studying at professional and agricultural schools, and were admitted only to schools of commerce and of arts [*sic* artisans] and trades — with a 20 percent cap on the total number of resident aliens in the student body. And those who got in faced an exorbitantly high tuition fee. Authorities hounded the schools that the Jews established for their children:

> When Jews founded schools of their own, obstacles were thrown in their way, and finally, contrary to the law, they were prohibited from teaching on Sundays and Christian feast days, and were forced to keep their schools open on Saturdays and Jewish holidays. The children are forbidden to cover their heads during the lesson in Hebrew.

Despite and perhaps because of its large Jewish population, Jassy was a hub of antisemitic ferment. A profile of the history of Jews in the city published in 1982 by the Diaspora Museum's genealogy center Dorot described the situation in Jassy during this period:

> Towards the end of the 19th century, Jassy became the center of anti-Semitism in Romania. In 1882 and 1884 two economic congresses were held there with the aim of promoting a boycott on Jewish commerce and industry. During

200. The *American Jewish Yearbook 1901-1902* (67) put the number of Jews found worthy of being granted Romanian citizenship for their military service in 1877 at 940 who were naturalized in 1880 (following independence). Only another 85 Jews in the following *21 years* (up until 1900) were added to the list of Jews with Romanian citizenship. A drop in the bucket.

> this period, 196 Jewish shops were closed down in 1892 and many Jewish tradesmen were expelled from the town. The University of Jassy became the center of anti-Semitism in Rumania with A. C. Cuza, who taught at the university as its main proponent.

More and more Jews slowly got the message.

At first, between 1878 and 1888, those leaving were a dribble — "sporadic" and "spasmodic" in the words of the *Yearbook*'s author. The turn of the century, however, was a watershed. The departure of Romanian Jews to America reached "amazing proportions". The increase in Romanian Jews heading across the Atlantic was clearly the reason the *American Jewish Yearbook* chose to devote 90 pages of its 1901/2 edition to the situation of Romanian Jews.[201] The piece noted the nature of the exodus in the 1880s and 1890s:

> Many [of the economically disenfranchised] directed their steps towards the United States, others towards the principal cities of Europe, in which they founded important colonies, notably in London[202] and in Paris. The movement revived again in 1886–1887, seven thousand persons emigrating during those two years. The [new anti-Jewish Romanian] laws whose enactment followed in rapid succession increased the number of candidates for starvation, and emigration became regular and continuous. [...]

---

201. While some of the English is a bit stilted, and here and there choice of words is over-the-top, the author of the essay (Elias Schwarzfeld) was a respected Jewish Romanian historian, and the historiography is backed up by an impressive bibliography of sources.

202. According to the 1902 census (believed to underestimate the number of Jews by a large margin, at least by 25 percent), there were 3,296 Romanian-born Jews in the UK; 2,106 in London. It is believed there was widespread census-dodging among immigrants, and children born in the UK were not included. See Andrew Godley, *Jewish Immigrant Entrepreneurship in New York and London 1880–1914* (Basingstoke, Hampshire: Palgrave, 2001), 30 (Table 3.1A). Excerpts on Google Books.

It is estimated that out of 218,000 Jews in Romania in 1876, some 45,000 emigrated between 1882 and 1894.

The financial-economic crush in Romania reached a crisis level in 1899–1900 as the circle of Jews losing their livelihood grew wider — labeled a "fever of emigration transformed into a delirium" in the 1902 monograph. Many of the emigrants were penniless, but others left with "a few remnants of their fortune" heading for Turkey, France, England, Canada, and more and more, to the United States. A 1992 study of the exodus of Romanian Jews by I. C. Butnaru[203] explained the psychological impact when two decades of amplified discriminatory economic pressure meshed with the realization that the door to Romanian citizenship would remain firmly shut, perpetuating the status of Jews as foreign aliens. The highest estimate is that 2,000 Jews were naturalized, but it was stipulated that even these recipients — unlike other Romanians — couldn't pass on their citizenship to their spouses or their children. Not only that. At one point Romania persuaded Austria and Germany to withdraw *their* citizenship from Jews living for years in Romania![204] The message was clear for countless Romanian Jews, including those like the Ehrlich brothers who were not penniless at all. As Butnaru summed it up: "The emigration of Jews from Romania then [from 1879] and thereafter did not stem from any adventurous spirit [...] or out of desire to settle among strangers. They left Romania because they could no longer endure their living conditions being considered aliens and treated as enemies".

How many Romanian Jews uprooted between 1880 and 1914 (after which the outbreak of the First World War disrupted immigration)?[205] Were the *American Jewish Yearbook*'s predictions of panic ('delirium') exaggerated or over-optimistic? It depends how you look at it. Subsequent

---

203. I. C. Butnaru, *The Silent Holocaust: Romania and Its Jews* (New York: Greenwood, 1992), 20–3.

204. "Romania Virtual Jewish History Tour", Virtual Jewish Library, https://www.jewishvirtuallibrary.org/romania-virtual-jewish-history-tour.

205. The drastic drop during the 1914–1918 war years was followed in 1924 by legislation that brought an end to unfettered immigration into the United States; its geographical quotas and the way they were arrived at (based on

data cited in a 2010 study of Romanian Jews in America and Canada[206] says 75,000 out of Romania's 218.000 Jews in 1887[207] arrived in America — how many went elsewhere is hard to estimate.[208] Other sources break the numbers down saying that of the 67,057 Jews who came to America between 1881–1910, 6,967 arrived between 1881–1890, and another 47,300 between 1901–1910, adding that this exodus was also fueled in part by an 1899–1900 financial crisis in Romania[209] that further worsened the economic hardships of Jews.[210] In short, *34 percent* of Romanian Jewry emigrated from Romania to America alone during the decades of heightened economic and continued political disenfranchisement that followed Romanian independence, and tens of thousands others left in the decade that followed.

There is an irony to history here — even a double irony: In essence, the actions of a viciously antisemitic regime whose actions sent a large proportion of Romanian Jews westward to seek a permanent home elsewhere would prove to be a lifesaver in disguise. During the Holocaust, half of Romanian Jewry — some 380,000 Jews — would perish. Yet, far from hemorrhaging to death as a result of the exodus between the 1880s and 1910, Romanian Jewry was replenished by the influx of Jews in even more desperate circumstances fleeing conditions in Poland and particularly pogroms in Russia — the same Soviet Union that a few short decades later, unlike the United States, did not close its borders and offered shelter to Jews expelled or fleeing eastward during

---

1890 figures before Jews began arriving *en masse* from Eastern Europe) effectively 'locked out' Eastern European Jews — the largest Diaspora community.

206. For more updated historical input, see independent scholar and ethnologist, Vladimir F. Wertsman, *Salute to the Romanian Jews in America and Canada, 1850-2010* (USA, 2010).

207. In 1899 –1900, in the midst of the exodus, there were 300,000 Jews in Romania — 43,000+ in Bucharest.

208. Going elsewhere in Europe, to South America and to Israel.

209. Overspending by the Romanian Government on massive infrastructure improvements that cascaded into a first-class financial crisis.

210. Dana Mihăilescu, *Eastern European Jewish American Narratives, 1890–1930: Struggles for Recognition* (Lanham: Lexington, 2018), 24.

the Second World War and the Holocaust[211]...including some of the children of Harris and Jake's sisters — Hannah and Rivka Ehrlich! But during the first decades of the 20th century the movement of Jews was *out* of Russia *into* Romania.

With the influx of Jews from the east, by 1930 a national census showed 757,000 Jewish residents in Romania, making Romania the third-largest concentration of Jews in Eastern Europe on the eve of the Holocaust (after Poland and the Soviet Union). Moreover, despite the decades of oppression, and although Jews constituted only 4.2 percent of the overall population of Romania, in 1930 a third of Romanian Jewry was engaged in commerce, 20 percent in industry and four percent were professionals. That year reform of the constitution fully enfranchised Romania's Jews *en bloc*, half a century after equality was promised as a 'package deal' in exchange for Romanian independence.[212] In 1931 five Jewish parliamentarians were already serving in the parliament. This optimistic picture, of course, was short-lived. Two years later in 1933,

---

211. Some European Jews fled eastward from the Nazi advance. The majority of them were simply shipped to the east in transports — travel and living conditions that were far from a picnic, but saved many lives. Jews flooded places as far east as Tashkent, with some 8,000 (i.e., Ashkenazi Jews) in Kazakhstan. And a handful even went farther overland to Shanghai in China (Leah Abbott's family among them). It is estimated that ten percent of Polish Jewry survived by crossing over to the Soviet zone in 1939 after Poland was swallowed up by Nazi Germany and Soviet Russia. After Hitler invaded Russia in June 1941, "more than a million Soviet Jews fled eastward into the Asian parts of the country" thus, despite killings and deportations by Stalin to Siberia or Asia, those Jews who escaped to Russia "constituted the largest group of European Jews to survive the Nazi onslaught". See United States Holocaust Memorial Museum, Washington, DC, Holocaust Encyclopedia, s.v. "Escape from German Occupied Europe", https://encyclopedia.ushmm.org/content/en/article/escape-from-german-occupied-europe.

212. Although the 1919 Treaty of Paris again required Romania to grant Jews civil rights, this was guaranteed on paper in the new 1923 constitution but with no tangible results: The Romanians made receipt of citizenship on an individual basis, not an *en bloc* process, using red tape to avoid implementation. Only with the amendment of the constitution in 1930, did Jews receive equal civil rights.

Hitler came to power in Germany and the clock was ticking.

As noted, on the micro-level, we know little about the specifics of the Ehrlich's lives in Jassy — their occupations or circumstances prior to the Ehrlich boys choosing to move out. Yet, it is clear that Harris Ehrlich's departure for London around 1897–1898, and later for the United States approximately seven years later in 1905, as well as brother Jake's decision to head for America in 1907–1909 (from wherever he was living in the meantime), was part of a much larger human drama — the fate of Rumanian Jewry.

There were Romanian Jews who died at the hands of the Nazis while the Romanian regime vacillated back and forth between collaborating with the Nazis and initiating their own killing fields at the hands of Romanian troops and police, and protecting Romanian Jews from being handed over to the Nazis for liquidation.[213] The overwhelming majority of Holocaust survivors would go to Israel as soon as they could.[214] In the meantime, both of Hannah Ehrlich Weiss' European aunts — Hannah Tova and Rivka — and a third of her European first cousins perished during the war years. Combined, only half the

---

213. The Romanian government under Antonescu between 1940–1944 was both an enthusiastic collaborator with the Nazis while also 'independently' engaging in mass murder of some 300,000 Jews in Bukovina, Bessarabia, and Transnistria (ethnically-Romanian areas beyond Romania's border to the north) while concurrently preventing most of Romania's 'own Jews' in the south within Romania proper from being slaughtered wholesale by 'Romanian Nazi' troops, or being transported to death camps in Poland (a change of policy that came only after the Nazi defeat at Stalingrad when it was becoming increasingly clear that Nazi Germany would lose the war...). Both attitudes were experienced in Jassy in Moldavia to the south: A massive 1941 pogrom and sealed death trains orchestrated by the regime (13,000 deaths out of a Jewish population of 45,000 in Jassy) — including, as already noted, Harris and Jake's nephew Avraham Sacomsky. However, Romanian authorities also prevented many others being shipped to extermination camps in Poland. An estimated 375,000 Romanian Jews survived. See Robert D. Kaplan, "The Antonescu Paradox", *Foreign Policy*, https://foreignpolicy.com/2016/02/05/the-antonescu-paradox-romania-world-war-ii-hitler/.

214. Immediately after the war, few could enter due to continuation of British war policy ('the White Paper' limiting immigrant visas for Jews to a dribble to

Ehrlichs who remained in Romania survived the Holocaust—and a third of them disappeared from the radar and are 'somewhere in Russia' even after a million Russian Jews emigrated to Israel in the 1990s. Other family members found refuge in Israel in the early 1950s or the smaller wave of Russian immigration in the 1970s, rebuilding their lives in the Jewish state.[215]

~

To return to the 'founders' of the American branch of the Ehrlich family. In the broadest sense they were part of an exodus greater than the Romanian exodus: Between 1880 and 1914 a third (!) of the Jewish population of Eastern Europe immigrated to the United States.

Nothing specific was known about the Ehrlich brothers' lives when they first arrived in America—save a photo in Bernie Weiss' family album: A studio photo of six Ehrlich children and their parents dated 1905—which appears to have been taken after their arrival in New York.[216] The existence of a photo and the apparel worn seemed to indicate they came from a family of at least modest means, however, studio photos of the period—staged by the photographers—are sometimes deceptive.[217] This, however, does not seem to be the case for Harris

---

appease the Arabs) and this policy remained in effect until the British completed their withdrawal from Mandatory Palestine. The Romanian Government began putting barriers and quotas on the exit of Jews just as the gates of the Jewish State were being thrown open in mid-May 1948. Money under the table to the Romanian Government worked to obtain the release of some Jews, but the majority of the remnant of Romanian Jewry remained 'trapped' behind the Iron Curtain until 1951.

215. For details on the fate of this or that member of Hannah Tova and Rivka Ehrlich's branches of the Ehrlich family, see the URL to the family tree on Playingdetective.com in the Appendix.

216. It is known that Hannah, born in December 1897, was eight when they arrived in 1905 but an Ellis Island record was not found.

217. By the outset of the 20th century, not just the well-to-do were posing for studio photos. Photographers staged such photos with props—including, for example, photos of illiterate persons with a book, explain historians

Ehrlich: First of all, in 1902 between 40 and 65 percent of the arrivals in America came on prepaid tickets (who paid for the ticket is noted on ship manifests) or with money sent from America to buy a ticket.[218] Often the head of the household would go first, to prepare the way for bringing over his family and paying their passage (as was the case with Nana's father). Later, the oldest son would be sent a ticket, and once in

Ehrlich clan, 1905

---

of the photographic image. Thus the Ehrlich's fine apparel could be misleading...or not.

218. "The Immigrant Journey" (see note 43). There were not only ticket agencies for each passenger line; roving ticket sellers went from village-to-village selling third-class ('steerage') tickets from Bremen or Liverpool to America.

America — go to work, toiling to help save money for a ticket for the next-in-line. In sharp contrast, according to census data, Harris Ehrlich's family arrived *together* in 1905 from London — two adults and six children (two more were born in America) — and this is a clear indication of the state of family's finances. Further confirmation of such circumstantial evidence came later from distant kin in Israel[219] who confirmed: Yes, the family was financially comfortable in Jassy — even well off. They traveled abroad on vacation. They lived comfortable lives.

Further circumstantial evidence can be found in business directories and other archival sources: As already noted, the *1891 Galica Business Directory* suggests the family of Pearl's father — the Schwarzers from Jaroslaw in Poland — dealt in textiles before going to America, where Michael Schwarzer's half-brother Esriel became wealthy importing silk. Likewise, it wouldn't take a great leap of faith to assume that Hannah Ehrlich's older brother Isador ('Izzy') establishing a business manufacturing ready-made dresses in New York[220] was tied to an occupational orientation and skills possessed by the family in Europe: According to oral history among Izzy Ehrlich's descendants, in Europe the Ehrlichs were engaged in "some aspect of the needle trade". That suggests the younger generation might have been merchants dealing in small lots of textiles if they were economically comfortable, while earlier generations may have engaged in less lucrative but relevant occupations, as tailors, furriers, hatters and so forth.

Some immigrants were able to upscale such skills in America (and even more worked in the sweatshops), making New York the center of the garment industry. As Yiddish-American short story writer and journalist Lamed Shapiro once commented in a pithy essay about the differences between the gentiles who built the railroads and mined the coal and the Jews who congregated in urban centers: "Others came with the pickaxe, the Jew came with the needle".[221]

---

219. From Nisana Gross — the great-granddaughter of Harris and Jake Ehrlich's sister Hannah Tova (née Ehrlich) Sacomsky, who lives in Haifa.

220. And for two of his four children to continue this family tradition, one as a manufacturer and one as a wholesaler of women's apparel.

221. Lamed Shapiro was born in Radekhiv — the *shtetl* where Pearl's mother

In a *1924-1925 Romanian Business Directory* (there is no earlier directory in archives) there are two Ehrlichs listed — both merchants. Jewish names abounded in commerce under listings such as 'ganlenterie' (haberdashery) and 'textil'. Closer to home,[222] according to testimony from Yad Vashem about at least one Ehrlich descendent, Avraham Sacomsky who perished in the Holocaust had been a merchant.[223] All these independent sources of oral family history confirm from different perspectives that the Ehrlich family photo from 1905 was not staged wealth (the term 'staged wealth' should not be interpreted as suggesting they were very rich, only that they arrived with some monetary assets). Although no one could provide any details about how the Ehrlich boys made a living up to this point in Europe one thing is clear: Harris (born 1860) only left Jassy when he was 37 (estimated 1897 by Hannah's birth year in Jassy) — with six children in tow. Such uprooting takes guts.

One could conclude with a fair degree of certainty that against the backdrop of increasing institutionalized antisemitism in Romania, the men in the Ehrlich family decided to 'get out while the getting was good' — to seek a more hospitable home for their families in the West before things got worse for Jews in Romania, despite the difficulties. When the girls married, as was the pattern at the time, they followed the inclinations of their husbands to stay in Europe, in essence, sealing their fate, and scattering the remnants of their families between Russia and Israel.

As for Harris and Jake, although relatively comfortable, their decision to leave was not out of desperation or abject poverty like so many other Jewish émigrés of the times, but in other ways — from a 'sociological' perspective — they were typical of all their Jewish brethren. Harris Ehrlich's brood may have been larger than the average family immigrating to the United States at the outset of the 20th century, but they were typical in the sense that Jewish immigration to America was "a movement of families" typified by an inordinate number of women

---

(Nana) was born. See note 9 for a description of Shapiro's work.

222. Submitted by his mother Rozika/Shoshana and his brother Meir.

223. In the *1924 Business Directory* Mordechai was listed as a grocer in Falisht.

and children in the mix. Moreover, for Jews it was a "permanent move" to quote one observer. A third of other immigrant ethnic groups went back to the Old Country (a significant percentage of the men who were dominant among many other immigrant groups, came alone to America to make some money and go back to their families in Europe after saving up a modest nest egg), while 94.8 percent of the Jewish immigrants between 1908 and 1924 had 'come to stay' no matter what.

What was life like in America for Romanian immigrants in New York at the time?

Here, again, the *American Jewish Yearbook* offers a few clues about their lives in macro: Although religiously observant (i.e., 'Orthodox'), the synagogue was not the primary hub for Romanian Jews arriving in America. Overwhelmingly urban, Orthodox but lax in their daily devotions relative to Jewish brethren from elsewhere in Eastern Europe, the Romanian Jews' first contribution to American culture was culinary. The institutions that served as a social hub were the Romanian coffee-houses, wine cellars and restaurants they established, more than 'Romanian synagogues'. Thank the Romanians for the all mighty pastrami sandwich...[224]

In addition, Jews had been active in the emergence and promotion of Romanian literature and culture throughout the 19th century in the Old Country, and Romanian Jews are credited with already playing a core role in the introduction of theatre and opera to the Lower East Side in the 1880s.[225] Even the grand 2,000-seat Romanian synagogue on the Lower East Side became a music hub — dubbed 'the Cantors' Carnegie Hall' — in its heyday. Romanian Jews — having been marginalized politically as resident aliens in their place of birth — are said to have sought naturalization as Americans earlier and in greater numbers than other ethnic communities; one, indeed, sees this pattern among the Ehrlichs as well.[226] Romanian Jews founded a plethora of political

224. The name 'pastrami' comes from Romanian *pastramă*, a declination of the Romanian verb *păstra* meaning "to conserve food, to keep something for a long duration". Corned beef is another story.

225. The Romanian Yiddish Theatre founded in Jassy in 1876 already had a sister theatre in New York by 1880.

226. For example, Jake's boys who came in 1907 and 1909 were already

and patriotic organizations. The *Yearbook* says that having been barred from higher education and the free professions in Romania by institutionalized discrimination, a proportionally high number of Romanian Jewish immigrant youth who came with their parents to America went to college to become physicians, lawyers, dentists and engineers.[227] According to the *Yearbook*, by 1901 ten percent of the Lower East Side's lawyers and physicians were Romanian Jews. This went hand-in-hand with the Romanian Jews' urbanized character: That is, while they only constituted 3.3 percent of the Romanian population at the turn of the 19th century, Jews made up 14.6 percent of Romania's city dwellers, 32 percent of the Moldavian urban population and 50 percent of Jassy's population.

How did Harris and Jake's families fit into this mold?

The one and only 'sighting' in the archives of Harris Erlich (note spelling[228]) is in the 1925 New York State Census: 66-year-old Harris and Fannie (Harris would die in mid-1928 and therefore left no further paper trail, save his grave site).[229] By then they were almost 'empty

---

American citizens by 1917. Yes, they were nominally Russian citizens it seems, but Romania made them ineligible for Romanian citizenship. In contrast were those who had never faced such disenfranchisement — Pearl's kin who were Austrian citizens — her grandfather Jacob Reiter only sought American citizenship 19 years after he arrived. Pearl's father Michael only applied 20 years after his arrival (but died before he could complete the process). It took Michael's half-brother Esriel 15 years to request American citizenship for his family. Pearl's mother (Nana) only became an American citizen 35 (!) years after her arrival (see note 7 for details).

227. Data is fragmentary about many descendants, but it seems this pattern can be found, at least in part, among the Ehrlichs. One needs to keep in mind that girls dominate the Harris branch and only a handful of women of this generation went to college — most women being housewives.

228. In the course of the research Ehrlich was found spelled Erhlich, Erlic, Erlick and many other spellings. In most cases (Schwarzer without a 't' is an exception) it is important *not* to limit searches in archives to 'exact' spelling. Choose 'sounds like' options. And in initial searches, give a year's leeway on date of birth (Harris' is listed here — estimated 1859).

229. Harris was buried, as is customary, under his Hebrew name

nesters' with only the youngest, 18-year-old Sara (AKA Shirley, born 1907), still at home.[230] Harris gave his occupation in the census data as "furrier". No information was found about Jake following his arrival in America (keep in mind, each branch arrived separately — Harris in 1905, Jake's family in 1907 and 1909). Neither Jacob and Harris, nor their children, left oral or written testimony about their lives. Nevertheless, it was possible — based on four decades of American census data between 1910 and 1940 — to piece together how their sons and daughters, most born in Europe, built their lives.

The raw census data reflects, for example, how Isador's branch of the family built their garment business (where nephew Gil Weiss would subsequently work as a shipping clerk while going to college). Harris' son Izzy (born 1888[231]) was already 17 by the time his family arrived in New York seven or eight years after leaving Jassy for London. As already noted, Isador reported in a later US census that he had only a 5th-grade education, and apparently never went to school in England. Five years after arriving in America, in the 1910 Census, Izzy Ehrlich reported he was a "wage earner" employee in a "ladies suit shop" but by 1920 he was a "tailor" with his "own shop". By the 1930 Census Izzy was already a "proprietor" of a dress shop (he was no longer 'behind a sewing machine') and his 20-year-old son Richard ("Dick") had entered the business as a "buyer" of ladies' suits and coats. Come 1940 Isador had advanced to the status of "dress manufacturer" with two adult children 'in the business'–21-year-old daughter Annette managing stock in their retail dress store, and 29-year-old Richard (already

---

Asher — spelled Acher Erlich in the records — in Mount Hebron Cemetery in Flushing, New York in the same Kishineff Congregation and Kishnever Congregation sections as his brother Jake and several of Jacob's sons, including Isador. Fannie was found kitty-corner to Harris in the same block and section but in the next row. One can almost imagine all these Ehrlichs (in fact, the entire Kishineff/Kishnever Congregation section), all gathered, 'sipping tea and conversing in Yiddish about the Old Country'...

230. They claimed they had been in the United States for 25 years, but apparently they added five years.

231. According to his marriage certificate he was 22 in December 1909 when he married.

married) a "distributor" for the Ehrlich's dress factory. According to family lore, Isador died while playing poker with his cronies.

Already in 1900, a tendency to turn to commerce was marked among approximately 40,000 Romanian Jews in America (half in New York), while 35 percent of the immigrants had initially arrived as small-time artisans — chiefly tailors, shoemakers and carpenters in Europe. It seems the road taken by Harris Ehrlich in leaving Jassy — to London, then to America, was a relatively well-worn path taken by other Romanian Jews, and Gil's Uncle Izzy Ehrlich's dress factory[232] followed a pattern that typified Romanian Jews.[233] By 1905 half the ready-made clothing produced in the United States was made in New York. Jewish men not only dominated the needle trade as employees, they also owned and operated the sweatshops and loft factories. A 1905 study of the clothing industry in New York says:

> [...] Eastern European Jews who had spent time in London learn[ed] not only the tailor's craft but also English language and customs. These tailors broke into the production business and paved the way for future immigrants. The clothing industry thus became one of the few in which Jews were employers.[234]

A 1890 report on the state of the garment industry noted that little capital was needed in order to establish a modest clothing operation

232. Ada's Dresses, which Richard ('Dick') Ehrlich named after his mother.

233. While Dick took over his father Izzy's business, his brother Benjamin ('Benjie') Ehrlich was a wholesaler of apparel, who eventually established his own dress manufacturing business in Florida — the Miss Rubette line — which a daughter continues to operate (the brand's 1960s and 1970s apparel is sold online as vintage clothing...)

234. Dwork, "Health Conditions of Immigrant Jews on the Lower East Side of New York 1880–1914" (see note 52), citing Jesse Eliphalet Pope, *The Clothing Industry in New York* (Missouri: University of Missouri, 1905). For vivid descriptions of the role of Jews in the needle trade and prevailing conditions, see Howard Sachar, "Jewish Immigrants in the Garment Industry", https://www.myjewishlearning.com/article/jewish-garment-workers/.

since (at least at the time of the report) workers had to furnish their own pedal-powered sewing machines, although this practice may have changed by the time the Ehrlichs arrived. The fact is, the primary capital such immigrants carried wasn't modest seed capital, it was intellectual capital — knowledge of English and Western customs and familiarity with 'how the system worked'...and a head for business. Thus, these Ehrlichs were a small part of this pattern.

As for pursuit of or aspirations for a university education and/or a head for business, this inclination can be found among at least parts of the Ehrlich family, including Jake's side of the family, for example. This emerges from four decades of census data where I sought (unsuccessfully) to locate living descendants who might be able to shed light on the family's history. Jake was 42 when he arrived in the United States in 1907; it isn't clear how *he* made a living, but the paths four of his six children took emerged from the data: George (born 1891), who was about 18 when he arrived in America, went to college for two years and in 1940 he was found in the census running his own electrical contracting business. Herman who was six when he arrived in 1909 became a physician. Louis, who was a teenager when he arrived, became a traveling salesman,[235] but two of his three boys got a university education.[236] Moe was 20 when he arrived at Ellis Island; with an 8th-grade education, Moe, like his cousin Isador, also built a business from scratch. According to the 1920 Census, at first (in his early twenties), he made a living as a pharmaceuticals salesman (apparently taking orders from drugstores), by 1930 was working in a drugstore as a "druggist", and by 1940 he was the owner of a Riteaid Pharmacy. Moe's children went on to get a university education — the eldest

235. No, not the Fuller Brush man, Louis sold lampshades... (Fuller Brushes that in its heyday had 35,000 door-to-door salesmen selling hair brushes was an iconic brand that was even the catalyst behind a 1948 movie: "The Fuller Brush Man", YouTube video, 2:46 minutes, 2017, https://www.youtube.com/watch?v=vxMRdEooTPw.

236. The third dropped out of high school, joined the army during the Second World War, and seems to have become a machinist — a die-cast specialist in an auto factory in Philly — if the Martin in a 1930 Census is the 'right' Martin Ehrlich.

Eugene becoming a dentist.[237] And according to one of Gil's notations, Jake's oldest — Abraham ('Avrum') was a pharmacist.

Parallel to the lives of all these Ehrlich cousins,[238] Isador's sister Hannah — my paternal grandmother — would marry Ben Weiss in 1912, and the two would move to New Jersey where they started out running a grocery store for a food chain, then bought their own grocery. After the family returned to New York, Ben Weiss would operate his own battery and tire garages in the Bronx to put food on the table and raise a family — lives that occupy a central place in this family saga, detailed further on.

~

As already noted in passing, a last-ditch attempt to shed some light on the Ehrlich family's life in Jassy (and their circumstances) at the close of the 19th century led me to a separate branch of the Ehrlich tribe, ironically, closer to home — the Israeli Ehrlichs in Haifa who were distant relations with whom I hadn't been in touch since the 1970s. Nisana Gross[239] and others are the descendants of Harris and Jacob Ehrlich's two sisters — Hannah and Rivka Ehrlich. Both married and both women also had large families — six children each. When the Ehrlich boys chose to immigrate to America during the first decade of the 20th century, Hannah Tova and Rivka remained in Europe.

These Other Ehrlichs, if you wish — at least those who survived the Second World War, the Holocaust and Stalin's purges — either remained

---

237. Moe's son Albert couldn't be traced.

238. In tracing the lives of all the other descendants of Harris' other children to paint a composite picture — the girls are harder to trace due to name changes. Most were housewives in any case, and finding them would have been too time-consuming.

239. Nisana Gross (and her brother Avrum Frumowitz and I are great-grandchildren of two of four siblings — brother (Harris Ehrlich) and sister (Hannah Tova), the children of Mann Ehrlich. Despite being distant relations, Gil invited Nisana's mother and father Rozika and Mendel Frumowitz from Haifa and another pair of distant cousins through Harris' sister Rivka — Rivka's daughter Yehudit and Josef Buzminsky, to our apartment wedding in 1972.

in Russia where they had fled, their whereabouts unknown, or went to Israel after the gates for immigration were thrown open in 1948. Several were stymied by the Iron Curtain and only came in the early 1970s from the Soviet Union after the Kremlin lifted its ban on Jewish 'refusenik' emigration.[240] Nisana's mother Rozika (also called Shoshana) arrived in Israel in the early 1950s, as did several other surviving descendants of the Ehrlich family.[241]

When Gil and Pearl met these distant relatives in Israel (Jake's sons Moe, Herman and George had visited them in the 1950s/1960s, traveling to Israel by ship), Nisana's mother Rozika told them about someone who remembered as a child pushing grandma Hannah Ehrlich in a baby carriage in Jassy, but that was about it. All that Nisana could do was add more recent generations to the family tree and fill in some missing details.

~

A detailed personal history of the family, of both the Weisses and the Ehrlichs, only reappears in 1912/1913—eight years after that 1905

---

240. *Refuseniks* were Jews who were thrown out of their jobs for requesting to leave Russia to immigrate to Israel, requests that were 'refused' (turned down) on security grounds. Overall, between 1970 and 1988, some 291,000 Soviet Jews were granted exit visas—the only ethnic group allowed to leave the USSR. The proviso was that they were leaving to be repatriated to the Jewish homeland, but once at transit centers in Vienna, vested interests in HIAS and the JOINT in cahoots with the rabidly anti-Zionist Austrian Chancellor Bruno Kreisky, 'convinced-assisted' 126,000 under the guise of 'free choice', to become dropouts by applying for and receiving visas to the United States in order to bolster American Jewry. Thus, only about half of the Jews allowed to leave specifically for Israel—165,000—actually did so, most in 1973.

241. Rozika's grandmother Hannah Tova, her father Avraham/Avrum (there is no record of her mother's name or fate) and three of her six maternal aunts and uncles died in the war years. While Rozika—in her late 90s, was still alive in early 2019, unfortunately due to memory impairment she couldn't add anything, and Nisana—like the rest of us—had never asked her mother for details about her family's life in Europe.

studio photo was taken of Harris and Fannie Ehrlich with six of their eight children. Not long after Hannah Ehrlich's marriage to Ben Weiss in 1912, Ben and Hannah reappear as a family of four, following the birth of their eldest son Bernard ('Bernie') Weiss born in early 1913, then my father Gil — 18 months later. The event that renewed the paper trail? In July 1917, after America entered the First World War, Benjamin Weiss registered for the draft in Perth Amboy, New Jersey — with three dependents. The next time the Weiss family pops up is in the 1920 US Census — by then living in Avenel, New Jersey with three kids. From here on, the narrative is enriched by oral history and detail extracted from hours of audiotapes...and an unexpected and priceless source — the short-lived local paper, the *Avenel Bulletin*.

Growing Up as Second-Generation Americans

Gil's Childhood in Avenel, New Jersey and the Bronx

There is a detailed Ehrlich family tree that Gil constructed, but no one among the Weiss descendants seems to know anything about the childhood of either Benjamin Weiss or Hannah Ehrlich, or how the two met. Grandson Randy Swiss[242] seems to remember being told by his grandmother Hannah that Pop Weiss saw her somewhere and went to her father to ask to marry her...and her father Harris agreed. What is known for sure is that Hannah and Benjamin Weiss married when Hannah was about sixteen and Benjamin was 21, about five years her senior.

After they married in 1912, the couple settled in Perth Amboy, New Jersey where they ran stores for grocery chains. In June 1917 Ben Weiss reported to the draft that he was married with two kids, and was working for Jacobson and Co. as a "salesman" (i.e., running one of their grocery stores). Later he would open his own grocery stores although it's not clear exactly when.

Gil was a 'sandwich child' born on 3 May 1915 in Perth Amboy, eighteen months after his brother and four years before his kid sister

242. The eldest son of Gil and Bernie's kid sister Millie Swiss.

Mildred (born 1919). In 1915 when Gil was a baby, while still working in the grocery business in Perth Amboy, Pop Weiss and his family moved to a small New Jersey town called Avenel. Gil recalled in a tape:

> Avenel was a small town with a railroad station with one big factory that made steel file cases called 'something Steel' and Pop ran a grocery store right across the street from the factory. A couple of years ago [in 1991 — DA] we detoured off the main highway and went through the town. The grocery store and everything was still there.
>
> Pop Weiss was a volunteer fireman in Avenel. The fireman had a hand-pulled pump and since Pop had a truck (not a horse and wagon) that he delivered groceries with, Pop would run with the truck to pull the hand-operated fire pump.[243] When they wanted to build a firehouse, we all worked on it and I lost a boot in pouring the foundations for the firehouse.

The 70-gallon chemical hand-drawn pump was eventually replaced by a real fire engine when the first firehouse was built in 1919; Pop Weiss served as the driver. The 'lost boot incident' apparently occurred when Gil was 14, in 1929 when according to town records a new firehouse (still in use today) was built. But by the spring of 1930 the family with their three children in tow, had relocated to New York City.

The *Avenel Bulletin*, which was published between 1922 and 1923 fills in a lot of blanks and corrected the chronology of events. The local paper (which folded after two years) is a time capsule for history buffs — with advertisements for button-lace ladies' shoes at $3 a pair and a Studebaker roadster for $975. It also contains a series of ads for Ben Weiss' Economy Grocer and Butcher shop.[244] While the family

---

243. Only replaced by a motor-driven fire engine in 1921. For the history of the Avenel Fire Department, see "History of the Avenel Fire Company", Avenel Fire Company, https://www.avenelfire.org/index.php/2017-12-27-17-48-36.

244. Read the *Avenel Bulletin* in pdf files online at the Woodbridge Public Library, http://www.digifind-it.com/woodbridge/ab.php.

Top: The Siessel Deli and Grocery in Perth Amboy
Bottom (L to R): Ben and Hannah Weiss, Avanel Volunteer Fire Department, 1929

only left Avenel in 1930, it turns out the Weiss family lost or closed the Economy Market much, much earlier — in January 1923 — when the grocery in Avenel failed to make a go of it.

How did Ben and Hannah end up in this tiny township? I had, in essence, already 'closed the manuscript' when in April 2019 I received a reply from the Woodbridge Historical Society which I had queried about the population of Avenel in the 1920s. As a courtesy, I had attached two vintage photos of the store and the fire truck from Bernie Weiss' album for their archives. Board member Tracy Billings wrote me:

> First of all, let me say how *thrilled* I am to see the old photo of the Economy grocery store! Old photos of Avenel are few and far between and when we come across one such as this, they are like rare gems. [...] Avenel was the 'bread basket' of the [Woodbridge] township — scattered small farms — so there was no real 'town' history to speak of. Avenel was/is basically known for the East Jersey State Prison (formerly Rahway Prison) which began as the New Jersey Reformatory at the turn of the century (1900, that is) and is pretty much

> located on all Avenel property, and then the Security Steel factory built in 1916. Even when I have the opportunity to speak with some 'old-timers' about life in Avenel and I ask if they have any old photos, I'm told that most of the families didn't even own cameras back then.
>
> [...] Security Steel Corporation, the major employer in Avenel, was located across from Economy Grocery. The factory was a focal point in our town for 100 years, being eventually taken over by General Dynamics Corporation,[245] but was sadly demolished a few years ago.

In fact, Tracy Billings 'knew' Ben Weiss! And she told me how:

> [The Woodbridge Library] has copies of the local *Avenel Bulletin* from 1922 and 1923. If you haven't 'discovered' this wonderful little local newspaper yet, let me know and I can direct you there. There are several advertisements for your grandfather's store *and* a few articles on him, too. And one article from December 1922 talks about him 'retiring' from the grocery. I peruse these newspapers regularly and that's how I first knew about Ben Weiss and his time in Avenel.

It was only when I began reading the *Avenel Bulletin* that I realize Avenel was so near Perth Amboy–11.5 km (7.2 miles) away. Perth Amboy (population 32,121 in 1910 and 41,707 in 1920) was the 'big city' for residents of Avenel. Therefore many ads in the *Avenel Bulletin* were placed by Perth Amboy merchants, although the local Avenel paper was a firm believer in residents 'keeping their business at home' and even editorialized to this effect.

A lengthy front-page profile of resident Ben Weiss, the proprietor

---

245. The factory manufactured large motors, generators, and electrical ship control components, and although it closed in 2000, because the process involved a lot of asbestos dust the owners were being targeted several years ago for legal action. See "Asbestos Exposures at the General Dynamics Plant — Avenel, New Jersey", Levy Konigsberg, https://www.levylaw.com/asbestos-exposures-general-dynamics-plant-avenel-new-jersey/.

of the Economy Market, appeared in the *Avenel Bulletin* on 20 October 1922 under the headline "Benny Weiss Celebrates Fifth Anniversary Here". It filled in the blanks about Ben Weiss' whereabouts after he got off the boat at age 14—a green immigrant, and why he went to Avenel. He and Hannah moved there sometime in 1915 and apparently opened the Economy Market in the fall of 1917. He saw Avenel as a business opportunity.

When the *Avenel Bulletin* began publication, Ben began advertising in it. Each of his ads (he probably used other forms of advertising prior to that) began to appear in the fall of 1922 with the paper's first editions. They included a one- or two-sentence 'editorial' at the top—a common advertising format at the time. In the first, he said he

B. Weiss Economy Grocer and Butcher, circa 1920

was "waiting patiently for Avenel to grow". Ben thought he recognized potential in the area — with Perth Amboy just across the river from Staten Island, sooner or later, the area was sure to become part of the New York metropolitan area. Avenel already had a train station linking it to New York City. Hopeful newspaper profiles about the area's potential spoke of 'commuter homes'. In June 1917 an article in the *Perth Amboy Evening News* under the headline "Avenel Growing Fast–Pictures Tell Story" said new building lots up for sale in Avenel Park[246] were the next best thing due to the "nearness to New York" adding that Avenel was "one of the fastest-growing communities in the state" and could "give the children their chance to enjoy real country air; to be away from the noise and grime of the city".[247] Not long afterward Ben opened the Economy Grocer and Butcher two years after the Weisses moved to Avenel. Remember these were the Roaring Twenties when the economy was booming.

Armed with a drive to succeed, Ben sought to combine an entrepreneurial spirit with a social conscience as a 'brand' to build his client base. Did this ethic go beyond selling himself as the 'friendly grocer' who didn't overcharge? That is, was it part of his worldview? The profile in the *Avenel Bulletin* wrote:

> Benny came to this community from Perth Amboy in 1915 [...] at the age of 25 [...] he got his apprenticeship in some of the best groceries and city markets of Perth Amboy [...] For nine years he worked for those Perth Amboy merchants, from the time he was 16 until he was 25. Weiss is a self-made man, having come up from the ranks [...] Consequently the bargains which he has to offer, are the

---

246. At $300 down, and $15 a month from a Perth Amboy real estate company.

247. The Library of Congress has a project called Chronicling America — Historic American Newspapers with free access to searchable online copies of local newspapers throughout America by state, year and keyword, https://chroniclingamerica.loc.gov/. Keying in 'Hannah Weiss' brought up a September 1920 edition reporting a $3,500 damage suit by Hannah Weiss over an auto collision in which six-year-old Bernie was injured.

> result of his years of experience as a grocer and butcher to the better classes.[248]

Pop Weiss told the paper that in May 1912 he met Hannah — "a New York girl" — and he married her five months later in October 1912. Ben recalled:

> We did not have much except love to start on, and so we decided that Avenel was a pretty good place for an adventure of that sort. And that is how I started here, when there were only a few houses over in this section [of Woodbridge Township that is a cluster of nine small communities, one of them Avenel]. In the beginning I worked outside to keep things going and Mrs. Weiss ran the store alone. [...] Avenel was then very little developed, and my store was then also pretty small. But it has improved and so has Avenel.

By 'work outside Avenel' while he could have meant working for Jacobson it is more likely that by then Ben was already running his own market in Perth Amboy — the Crescent Market — since there is definitive evidence that the Crescent Market in Perth Amboy and the Economy Grocer and Butcher in Avenel were *both* operating under Ben's management in 1921/22. The vintage photos of the Crescent Market business testify that business was thriving: There are several employees in the photo including a salaried cashier, not he and Hannah running the show. What is clear is when Ben and Hannah moved to Avenel in 1915, Gil was a baby, and the Avenel grocery photo shows sister Millie (born 1919) as a toddler (perhaps three years old). The family remained in Avenel until Gil was 14.

In Avenel, Ben set about establishing a reputation for his store as a discount market, beyond the name he chose: Economy Grocer

---

248. According to the paper, he worked for "well-known concerns as Greenspan Brothers, the Perth Amboy City Market, and Scheurer & Son" from age 16. 'Siessel' cited in the photo caption on page 123 for a Perth Amboy deli Ben ran was an Avenel resident (see page 136).

and Butcher. While noting that in bad weather, his shop was the only grocery locals could frequent, his business plan was to offer the same amenities locally that the big chains in Perth Amboy offered, including "an electric coffee mill, electric chopping machine, good scales,

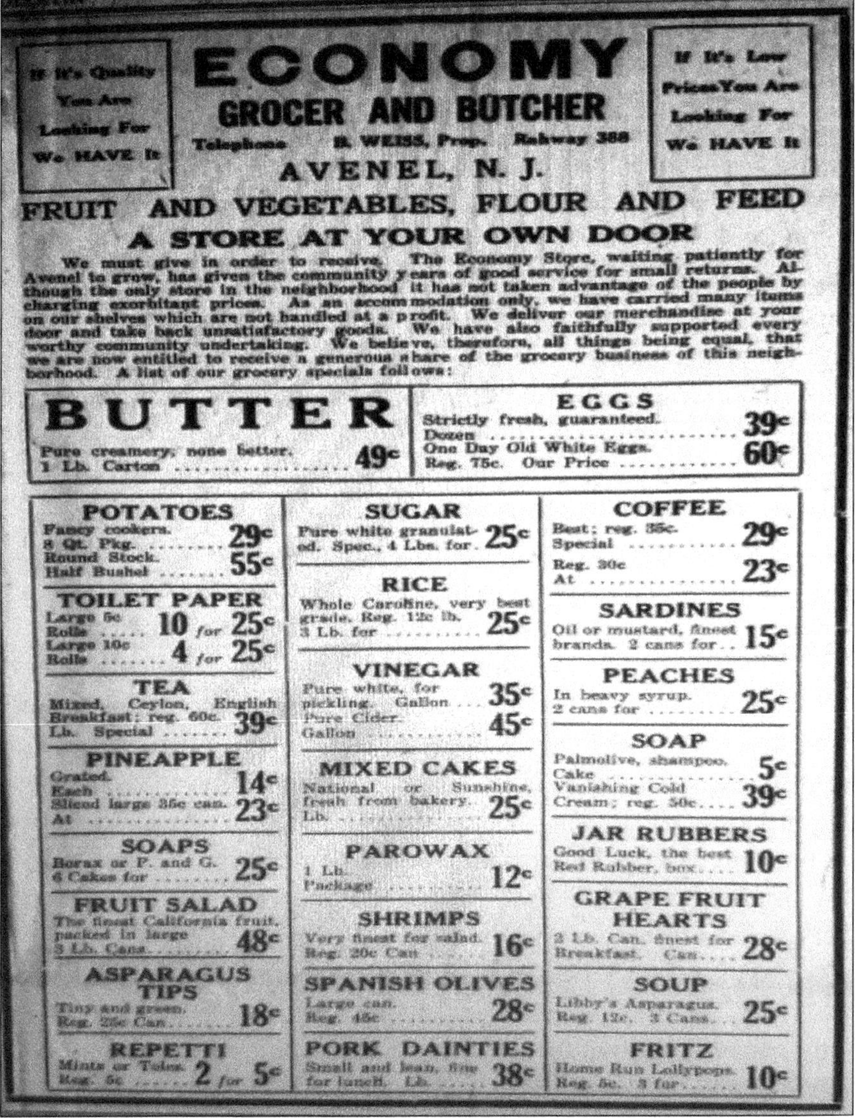

Economy market ad

slicing machines for lunch meats, good showcases" that he bought, adding that his objective was to plow profits back into the store, underscoring that he was proud not to charge 'exorbitant prices' typical of small indie groceries. Such mom and pop establishments offered credit until payday to attract a 'captive clientele' that couldn't afford to pay cash, but sold their stock at jacked up prices because they could (and couldn't demand reductions on price for volume from suppliers, like the chains).

Ben tried to 'educate' the public in his "mini-editorials' at the top of the huge ads he took out in the *Avenel Bulletin*, explaining, for example, that paying cash in his grocery would save them money in the long run. But ultimately he had to offer credit like the other groceries because that was how most of the residents — blue-collar workers at the file cabinet factory or the hollow tile and firebrick-making foundries — managed to get through the month.[249] He told readers that going to Perth Amboy to shop (by public transportation, few had cars) turned them into "pack animals" in bringing home the bacon, while he could make their lives easier with "quality products at low prices"...and free delivery. He branded the Economy Grocery a "Store at Your Own Door".

He sold certain items at cost to offer variety not found in normal mom and pop operations. He sold cigars. He sold ice cream. He did catering. He installed a telephone booth. In another expression of business acumen, Ben Weiss teamed up with another merchant — E. A. Adams — in a win-win arrangement where the store doubled as a miniature 'showroom' for the home appliances which Adams could get at deep discounts ("bargain prices") in New York City; an electric sewing machine, vacuum cleaner, a toaster and a washing machine served as floor models but also as come-ons to bring in more customers. In the last quarter of 1922, over a number of months, the Economy Market offered a three-month subscription to the new local newspaper to

249. This area of Jersey was rich in the fine clay used in tile-making. The reformatory (prison) at the edge of Avenel most probably employed some locals as well. That the grocery offered credit is evidenced in a call on "those who had purchased on credit" to pay up in order to be eligible to participate in a raffle Ben was running, and the fact that there were those who still owed him money when he closed or sold the store in January 1923.

anyone buying a one-pound box of chocolates (49 cents), a ploy that brought in 40 new subscribers (and perhaps some new customers). He sold 'key-like raffle tickets' for a fancy Victrola to the first two thousand customers buying $2 worth of groceries in the weeks leading up to Christmas and met his quota despite the small size of the town and its hinterland. Things seemed to be looking up.

It was as if Ben Weiss was 'on a roll'. In the beginning, he had claimed his sales had doubled on Saturdays due to the ads, and swore that for every dollar of advertising he reaped three dollars in sales.[250] But then, in November 1922, Ben initiated his most ambitious scheme — that in retrospect may have been 'a bridge too far' for Woodbridge:

> WEISS BUYS SERVICE CAR — FREE RIDES FOR ALL
> A brand new service car large enough to accommodate passenger is a new idea in retail store service introduced by B. Weiss, manager of the Economy Grocery. [...] Not only will this entrepreneuring grocer call at the homes of people for miles around for orders and deliveries [...] His conveyance will be at the disposal of shoppers within a radius of from three to five miles of Avenel of persons who wish to come in person to his store and select their groceries from his large stock. In other words, he will open a free bus line between the Economy Store and any home in the northeast sector of Woodbridge Township.

It was like an airplane in a steep climb (against all odds) — the nose too high, the airspeed too slow: Things seem to have suddenly stalled in mid-air.

---

250. It's hard to know if this was accurate or amplified for mutual benefit. He and the editor Dirk P. DeYoung were apparently friends or at least allies, each promoting the other's business, and clearly saw eye-to-eye in encouraging residents to do their shopping locally. Logic says he must have seen a dramatic increase in sales if he took that last gigantic 'win or die trying' move in merchandising — buying a no doubt very pricy vehicle (I'm assuming this is not an editorial error when it says a 'brand new service car' not a 'brand new service').

The ads dropped off. Did Ben find himself in cash flow woes with such outlays after buying this vehicle, because his sales in a limited market failed to keep pace? Had he underestimated the attraction and clout of Perth Amboy's stores? Had locals failed to take the bait to shop regularly at the Economy Market? Or had the big boys in Perth Amboy decided to play hardball, and reduce their prices to eliminate an up-start? Or all of the above. We'll never know. But the ads — which had grown to half-page ads, suddenly stopped appearing entirely.

It seems Ben Weiss decided to cut and run. In January 1923 he announced he was 'retiring' from the business. The paper carried the following announcement:

> Benny's Farewell Gathering * * * AVENEL–Don't forget the free entertainment at the Progressive Club House, Saturday night, January 6th, at which Benny Weiss, who retires from the Economy Store, will give all Avenel people a fine reception. Music, dancing, basketball and refreshments. The Victrola will also be given away then. Be sure and get your key beforehand.

He was 33 years old. In mid-January the following item appeared in the *Avenel Bulletin.*

> 'NOTICE. Having business interests which take me out of Avenel much of the time, I have put my accounts in the hands of Harry S. Abrams, who will look after my collections. Please report to him for payment. B. WEISS

The next week, on January 26, 1923, there was a correction:

> NOTICE Through a misunderstanding a notice was inserted in the Bulletin last week notifying all people owing me at Avenel to pay H. Abrams. Please ignore that notice and report to me at 182 Smith Street, Perth Amboy, NJ., opposite Crescent Theatre.

Apparently, the Crescent Market (opposite the Crescent movie theatre) was the 'business interest outside Avenel' Ben Weiss spoke of.

Eight months later, in August 1923, an item appeared in the *Avenel Bulletin* that mentioned in passing an insurance claim 'adjustment for a loss' at the Crescent Grocery in Perth Amboy run by Ben Weiss (maybe water damage, maybe a fire). The *Avenel Bulletin* folded soon afterward. Was Ben's ownership of the Crescent Grocery in Perth Amboy in the background during all these years, and was this the place where Ben had 'worked outside' at the beginning while Hannah ran the Avenel store? From the looks of it, the photo was taken when Gil and Bernie were perhaps ages six and seven and a half (circa 1921) when the store in Avenel was still operating. We know the family continued to live in Avenel for another six years, until 1929 or early 1930 (reflected in the 'lost boot episode' and other oral history).

Ben's Crescent Market (outside), Perth Amboy

In the one vintage photo of Avenel in Woodbridge archives — from 1922, the main street, Pennsylvania Avenue — where the Weiss' grocery was situated at a corner of Pennsylvania Avenue and Avenel Street — was still largely undeveloped. The grocery, just across from the factory, was a prime location...but only if one envisioned the potential. Yes, more stores in the center of town did follow but in 1920 the population of Avenel (according to a very rough 'guesstimate' supplied by a local in Avenel today) was in the vicinity of 750 persons.[251] By 1929 just before the Weisses moved to the Bronx, the population had doubled to

Ben's Crescent Market (inside), Perth Amboy

251. Based on a local resident's knowledge of Avenel's early days, and extrapolation using census tools, although there is no official data for the town alone.

Avenel, 1922

approximately 1,500.[252] The potential of Avenel was eventually realized and today Avenel boasts a population of 15,000. In 2015 the old factory building (empty since 2000) was demolished to make way for Station Village (a combined commercial, cultural and residential complex on the factory's former 27-acre site). The Economy Grocer and Butcher's location is now prime real estate—right across from the New Performing Arts Centre that opened on 1 May 2019, and a one-minute walk from Avenel's commuter train station. Ben Weiss was there first, only 100 years too early.

Reading the *Avenel Bulletin*, I gained a new respect for this grandfather of mine whom I barely knew and whom I associated with a tiny grimy hole-in-the-wall 'garage' selling tires and batteries in the Bronx.

Not only that. The newspaper offered glimpses of Hannah and Ben beyond their work lives, reported in the pages in the *Avenel Bulletin* devoted to local news. In the half-page weekly feature called Local Briefs, about the most exciting local news to hit the presses in the

252. Many thanks to Tracy Billings for extracting the demographic data at the local library. The population in 1929 was extracted from the *Historical Booklet of the First Presbyterian Church* in Avenel, compiled in 1952, that approximated the population of Avenel in 1929 when the church was built as around 1,500 residents.

paper's two-year existence was a piece about a dog who showed up with a wad of bills between its teeth, dropped by a town merchant:

> DOG FINDS MONEY LOST BY DREVICH FAILS TO ACCOUNT FOR TEN DOLLARS
>
> A dog belonging to the Siessel family on Burnett Street was caught with a bank-roll in its mouth last Monday morning, the amount, which it had evidently picked up in the street, at the time it was taken from him being $30 in bills. B. Drevich, grocer on Avenel Street, reported $40 missing a little later in the day, from which it is concluded that the canine must have eaten a ten-dollar bill, probably claiming that as a reward for finding the money. Mr. Drevich dropped the roll while delivering goods in that section.[253]

If someone so much as sneezed, it made the papers... Indeed in September 1922 Local Briefs reported that "Mrs. B. Weiss has been suffering from a severe cold with symptoms of grippe the past week. At the time of writing, she seems much improved". But she gave her cold to hubby, and three weeks later, it was reported that "Mr. Benjamin Weiss has been confined to his home, being in the grip of a severe cold".

While living in Perth Amboy, Ben was an active member of the YMHA (the Jewish YMCA) in Perth Amboy, and cited as a competitor in a 1912 pool tournament and other local activities such as a baseball team of Greenspan grocery chain employees.[254] As soon as he moved to Avenel in 1915 Ben joined the fire department which drilled twice a month—his truck pressed into service to replace the team of draft horses employed since establishment of the fire department in 1913. Every year, Ben bought Avenel's annual Christmas tree which locals gathered to decorate and sing Christmas carols around. He was also an active member of the Progressive Club founded in 1920 that despite the name was *not* political; the Avenel Progressive Association was a non-profit "formed for the purpose of aiding its members socially, in

---

253. *Avenel Bulletin*, 27 October 1922.

254. From the *Perth Amboy Evening News*, not the *Avenel Bulletin*. See note 247.

business and economically" according to its charter — sort of a combination 'chamber of commerce' and 'citizens' organization' that in the name of progress, built a modest community center called the Progressive Club House "where local events could be held, a needed facility for the small town" according to Avenel archivist Tracy Billings. Avenel having its own newspaper was also seen as progress, and Ben supported this endeavor with ads in the fledgling weekly, which in turn lauded him as "a public-spirited man" who "deserves the patronage of his neighbors".

Boy Scouts—Gil (L) age 10 or 12 and brother Bernie (R)

All the Weiss grandchildren remember Pop Weiss as a person almost chained to his garage which was open six-and-a-half days a week. But the *Avenel Bulletin* captures a more prosperous period in the lives of the Weisses in 1922 and 1923: "B. Weiss and family spent Labor Day in Perth Amboy". One of the next editions reported: "Mr. B. Weiss and family motored to Stamford, Connecticut, on Saturday evening to attend the wedding of a sister of Mrs. Weiss, They returned on Monday morning". A few weeks later the paper reported "B. Weiss and family motored to Bronx Park on Monday to visit the Zoo. The children were delighted with the animals that they saw there". This was followed by a report that "B. Weiss and family drove over to Dreamland Park[255] last Sunday night". In between, Bernie and Gilbert got their names in the paper with other 3rd grade children for perfect attendance... And there were glimpses of a young fun-loving couple we never knew:

The Barn Dance held by the Avenel Fire Company on

255. An amusement park in Elizabeth/Newark, New Jersey that operated between 1922–1939.

> Saturday night was quite a success, but the dances ran more to the modern steps than to the old-fashioned dances planned for by the management. About 100 were present, and a very good time was reported by those who were there. [...] B. Weiss, according to some who are critics of the art of dancing, did some very fast and fancy stepping.

Ben Weiss — whom it turns out none of us really knew — lost the battle in a dream of making it big in food retailing through enlightened capitalism. As he 'editorialized' in a 15 September 1922 ad:

> Henry Ford made his fortune by large sales and small profits. Teach your dollars to have sense. Your dollars buy more for cash than on credit.

Yes, he hoped to expand his special brand of business ethics into a full-blown discount chain, but this was not to be. In part, it was due to competition from chains in Perth Amboy, in part due to competition from three other independent groceries in the vicinity, in part due to the town's failure to grow at the rate he expected/hoped for... and in part due to a fascinating, indeed heroic attempt to 'change the rules of the game' with innovative advertising, unique come-ons and far-reaching strategies to attract market share. Too many forces were stacked against him.

All the more tragic, Ben probably lost the Crescent Grocery in Perth Amboy following the 1929 crash, considering the timing of their move from Avenel to the South Bronx which was hardly a desirable neighborhood (where they could be found in the April 1930 Census).

The stock market crash on 29 October 1929 plunged the economy into a tailspin. How did events affect small businesses like Ben's that ran on a shoestring?[256] In response to the credit boom of the 1920s which

---

256. A source that traces the rise of the chain stores during the Depression claims that in 1929 more than one-quarter of food retailers in the United States had annual sales of less than $5,000. See Javier Escribano, "The Great A&P, The Supermarket Chain that Conquered USA at the Beginning of the XX Century", *Medium*, https://medium.com/@fesja/

was typified by inflation in the number of banks but also easy credit to open new businesses and an aura of optimism, in 1930 after the crash, credit became tigh, spending came to a halt, and prices plummeted, sending the country into the Great Depression. Was Pop Weiss unable to get credit to stock his shelves because his bank had failed or suppliers went under or demanded cash for goods whose prices kept dropping, while profits were disappearing as even grocery customers tightened their belt? Or had too many clients been thrown out of work and they couldn't even pay what they owed him–or all of the above?

Indicative of the economic climate, a January 1935 issue of *Progressive Grocer* reported total retail sales of food stores dropped by 37 percent between 1929 and 1933, while sales of all goods sold through all types of stores declined by a whopping 49 percent in the corresponding period.[257] Ironically, studies of small businesses during the Depression show the ones that survived were the ones who diversified — that is, Ben Weiss' business model in Avenel was logical but badly timed and apparently he became but one of countless businesses that failed during the Depression.[258] He'd just turned 40.

Once in the South Bronx, Pop Weiss made his living selling tires and batteries he acquired pretty much on-the-spot whenever a customer showed up, without any real stock. The South Bronx neighborhood's

---

the-great-a-p-the-supermarket-chain-that-conquered-usa-at-the-beginning-of-the-xx-century-b46ed605e3b8.

257. See Jenny McTaggart, "New Deals of the 1930s", *Progressive Grocer*, https://progressivegrocer.com/new-deals-1930s.

258. See Emek Basker, Chris Vickers, and Nicolas L. Ziebarth, "Competition, Productivity, and Survival of Grocery Stores in the Great Depression", *International Journal of Industrial Organization* 59 (2018), 282-315, http://www.auburn.edu/~czv0008/files/COD_survival_BVZ.pdf. Not only were chain stores set up to allow customers to shop without the intervention of the clerk (= more sales volume with less staff/overhead), they had "lower prices" and a "wider range of nationally branded products and more varieties within a product category than independents" (not to mention chain outlets being located in wealthier locations, an additional advantage in a tough market). The Avenel grocery was an 'independent' mom and pop operation — not even part of the nascent New Jersey chains Ben Weiss had worked for in Perth Amboy.

beleaguered police station was dubbed 'Fort Apache' because it was such a rough neighborhood... Gil's older brother Bernie—who was short and stocky but 'a scrapper', protected 15-year-old Gil from neighborhood bullies.

The two boys used to hang out together, and one classic family tale tells how as teenagers, the two decided to take a 'shortcut' from the Bronx to Manhattan on foot—via a railway trestle—but about two-thirds of the way across the East River they realized a train was coming... Gil, a sprinter, outran the train and made it safely to the other side. His brother Bernie realizing he wouldn't make it, managed to suspend himself below the tracks, hugging one of the railroad ties or a bridge support beneath the rails until the train passed over him, then climbed back up onto the tracks. When Pop Weiss got wind of this caper, he was, not surprisingly, fit to be tied...

While still in Avenel, at age thirteen, Gil was bar mitzvahed, sort of. Pearl recalled:

> Pearl: When Gil was 13 they had a rabbi come to the house to teach him his Torah portion by rote without him understanding what he was saying. For his bar mitzvah—my father-in-law couldn't close the store—my mother-in-law Hannah and Gil went to New York to her father and mother, and Gil's grandfather [Harris/Asher Ehrlich—DA] took him to *shul* that day and they told him to stand up and say these words that he knew by rote...and that was it. No gathering of a clan or of relatives. Nothing.
>
> Gil: Pop Weiss wouldn't have been caught dead in a synagogue, but my grandparents were very Orthodox and they wanted me to have a bar mitzvah.
>
> There was a community center in Avenel that doubled as a church—and sometimes I went to church services (I was walking by and heard this beautiful music and went in...) This was long before I knew there was such a thing as a synagogue because Pop was a complete atheist... We were the only Jews in town, but in any case we were totally non-observant.

What is interesting is there *were* other Jews in Avenel! First of all, there are patently Jewish names that stand out in the ads in the *Avenel Bulletin* placed by local merchants such as Greenspan & Schlesinger who ran a general store, or F. H. Abrams a real estate and insurance broker. Secondly, a pamphlet entitled *Woodbridge–New Jersey's Oldest Township*[259] notes that the first Jewish families — the Sterns, Demblings, Grossman and Schillers — arrived in 1906. Yet, organized Jewish life was indeed ephemeral — mainly organizing *ad hoc* a place to meet on the High Holidays for services (some held in the Avenel Hotel...) although officially a congregation (named Adath Israel) was incorporated in December 1913, headed by a storekeeper and milk distributor named Levy Najavits.

While Gil was raised totally non-observant, it is nevertheless very strange that he didn't recognize there were other 'Members of the Tribe' in Avenel (this, despite Gil's father apparently being close to another Avenel businessman named H. Abrams mentioned above). When Gil said he got zero Jewish education as a child, apparently that is part of what he meant. Yet, in 1922 even the local newspaper considered it newsworthy to note the activities of "people of the Jewish faith" in Avenel, reporting:

> The Rosh-Hashana or Jewish New Year was observed by the people of the Jewish faith in Avenel. Services were held in the Synagogue on Saturday and Sunday, September 23 and 24. They also will observe the Day of Atonement, which begins at sunset on Sunday, October 1, and ends on Monday, October 2, at sundown.

So, there *was* a synagogue in town (unless this refers to the one in adjacent Woodbridge); it is quite strange Gil had no recollection whatsoever of such an institution's existing in the vicinity (regardless whether he attended or not and whether it had its own building or not). There are definite signs that Ben Weiss was totally non-observant: Elsewhere in

---

259. Virginia B. Troeger and Robert James McEwen, *Woodbridge — New Jersey's Oldest Township*, (Charlston, SC: Arcadia, 2002).

the *Avenel Bulletin* under local news, the paper informed readers that one of the local grocers would be closing his shop over Yom Kippur ("B. Drevich will close his store on Sunday at 4 p.m. and will remain closed on Monday until 6:30 p.m."); there was no such notice that the Economy Grocer and Butcher would be closed on Yom Kippur and, in fact, a week earlier Gil's father announced in the local weekly in its News Briefs that his grocery would be open all day on the first day of the Jewish New Year and closed the next day ("We will be open all day Saturday; the 23d, closed Sunday. B. WEISS").

Nevertheless, there is a 'B. Weiss' mentioned as having contributed $5 to the building fund for a Conservative synagogue in nearby Woodbridge (Adath Israel).[260] Does this suggest something? Not necessarily: In fact, it wasn't incongruous that Ben Weiss, as a local merchant, would buy the Christmas tree for his Christian neighbors

Ben's Tire and Battery Store

260. Some history of the synagogue — which was incorporated in 1913, but only constructed its own building in 1923 — can be found in an oral history interview with Sandy Spector Goldberg archived in the Woodbridge Public Library's Oral History project, http://www.digifind-it.com/woodbridge/oh_pages/goldberg.php.

and also open his wallet, if approached, to solicit a donation to build a Jewish house of worship, although he himself, as Gil testified (albeit offhandedly) 'wouldn't be caught dead in a synagogue'.

After leaving Avenel, from then on the Weisses and their children lived in various parts of the Bronx. Ben's tire and battery garages also moved from location to location. Pearl recalled:

> Bernie and Gil both started working in their father's tire store. Gil was driving a car without a license for years from age 14 or 15 because when Pop Weiss would have to get a new tire for a customer—he didn't have money to keep stock—he'd send one of the boys to get one. [...] They never worried about the Law. It's a miracle they never got caught... They would do stuff like driving in and out between the posts holding up the El.[261] [...] You could only get a driver's license at age 18 in New York.
>
> [...] One time we were going out to City Island to 'spoon'[262] because we were too late to go to the movies. [...] By mistake, on the way back, Gil got on the line for the ferry [...] and all we could think was 'Oh my God, there are so many police around [and he didn't have a license]. Pop would give him the car [to go on a date] because Gil was chronically late; it was a way of saying—'I'm sorry, but you had to make a buck where you could make a buck'.

~ *Pearl's Childhood in the Shadow of Poverty*

As already noted, Michael had a half-brother who was very wealthy. After Michael died there was practically no contact with these kin, except an occasional query from one cousin. Pearl recalled:

---

261. The elevated subway lines.

262. The term at the time for kissing and cuddling. City Island was a small one-and-a-half by half-mile island on the western side of Long Island Sound, just off the Bronx, connected by a bridge and ferry.

> He was the only one from the Schwarzer family who was in touch with my mother after my father died. My mother stopped talking to them after that. She said 'they panicked when my father died'. Now this is my mother's version of it, of course... That they thought she would be dependent on them — with a two year old and a ten year old...and without any job skills. And she told them, "You don't have to take care of me. I can take care of my own children!"

The first and last time Pearl would meet the Schwarzer aunt whose name she couldn't remember (the uncle was already dead) — was when she was ten years old and in middle school. After Nana was widowed in 1918, Pearl's mother worked in a host of jobs to make a living and support her two remaining children — Ruth and Pearl. She moved to Cleveland, Ohio a year after her husband Michael died, where she ran a grocery store with relatives. Pearl reminisced in one of the tapes:

> Aunt Hannah and Uncle Abe were living in Cleveland at the time and they had a grocery. My mother had been left the 'magnificent sum' of $2,000, which was what my father's life insurance policy paid,[263] and she decided to 'go join the business' after they invited her to do so. My Uncle Joe was also in this business–going around the neighborhood with a horse and wagon selling fresh products. I don't know how they figured that that many people could be supported by this grocery store, and of course they figured poorly, but my mother joined them and took us to Cleveland. I was about three when we arrived. I remember Cleveland was like heaven. [...] But the business didn't do well, my mother's $2,000 was gone and we had to go back to New York.

Nana said in the tapes that the damp weather in Cleveland left her repeatedly unwell and a physician told her she ought to leave if she wanted

263. It was common in those days even for poor people to have an insurance policy — even be it meager — should calamity strike the breadwinner.

to stay alive, but it is likely the real reason was there, indeed, was no way this one little grocery could support so many people. Pearl recalled:

> I remember crying when we left Cleveland. I only wanted to go back to Cleveland — not to go back to New York. My sister remained in Cleveland for months, apparently until the end of the school year and until Momma could find an apartment. [...] There was a shortage of housing and no apartments, so we ended up sharing with another family until Momma found an apartment on Delancy Street [on the Lower East Side], just where the Brooklyn Bridge hits Manhattan, where she became the building janitor.

The one legacy of Pearl's year or year-and-a-half in Cleveland was a lifelong fear of cats:

> I was only a little kid. I didn't realize that the [grocery store] cat was sleeping. I went to pet the cat and the cat jumped on me. My Uncle Abe was up on a ladder — the shelves were very high — and he reached for a can of something and threw it at the cat to get the cat off me... For most of my life cats literally made me shutter. I only got over my fear of cats in my old age.[264]

After returning to New York Nana also worked as a janitor in a school, cleaned house for a dollar, then ran a lice-ridden chicken stall in New York, and got a job as a sweater cutter in a sweatshop on the Lower East Side. Pearl said, looking back, "How she managed, I don't know", recalling one such venture to support her children that lasted two years[265] — the chicken stall:

---

264. After staying as house guests with some friends in Israel (Miri and Yossi Rosen) "who had a beautiful Persian cat. Then Wendy got a cat. And Lisa got a cat. And I adjusted".

265. According to census data, Nana's maternal uncle Morris Sahn was in the retail chicken business. For Pearl, watching her university-educated daughter

> At one point, she went into business with Uncle Saul (Yetta's husband and Nana's brother-in-law] — the chicken business. It was a chicken stall in a market and they would have the chickens ritually slaughtered by a *shochet.*[266] [...] People would come and buy them and the stall proprietor would have to 'flick' the feathers off. [...] Oh God, she would come home and immediately take off all her clothes and get in the laundry tub because we didn't have a bathroom, and wash herself and then she would wash her clothes that she had been wearing. She was absolutely immaculate but I don't know how she could do this. It was a 'cold water flat' and we heated the water on the stove.
>
> [...] I once had a chicken as a pet (!) but finally they told me I had to give it up. I was very disappointed because I lost my one pet. I don't think I was allowed to keep it in the house... All the chickens in those days had lice, and it's very vague in my mind, but I know I had a chicken as a pet.

Pearl recalled how fueled by pure *chutzpah* and desperation, Nana got a job in a sweater factory:

> One day she came home and said she got a job. What kind of a job? "I'm a cutter of sweaters". My sister and I say — 'Momma, what do you know of cutting sweaters?' I think this was later on and I was able to verbalize "you don't know how to cut sweaters". And she says, "Now I do"... So we ask "How did you get the job?" and she says,

---

raising broilers on our farm in Israel...all the more so witnessing how I would slaughter and clean dozens of chickens for the freezer, was personally traumatic. It remained a disgusting, smelly and exhausting but necessary chore if we wanted to have meat on the table, although our chickens didn't have lice.

266. A religious slaughterer. Nana related in the taped interview how she had to buy the live chickens in the wholesale market (where, is unclear), take them to a Jewish ritual slaughterer on the other side of Brooklyn, then *schlep* the kosher chickens back to the Lower East Side to their stall to sell them to customers.

> "I told them I was experienced. So they put me next to somebody and I told him the machine was a little different from the machine I'd worked on, and he showed me what he did — how he'd pile up the fabric and press this machine into it and it would cut x-many sweaters at the same time".

Pearl added:

> She had no skills. She had no education. And whatever she could get, she did [...] Yet, there were times she didn't have enough money to pay the rent, so she would put her furniture 'in storage' [and move in with a relative temporarily]. Of course, we didn't have any living room. And only the few sticks of furniture she had would go into storage...and I would go to live at my Aunt Hannah's.

Being repeatedly shipped off to live at Aunt Hannah's was not the worst thing that could happen to a child in those days. Recalling when she was working as a research assistant (see the section on her career), Pearl said one of Dr. Pintner's personal projects dealt with finding out more about the fears children harbor — what they worry about:

> I still remember when we started that project I said "Ohhhh, I know what *my* fear was. Financial disaster... Not having enough money for food. I know that I never went hungry. I don't ever remember my mother saying 'we don't have any food in the house' but the fear of being put out on the street... Everything related to survival. I used to get very worried about it. When they would dispossess you for non-payment of rent, they would put your belongings and your furniture on the sidewalk... It didn't happen to us, but it happened to people around us. Evelyn[267] and I talked about this and she said "it was the *shame* of being

267. Pearl's younger first cousin and Nana's niece — the daughter of Nana's sister Yetta and Sol Cantor.

> put out on the street". As if it was their fault. It was a crazy ethic. If you passed by and there were people watching their belongings, probably waiting for someone to come and take them, otherwise they would disappear [...] you would avert your eyes so you weren't looking at them because you didn't want to embarrass them by looking at them. I still remember that so vividly as if I was still eight years old. And people were ashamed to go to Home Relief for assistance. There was no feeling of 'entitlement'. You were glad to have what you had.

Later, Nana got a job working for an obstetrician in Brooklyn — Dr. Levine — a live-in position that required Pearl at age ten (as noted, not for the first time) to go live with her Aunt Hannah and Uncle Abe and Pearl's three boy cousins while her mother earned a living as both housekeeper and nanny for the doctor's family and assistant to Dr. Levine in his practice, including helping deliver babies. The two years that she worked for Dr. Levine gave Nana the skills to make a living by 'going out on cases' as she called it. Dr. Levine would recommend her to his pregnant patients, and she would serve as a live-in practical nurse for weeks at a time with the newborn and new mother...who in keeping with medical practices of the day, was 'in confinement' — that is, kept in bed for over a week after giving birth. By the time her mother became an independent practical nurse, Pearl could be left at home with her sister (who was more than eight years older than Pearl) while Nana disappeared for weeks on end:

> We would accumulate dishes for God knows how long. We never cleaned and then when we knew Momma was coming home... How we lived was up to my sister, of course — what we were doing...and not doing. All I know is, Momma would somehow let us know 'I'm coming home tomorrow' and we would get busy cleaning up the mess.

Pearl said that even prior to Nana living at Dr. Levine's, her sister "got involved in earning a living and having a good time". Ruth was a wiz at math and worked as a bookkeeper, at one point taking classes at night at City College:

> She was wild! She was a 1920s 'flapper'. That was my sister! [Her red hair] in bangs. She'd have friends over [when Nana was out working] and she'd tell dirty jokes. I'd be hiding out somewhere and listening and I didn't have a clue of what these jokes were about. That was one of our more 'affluent' periods and we were living in a very nice neighborhood, a very nice apartment. I don't know where my mother was working that this occurred, but even with Ruth working, nevertheless, we were always teetering on the edge of economic disaster.
>
> [...] Ruth and her friend Selma used to go out and get picked up by guys and I don't know where they went. All I know is that my mother was up all night waiting for my sister and I'd say "Momma, what are you doing?" and she'd say "I'm waiting for Ruthie to come home"...
>
> Selma was a tall nice-looking gal. She met this [Italian] guy and he got her an apartment and she was literally his 'kept woman' — in short, his mistress. He had a private plane. He was rich-rich and bought her gorgeous clothes, until he killed himself in an airplane crash. Selma would give me her castoff clothes. What I must have looked like — short little me, in these dresses that were designed for a tall person, you can only imagine. I would 'blouse out' the tops to get the waist somewhere near my own waist... but at the time, I felt all dressed up.

In April 1935 — when Pearl was almost 19, already in college but living at home, Anna Schwarzer (that is, Nana) remarried, without telling anyone in advance...

The groom was David Lefkowitz — a garment worker and widower with five children of his own — four still at home.[268] The 'newlyweds' — in

268. Rose was married and out of the house; Hy, Charlie, Pauline and Bessie

their forties — moved their respective families who were total strangers to one another, into a common two-bedroom apartment.[269] Pearl recalled the shock of this 'development':

> She came home and said she'd gotten married, and my sister was absolutely stunned. ("Where?! Who did you marry?!")
>
> [...] Ruth moved out after a week or two...but I was one of these kids who wherever I was sent I adapted to the situation. I didn't know there was any other way of being.

Dave Lefkowitz and Nana, 1935

Why hadn't Nana remarried before? She had watched as her stepmother had one child after another after remarrying — another four pregnancies in addition to the six previous offspring between her father Jacob Reiter and Rose Raubfogel, making it harder and harder for her father to support his family and accommodate more children in their already cramped household. Nana was barely making a living supporting her two girls, and apparently was not about to fall into the trap of thinking 'combining households' would necessarily better her situation (including having already experienced firsthand finding herself suddenly widowed with small children). She recalled in the tape:

> I had many chances to remarry, but I said "no thank you". I can take care of them [my daughters] as best as I can,

---

were still living under their father Dave's roof.

269. Ruth — who was already working, took one look at the 'arrangement' — four girls in two double beds and two totally strange adult boys sleeping in the living room and promptly got her own apartment with a flat mate (her good friend Ida, called 'Half Pint' because she was so short). Pearl accepted this extended 'instant family' in one small apartment — not that she had a choice...

> but I don't want more, and if I get married there will be more children. In those days you didn't know, and you took what you got.

As fate would have it, for Nana, 'what you got' included Dave being diagnosed with cancer a few short years into their marriage. Thus with Dave unable to work, the full burden of raising her own children and his youngest children fell on Nana, who parallel to this task (and caring for an incapacitated husband at home for six years), went out to work — at one point even working in a defense plant during the Second World War. Pearl recalled:

> She was the epitome of 'Rosie the Riveter'.[270] I don't even know what kind of factory it was and I'm not sure she knew what they produced. But I remember she had to cut her hair — her hair was long — because of the machinery. I remember I was very upset.

Asked about her life in a taped interview when she was 88 — whether there was something she would have done differently — Nana replied frankly that "Dave was a decent person" but "the second marriage was a mistake":

> I had to divide the little that I had left between mine and somebody else's children because I had to be a mother [to them]. After all, these children weren't guilty. [...] I brought up his children. It was hard, but I survived. David's youngest [Bessie] stayed with me [after he died in 1943] until she had her first child.

Free of obligations to Dave and his family, in 1944 Nana could move to

270. The women who went to work in heavy industry, occupational domains once reserved exclusively for men. See the story of the 'real' Rosie the Riveter in the short documentary clip, "Ask History: Who Was Rosie the Riveter?" YouTube video, 2:40 minutes, 2015, https://www.youtube.com/watch?v=jhCEdhxdJUc.

Washington, DC, to open a grocery business in partnership with Ruth and Dan Platt (her eldest daughter and son-in-law). Dan, a Polish-born mattress maker 14 years older than Ruth and pushing 50, had been out of work (they are registered as living with Nana and Dave Lefkowitz in the 1940 census). But in 1944, Dave Lefkowitz had died and Ruth had just had a baby, thus Washington beckoned, but the 'partners' in this grocery store were, of course, totally ineligible for a commercial business loan:

> There was this Jewish grocery chain owner in DC — Fred Kogod[271] who on the side acted as a private financier, setting people up in small businesses (dry cleaners, delis, corner groceries, etc.). He found the businesses and financed people who literally had nothing, for a good interest rate. All people wanted in those days was to put food on the table and have a roof over their head. Kogod had set up Julie Schwartz's[272] parents in the grocery business on Georgia Avenue at that time — and they were making a living.
>
> My mother came down from New York. Kogod took her to see different stores and within two or three days she said: "Pearly, I found the store. It looks like it is well run... and there were customers coming in". It sold groceries and beer and wine. A beer and wine license was very hard to come by. My mother went back to New York to take care of the baby [Michael] and my sister Ruth came down to

271. An Eastern European immigrant (1899–1954). Kogod settled in Washington, DC where he went into the grocery business (the District Grocery chain). In the 1920s Kogod expanded into real estate (a bit of sleuthing revealed he also built Skyland Apartments in the 1940s — something apparently Pearl and Gil didn't know!). Kogod then fell into the movie theatre business by chance, founding K-B Theatres, a movie house chain in Washington, built together with partner/brother-in-law Max Burka (including the Naylor Theatre where Wendy and I went to the movies as kids...) Another quirky tidbit: Fred Kogod also air conditioned the White House and Supreme Court. A prominent Washingtonian, he served as Commissioner of the District of Columbia before Washington got self-rule.

272. Friends Julie and Leo Schwartz who later moved to Aberdeen, Maryland

> stay in the store for a few weeks and by instinct, see if the account books were 'cooked' or not [...] staying with the owners — the Cohens — who lived above the store, because they would get up at six in the morning and the store was open until late in the evening. They didn't close at 6:00 in the evening because there was a lot of business from 6:00 to 9:00 or 10:00 PM. As far as Ruth could see, the store could turn a profit.

Ironically, as mentioned earlier, Pearl became the front for Max's Delicatessen, because neither Ruth, nor Dan nor Nana — as newcomers to the District of Columbia, could qualify for a liquor license, and beer and wine were a major part of the business. Nana and Ruth and infant Michael arrived in Washington in a blizzard in December 1944... having arrived by bus and taken a taxi to Pearl's, after Dan's car broke down somewhere in New Jersey.

Nana not only worked long hours in the store in DC, she had a tendency to overwork herself to a point of exhaustion and even served homemade soup in the back of the store to rooming house customers in the neighborhood who had no cooking facilities:

> My mother — she was like this all her life. Nobody could do things for her, and in everything she did, she undertook too much... In the store, if it wasn't done her way, it wasn't good. I recognized that this was very difficult for Ruth, especially — while Momma was also 'falling off her feet'.

In early 1946 — exhausted and unwell, Nana moved in with Pearl and Gil and their two small children for a period:

---

where Leo ran a pharmacy. Families during the Cold War were supposed to have an agreed-upon address where they would 'reunite' if Washington was nuked. Ours was the Schwartzes in Aberdeen, Maryland, although in retrospect this was a strange choice, considering Aberdeen was a strategic location and home to the Army Proving Grounds where all new ordinance for the armed forces was tested.

> I got her back to normal... This was about a year after they had gone into the business. It was supposed to be temporary that I was taking my mother to live with us, but by the time I'd finished, she didn't *want* to go back...so we made some financial arrangement where they paid her off (for her part in the business) — a few thousand dollars.

Thus, a stop-gap measure became a permanent living arrangement after Pearl and Gil requested to exchange their two-bedroom rental apartment in Skyland for a larger three-bedroom, where there would be a bedroom for Nana. Nana would live with her daughter and son-in-law in the same household, an integral part of the Weiss family when Wendy and I were growing up and into early adulthood.

The legacies she left are recaptured in Chapter V in Life with Nana. It both hallmarks her remarkable strength of character and role as a nurturer, and shares flashbacks of special 'Nana moments' and memories with an in-house grandmother — from Nana's trademark expressions and sayings to the reactions and interactions that defined her *and* the tenor and the flavor of the Weiss household, including recollections of Nana's kitchen...and thanks to a sudden flash of recognition on my part — the keys not only to her feather-light *kneidelach*, but also Nana's long-lost *rugelach* recipe.

In approximately 1966 or 1967, after some 23 years or so living with the folks, Nana announced she was 'moving out' and got her own subsidized apartment for senior citizens in the center of Silver Spring — $57 a month from the Housing Authority of Montgomery County.

This was a few short years after Wendy moved back home with baby Lisa, taking up residence in the basement recreation room in the fall of 1964. Four generations under one roof was tense. Having just returned from a gap year in Israel, I was sullen and withdrawn, one unhappy camper to be back in the States — unhappiness in the midst of my first year at American University that was jacked up by having to undergo emergency knee surgery and rehabilitation for a knee injury sustained in Israel. Wendy having fled an abusive ex-husband who was stalking her despite their separation, found herself at odds with prudish Gil trying to impose his own 'sense of propriety under his own roof' when Wendy — a consenting adult — returned to the dating scene... It was not an easy time for the Weiss household. Pearl and Gil hired full-time daily help — Bea Foster — who took over the cooking (marked by a shift to scrumptious fried chicken once a week) and the childrearing (caring for Lisa), as well as the house. I transferred to Temple University in Philly the next year.[273] Bea's presence allowed Wendy to go back to school with the goal of getting a fine arts degree. Looking back, Pearl surmised that Bea essentially *usurped Nana's place in the family* as the in-house nurturer, and she probably felt unneeded and merely 'underfoot' so to speak, when Nana decided to move to her own apartment.

I remember visiting Nana in 1967 soon after she moved in:

> Nana had a *schmatteh*[274] of a throw rug just inside the door to her apartment that worried Pearl, which Nana stubbornly refused to part with. I promised my mother that I would 'solve the problem'... At the time, I was in the midst of a modified judo self-defense course in my last year at Temple University in Philadelphia that had taught how to fall to the ground while breaking your fall to throw an assailant off balance. I faked slipping on that throw rug — telling her ruefully: "I'm ok, but I almost broke my neck"...the only thing that convinced strong-willed Nana to get rid of that ratty rug.

---

273. I returned home to Silver Spring in September 1967 for six months, after spending the Six Day War in Israel. Armed with a BA in sociology — I worked as a research assistant to save up some money before immigrating permanently to Israel in March of 1968. As fate would have it, while working for the Washington Health Facilities Planning Council, one of my projects was an in-depth survey that served as foundation for Olney Hospital... including recommending a strong geriatrics department, in part in light of demographic trends in Montgomery County, in part due to plans on the table to build Leisure World. More than once, Pearl ended up in Olney Hospital with medical issues.

274. Rag in Yiddish.

After doing the math, it seems she lived at Fenwick Lane for about seven to eight years. In 1969 or 1970, while visiting the folks (by then I was already living in Tel Aviv) Nana asked me to accompany her to the Fenwick complex's weekly social gathering in their clubroom, to show off 'her visiting granddaughter from Israel' to the other residents:

> The only thing Nana forgot to tell me was that I was slated to be the speaker for the day...a fact discovered after the director introduced me to the group, everyone clapped and then there was this awkward silence and the director half-whispered: "You're the speaker today, didn't you know?!" So, I found myself giving an impromptu talk about 'the elderly in Israel' sharing my experiences running a municipal clubhouse for seniors in a Tel Aviv slum...

Later (approximately 1975) Nana moved to the Hebrew Home in Rockville, where she lived the last eleven years of her life, until her death on 11 October 1986. When she passed away, Nana was apparently 94, not 96 (*if* the Ellis Island records are correct). Pearl recalled that last decade:

> When she first got there, she was in pretty good shape. There were a lot of activities outside the Home but she didn't have many friends — didn't have that skill. Once Dad and I retired, we volunteered to drive — for example, to the theatre. They would invite residents to go to a play, and to other entertainment. [...] We could volunteer two cars — each with say three people, each with their walkers. She didn't have any outstanding illnesses. Her memory was going towards the end, but she would cover it up beautifully, greeting people with–"Darling, how are you? And how are the children?" That was a 'safe one'... She loved having company.

Chapter II
The Lost Art of Letter Writing

We don't realize how much is lost through instant communication and the price humanity really pays for cell phones and e-mail, Messenger and Whatsapp, that leave no permanent records for posterity. The letters Pearly and Gibby wrote each other in the 1930s when they were courting, and living apart even as newlyweds; the letters from people at war; the letters Wendy and I wrote from sleepover camp in the 1950s; vintage telegrams and greeting cards from the 1930s and 1940s; and some 30 years of aerogrammes that I wrote from Israel[1] and a host of other correspondence would never have existed had there been instant communication.

Gil and Pearl — The Letter Legacy

There are two shoeboxes of letters Pearl and Gil sent to one another. Sometimes they came fast and furious both when they were courting

1. From my 1963/4 gap year and from March 1968 onward after I immigrated to Israel (until the arrival of the home fax machine in 1995 that brought 'instant communication' — long letters that unfortunately faded on thermal paper). There were almost weekly letters, augmented by audiotapes — particularly between 1973–1980 after Rafi and I bought a farm in the boondocks, and found ourselves on a 'waiting list' of the then state-run telephone monopoly for *seven years* before we got a telephone...a period marked by a '100 meter dash' across the road to our nearest neighbors to take rare telephone calls from the States! In fact, some of my first writings as a journalist in 1986 (before personal computers and spell-check software) weren't submitted until I completed the month-long process of sending them to Pearl by snail mail for proofing and receiving them back with corrections by snail mail.

but living in different neighborhoods and going to different schools, and after they were already (secretly, then officially) married but 'separated' by economic necessity, or when Pearl went to NYC from Washington, DC, to visit the relatives.

When they were courting in 1932, Gil would send letters from Cypress Avenue to Pearl on Washington Avenue, because he was working during the day and going to school at night — so most of the time, they would meet face-to-face only once a week. They asked how school was going, planned their dates and what they would do — by letter, even sending (rare) special delivery letters announcing there was a glitch in plans.

It seems that Pearl took charge of choosing Gibby's wardrobe early in the relationship. A postcard dated 2 July 1934 reads:

> Hon, Please be at my house early... Wear your knickers[2] even if they are dirty. See you tomorrow — Always Pearl.

Letter Writing—Once an Art in Every Sense

---

2. Loose-fitting men's trousers gathered at the knee or calf in 1930s America... *not* the British term for a woman's or girl's underpants...

There are dozens of letters that Gil sent from Keyport to his wife in the Bronx in 1938 after he got his first job with Burnelli Aircraft, located in the boondocks of New Jersey. Nine months later Gil went to work at the Naval Aircraft Factory in Philly while Pearl was working in New York homeschooling homebound kids — a Depression (and depressing) job. Gibby would get a ride into New York with one of the guys once a week to visit Pearly. The rest was left to letters for the time being.

Pearl addressed her letters and Valentine's cards simply "To The Dearest Boy in the World". Gil called Pearl "his pal" — and always signed his letters and cards with a special seal: A doodle of a biplane and the closing salutation that became a personal trademark, "happy landings". A 1938 birthday card to Pearl signed "as ever always your loving Gib" explains the source of the signature: Living in different places, they met 'on the wing', weekly meetings, brief weekends even when married, dreaming of sharing the same pad. Written on the back of the card he declared:

Gil's Closing Salutation

> The happiest day of my life, my Love, is when you said 'yes' and became my wife. May the future for us be one "happy landing" after another until we trade in our 2-place ship for a larger one 3 or 4 — then we'll stay on the ground and say in squeaky, old voices, I still love you, darling. Gib.

Most correspondence was filled with expressing their love and longing for one another. Pearl opened her letters with "Dearest Gibby" and he would respond "Sweetheart" and even in one letter "Dearest most adorable, loving, sweet, honey, darling sweetheart" when he was feeling particularly lonesome and horny — explaining that the salutation was because:

> I missed my goodbye kiss this morning and my 'hello kiss' just now. I'm getting fed up on 'mental kisses'. I want the real thing or nothing.

For their first wedding anniversary, 21 March 1938, when Pearl was in NYC, she sent a card in the form of a diary to Gil in Keyport. The card, bought in 1931—after they first met in a drama class in 12th grade, contained a series of separate yearly entries. A February 1932 entry says:

> Last 'nite I graduated High School... Gilly, whom I mentioned before is so adorable... He shook hands with me and said, "How sweet you look tonite." The tears just rushed into my eyes at the thought that I might never see him again.

By 25 May 1932 she wrote:

> I'm in love. Can you guess whom it is. Well—it's Gibby.

Squeaky kisses and duct tape

In a September 1932 entry, Pearly — at the time just over 16, had written:

> This is not a mere infatuation or liking — Gib and I really intend to get married. I love him so. We expect to become engaged when Gil's about 20 and to get married in about 6½ years. I know that it's a long time but if this is true love I guess it will last that long. He loves me as much as I love him.

In a 17 April 1939 letter, two months after Gil moved to Philly when they were already officially married but living apart, Gil wrote:

> Honey,
>
> Surely it should be Thursday — that dull ache couldn't be here only 1 day after I left you. Darling — those 2 months really do seem like 2 years. It's such a terribly long time.

Pearl mixed romance with radical politics noting in a 31 May 1934 entry in a diary she kept:

> Will we be able to get along together? He has a distinctly bourgeois outlook upon life. His reaction to the word communism is one of definite antagonism and even contempt. I hope he will take a definite turn to the left and know what it's all about.

A 25 September 1934 letter from Pearl to Gil (when she was 18 and at Hunter) is a mixture of personal aspirations and class consciousness (more about the latter below in the section Two Letters from Spain Reveal Much Much More):

> I often wonder what it would feel like to have no financial worries at all. I don't mean fabulously wealthy, with maids and wardrobes of 50 dresses. I mean to have enough clothes to satisfy me — don't laugh — I could be satisfied with very little. Not to worry when I need a new pair

> of shoes or the old ones fixed. And at the beginning of the school term to be given $5 or more for supplies, fees, S.A.B., etc. And one more thing. To be able to eat lunch out. To have a weekly allowance that would enable me to go to the restaurant for even a 25 cent lunch. But I am dreaming, am I not, the dream of the working class the world over. I don't suppose it is just my own special dream. People in my class have been dreaming of this security for centuries probably—And shall they go on dreaming it or try to achieve it through action. Don't mind me darling, I am merely trying to get myself straightened out. And to whom—but you—could I talk to this crazy way. Dearest, I love you, All Your Own Pearl.

Gil, for his part, primarily mixed romance with daily comings and goings, literally and figuratively. Most letters were written on the move—on the subway or the bus or before going to bed. As graduation from college approached, he worried whether there would be a job:

> The fellows were talking about what they expected to do after graduation. Some don't feel so enthusiastic over finding a job. If they don't, so what—they just won't be engineers. The very thought doesn't seem to send chills down their spines. Imagine spending so many years and not practicing.

Although he and his friend Mike Frankel ranked 2nd and 3rd in their engineering class, none of their letters of inquiry about employment were answered by Boeing or McDonald, apparently because of their clearly Jewish names. Even a 1936 appeal from Gilbert Weiss to his congressman to help him get a civil service job as an airplane inspector was to no avail. Yet, when Gil did get his first job at Burnelli, his promise was quickly recognized: Writing from Keyport in an undated letter, Gil was elated by news of a 20 percent raise:

> FLASH!
>
> I was told today by Murray that I am one of 3 getting a $5 raise this week.[3]

Once they moved to Washington in 1939, Gil became involved in woodworking, which not only filled his leisure hours but also his letters. A letter from DC addressed to "Mrs. Pearl Weiss and the Princess,[4] c/o Mrs. Ruth Platt, 2690 Morris Ave., Bx, N.Y" dated 8 October 1942, goes into details of the bookcase Gibby planned to build, describing

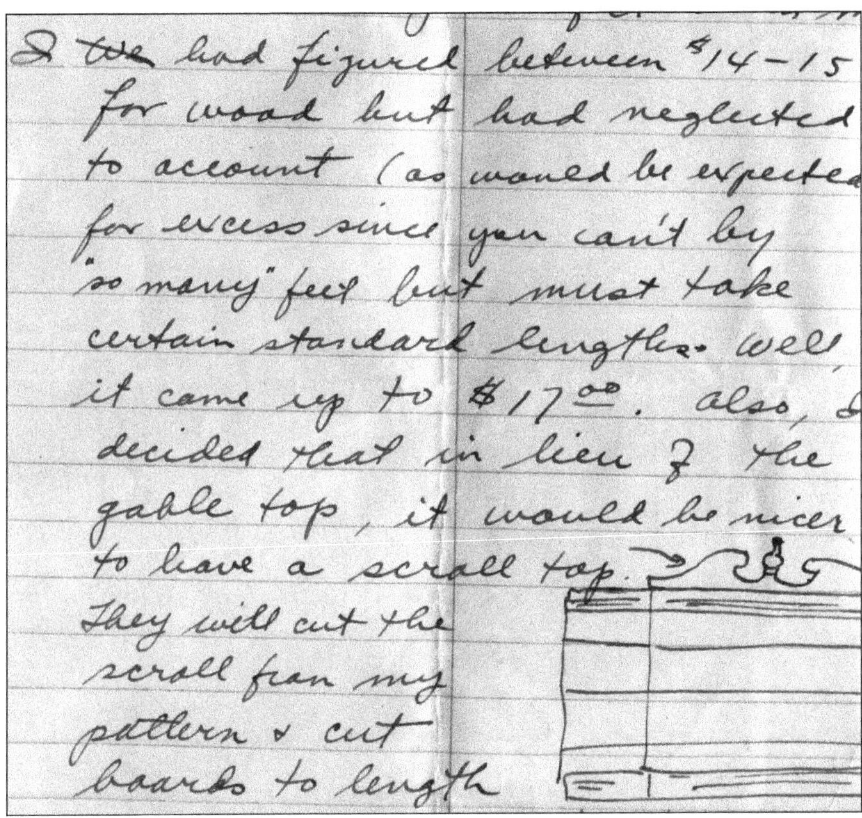

I ~~we~~ had figured between $14–15
for wood but had neglected
to account (as would be expected
for excess since you can't by
"so many" feet but must take
certain standard lengths. Well,
it came up to $17.00. also, I
decided that in lieu of the
gable top, it would be nicer
to have a scroll top.
They will cut the
scroll from my
pattern & cut
boards to length

The bookcase project

3. Pearl was making $27.87 a week with her WPA-funded job.
4. 'The princess' was four-month-old Wendy.

The bookcase—complete

the $20 in material he'd purchased, with sketches, including the scrolled top, asking Pearl's opinion on the aesthetics of this enhancement of the original plans he'd torn out of the newspapers.

In a 1943 letter to Pearly in NYC the next year, he reported:

> [...] Worked 'til about 7:00 Friday eve and decided to go to Basskin's for a deli supper. However, there on the menu was tenderloin steak and F.F. [French fries] for 85 cents so I grabbed it... I can now call the footstool project[5] really complete because I finished it up last night... I sent in a 50 cent sub[scription] for 1 year of "Deltagram" the magazine that deals with all sorts of woodworking projects. Also ordered a few small project books 49 Fine Tables, 19 Fine Chair, Toys, Games, and Playground Equipment.[6]

The dates of these letters — between 1942 and 1944 at the height of the Final Solution — sound jarring in retrospect (at least in Israeli eyes). American Jewry at the time was not only fragmented, weak and politically powerless...but also meek, insolated and quite insular and self-occupied. Concern over Jewish issues focused more on nightmares over the thirty million supporters-listeners to the pro-fascist antisemitic radio broadcasts of Father Coughlin[7] than whatever filtered out about the fate of European Jewry.[8]

---

5. A bulky deep steel blue two-step footstool with black rubber treads — made for Wendy, who by then was 18 months old, so she'd be able to reach the bathroom sink to brush her teeth.

6. All were still around more than 50 years later.

7. The most damning and typical Coughlin radio speeches uploaded by Old Time Radio were removed from YouTube in 2020 flagged as Hate Speech... The only remaining documentation open to the public on the Internet is a sound-bite length segment, "Father Coughlin on Communism and Jews", YouTube video, 1:56 minutes, 2013, https://www.youtube.com/watch?v=igsGXwcZ9hI. While Coughlin's broadcasts were forced off the air in 1939 — he continued his harangues on other platforms. His sentiments and their popularity was a barometer of a strong antisemitic undercurrent that existed not only in Europe, but in America, as well. For a short overview on "American Jewry and the Holocaust", Shoah Resource Center, https://www.yadvashem.org/odot_pdf/Microsoft%20Word%20-%205738.pdf.

8. Recently studies unmask the deep systematic and personal role of FDR in keeping Jews fleeing Hitler out of America, in preventing the bombing of Auschwitz...and in keeping American Jews clueless and silent about the

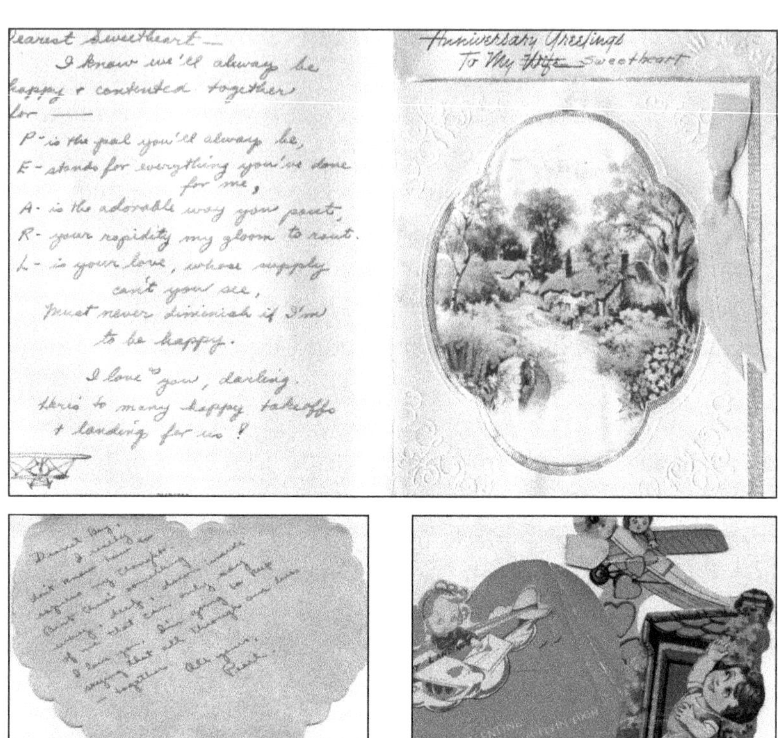

Vintage cards

Also among the period gems among Gil's Miscellaneous were earlier 1930s vintage Valentine Day cards with airplanes for Gibby. In

extermination camps. See this overview of recent scholarly research in Sol Stern, "Franklin Roosevelt Betrayed Europe's Jews", *Tablet*, 30 January 2020, https://www.tabletmag.com/jewish-arts-and-culture/297806/franklin-roosevelt-holocaust. Pearl, who like many of her generation simply idolized FDR, would have been devastated to learn the truth.

another class entirely were the exquisite ornate laced birthday and anniversary cards that are both period pieces and a reflection of 'the linguistic art of loving'.

When they were already in their eighties, Pearl and Gil were still holding hands when they took a stroll, and Pearl was still yelling down to the basement before every meal "Gibby, the food's getting cold!"

OTHER LETTERS AND PERIOD PIECES

Among the letter were other surprises. The shoebox also held typewritten letters from Miriam — Martin Sahn's sister[9] who had *hitchhiked* across the country to California in 1929 four months before the stock market crashed, visiting the Grand Canyon and Yosemite, eliciting a typewritten reply dated 27 June 1929 from Pearl's sister Ruth, saying:

> For heaven's sakes, stop it! If you keep telling me all the wonderful and interesting things you are doing you will be solely responsible for a bad case of discontent... Oh Miriam, will I ever meet those interesting people that you delight in writing to me about.

During the Second World War there were also letters from Gil's brother. Earlier letters from Cpl. Bernard Weiss 32983153 sent from Ohio had "IDLE GOSSIP SINKS SHIPS" emblazoned on the envelope in red, postmarked 6 March 1944. Later letters sent from the south of France via "V-MAIL" — short for Victory Mail, were 'shrunken facsimiles' of handwritten letters, the size of small index cards, passed by military censors. Each carried the message "Penalty for private use to avoid payment of postage $300" embossed on the tiny envelope where the stamp should be. The contents focused on the war and the home front from the perspective of the boots on the ground. In a December 1944 letter Bernie wrote:

---

9. Nana's first cousin (Zand, Sahn). Miriam (born 1894) was ten years older than Martin.

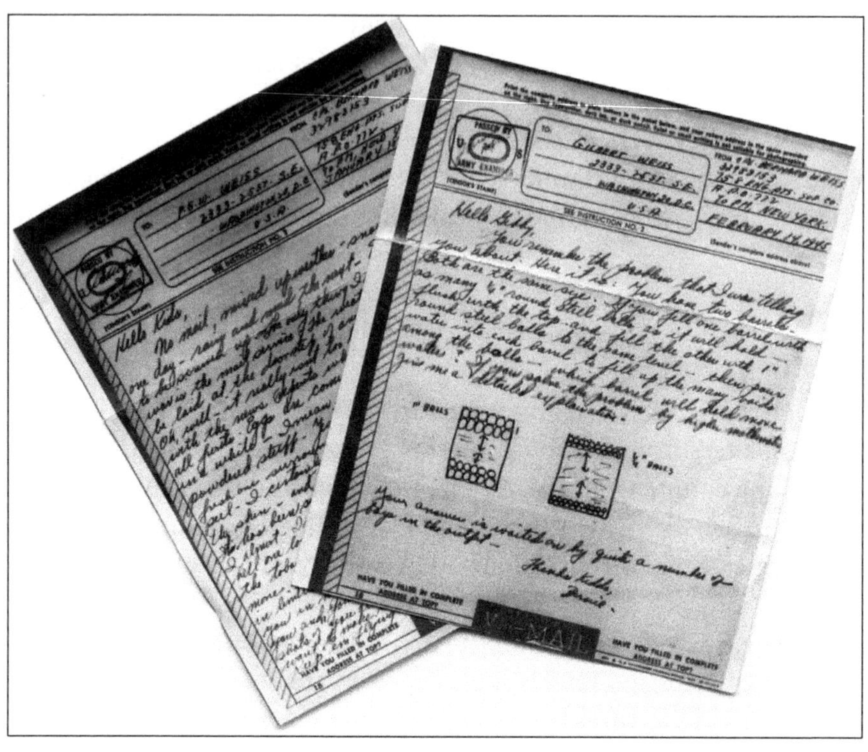

WWII V ('victory') mail

> As for voting overseas is concerns—judging all by my unit's action as well as news from the army information bureau—I would say there was an enthusiastic, numerically great response. Unfortunately, as I see it, a great number of votes will be lost but because they don't reach the polls at the stated deadline time, they won't be honored.

An 18 January 1945 letter was devoted to more immediate concerns for grunts in the field: Describing in minute detail the pleasure of peeling and eating a fresh orange, adding, from wherever they were presently but momentarily encamped, that "eggs are coming thru now, every once in a while—I mean eggs with shells, not the powdered stuff".

In the shoebox were also letters from another type of camp—summer camp: A letter from nine-year-old Wendy from Camp Louise[10] in Maryland in 1950 complained:

> Dear Mom and family, How are you Almost all the Bunk is againest me, mostly myrna.[11] I just can't Wait till I get home. Love and Kisses, Wendy.

And the ones I (called Diana, not Daniella, at the time[12]) sent at age ten from Camp Onas in 1955, a Quaker camp in Bucks County Pennsylvania that I adored,[13] unfazed by the Spartan conditions such as open latrines, wormy garbage collected once a week, swimming in a swampy creek and, not surprisingly, a raging impetigo epidemic:

> Dear focks. How are you I am fine. Guess what. We

10. A Jewish camp for girls, with the mirror Camp Airy for boys 'across the lake'.

11. Pearl and Gil's best friends the Abbotts had two girls—the eldest Myrna, the youngest Glenda—the same age as their kids.

12. Changed at age 14 after joining a Zionist youth movement—Habonim.

13. Having gone to Camp Louise for two weeks—populated with snotty little JAPs (Jewish American Princesses)—I hated it as much as Wendy did.

> PASSSED OUR Deep End test.[14] Heidi[15] still wants to go home. PS Please send some stamps. 3 cent ones [...]
> Did you get the Dog yet? Did Wendy find any more Boys yet?

Or another gem:

> Dear mom and Dad, I am haveng a nice time at camp by the way, how are you? We haven't gone swimming. I had a nose bleed. I cant Think of something els to say.[16] Love Diana xxxxxxx

What's amazing is *both* camps still exist.[17] (Camp Onas hasn't changed at all in terms of activities or ambience — still based on 'Quaker values of simplicity' with the same activities, although there are no longer latrines.

---

14. Permission to swim in the deep end of the new pool — which apparently had no filtration system (they periodically dumped tons of chlorine in over the side), not surprising considering it was filled the first time with brown-greenish creek water pumped in by the fire department.

15. Heidi Steffens who lived in nearby Newtown, Pennsylvania (whose mother Dorothy was Nana's niece) was perennially homesick and much to my frustration, I was always placed in the younger cabin or tent to keep her company, despite being a year older than Heidi.

16. Hummmm. *Nothing* to say??? Spelling aside, they always said I was a late bloomer. No inklings of the writer...or the adult with an opinion on everything, an attitude capsulated in a meme penned by artist Brian Andreas: "I predict the future a lot, she said to me, & I'm never surprised when I'm right, but that's because knowing it all has been one of my issues from the very beginning".

17. Camp Louise website: https://www.airylouise.org/, and Camp Onas website: http://camponas.org/.

Letters from Israel: A Time Capsule of Times Past

For decades, long letters and countless audiotapes flew back and forth between Israel and America — hundreds of them — until the advent of home fax machines in 1995. Pearl and Gil's, which were not saved, contained news of the family, questions to the kids, news clippings for me, and from time to time, a much-welcome check (that took two months to clear). But Gil — bless his heart — saved every one of the letters from Israel (mine and the kids') in a neat thick six-inch-high stack as well as a huge box of (unplayable) microcassettes in their mailing sleeves. I only took a handful of letters back to Israel[18] that, it turns out, reflect fairly accurately what life was like during the chaotic period from 1977 (when the Likud came to power) through the early 1990s as Israel struggled to transition from a centralized socialist economy to a liberal market one.[19] Nowhere was the economic turmoil and hyperinflation that accompanied this changeover more dramatic than in the agricultural sector.[20] A year after we married in May 1972, Rafi and I had bought a 60-dunam (13 acre) farm on a moshav east of Ashdod, Kfar Warburg — bought with the proceeds from the sale of our small two-bedroom fourth-story walkup in a Ramat Gan *shikun*[21] — the

18. Most probably, the others were discarded in downsizing in anticipation of Pearl's move to Leisure World. The ones taken were mementos for the kids of their correspondence with their grandparents, and a few of mine with 'telling passages' about the kids from quickly thumbing through the stack.

19. If one needs a touchstone of how a centralized economy operates, it was epitomized by the prohibition for ordinary citizens to hold foreign currency that led every Israeli family to stash black market dollars under the floor tiles and forced travelers to hide hundred-dollar bills in their shoes when going abroad. In December 2019 Israel's foreign currency reserves stood at a new record high of $126.023 billion, 32 percent of the GDP.

20. Up until 1985, costs of goods and wages were linked to the Cost-of-Living Index including farm inputs...but farm outputs/prices and farmers' income weren't part of this vicious cycle of automatic adjustments that fueled inflation.

21. *Shikun*: a term for standard apartment clusters built in the 1950s and 1960s in Israel, housing 'blocs' — each with four entrances, 16 families to an entrance.

tractor included. This was my 'doing': I had always wanted a farm and Rafi was clearly at loose ends — not sure what he wanted to do in life after dropping out of university[22] so it seemed to me to be a perfect fit. We hadn't a clue of what we were getting into...

Yes, there are plenty of articles about this difficult period on the macro level, but these letters (from a single aerogramme to typed single-spaced eight-page letters) that Pearl and Gil received weekly with family news, provide a unique prism in micro — at the family level. During this period Israel would witness not only countless devaluations but also the introduction of new currencies *twice* in the short space of six years–the first time when the Israeli pound or Lira (IL) was replaced by the Shekel (IS) in February 1980, at a rate of one Shekel = ten Lirot (nevertheless hyperinflation ensued peaking at 445% in 1984–1985) sparking introduction of the New Shekel (NIS) in January 1986 at the rate of one New Shekel = a thousand Old Shekels. An April 1980 letter — two months after the Shekel replaced the Lira, described the struggle to survive, even simply to put food on the table:[23]

> Rafi is working 13 hours a day on a wheat harvester...to make some money as long as there is work. So I had to take care of sending the chickens to market, the first time I had to do this. Waited up until 2:00 AM forcing the chickens

---

22. In retrospect, he should have been in a history or political science program (a passion we have always shared) but he'd enrolled in engineering.

23. I remember vividly circling the one aisle of the village's tiny grocery, sometimes for up to half an hour or more, eyeing the merchandise trying to figure out what to buy this week that would allow me to feed the family on the limited monthly credit at the 'company store' that we received from the moshav. There was always food and the kids often brought home friends from school ('extra mouths'), but the financial strain was tremendous. For many years, at most we could afford to buy this or that child a pair of sandals in April; the others had to wait their turn in coming months... The chronic shortage of cash for basics was eased temporarily three times a year by secretly selling (under the radar of the centralized marketing system) several dozen chickens from each flock we raised, to the owner of a chicken stall in nearby Kiryat Malachi. It was not an easy time.

> to eat in hopes that [the Arab buyer] would come but he arrived only at 5:30 AM after dawn (so you have to run after each chicken, while in the dark you can pick them up like mushrooms). [...] Afterward I slaughtered and cleaned what was left (34 chickens) in five hours, for the freezer. [...] The damned Government didn't raise the price for broilers[24] despite the fact that the price of feed went up 40% — so we barely broke even for three months work! Some farms are paying 82% interest, some are paying 104%. [...] The price of petrol went up yesterday 38%. [...] We can't make enough money from the lemons, wheat, etc. to pay our interest, not to mention our living expenses. [...] We are undecided between [planting] watermelon and cucumber. The latter is a real gamble–lose money or make a fortune.
>
> The ironic thing is the deeper you get into debt, the higher risk you take to get out. [We grew cucumbers and by a small miracle made a killing, which was enough to keep our debts from spiraling out of control. — DA].
>
> [...] We probably have no choice but to continue to grow chickens. A risky business, but as long as Rafi hasn't found permanent work outside the moshav we have no choice.

This letter was written on 24 April after Holocaust Day (*Yom HaShoah* in Israel) and Memorial Day (*Yom HaZikaron*, the day before Israel's Independence Day), remembrance days spaced seven days apart:

> Efrat has started asking questions about the world around her that sometimes leave me exhausted, startled, embarrassed, and God knows what...and as a 6 year old, she wants answers that are true, clear, and black and white. [...] How old was Savta Aviva's brother when the Nazi's killed him? How could Savta leave her family in Europe and come to Israel? [when they were in danger]? [...] Will Savta Pearl

24. One of the last vestiges of the old system was Government price controls which rarely reflected realities at the farm.

> come to live in Israel only when it will be bad for the Jews in America? Why won't she come now? [...] Why do Arabs like Salach[25] build houses for us and don't want us to live in them. If they don't want us to live in them, how do we sit and have coffee with them?! Before she fell asleep on the eve of *Yom HaZikaron* she called me into her room—looked me in the eye with a pleading look and asked: *Ima* why *dafka* the Jews?—closed her eyes and said good night. [...] Luckily she didn't demand an answer!
>
> [...] Thank God Asaf is still 4 and not asking questions! When the siren sounded for a two minutes tribute on the eve of *Yom HaZikaron*, Asaf suddenly got quiet, stood up at attention, puffed out his chest and froze. Rafi and I and Efrat couldn't help but smile, he was SO serious.

In 1989 things were looking up financially. I was being published widely and raking in a modest income as a freelancer, and Rafi had just found salaried work at a geodesic engineering firm in Tel Aviv interpreting and digitizing aerial maps—all this parallel to running the farm which was limping along.[26] In January 1989 I wrote Pearl and Gil's friend Judy Summers who did not have any grandchildren of her own[27] and every year sent $25 in Hanukah *gelt* to the children:

> Rafi has found work outside the moshav with an engineering

---

25. Our building contractor from Gaza, Salach al-Baneh, a devout Muslim for whom Asaf (three years old at the time) once ran to bring a pillow when he saw Salach kneeling down for prayer.

26. For two decades, Rafi would work a full eight-hour job in Tel Aviv plus the 40 minute commute each way, working either the morning or the evening shift, parallel to picking fruit in our orchards from dawn to mid-morning three times a week in harvest season—until our orchards were played out. This punishing schedule, along with my writing income, enabled us 'to come out owing nothing' when there was a partial cancelling of farm debts as part of the 1992 law that dismantled the moshav system, while many of our neighbors continued to pay off the balance of what they still owed for decades.

27. The kids, in turn, always visited Judy on their trips to the States.

> firm in Tel Aviv so I am back to worrying about [*sic* dealing with] the farm. It's not the physical work. It's the time *thinking* about it. [...] Many of the things I write about in my column [a weekly column of satiric commentary] cover a very wide range of subjects that require a period of time to develop between the event that ticked me off and what I want to say about it. [...] I'm harassed for time and a clear mind unoccupied whether the automatic feeder in the poultry run will stop when full or I'll find two tons of feed on the floor because I didn't check. Rafi has been working in Tel Aviv for a month now — so either I will adjust...or collapse.

No, it was not an easy time for us. Nor for Israel as a whole. Nationally, this was part of the painful above-mentioned transition from a socialist to a capitalist economy, but there was more to it: A gap between lofty ideology, and actual economics and human nature that led the moshav (and kibbutz) model to implode under the combined weight of built-in contradictions, unsustainability,[28] mismanagement

---

28. Thirteen-acre farms throughout the world (and most Israeli family farms are even smaller) are not economically viable as a business. Under Labor-led governments, they were kept afloat artificially — in fact, booming — with massive financial support and subsidies.
For those unfamiliar with the differences in these two constructs, in brief, at the risk of being simplistic: The kibbutz was a utopian collective community where all means of production (fields and factories) were collectively owned by the members and where in theory, daily life operated on principles of 'each according to his abilities — each according to his need'; children in most kibbutzim lived separately from their parents — raised 'collectively' in groups by the community. The moshav setup was an ideological compromise in Zionist land settlement, designed for those who aspired to become Jewish farmers but were unwilling to forego regular family life and wanted more latitude for individual initiative and reward; it was based on a semi-collective village framework governed internally (like the kibbutz) by direct 'town hall' democracy, comprised of individual family farming units of fixed and equal size, cushioned in theory by centralized purchasing and cooperative marketing machinery and the pooling of working capital, said to prevent

and simple greed.[29] Only when the moshavim began to collapse financially leaving every farm to operate independently, culminating in 1992 legislation that dismantled the 'shared liabilities' system, did we begin to suddenly turn a profit.

These vintage letters reflect a different Israel from today's Israel: A high-tech driven liberal market economy on the European model in terms of social legislation,[30] a strong local currency and huge foreign currency reserves, membership in the OECD, a per capita GDP of $45,000 at the close of 2019 (surpassing the UK and France, not just Italy and Spain) and an annual growth rate of almost five percent according to *The Economist*. The standard of living, despite high taxes and high prices, is equal to most countries in Europe. With a population of 9.1 million at the close of 2019 — Israel's population is equal in size to Austria and Switzerland and larger than all the Scandinavian countries — young and still growing. These figures are without taking into account the flow of capital from off-shore natural gas revenues in coming years. We still live in Kfar Warburg but like most, no longer

---

victimization/exploitation of individual farmers by market forces or capitalist entities (based on the same logic behind labor unions that 'there's power in numbers'). Both the moshav and the kibbutz had a strong, at times overbearing, sense of community.

29. In Kfar Warburg it was a case of the classic Three Shell Con Game. A sleight of hand on a grander scale based on mouthing the three moshav principles of "mutual assistance, shared liabilities and joint marketing of crops" to keep the 'clueless suckers' off guard... Those responsible for the moshav's centralized accounts — dairy farmers who by their sheer numbers were repeatedly elected to run things — were able to keep poultry farmers in the dark, while for years they had their hands thrust deep in our pockets. 'Pooling' resources actually meant our village's dairy farmers were secretly benefiting from interest-free credit that poultry farmers were receiving from hatcheries and feed mills for chicks and feed, that would have spelled a profit during years of hyperinflation. Instead, with no revenue from our broilers — barely breaking even on flock after flock — our debts mounted.

30. For example, high taxes to support a compulsory universal public health system, based on graduated income-based premiums, and European-style social legislation (severance pay, maternity leave, paid leave, etc.).

farm.[31] And the village is almost part of Tel-Aviv's growing metropolitan area stretching south to Ashdod — the fifth largest city in Israel only a 12-minute drive from the house. No longer the boondocks, it's only 35 to 40 minutes to the heart of the Big Orange by superhighway and there are three commuter train stations to choose from, 12 to 15 minutes from our house, with a modern mall five minutes away.

Perhaps just our timing, in terms of economic change, was incredibly poor.

Two Letters from Spain Reveal Much Much More[32]

In retrospect, the most amazing and moving letters squirreled away in a shoebox were two letters from a friend named Ben, a volunteer in the Abraham Lincoln Brigade, sent from the front during the Spanish Civil War, opening "Dear Pearl and Gibby" and signed "Salud! Ben".

In one, dated 10 January 1938, Ben started his letter to Gil and Pearl during a lull in the fighting, writing:

> At present it is fairly quiet if you discount the constant boom of cannon and the riveting gun noise of the machine guns which keep up an incessant chatter. We are in the front line. It is bitter cold. 5 degrees above zero in fact. The water freezes up in our canteens a few minutes after we fill them up.

---

31. Ending the huge surplus in farmers and chronic overproduction (driven in part by massive subsidization of cheap 'agricultural water' for the farm sector that encouraged wastage of a precious resource in a semi-arid region — in essence sanctioning 'exporting water' in the form of low-profit tomato paste, cotton, etc.

32. Chronologically, the 'much much more' puts the cart before the horse, and chronologically doesn't belong here before Growing Up during the Depression — but this aspect of Pearl and Gil's lives is intimately entwined with these two letters and where they led.

Ben had to leave the old abandoned house where they had sought some shelter from the cold when the battle suddenly resumed:

> The call has been sounded for all men to keep down as *avion*[33] has been sighted. They have many planes but we shall win in spite of them. [...] The planes are overhead & I can hear the bombs falling not more than a half kilometer away. The explosion is terrific. Lapse of 15 minutes. The planes were headed this way so we left the house to take cover in the open territory. It's safer there. They're gone now [...] Boy, It's a funny feeling to lie there with those things dropping all around. Not knowing whether the next will land right beside you. The worst is there is little you can do to get back at them. Rifles and machine guns are almost useless.

Yet, Ben wrote Gil and Pearl optimistically:

> [...] on this front the fascists have attacked 20 times but we have driven them back each time. They are becoming desperate. Their losses must be tremendous ours small by comparison. It is now another year, a new one, a year in which fascism will be defeated on all fronts, Spain, China and we hope that it shall receive those death blows which shall cause it to disappear even in Italy & Germany from the onslaught of newly reborn democracy.

The second letter was a faded farewell letter written in pencil and dated 8 April 1938, Spain — when the author thought he wouldn't make it home:

> Hello Pearl and Gibby,
>
> [...] As you probably know from the papers, we are in

33. French and Spanish for 'airplane' (powered fixed-wing aircraft); derived from Latin, *avis* (bird).

the midst of the most difficult and important battles this war has yet seen. Our men fight and die heroically in the face of superior arms and equipment. Almost bare-handed you might say they are prepared to fight to the finish. As long as one of us is left alive, this war will continue. The last month has been one continual round of desperate fighting, often hand to hand. When you consider it is a sequel to two long months of continual campaigning, you begin to realize what our boys are made of. This is the first time in modern warfare that any soldier has been asked to spend more than 8 or 10 days in continuous action on the front line & we have been in it now for 90 days without let-up. But we are not complaining. The boys are really to go the limit and many have already.

I would like to write a real long letter but I am mentally as well as physically exhausted. I know you will excuse me if I don't try to make this letter a piece of prize revolutionary literature [...] In case it should happen that the next letter never materializes for good and obvious reasons, you will know that my intentions were good any-way so until then best regards and Salud!

As ever
Ben

Ben survived the war. LOL, he came home from Spain just in time to vouch under oath that Pearl's mother was not a communist, when Nana finally applied for American citizenship 35 years after she came to America...because Nana's half-sister Estelle had gotten sick that day.

Back in 2003 when I wrote the part about the Lost Art of Letter Writing as the first version of this work was being assembled, these two letters had been lauded as 'timepieces' — but they turned out to be much much more. Fast forward to 2018: From childhood, I was always told that I (Diana at the time, Daniella today) was named in memory of a friend of Pearl and Gil, a fellow named David who fell in the Spanish Civil War. I added this fact in a footnote as nothing more than a piquant enhancement to 'Ben survived the war'...but then asked myself, was that enough?

Who was this David? Despite being a lifelong history buff, I had never asked his full name and now, there was no one to ask. Could I 'close the book' on *Playing Detective with Family Lore* without at least an attempt to find out whose name I carry? And what were the odds of finding this man, out of close to 3,000 volunteers from North America fighting the fascists?

I extracted a list of 44 volunteers on the Abraham Lincoln Brigade website named David or Dave. Then by a process of elimination (seeking peers of Pearl and Gil — to be more specific, members of the Brigade born in 1915/16 or thereabouts, who also came from NYC, and who had been killed in action). I narrowed the list down to three...all from the Bronx: David Leonard Hellman, Abraham David Barsky and David Raphael Lipton.[34]

No fluke, records show a third of the 3,000 American volunteers were Jewish (and a third of the Lincoln Brigade was killed in action!). Jews were also prominent among an estimated 41,000 members of all the International Brigades including half the Poles and 20 percent of the Brits and even half the nurses. All told, out of the sum total of

---

34. For better or worse, it seems Jews make good True Believers due to a messianic streak passed on in the DNA. Members of the Tribe tend to pop up in impressive numbers in every utopian and messianic movement that believes it holds the keys to the salvation of humanity (broadly construed), from followers of Jewish false messiahs such as Shabbetai Tzvi to supporters of messianic political dogmas. There were not only a disproportional number of Jews in the International Brigades. There were disproportional numbers of Jews in the Russian Communist Movement infrastructure at all levels — from the ideological scaffolding and senior leadership, down to the commissars, *politruks*, and *apparatchiks* — including many Jews running gulags not just imprisoned in them, see Yuri Slezkine, *The Jewish Century* (Princeton, NJ: Princeton University Press, 2006) (Slezkine is a serious scholar, not a loose cannon.) For more on Jews in the Spanish Civil War see excerpts on Amazon.com from Gerben Zaagsma, *Jewish Volunteers, the International Brigades and the Spanish Civil War* (London: Bloomsbury Academic, 2017).

international volunteers, modest estimates put the number of Jews at between 6,000 and 8,000 or just short of 15–20 percent.

Dave Lipton (originally Lifshitz in Russia) — who had only come to America from Riga in 1927 at age 11, came from a middle-class Russian-Jewish family steeped in European Bolshevism on his mother's side. He had been very active in the Young Communist League in the Bronx. He seemed the least promising of the three. Nevertheless, I sent an email to Eunice Lipton who had researched and written a book about the uncle she never knew, who fell in the Spanish Civil War: *A Distant Heartbeat: A War, a Disappearance, and Family's Secrets.*[35] She replied that Dave Lipton had, in fact, at one point attended the same high school as Pearl and Gil — James Monroe (and graduated from George Washington HS, where Pearl went to summer school). I asked Eunice about social circles where their paths might have crossed (from Camp Marshall Field to the drama group where Pearl and Gil first met during high school), a query that revealed Dave Lipton also had a keen interest in aviation and had gone either to City College or NYU at night to study engineering, possibly aero engineering, like Gil. "He might be your guy", wrote Eunice.

But such linkages rested heavily on conjecture and were hardly conclusive.[36] In fact, it turned out all were irrelevant. The clincher came when I shared, in another email with Eunice in the space of a few hours, the name of a friend of Pearl and Gil's who flew with the Loyalists in Spain — Eddie Lyons, and the above excerpts from Ben's letters, and she replied briefly, in the midst of packing to leave for Paris the next morning:

---

35. For an excerpt from Eunice Lipton, *A Distant Heartbeat: A War, A Disappearance, and a Family's Secrets* (USA: University of New Mexico Press, 2016) see the Kindle edition on Amazon.com. For the book trailer "A Distant Heartbeat–Book Trailer", YouTube video, 2:38 minutes, 2016, https://www.youtube.com/watch?v=GCMpNPS47Go.

36. In fact, Dave went to City College for a short time studying regular engineering. He'd taken airplane mechanic courses elsewhere at a technical school, driven by the desire to become a genuine ('toiling') member of the proletariat. But the possibility of an aeronautical connection prompted further correspondence with Dave's niece that led to a real connection emerging.

> ...just one more thing for now. Dave did have a friend named Ben Katine. I don't know if Ben wrote letters home.

By now it was after midnight in Israel but I pulled out the two letters from Spain I had taken home to Israel with me.[37] The farewell letter was signed simply Ben — as I remembered. But when I opened the other letter Ben had sent three months earlier in January 1938, my heart jumped when I realized this letter had been signed Ben Katine, not just Ben. If further confirmation was needed, I subsequently found a photo online of Ben Katine (L) and Dave Lipton (R) taken in 1938 in Spain

While it is hard to know how close Ben and Dave were, there are strong suggestions they knew each other well — both in New York and in Spain and this was not just a random photo of many that Ben took while serving with the XV International Brigade's Photographic Unit. According to the Lincoln Brigade database, both were very active in the Young Communist League in the same Bronx 'unit': Katine was even president of the Bronx chapter in 1935, and Dave Lipton organized demonstrations, sold copies of the *Daily Worker* and participated in Marxist study groups in the same Bronx chapter (which was hardly a mass participant organization...). Both served in the same brigade, but in different capacities: Dave Lipton was a low-ranking soldier in Company 3 — and only three months in Spain when he was killed; Katine had been in Spain since June 1937 where he was assigned to the XV International Brigade Photographic Unit. However, from what I read in the memoirs of the chief photographer of the Unit Harry Randall

37. As a history buff, I viewed them as a precious primary source I couldn't bear to leave in the shoebox filled with the other letters, stuffed in a closet in Leisure World. I planned to frame them for my office...but (shades of Gil?) never did.

and others about their work,[38] the three-man Photographic Unit was closely embedded with the men on the front line such as Dave. Moreover, it was Katine who wrote Eunice's father a letter — just before the volunteer forces returned to their native countries, telling him Dave had been killed in action. Those returning to the United States on the *S.S. Ausonia* arrived in New York on 20 December 1938; Eunice's father met Ben Katine at the dock. For a host of complicated reasons, Lipton was still hoping against hope that it was not true that his brother had been killed. Among his meager baggage, Ben Katine had brought with him from Spain Dave Lipton's personal effects for the family — including Dave's harmonica. Last but not least, Dave sent a photo postcard with the image of himself and Ben Katine to Belle and Mike Zykofsky dated July 1938 saying:

> Mike and Belle — my dearest and most beloved comrades who are also fighting fascism back home. Love David Lipton.

Mike and Bell were very good lifelong friends of Pearl and Gil. Clearly, I had been named in memory of Dave Lipton.[39]

I only went to sleep at 4:00 AM. Googling 'Dave Lipton' brought up a number of poignant articles by Eunice Lipton about her quest to bring her uncle to life, and skeletons in the closet she found in the process. David Lipton had been both an excellent student and an able athlete,[40] earnest and committed to his worldview, but he was best remembered by those who knew him in America and Spain as a tall but slight-built, gentle, kind, soft-spoken non-demonstrative man — a *mensch*[41] who read books and thought deeply — very different from Eunice's fun-seeking, impulsive, verbose, *macho* father, who oft commanded the limelight

38. Google "Harry Randall" and "XV Brigade" for a host of sources.

39. A Jewish commemoration practice that I share with Eunice's brother — David Lipton.

40. It never occurred to me that studying Spanish in high school — a choice shared by Gil and Dave — might have had political overtones.

41. Yiddish for 'a decent person'.

in his family. There were also two articles by comrade-in-arms Bill Wheeler, who had been with Dave Lipton at the very moment he was killed by a sniper's bullet on Hill 666 at the beginning of the Ebro Offensive, a death that had haunted Wheeler ever since.[42]

> We were at rest the evening before the crossing. Dave handed me a letter written in Yiddish, asking me to mail it to his brother (as I recall) if anything happened to him. I remember telling him, "You will make it OK. Just remember to keep your head and fanny down". The next morning he asked for the letter back and tore it to bits.
>
> That morning we crossed the Ebro and proceeded on a three-day march with no food or water to the first town abandoned by the fascists. As we approached, we found some food, cans of salty fish, but were unable to drink the water as the fascists had contaminated the wells. Tired, parched and hungry we moved on to Hill 666; a rocky height, completely barren of any vegetation due to the repeated bombardment; not enough soil to dig trenches, the parapets piled-up rock that added to the danger when struck by artillery shells. Company Three occupied the right flank of the battalion's position. One of our squads was short-handed and requested a replacement. Dave's sergeant sent him to reinforce the squad. While with that squad, Dave was sent with a detail to the bottom of the hill for grenades, much needed in the event of an attack.
>
> It was shortly after this that I was checking our position at the front [Wheeler was a lieutenant with the unit — DA] when Dave walked over towards me asking if he could return to his regular squad. Just as I yelled to him to get

42. See, for example, Eunice Lipton, "My Dad's Spanish Civil War Secret Tore Our Family Apart", *Daily Beast*, 27 March 2016, https://www.thedailybeast.com/my-dads-spanish-civil-war-secret-tore-our-family-apart and an article in the Lincoln Brigade's periodical, *The Volunteer*: Chris Brooks and Liana Katz, "A Death on the Ebro by Bill Wheeler", *The Volunteer*, 31 March 2015, http://www.albavolunteer.org/2015/03/blast-from-the-past-death-on-the-ebro/.

> down, he was struck by a sniper's bullet, sinking slowly to the ground in front of me.

Wheeler described that indelible moment:

> He stood there yelling, No, no, no, and fell right there at my feet.

When I told Eunice what I had found in Ben's letters — that 'her Dave' was 'my David' — both of us were very moved.

She added in another email that at the memorial service held in honor of Dave Lipton on 18 January 1939, donations were made in her uncle's name and there's a list with the names of people who contributed even the smallest sums. Gil and Pearl were not on the list, but the list did provide further proof that Dave Lipton was 'my David': Besides the mutual tie to Ben Katine, Pearl and Gil's good friends Mike and Belle Zykofsky, as already noted, were also close with Dave Lipton.[43] Their daughter Diana Anhalt later told me that Mike and Belle attended discussion groups of the Young Communist League. Had Pearl also attended any of these discussion groups that Dave Lipton organized? I scrutinized the photo in an article about him of Dave Lipton leading a discussion of young people — but it held no clues. Neither Gil nor Pearl, nor Mike and Belle were among the handful of participants in the photograph with Dave Lipton. But the typed list of contributors at the memorial service for Dave Lipton that stated each donor's full name — showing Belle and Mike had each given a small donation (to help returning wounded veterans of the Lincoln Brigade) — confirmed something else mentioned in Eunice's

43. Dave left for Spain on 18 May 1938; he fell on 20 August 1938. Ben Katine only returned to the States in late December 1938. With the war a lost cause, the remainder of the International Brigades had been sent home, only a few weeks before Franco took Barcelona in January 1939 (though the beleaguered Spanish Loyalists continued to fight on for another five months.). The dates explain the 'late' date of the memorial service at PS 67 in the Bronx under the auspices of the local Friends of the Lincoln Brigade Provisional Committee, which was named after David Lipton.

book. It definitely was they who had served as the alternate address Dave had used as his own for a doctor's note — written before Dave Lipton's departure for Spain in May 1938 — a draft of what Dave should tell the examining physician to write: "This is to certify that

Daniella's Namesake—The 'David' Killed in Spain

I have this day examined Lipton, c/o Zykofsky, 816 E. 179th Street and found him in good health".[44] There is little doubt that Dave Lipton, Ben Katine, Mike and Belle Zykofsky and Pearl and Gil Weiss were good friends. Nor is there any room for doubt now, that in July 1945 — almost seven years to the day after Dave fell[45] — Gil and Pearl named me Diana in Dave Lipton's memory.

~

In Hebrew there is a quip that "anyone who wasn't a communist in their youth has no heart — anyone who remained a communist has no brains".[46] No memoir would be complete without expanding on Pearl's 'hidden radical past' reflected in the diary entry about Gil's 'distinctly bourgeois outlook upon life' and letter to Gil about 'class consciousness' in this chapter on The Lost Art of Letter Writing.

It was only when I was making *aliyah* — literally in the car on the way to New York to sail for Israel in early 1968 — that I dared ask my parents: "I know there's some dark secret about your background you never talked about. Were you socialists?" They laughed, and Pearl

44. Eunice mentions in her book on page 115 this slip of paper found among Dave's personal belongings with the names of two doctors on one side and how to word the note for the Lincoln Brigade screening committee on the other side...using a 'borrowed address' because initially, he was hiding his plans to go to Spain from his parents.

45. Dave fell on 20 August 1938; I was born on 9 July 1945.

46. My husband Rafi, who grew up in a Stalinist-oriented kibbutz has a 'doctorate' on attempts to forge a New Jew just as the Bolsheviks strove to forge a New Soviet Man. He noted, ruefully, that while the Bolsheviks had to brutally impose the vision of collective farming communities (where in the Ukraine and in China tens of millions of peasants lost not only their livelihood, but their lives, in forced collectivization). Jews in Israel, were the only people on the face of the earth who *voluntarily* adopted this warped system of social organization and experiment in social engineering in the kibbutz and moshav models. For a look at the seeds of the moshav model, see a brief description of the Soviet collective farm — the *kolkhoz, Encyclopaedia Britannica*, s.v. "Kolkhoz", https://www.britannica.com/topic/kolkhoz.

retorted, chuckling: "Of course not. We were communists!"

They lived their entire lives with the fear of being 'found out' — the fear of being fingered during the McCarthy Era as 'communist sympathizers' in their youth for having the 'wrong friends' who were card-carrying members of Communist or Socialist parties; for supporting the wrong causes such as the Left-wing Soviet-backed Loyalists in Spain; for attending some meetings/discussion groups with Marxist content and reading 'subversive' books. Even decades later the fear lingered of losing their government jobs, even going to jail for perjury after signing Loyalty Oaths,[47] thus bringing economic catastrophe down on the heads of their family.

Pearl and Gil spoke in the tapes about how they were plagued with the knowledge that one of Pearl's Left-wing teachers in political science and economics at Hunter — who knew of Pearl's leanings, had once invited her to a meeting of the inner circle in the parlor of this professor's Brownstone (which Pearl missed because she couldn't find the address). This faculty member — Professor Bella Dodd — was a key member of the Communist Party who was expelled by the party in 1949 and subsequently became a star informer during the McCarthy Era in hearings before the House Un-American Activities Committee, repeatedly 'naming names'.[48]

It's hard to fathom just how unhinged the witch hunt for 'subversives' had become in the early 1950s, but a good place to start is simply to read some of the original transcripts of one such hearing held in Ohio by the House Un-American Activities Committee in June 1953, where Dodd was a 'keynote informer'. Congressman Hon. Gordon H. Scherer from Ohio who presided over the hearings whose objective was to ferret out subversives in the labor unions (often based solely on 'guilt by association'), defined the threat. To quote directly from Scherer's opening statement, such people were behind "a Communist

---

47. In Maryland (up until 1968 when the wording was declared fuzzy) one could be sentenced to up to ten years in prison for perjury — for having lied about being a "subversive person".

48. For a profile of Dodd, see *Wikipedia,* s.v. "Bella Dodd", https://en.wikipedia.org/wiki/Bella_Dodd.

conspiracy [...] for world domination" aimed at "infiltration of every field and phase of American" including "to cause people to be suspicious and distrustful of the Government" [...] "and make them dissatisfied with the American way of life".[49]

Aside from Dodd, Pearl and Gil had peers, good friends who attended meetings of the Young Communist League, such as Dave Lipton and Ben Katine. Ben was even a card-carrying member of the Communist Party, not just active in the Bronx Young Communist League. Mike and Belle Zykofsky were members of the American Labor Party[50] who also attended YCL discussion groups. The Zykofskys were so spooked that they felt compelled to flee to Mexico City in the 1950s when the socialist ALP was accused of being "an adjunct of the Communist Party" or "a Communist front". The work by their daughter Diana Anhalt[51] — autobiographical in part — fills in the blanks about the sheer terror that propelled her parents to flee, and the same uneasy undercurrent of fear that accompanied Pearl and Gil throughout their lives. My reticence not to 'ask questions' (totally out of character) reflected this undercurrent. Diana Anhalt would write to me in an exchange of emails:

> I am sure my parents felt that the less I knew the safer we'd be. That, of course, explains why after they died I researched and wrote *A Gathering of Fugitives*...searching for answers.

Their rationale resonated with me, as did Diana's, explaining in part how I ended up in the same role as family memoirist. In the course of researching this book, I found myself querying Cousin Gina Burrell about her branch of the Ehrlichs (her father Henry was one of Isador's

---

49. Read the transcript of the 17–18 June 1953 hearings "Investigation of Communist activities in the Columbus, Ohio, area. Hearings", Internet Archive, https://archive.org/details/investigationofc1953unit/page/n3.

50. Mike even ran for office on the ALP ticket.

51. Diana Anhalt, *A Gathering of Fugitives: American Political Expatriates in Mexico 1948–1965* (Santa Maria, CA: Archer, 2001), https://www.amazon.com/dp/1931122032/ref=rdr_ext_tmb.

sons and Gil's first cousin). Gina related how her father — a lawyer on his way to take up a job in LA in the film industry — had to change planes in Mexico City (as fate would have it, he was routed that way, because there were no seats available on a more direct flight). So Henry Ehrlich went to explore the city during his layover, fell instantly in love with Mexico...and never got on the plane to LA. Gina and her two sisters were born and raised in Mexico City totally submerged in Spanish culture. Of course I immediately asked whether she knew the Zykofskys... "Of course!" she replied., "How do *you* know the Zykofskys?!" Gina went on to describe their unusual upbringing among the American expatriate community where her father Henry socialized with legendary figures such as Dalton Trumbo:[52]

> He fell in love with Mexico, married my mom, took her there on their honeymoon and hoped she would like it there. Neither spoke a word of Spanish. This was 1945. Exciting time in Mexico with all the blacklisted filmmakers, ex-pat communists, artists Frida Kahlo and Diego Rivera, etc. He couldn't practice law in Mexico but went back to New York on occasions for legal work. He became good friends with the film and the art community — got involved in film production, producing Spanish filmmaker Luis Bunuel's only English-speaking film *The Adventures of Robinson Crusoe*, worked with John Huston, Budd Boetticher, and eventually distributed films through Central and Latin America.

Although Pearl and Gil didn't talk about their radical past, there were

52. American novelist (*Johnny Got His Gun*) and screenwriter (*Exodus*, *Spartacus*, and *Thirty Seconds Over Tokyo*, for example), was one of the Hollywood Ten who refused to testify before the House Un-American Activities Committee (HUAC) in 1947 and was subsequently blacklisted by the movie industry and lived in Mexico. For a taste of the times, see the 2015 Hollywood movie *Trumbo*. For a more serious look, see Larry Ceplair and Christopher Trumbo, *Dalton Trumbo: Blacklisted Hollywood Radical* (Kentucky: University Press of Kentucky, 2015).

ample 'clues' about the house — such as journalist Edger Snow's *Red Star over China* (1937) and *People on Our Side* (1944) (removed from the bookcase when the FBI came to renew Gil's top-level security clearance). Pearl recalled in one of the tapes the hysteria at the height of the witch hunt, including what McCarthy labeled "fellow travelers":

> I remember destroying books... Something by Lytton Strachey.[53] One time we got rid of them on the way to New York...dumped them in a toilet or something.

Yes, throughout his entire career, Gil had his top security clearance renewed periodically...including one time[54] that FBI agents came knocking on the door of Pearl's first cousin's[55] house... Dot and Gerry Steffens, who'd lived not far away from us, with whom the Weiss family had always been very close even when they were living in Pennsylvania. Daughter Heidi Steffens recalled:[56]

> I clearly remember the entire Steffens family — incredulous, when the FBI came to our door. This was because they were doing an investigation for your dad's security clearance renewal or some such — and they asked my parents if Gil and Pearl were loyal US citizens. Needless to say, Dot and Jerry assured them the country's fate was in good hands with Gilbert Weiss. They closed the door — and we

53. A founding member of the Bloomsbury Group at Cambridge immortalized in the 1995 film *Carrington*.

54. This was in 1961 about the same time I was plastering the halls of my high school with posters advertising debate of the question "Should the United States recognize Red China?" which didn't even make a ripple.

55. Dorothy was Nana's niece — the daughter of Aunt Yetta, and five years younger than Pearl. According to Heidi, her mother told her "it was her older cousin Pearl who first introduced her to progressive thinking"...

56. From a January 2018 email, after I shared this section of the manuscript with Heidi (we are both writers), seeking more information about my parents' radical past.

> looked at each other in astonishment. My father had been blacklisted forever.[57] He'd been fired from one job, literally escorted off the premises, refused others, including during the 1960s, a United Nations position because one needs approval from one's government to work for the UN. Both my parents had FBI files inches thick, I still have parts of them. This was the vaunted FBI, asking two presumed communists if someone with a security clearance for military work was loyal?

The Weiss household did not nurture anything close to "Red Diaper babies"; in any case, by then Pearl's[58] political sympathies had mellowed, and because they were civil servants, both were forbidden from engaging in any overt political activities of any kind even something as benign as openly working for Democratic Party candidates. But Pearl's efforts to nurture *social* consciousness in her comfortable middle-class children were not lacking.

As early as 1952 Pearl 'convinced' her seven and eleven-year-old daughters along with another 12 neighborhood kids to forgo Trick-or-Treating at Halloween armed with a cardboard sign (which Gil saved...) "I am collecting for CHILDREN'S HOSPITAL — please give me your change instead of a Treat. Thank You" — collecting the princely sum of $30 that got everyone's names mentioned in the newspapers, including

57. For more about Dot and Jerry Steffens, see this two-page obituary "Jerome Steffens Aeronautical Engineer", *Washington Post*, 10 March 2005, http://www.washingtonpost.com/wp-dyn/articles/A22169-2005Mar9.html and about Dorothy's work as executive director of the Women's International League for Peace and Freedom in the 1970s in an obituary "Peace Activist Dorothy R. Steffens dies", *Washington Post*, 1 July 1999, https://www.washingtonpost.com/archive/local/1999/07/01/peace-activist-dorothy-r-steffens-dies/075c5c53-d2e4-4efc-9327-aaf7b151db94/.

58. Gil, as Pearl noted in her diary entries and letters, was far more 'bourgeoisie' and more interested in woodworking than politics although his experiences in the work world on a production line — while working his way through college, no doubt left him feeling the system was rigged against working people.

'Windy Weiss'.[59] On a road trip in 1957 to Williamsburg and Jamestown — colonial theme parks in Virginia, Pearl and Gil made it a point to drink from the "Colored Only" water fountains as a form of protest. In 1958, Pearl 'volunteered' her daughters to teach mentally-challenged children and polio victims to swim, lessons held several times a week in a wealthy Jewish family's private pool. Pearl recalled:

> They were mainly kids who were mentally handicapped[60]... We wanted you to do something with your summer that was not just entertaining yourselves... I thought that was very important.

Another summer in June 1960, Pearl and Gil and a group of their friends carpooled carloads of their teenagers to Glen Echo[61] every weekend for five weeks straight, to picket the segregated amusement park until it was forced to desegregate. It went without saying that any wearing apparel bought for the Weiss household had to have a 'Union Label'.[62]

Undoubtedly these experiences and values helped set the stage for my decision[63] to spend a summer during my university studies as

---

59. One little girl, Sharon White, not only got her name in the papers, she also got polio the next summer and ended up in Children's Hospital.

60. At university, this experience helped me land weekend employment working as a teacher for the Sunday School Society which ran a special Sunday activities program for Jewish residents of Elwyn outside Philly, a home for institutionalized severely mentally-challenged children and adults.

61. See a recap of the 1960 picket, Brigid Schulte, "Protest on a Sculpted Horse", *Washington Post*, 29 June 2004, http://www.washingtonpost.com/wp-dyn/articles/A13304-2004Jun28.html.

62. Sewed into the garment, testifying it was made by organized labor — this was decades before the textile industry migrated to Bangladesh and Indonesia.

63. Joining VISTA (Volunteers in Service to America) was motivated not only by a sense of commitment to be socially engaged, but also a personal identity quest designed to take me as far away as possible from everything Jewish before finalizing whether to immigrate to Israel... Some experiences and events in Eckman — personal and the project itself — appear less starkly black and white in retrospect than they did at age 21.

a community organizer with the Appalachian Volunteers in a racially segregated coal mining community in West Virginia under the auspices of VISTA — the 'domestic Peace Corps'. My fellow volunteers and I ran an integrated summer camp in the back of the African-American AEM Church which preceded integration of the schools in McDowell Country which only took place in the fall of 1966 — 12 years after *Brown vs. Board of Education*. Besides showing kids how to wind donated wool around tin cans to make vases for their moms, in the evenings we sought to bring together the white inhabitants up Eureka Hollow and the African-American residents down in Eckman-Landgraff to solve common problems and meet socially around mutual hobbies — an experience that Pearl was able to share vicariously through my lengthy and detailed letters — which, naturally, Gil saved.[64]

Considering all the clues around the house and attempts to nurture socially-engaged offspring, it was not all that surprising that earlier — in high school — I also went through a 'Red period' kick-started by reading one of Howard Fast's[65] historical novels in the bookcase. The book was *The American*, about a travesty of justice in the struggle for the right to unionize in America. Subsequently, I got special permission (as a 10th grader) to gain entrance to the Library of Congress to read the original trial transcripts and other primary sources (material I naturally

64. The letters were the foundations for another writing project on my bucket list, worked on in fits and starts for over a decade — a major unfinished feature titled "A Story in Black and White" about the community then and today — based solely on Internet research and people I reconnected with 40 years down the road — by email or phone, meshed with the vintage letters, a diary I kept and a pack of black and white photos I took that summer, some that look like they could have come right out of *You Have Seen Their Faces*, the iconic 1937 book by photographer Margaret Bourke-White and novelist Erskine Caldwell about the back roads of America.

65. A prolific Jewish 'progressive novelist' who, as a member of the Communist Party, was jailed for Contempt of Congress in 1950 after refusing to divulge to the House Committee on Un-American Activities the names of contributors to a fund for a home for orphans of American veterans of the Spanish Civil War. For a decade, Howard Fast was blacklisted by the major publishing houses (until 1958) and by Hollywood (a ban only broken in 1960).

put in writing and turned-in as a term paper...[66]). Politically driven and humorless, my first 'published work' was a curt letter-to-the-editor following the 1962 Cuban Missile Crisis — coauthored with my cousin Heidi Steffens and published in the *Washington Post* that pilloried a speaker about civil defense who dressed up his talk to an auditorium filled with bored high schoolers by cracking a few jokes about nuclear war. The second was a lengthy take-no-prisoners letter-to-the-editor in the *Montgomery Country Sentinel* about separation of church and state. But a writing career never crossed my mind. There had been a silent nod of approval from Pearl and Gil when I first joined a Labor Zionist youth group in 9th grade...initially attracted by the *Labor* — not the Zionist. Nevertheless, I never asked for details about their hidden past until I was 'safely on my way to Israel forever' — which at the time (no telephone, not just no Internet) was about as far away as the moon.

To return to Ben's letters and the discovery of Dave Lipton — in memory of Dave Lipton, a photograph of Dave and Ben in Spain (taken on 4 July 1938, a little over six weeks before he was killed) has been added, with Eunice Lipton's blessings, to the L-shaped wall in our eating alcove — the hub of family life and the site of an eclectic and far from formal collection of several hundred Ashkenazy family snapshots in various size frames that span six generations and people in all sorts of states[67] and stages of life.

Chapter III that follows takes a step back in time to recap — often in their own words — what it was like for Pearl and Gil as children of Jewish immigrant parents from Europe, growing up in households struggling to make a living (and in Pearl's case, genuinely poverty-stricken at times — with all the hardships and insecurity that entailed), then to

---

66. How could it be otherwise, 60 years later I still have that typewritten paper and other course papers from college. And like Gil saving our Second World War ration books 'just in case', I find myself unable to simply trash my more than 60-year-old manual Olympia typewriter in its signature wooden molded case.

67. From formal studio pictures of grandparents, to a shot of my husband Rafi caught on film cutting the grass on a ride-on lawnmower, clad only in a pair of BVDs.

mature into adulthood during the Depression[68] including the struggle to get the college education which would provide passage to upper middle class status...also providing a partial answer as to why Gil and Pearl got married — not once, not twice — but three times!

68. A life story shared not just by Gil and Pearl, but by an entire generation — shaping their worldview.

Chapter III

Growing Up during the Depression

Childhood and School days

After Nana lost her husband, the breadwinner of the family, life was arduous and uncertain during most of Pearl's formative years. Living conditions were stark. They moved frequently; she was sent multiple times to live temporarily with relatives. Historians note that some kids were even sent temporarily to orphanages by poverty-stricken parents 'put out on the street' due to their inability to pay the rent! Pearl went to eight different schools. Moving so frequently, and being younger than others in her class from 'skipping' grades, she had few friends. She recalled her childhood several times in the tapes:

> We lived on the Lower East Side in tenements when I was a child. We always lived on the top floor (a five-floor walk-up) because my mother always said it 'was cleaner'—too high for transients to come up and pee in your hallway or break into the shared toilet in the hall... And we moved almost every year (we only had a few sticks of furniture—a bed, dressers, a table and chairs) because when apartments were plentiful, landlords would give a month's free rent to attract new tenants.
>
> There were gas lights where you had to put in a coin and you would get a certain amount of gas for your quarter [sometimes they had to borrow the quarter to keep the lights on—DA]. These were one-bedroom cold-water

> flats — a bedroom and a big room [parlor], and a kitchen with a coal stove as the only source of heat. [...] It was frigid in the morning in winter. You heated water on the stove for once-a-week baths in a tin laundry tub in the kitchen. We had a lock on a toilet in the hallway which we shared with two neighbors — the Watzers and the Zuckers. Watzer was a barber and used to cut my hair. His wife had epileptic seizures and I would stay with her when my mother was at work and when she had a seizure I would run and get somebody and say "Mrs. Zucker is sick".
>
> Since everyone around us was as poor as we were, you really didn't know there was anything else — though I do remember my mother sometimes taking me out for the day to the Natural History Museum or the Planetarium on her day off. [...] Riding on the top of this double-decker bus [in Manhattan] we'd pass these mansions and she'd say "that's the Rockefeller's and that's the Mellon's house" [...] But being rich was an abstract thing to me because I really didn't know people lived like that.

Her Aunt Hannah's was almost a second home:

> When the Depression got very bad, my Aunt Hannah got a job as the janitor of this building on Washington Avenue and we moved there. The janitor in our previous building had a baby and my two-year-old cousin Bobby liked to look at the baby. It's funny the things you remember from your childhood. Bobby went to the window — and I still remember this — he called out "Janitor, where's your baby. I wanna see your baby!" And my Aunt Hannah burst into tears and said "I'm the janitor now..."
>
> This apartment had two bedrooms and a room that was a dining room and a kitchen. Because Hannah was the super who maintained the building [short for superintendent, or

> janitor — DA],[1] my cousins Milton and Harold and I had the job of collecting the garbage from each tenant, knocking on the doors saying 'Garbage! Garbage!' There was a dumbwaiter[2] in the hall and we would put the garbage from each floor inside to take it down, where probably my aunt was the one disposing of the garbage. We'd do this every day for all five floors.

Pearl's childhood was marked during one point by rheumatic fever that kept her bedridden for a month and a half, followed by a long convalescence:

> When I was 10, I was again living with my Aunt Hannah and their three boys in a tenement in the Bronx. [...] We were washing dishes for Passover, changing the dishes... and all of a sudden my lips started to swell. As I watched, it got bigger and bigger. Before I knew it, I was in bed and my aunt had called a doctor, who diagnosed me as having scarlet fever which was highly contagious and *very* dangerous. So my Aunt Hannah immediately called my mother (who was still out in Brooklyn, living at Dr. Levine's). Under such a threat, I had to be gotten out of the house.
>
> When my mother arrived, she assessed the situation and called another doctor, labeling the first one a *knubel doctor* — literally, 'a garlic doctor'...meaning he wasn't much of a physician.[3] He correctly diagnosed that I didn't have *scarlet* fever, that I had *rheumatic* fever. Rheumatic fever was nevertheless a lousy thing to have; if anyone even so

1. This included coal delivery and collection of rents and keeping the stairwells clean.

2. A small interior pulley-operated freight elevator for transporting small objects such as a food tray (or a garbage pail) between floors (not intended to carry people or larger cargo).

3. Reflecting folk 'remedies' such as hanging garlic cloves near a cradle to keep evil spirits away and ward off disease.

> much as walked in the room and there was a creaking floorboard, I was in terrible pain and this lengthy illness could permanently damage the heart. But rheumatic fever was not contagious, so my mother didn't have to take me immediately somewhere-we-know-not-where.
>
> This was a very difficult period. The only medicine at the time was aspirin and bed rest. So, there I was — unable to go to the library and bedridden for weeks on end. But one of my friends, Ruthie Katz, had an older brother who owned complete sets of Mark Twain and Dickens, and I asked to borrow his books — one at a time. Thus, because of rheumatic fever, at age ten, I was already reading *A Tale of Two Cities*.

Sleeping arrangements in tenements were always at a premium, and it was common for all the kids to be crammed into one small bedroom with shared beds:

> We had just moved into this apartment where Aunt Hannah had become the janitor for the building, which saved rent. There were a bunch of girls — the only time in my life that I had friends because we lived in one neighborhood for a long time. Well, someone asked me, "Where do you sleep?" and all of a sudden I couldn't tell them that I slept in the same bed with my male cousins. It was as if at that moment — I was 10 — that I became self-conscious about it.
>
> The reason my Aunt had me sleeping with one of the boys was that the boys used to fight and if one slept with me they didn't fight. My heart was pounding and I walked in and I told my Aunt Hannah, "I'm not going to sleep with Milton or Harold any more! The boys are going to sleep together, and I'm going to sleep on the folding cot". I was very nervous, but she just responded: "OK".

Another time — actually when Pearl was younger and living with her mom, who was eking out a living doing odd jobs, before Nana began working for Dr. Levine — Pearl had her tonsils removed and almost hemorrhaged to death:

> They took me to Bronx Hospital and I was presumably very lucky because this doctor was a good private physician who was in the clinic [for the indigent][4] and he took care of me. I was recuperating very nicely...so my mother took us to the circus. After we got home, suddenly, in the middle of the night, I started to hemorrhage... They took me back to the hospital and to this day, I can still remember those doctors trying to sew me up and not being successful.
>
> I remember my mother being on the payphone yelling and carrying on like a maniac, telling the doctor, "You're the one who operated on her, and you're going to come and take care of her, and if anything happens to this child, it's your fault". And the next thing you know, this doctor came in and stitched me up and was explaining to these interns (or whoever they were) how to do it.
>
> She was a tiger.

Keep in mind how terrifying this situation must have been for Pearl's mother. Nana had already lost a husband and child. She was not about to lose her daughter while she meekly stood by.

Pearl also changed schools umpteen times along with the fortunes or misfortunes of family finances (which had also sent her bouncing back and forth to live with her Aunt Hannah and her three male cousins — Harold, Milton and Bobby):

---

4. Both Bronx Hospital and the Lebanon Hospital were Jewish hospitals established in 1890 and 1909, open to all regardless whether a patient had the means to pay or not, and top physicians worked there *pro bono* treating the poor. For a short history on the two hospitals that ultimately amalgamated into one in 1962, see an excerpt from the *Bronx-Lebanon Hospital–100th Commemoration Book*, https://www.douggléner.com/docs/Bronx_abi.html and "A Brief History of Bronx-Lebanon Hospital" https://web.archive.org/web/20130403081216/http://blhcpediatrics.org/node/32.

> My mother *paid* Hannah for taking me in... It wasn't a matter of putting another kid on her to feed. [...] Aunt Hannah was very glad to have me — a girl. They treated me like part of the family — certainly not like a Cinderella [alluding to Nana's experience as 'Cinderella' with her mean stepmother — DA], but I do remember doing a lot of chores around the house.

Aunt Hannah's husband Abe made a relatively good living as a machine operator in a garment factory — a skilled job. They even had their own bathroom...with a tub, Pearl remembered. But her Uncle Abe was a terrible gambler — and Aunt Hannah would send Pearl to fetch him from his backroom poker game at the United Cigar Store. She would refuse to go home without him and Uncle Abe had his principles ("He didn't mind gambling away the food money, but he had his own standards of morality and didn't think it was proper for a girl to be in such a joint filled with men"). Consequently, he would give in and go home... Pearl recalled that her uncle also had a terrible temper:

> He had a strap hanging from the wall like you see in the movies. I was the only one who could control him. He adored me. I'd start yelling "Uncle Abe, don't hit the boys" when I'd see him going for the strap. And I'd start crying. And he'd say, "*Da pishta d'oigen*" (I'm peeing in my eyes). But it worked.

Pearl says her Aunt Hannah was also very glad to have her because she could babysit with her hellion cousin Bobby:

> I remember Bobby was maybe three years old. People used to bring their chairs out and put them in front of the building and sit out there and socialize.[5] Aunt Hannah had taken Milton [who was recovering from polio and had to be taken regularly to an out-patient clinic for physical therapy] and

5. Remember, there was no air conditioning and no television in those days.

> I was in charge of Bobby. Suddenly I hear someone yelling "Pearly! Pearly! Look what Bobby's doing!" That little kid was standing there with a concrete block and threatening two children — the Pupitzky kids who lived in our building who were 'deaf and dumb'.[6] My heart was beating and I went over and said "Put that down! Put that down, Bobby!" and luckily he did. I wasn't a very assertive person, but I sure was then...

Pearl recalled another indelible incident with Bobby at another juncture:

> One time, my mother was taking care of all of us. I don't know where my aunt was. Momma had made lamb chops. Bobby wanted more and she told him there was only one for each child. So Bobby threatened "he wasn't going back to school" if she didn't give him another one...so Momma called the truant officer! She told him that she has this nephew who refuses to go to school. He was in elementary school. My Aunt Hannah was furious at my mother for calling the truant office ("As if I don't have enough trouble with Bobby, you have to call the truant officer?!?"). But Aunt Hannah couldn't get Bobby out of the house and he kept screaming, "The other chop! The other chop!" Mr. Lucie the truant officer literally dragged him back to school by his ear.
>
> Amazingly Bobby didn't grow up to be a gangster. There were plenty who did. He was a 'big man'[7] who married, had a family, worked a regular job — selling furniture, had a bad heart and died relatively young from a heart attack. He was a smart kid but never used his potential, but all things considered — he could have turned out far worse.
>
> [...] When you think about the screwed up childhood I

---

6. The term which was employed widely at the time (along with 'deaf-mute') for deaf persons who did not use oral speech to communicate, carrying the assumption that such individuals were mentally defective (dumb).

7. Tall and big boned, with a build like a football player.

> had — I wasn't alone. Many people had screwed-up childhoods... What makes kids 'problem kids'? I know one thing was very constant in *our* lives: love. The hardships? That was your life, and you just 'lived it'.

As already noted, Pearl was already reading adult fiction when she was ten 'thanks' to rheumatic fever. As a result, she ended up as one of the youngest in her classes, finishing high school at age 15 and a half. Why? Because in elementary school, more than once, Pearly came home from one of the multiple elementary schools she attended in the course of being moved from pillar to post, reporting, "Ma, they skipped me again":

> Once we moved to a new dwelling (for a change...) and after the second day of school they checked reading ability and the next thing I know I come home and tell my

Pearl at PS 55, age 10

> mother, "Ma, they skipped me again. I'm going into 4th grade [directly from 2nd]". When they had a full class in 3rd grade and places in 4th they would skip the good students to even out the number of students. So Nana went to school saying, "How can they skip you, you just got there!?" But they tested kids and I tested very high on reading and comprehension. They wouldn't ask your parents and it was considered an honor.

Due to this practice, Pearl and Gil (who was also skipped, it seems, but fewer times) met in a drama class in their last year of high school, which was a windfall for Pearl socially:

> We put on a play that was so stupid — when I think about it, I blush. [...] I had only one line in it and it was: "Now you can go to hell!"
>
> What was nice was we — those in the drama group — used to meet in someone's basement after school. I was the lonely kid. No friends. No anybody. Didn't know anybody and all of a sudden I'm in this close-knit group. It wasn't just because we moved so often and I hadn't gone through school with these kids. I was a lonely kid. My sister was seven-and-a-half years older.

But Gil didn't take notice right away, and he was shy. They both graduated James Monroe High School in the Bronx the same year although they were born a year apart (and thanks to fate, for Pearl had begun high school at Hunter High in Manhattan, but after a year she quit due to the arduous commute).

Among a host of 'period pieces' that remain from their schooldays are Pearl's 7th- and 8th-grade report cards from Bronx Junior High No. 63 — with the As and Bs in English and history and a 65 in math and algebra...and a 61 and 66 in cooking. Every time they skipped Pearl in elementary school, she missed a year of arithmetic, recalling: "They didn't go back and teach you what had been taught in the grade before. I didn't have to worry about reading and comprehension, but in

REPORT TO PARENTS

Bronx 65 JUNIOR HIGH SC

Report of Schwarger Pearl
Last Name First Name

Term Ending June 1928 Class 8A[71] Teacher H. Youn

Ratings	Excellent A or 86 to 100	Good B or 76 to 85	Passing B or 60 to 75	Poor C or 40 to 59	Ver D o

SUBJECTS	Grade	1 Prelim-inary	2 Mid-Term Mark	3 Mid-Term Exam.	4 End-Term Mark	5 End-Term Exam.
Effort		a	B+		a	
Proficiency		B+	B+		a	
Conduct Self-Control		a	B		a	
Personal Habits		B+	B		E	
Times Absent						
Times Late						
Reading and Literature		B	89	88	85	86
Composition		a	75	75	75	86
Grammar		B+	70	80	75	92
Spelling		a	95	96	98	98
Oral Expression		B	89	85	85	85
Penmanship		B+	75	75	80	80
Arithmetic and Algebra		B+	90	94	90	84
History		a	90	100	95	98
Geography						
Shop Cooking		B	61	66	70	70
Science Sewing		B	80	75	95	90
Music		B	55	65	66	68
Physical Training		B	65	65	Ex	Ex
Drawing		B+	90	90	75	90
Foreign Language		a	80	75	85	94
Biology						
Community Civics						
Bookkeeping						
Stenography						
Typewriting						
Office Practice						
Rec		a	50	50	65	65
Club		a	95	65		

Promoted

Pearl's 8th-grade report card, 1928

math I had holes. I missed the year they learned fractions". (Luckily skipping was based on reading comprehension, not math aptitude and mastery or Pearly and Gibby may never have met...) The subjects included grades in subjects like 'penmanship' (80) and 'oral expression' (80).

Also found among the papers was Gil's acceptance into the Arista League — the pinnacle of excellence at Monroe High School which championed "High Character, Scholarship and Loyal Service"; his school letters for track sports, including the one hundred yard dash, and the February 1932 Commencement Exercises from high school that included gold medals in elocution, English and economics — the last won by Gil (and a prize that Pearl coveted for herself). Parallel to scholastics and athletics, Gil used to help Pop Weiss out in his garage after school.

According to the custom of the day, each girl who went to the 'Senior Promenade' — held 30 January 1932 — came equipped with a little red notebook with a tassel and a pencil attached in which she entered the name of her escort for the evening (one Milton Slatoff) and the Order of the Dances — where a girl would enter the names of the young men who had requested to dance with her. Gil wasn't there. The two knew each other slightly in high school — having first met in that drama class, but Gil was dating another girl named Pearl. As a

Arista Honor Society

Monroe sports letters

member of the Arista League, Gibby also tutored Pearly in geometry, but only became infatuated with her curves when they began dating after graduation. They were reconnected by fate at a post-graduation party that Pearl almost missed because she lost the address and got there late based solely on blind reckoning, while Gil got ribbed for repeatedly asking the host 'whether Pearly was coming'. Gilbert, who could never pass up a pun, signed some of his letters to Pearl when they began dating—"drama-tically yours, Gib". Even girls from poor immigrant families had Sweet Sixteen parties with printed invitations (Pearl's was held 23 July 1931). By then Gibby was courting Pearly—and

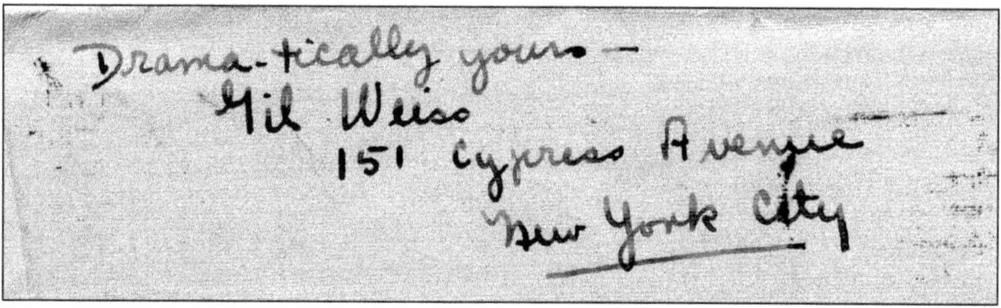

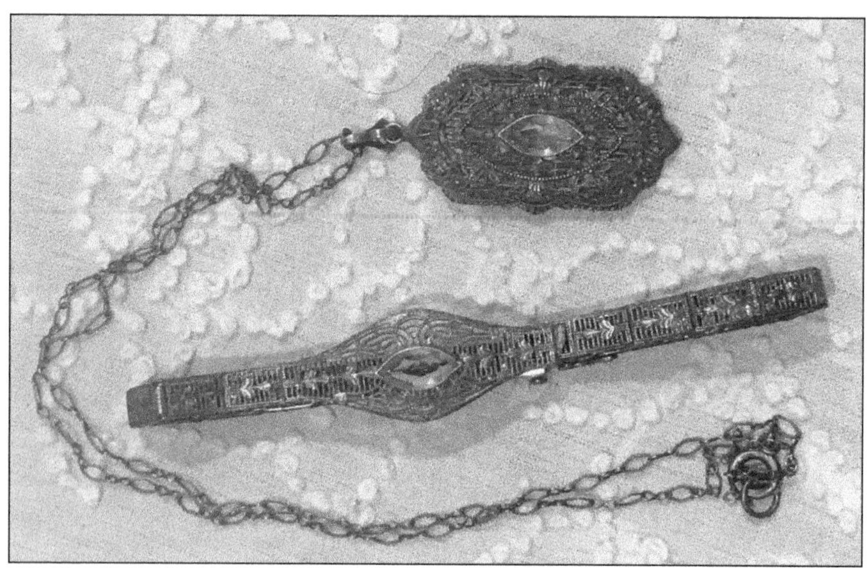

Top: Gil's signature
Bottom: Sweet-16 gift to Pearl from Gil

had bought her a lovely filigree bracelet and matching pendant set[8] with the help of his mother.

College Days

Armed with a 'College Entrance Diploma' from the University of the State of New York — a document crowned by an etching embossed with a gold seal and a far cry from today's mechanized computer printouts, Pearl began to study at Hunter College. At the same time, in February 1932 Gil enrolled in NYU's night school engineering program — an evening degree schedule spread out over six and a half years, with the last two semesters completed as a fulltime day student:

> Gibby was going to night school and for six months he was working for Uncle Izzy Ehrlich as a shipping clerk in their dress factory, Globe Garment Corporation, for $15 a week. There was this cousin Dick Ehrlich who *on purpose* would give Gil more work to do just before he had to leave for school: He'd tell Dick "I'll be late for my classes if I have to go mail these packages from the post office" and Dick would say "I don't give a shit about your classes" [...] so, Gil never had time to eat supper, or grab a milkshake or something before class — always rushing. [...] To top it all off, when Uncle Izzy went bankrupt, he had to file certain papers, and Gil found out that he was on the payroll for $18 a week [to jack up expenditures for tax purposes], and Gil was being paid $15. OK, Uncle Izzy gave him a job, but boy was Gil mad.

In New York City, by 1932 "half of [the city's] manufacturing plants were closed, one in every three New Yorkers was unemployed, and roughly 1.6 million were on some form of relief", according to the

8. Wendy still has it...in a 'memory box' that hangs on the wall that she made for Pearl years ago.

Tenement Museum. Having graduated at the outset of 1932 just as the Great Depression hit rock bottom, Gil should have been thrilled to have a job, any job that would pay for his tuition — even at three dollars a day.[9] Was Gil's cousin Dick jealous that Gil was going to school (and Dick's younger brother would do the same) while Richard Ehrlich was expected to take over his father's struggling business? In 1933, 25 percent of the workforce and 37 percent of all nonfarm workers were completely out of work, although by the second quarter of 1933, the economy began to improve, a recovery that largely stalled for most of 1934 and 1935.

From 1934 Gil held down a day job as a production line worker in a factory called S. M. Frank that made tobacco pipes. Pearl reminisced:

> He would have to break the pipe stems off from the mold. He did a 'time and motion' study of how he could do it faster, so he made a lot of money. In response, they cut the amount they were paying him per gross unit (!) so, Gil started to hide how much he had done, so he wouldn't earn too much in one week. When things were slow he would take them out and get paid for them, but he was earning as much as $40 a week — a good salary. [Afterwards, when Gil first started working as an engineer at Keyport, he was earning $25 a week... — DA.] But he had to quit [his factory job] in mid-1937 to go to day school. Tuition for the year was $500 [a princely sum in those days] — that had to be paid in advance.

During his last year at NYU as a full-time student — all the advanced engineering courses necessary to graduate were given only as day classes — Gil worked a part-time job to cover his minimal needs:

> [...] While going to day school, Gil got a National Youth

---

9. For striking photos of New York at the height of the Depression, see John Kuroski, "55 Harrowing Photos of the Great Depression in New York City", https://allthatsinteresting.com/great-depression-new-york-city.

> Administration job working 30 hours a month and was being paid $15 a month — half a dollar an hour. But because a lot of the guys who applied came from families who were moderately well off, they wouldn't work all their hours. Thus, the professor in the lab where Gil was working setting up lab experiments allowed Gil to work the hours that so-and-so didn't work... So he was able to earn $30 a month. But he was never 'free and easy' like a lot of the guys in his class who were being sent to school by their parents.

If Gil and his close friend Mike Frankel were such good students, why didn't they get scholarships? Pearl explained, in retrospect:

> We didn't know about scholarships! Everyone knew City College and Hunter College were free. Only many years later did we become cognizant there were scholarships at NYU... We didn't have counselors to advise us, and no one in the family knew about such things. By the time Gil met Clemens — who might have told them [the head the aero department — DA] — they were in their senior year.

Gil helping Pop Weiss, circa 1933

Gil graduated from NYU in June 1938—second in his class. The transcript shows 49 As and seven Bs including not only courses in Thermodynamics and Hydraulics but also studies that ranged from Elementary Surveying to Propeller Design, parallel to Effective Writing and Industrial History.

~

Looking back, Pearl recalled when she first decided she wanted to be a teacher:

> When I was a little girl, I couldn't have been more than six years old, I came home and I said I wanted to be a teacher when I grow up. At the time it was a ridiculous hope because we didn't have a dime. [...] I didn't think about how exactly I would go to college, but when I got older [...] I heard about Hunter and said [to myself], "I want to try to go there".
>
> Hunter had both a high school and a college. [...] I knew I had good grades and you could go to Hunter High—an elite school for free, and that there was a free college afterwards [admission being almost automatic for Hunter's high school graduates—DA]. But I only went to Hunter College High School for one year. [...] Hunter College didn't have very many programs—because not many careers were open to women at the time, so I never thought about anything but being a teacher.

Pearl says she never officially graduated from middle school because she was 'skipped' right into high school. She left Hunter High for two reasons: For one, she didn't like Latin, and Hunter required everyone to take four years of Latin in high school, but the main stumbling block was simply *getting* to Hunter High. Hunter College High School for Intellectually Gifted Young Ladies as it was officially called up until 1947 was situated on the Upper East Side of Manhattan and Pearl lived in the easternmost part of the Bronx. The hour-long commute each way cost only ten cents a day, but it was a grueling commute: taking a streetcar (tram) to the elevated subway, changing subway lines three (!) times, then walking three New York city blocks to school — all this at age 12:

> I was in the Hunter High School orchestra, and I played the violin and on practice days I had to carry my violin on the subway as well! I was just a small kid, with all my books[10]...*and* a violin case. We didn't have lockers in those days. Or backpacks. So I decided I wanted to go to a local high school, James Monroe, which was one short bus ride from home. I finished high school in three years — in January 1932 at age 15 and a half. [...] Why in three years? I didn't have anything to do in the summer, so I took courses — went to summer school in the summer of 1930 and 1931 at George Washington High School nearby — so I had enough credits to graduate high school in three years.
>
> To get into Hunter, we had to take exams and you were evaluated also by your high school grades — and I did very well, so I was accepted to Hunter College's teaching program. But the only reason I was able to go to college was that there were no jobs [Remember, almost 25 percent of the workforce was unemployed in 1932 and 1933 — DA] and there was no point in me sitting around at home. Once at Hunter, I was determined to stay.

How did she manage — even with free tuition, to pay for school supplies, books and so forth? During the Depression there was a program called the National Youth Administration that gave part-time work-study projects — 30 hours a month — to students to help them stay in school rather than joining the lines of the unemployed on the dole:

> You got $15 a month, and that basically kept me in college. My mother managed to scrounge together enough for my

10. American high school textbooks are lent to students by the school, and made to last: thick, sturdy hardback editions that can weigh a kilo each.

> carfare. She used to give me lunch to take along—and a nickel for milk with my lunch, and an extra nickel for a candy bar...and that was how I went to college, since tuition was free.

Thus, Pearl entered university at age sixteen, At Hunter she majored in education and minored in history, sociology and political science:

> My major in education included all sorts of education courses including...sewing by hand! [...] On Friday afternoon in elementary school classrooms, we used to have crafts with the children ['practice teaching'—DA]. We had courses in language arts, and presumably were taught how to teach arithmetic.
>
> [...] Most of the girls were very smart—smarter than

Hunter College

> I was...and my career at Hunter was not a stellar performance. I was a history and sociology and political science minor. Looking back on the history curriculum, it wasn't very good, although I know American history pretty well as a result, and we studied European history — but history was Anglo-centered. They were completely detached from the rest of world, and I was intensely interested in what was going on at the time in China.

Pearl was referring to the protracted two-decade-long civil war for control of China between the Nationalist Chinese under Chiang Kai-shek, and the Communist Chinese under Mao Zedong (and Zhou Enlai) that would culminate in the 1949 Communist victory and establishment of the People's Republic of China. But in 1932–1936 when Pearl was in college, events in China focused on the Red Army losing ground, hallmarked by the Long March of retreating Communist forces between October 1934 and October 1935 in which only 8,000–9,000 troops out of 80,000 survived, but demonstrated Mao's organizing skills, propelling him into the top echelons of the Chinese Communist Party.

Pearl Schwarzer's commencement from Hunter College in January 1936 (two and a half years before Gil graduated NYU) reveals that prizes for excellence ranged from $10 for excellence in geology and $15 in chemistry from the Chemistry Alumni Association and $25 for excellence in constitutional law to a whopping $100 prize for graduate studies for excellence in home economics...

Such scaling in prize money reflected the state of education for women at the time — based largely on 'female curriculums' where, throughout the 1930s, teaching and nursing were the top two avenues open to women to get a college education. Indeed, another popular major at women's colleges was a full-blown major in home economics (even at Hunter some home economics courses were required to get one's bachelor's degree as an educator — including sewing by hand!).[11]

11. Another requirement for graduation was to demonstrate one could swim. A sympathetic gym teacher at Hunter allowed Pearl to doggie paddle the length of the pool, stopping every few feet to grab the side of the pool and

Framed within the traditional role of women as homemakers and child raisers, a college degree in home economics didn't challenge the Social Order while at the same time it raised "homemaking to the status of a respectable–though definitely female occupation" to quote one scholar.[12] Furthermore, women of Pearl's era and before, even college-educated women, were *expected* to rear their children — at least until they were in kindergarten, before thinking of going out to work, and to take the back seat to the demands of a husband's career. Such social codes were symbolized by the quip that "so-and-so went to college to get her MRS" and women sometimes signing their names as appendages to their husbands ('Mrs. Gil Weiss'). Only about ten percent of women in the 1920s kept their jobs after marriage, most of them working-class women whose family needed their paycheck. Even Dee Sennett, Pearl's contemporary and friend at Leisure World — one of the first women journalism graduates, after a brief 'fling' as one of the first female radio journalists, ended up working as a salesperson in a department store after she and her husband came to Washington — due both to this hierarchy of priorities as well as the rarity of journalism jobs for women of her generation.[13] Nevertheless, for women — all the more so, the daughters of immigrants — a college education was empowering, a source of social mobility and what today is defined as 'social capital' even if they didn't cash in on the economic perks of a degree. But both Pearl and Dee were among the 900,000 youth — one-eighth of all young people ages 18 to 21 in the early 1930s in America who enrolled in colleges "partially attributed to the fact that there were few jobs available" at

push off again, since Pearl had had no opportunities to learn to swim in her upbringing, and indeed never mastered swimming.

12. John L. Rury, "Vocationalism for Home and Work: Women's Education in the United States, 1880–1930", *History of Education Quarterly* 24, no. 1 (1984): 21-44. https://doi.org/10.2307/367991.

13. Input and data from Margaret Nash and Lisa Romero, "'Citizenship for the College Girl': Challenges and Opportunities in Higher Education for Women in the United States in the 1930s", *Teachers College Record* 114, no. 2 (2012), 1–35, and Mary C. McComb, *Great Depression and the Middle Class: Experts, Collegiate Youth and Business Ideology, 1929-1941* (New York and London: Routledge, 2006).

the height of the Great Depression. As a result, enrollment increased by 12 percent in 1931—a phenomenon expanded on in discussion of Pearl's education and career in Chapter IV in the section Pearl–the Ultimate Mentor. Both women were part of a quiet revolution in the status of women when between 1900 and 1940 the number of female college enrollees in the United States spiraled from 85,338 to 600,953.

~

What did Pearl and Gil and others of the Depression Generation do for fun?

For one, they lived walking distance from one another. The usual two-dollar date was a movie (50 cents a ticket) followed by a stop at the ice cream parlor. They treasured meetings in Washington Square (in Greenwich Village, near NYU's engineering school), holding hands and exchanging adoring looks riding the subway, savored as 'stolen moments together' (along with close to two million other subway riders).

Eddie Lyons—just back from Spain!

In the late 1930s, there was a new enticing diversion: Eddie Lyons, who had flown with anti-fascist Loyalist forces in Spain[14] bought a two-seater biplane when he

14. Lyons, a former shoe salesman, first flew transports, then served for six months as a wing commander in a Loyalist bombing squadron, later specializing in ground strafing. It turns out Eddie Lyons (whose original name was Edwin Leibowitz) was also the first flight instructor for the Etzel underground's one and only 1939 pilot course at Lod Airport, a flight school called the Palestine Flying Service. See Marvin G. Goldman, "From Flying Camels to Flying Stars: Israel Reborn (1917-1948)",

Pearl and Eddie Lyons' biplane

returned. The guys — Gil, Mike Frankel and others, would go out to the airport with their spouses, to tinker with the plane and hawk flights to tourists at $5 a ride — the 'pay' being a free ride when business was slow. That iconic photo of Pearl's 'maiden flight' — photographed wearing a bathing suit and a leather aviator helmet — was the upshot of the girls having just come back from a nearby beach where they would go while the guys were working on the plane. Eddie had asked, "Pearly, you wanna go up for a spin?" And she said, "Sure!"

By then Gil and Pearl were married — just how long depends on how one does the math...

Just Married! Not Once. Not Twice. But Three Times!

Gil and Pearl Weiss were together — in fact, inseparable as a couple — for 66 years, and were married for 62 years...or 64, depending on how one reckons things.

In fact, they got married *three times* — once secretly on 11 May 1935 when they walked into a 5th Avenue synagogue accompanied

---

Israel Airline Museum, https://www.israelairlinemuseum.org/el-al-israels-flying-star/.chapter-1-from-flying-camels-to-flying-stars-israel-reborn/. Afterwards he flew briefly with the Chinese Air Force, before returning to the USA. After the Second World War he established his own flying school (Lyons Flying Service at Zahn's Airport on Long Island).

by Pearl's sister Ruth and her husband, and asked the rabbi to marry them, and the second time publicly in a unique 'double ceremony' a month apart. First they got married in city hall in Perth Amboy on 27 February 1937 using a fake New Jersey address so the WPA wouldn't get wind of the fact that Pearl was married, and fire her from her job.[15] The second time, a *second* Jewish wedding ceremony — but the first as far as the family was concerned, one accompanied by a *ketubah* (Jewish marriage contract), which was held at the Washington Palace on 21 March 1937. Suffice it to say, with a $25 rental fee and a $25 band, it was no palace. When they ran out of food for the 100 or so guests, Uncle Ben Reiter was sent out to get sandwiches from a nearby deli.

The reason (for one secret and one public marriage, not the sandwiches): Gil and Pearl were conservatives[16] — at least as far as sex goes, not politics. Having waited way too long to lose their virginity (four and a half years after they started courting), Gil was having quote "heart palpitations" that the family physician Dr. Greiver[17] said would only be cured by finally bedding his sweetheart, not just going out to an isolated spot with Pop Weiss' car to 'spoon'.[18] While not everyone

---

15. The Works Progress Administration was the most ambitious New Deal initiative, designed to keep the unemployed off the dole by employing them in public works' projects. WPA jobs (Pearl's teaching homebound children, then as a research assistant designing intelligence tests) were tailored for individuals who had no other source of income and if she married and her husband was working she would no longer be eligible for a WPA-funded job.

16. Other members of the family and friends were far less inhibited...and not just Ruth, the flapper. On the flapper subculture of the 1920s, see Sarah Pruitt, "How Flappers Redefined Womanhood (Hint: It Involved Jazz, Liquor and Sex)", History, https://www.history.com/news/flappers-roaring-20s-women-empowerment, and Liton Weeks, "When 'Petting Parties' Scandalized the Nation", https://www.npr.org/sections/npr-history-dept/2015/05/26/409126557/when-petting-parties-scandalized-the-nation.

17. The same general practitioner who had correctly diagnosed Pearl with rheumatic fever, not scarlet fever, when she was a kid.

18. 'Spooning' (and petting/necking/making out without quote 'going all the way') are innocuous terms for a host of activities deemed permissible by a couple (with widely varying margins) of what 'Everything but...' means. That

in their generation was straight-laced, in their minds full premarital sex was out of the question, so they secretly got married to have sex... secretly! But they couldn't afford to *live* together as Gil was still going to school. So, for two more years they met secretly at Ruth's apartment (party to their 'secret') and frequented $10 hotels signing in as "Mr. and Mrs. Weiss"... This situation — legally married but living apart and meeting at most on weekends — continued from May 1935 through June 1939.

---

can be incredibly varied and exceedingly erotic...or rather unimaginative and limiting — while in all cases thinking one is still 'a virgin'... Suffice it to say, I never pried as to what Pearl and Gil did and didn't do during this four-and-a-half year courtship, until they secretly tied the knot in order to have full intercourse, but 'heart palpitations' suggests — poor Gil — that the two of them were very Old School. A prudish attitude towards sex lasted well into the mid-1960s and beyond. As noted earlier, when Wendy returned to the dating scene after separating from her husband, our father clashed with Wendy over what two consenting adults could and couldn't do in *his* basement while also making it clear to me — twenty at the time and living in Philly — that it was 'improper' to have closed the door behind me when I went to wake my visiting boyfriend mid-morning (who was expected to sleep in a separate room) while the two of us were visiting the folks. By 1972, however, Gil had mellowed enough (by then I was 27 and in any case 6,000 miles away) that when Rafi insisted he needed to 'ask Gil for my hand' saying in his limited English over the phone, "Gil, I want to marry your daughter! It's OK, yes?", Gil quipped afterwards to Pearl: "Hummm, he didn't ask my permission to *move in* with her (we were living together); he only asked if he could *marry* her..."

Chapter IV

Building a Career and a Family

Gil — An Engineer in Every Way

Charles Lindbergh's flight across the Atlantic in the *Spirit of St. Louis* in 1927 when Gil was 12 years old was a pivotal event; it was then and there that he became determined to become an aeronautical engineer. It took him six and a half years to complete his engineering degree — course-by-course at night school at NYU while working as a factory laborer by day to support himself and pay his tuition.

When he graduated Gil still wasn't sure he would ever get a job as an engineer because of discrimination against Jews, His name was as 'Jewish' as they come...but he rejected the idea of changing it to Wallace, as others of his generation had done.[1] The job applications he sent out remained unanswered, despite graduating

Gil's 80th Birthday (1995), 'flying' a toy airplane present

1. For example, the Abbotts were originally Abrams. The most ironic case of name changing was the Summers — one of the Weiss-Jaffe-Silverman-Summers Quartet. Harold ('Curly') Summers was one of three brothers. Harold and Robert (the latter, an economics professor at the University of Pennsylvania) changed their last name to Summers but it was the *third* brother Paul Samuelson who won the Nobel Prize in Economics.

at the top of his class — *magna cum laude*. Pearl recalled those days:

> Gil got a letter from the head of the aeronautical engineering department Dr. Clemens sent to McDonnell about himself and Mike Frankel[2] praising them — 'about these two young men who had gone to night school and were his outstanding students' in the hopes this would help them get a job. [...] They couldn't get an interview — not at Boeing, not at McDonnell. None of the companies bothered to interview them. We think it was because they were Jewish. [...] Clemens must have been really aggravated [at the lack of a response from the top companies] if he told Mike he was Jewish.

Professor Clemens — a 'closet Jew' who had changed his name to hide his Jewish origins — didn't give up and it was he who helped Gil finally land his first job at Burnelli:

> Clemens had a previous student — a Jewish guy who was several classes ahead of Gil — and Dr. Clemens called him and said "find 'um a job". I don't know what else he might have told him but that's how Gil got his first aero engineering job — at $25 a week.

Pearl noted in a 2009 tape, the irony of the big aircraft manufacturers not even answering Gil's applications back in 1938:

> Gil [by then a well-regarded figure in naval aviation and a highly-placed expert in design and procurement processes] was offered a lot of jobs by private industry on the QT [off-the-record] since they were forbidden from trying to lure him away — the same companies that wouldn't even

---

2. Pearl related: "Mike worked at the Naval Aircraft Factory in Philadelphia with Gil, but left to work for Budd Engineering that makes cars and trains, including the special buses ['mobile lounges' or PTVs — DA] that transport passengers between planes and terminal and while he did well financially, he never had anything to do with designing an airplane".

> give him an interview when he finished college because he was Jewish...
>
> There were some jobs — one or two — that were very tempting, since they offered twice what he was making, but Gil liked where he was and we loved the security of a government job which was very important to us as Children of the Depression.

~ *Navy Through and Through*

Back in late 1938, Gil's first job as a design engineer at Burnelli Aircraft paid $1,500 a year. Nine months later he landed a civil service job with the Navy. Gil saved a draft copy of his Civil Service Examination — which is priceless. The questions ranged from "What's the speed of light?" to "What's the energy of a 64-gram body moving at a speed of 10 cm per second?" and "Given the frequency of Middle C is 256, find the frequency three octaves above Middle C". Gil wrote that the lowest salary he was willing to accept was $1,620...a year, and only east of the Mississippi, but he was willing to settle for as little as one, three or six months' employment. In any case, $1,620 was a significant advance from the $884/year he earned as a shipping clerk in the garment industry in 1932 or the $936/year he earned as a laborer in a tobacco pipe factory up until mid-1937, while going to night school at NYU.

In fact, Gil stayed with the federal government and the Navy not for three months, but for over three decades (March 1939–May 1970). At the close of his career as a civilian working for the Navy (before contracting as a consultant for private industry) Gil Weiss was a GS-16 or GS-17 'supergrade' — a special high-level rank in the federal civil service at $18,000 a year that had to be approved by the Congress. But he began his Navy career at the bottom of the pay scale — as a P-1 grade.

The acceptance letter from the federal civil service, dated 14 March 1939, said that Gil would be posted as a Junior Aeronautical Engineer at the Naval Aircraft Factory in Philadelphia — at $2,000 an annum. While this was accompanied by a period living at the YMCA, then a boarding house, the job paved the way for a glorious summer during which Gil commuted to his job in Philly by Navy barge every morning from the couple's tiny Atlantic City apartment on the ocean — the first time Pearl and Gil actually *lived* together as man and wife although they had been married since 1935. Enjoy the privacy? A family affair, the pull-out sofa on a little porch became the plush destination for New York family as a 'free vacation'. Pearl reminisced:

> In the summer you didn't teach. I got to Philly and I go to sleep in this room that Gil had [in a boarding house] and it was an attic room and I always wilted in the heat anyway. I was simply dying. I only stayed a few days... Kaplan[3] [Gil's boss, who lived in Atlantic City] suggested to Gil that instead of getting an apartment in Philadelphia for the summer, we look for an apartment in Atlantic City. [...] That's how we came to rent a cottage[4] on the ocean, and all the relatives got a free vacation. No, they didn't come for a weekend; they came for a week or two weeks at a time. The whole family got a vacation (except Pop Weiss who couldn't close his business).

In late fall 1939 Gil Weiss was promoted to a P-2 grade Assistant Aeronautical Engineer position and was transferred to the Bureau of Aeronautics at the Navy Yard in Washington with a salary of $2,600 per annum...but not before Pearl quit her WPA job and joined Gil in Philly, where they lived for six weeks in an apartment-hotel on Walnut Street feeling they had no other option but a hotel[5] while waiting for him to receive his transfer orders:

> It was hot and I slept by the window, and it was very noisy, because people were coming in and out of the hotel at all

3. Pearl never said anything in the tapes...but *Kaplan*? Was this also a case where a fellow Member of the Tribe helped Gil get a job as a Jewish engineer when he had a job opening — allowing Gil to demonstrate his worth?

4. Actually a one-bedroom holiday unit attached to the landlord's house.

5. They didn't know they could rent an apartment and legally break the lease without penalty, if Gil was ordered by the Federal Government to relocate.

> hours of the night. It turned out that the building was occupied by a lot of prostitutes...but the girls were very nice and pleasant in the elevator and we didn't get to know them personally.
>
> [...] One day, Gil came home from work with a ticket on his jacket 'Washington — Here We Come!' and he asks me: "Pearly, how would you like to go live in Washington, DC?" This was like going to live on the moon.

His orders from the Secretary of the Navy to report for work in Washington "at the earliest practical date" were dated 31 October 1939 — two months after the outbreak of the Second World War in Europe. The appointment letter told him:

> ...as this transfer is in the interest of the Government, and as it is more economical and advantageous to the Government you are hereby authorized to use your personally owned automobile in performing this travel, and you will be allowed expenses on a mileage basis at the rate of 3 cents per mile for transportation.

Gil began work on 1 December 1939, along with George Spangenberg[6] — who was recruited to BuAer's Engineering Branch from the Naval Aircraft Factory together with Gil. But George recalled (in his eulogy to Gil in 1998) that he receive $4.23 for the 141 mile trip between Philadelphia and Washington, while Gil received nothing because he had used a car registered to someone else... Ultimately, the pair (George and Gil) took up residence in the "W" building — one of the first prefabs built in the Naval Yard compound to accommodate the influx of new personnel — located within sight of the Reflecting Pool. Gil Weiss was one of the first Jewish aeronautical engineers to work for the government.

In his memoirs,[7] George Spangenberg recalled what made 'going to

---

6. Gil's boss at the Navy Yard.

7. The taped and transcribed interviews that constitute an oral history of

Washington' so attractive that rather than accepting any of the jobs he was offered at Lockheed, Glen Martin and McDonnell Aircraft[8] Spangenberg decided to stay with the Navy, accepted the job at BuAer, and remained there his entire career for a much lower salary:

> BuAer was one of the places that took a look at the whole airplane rather than pieces as you might get if you went to work [for one of the aircraft manufacturers] in a power-plant section or other specialty groups in those days. [...] Washington was obviously the best place to go [...] My boss [Frisbie] had been given the title of 'Design Coordination' and head of the 'Contract Airplane Design' section of the Engineering branch. [that evolved to become the Evaluation Division — DA]. I became his right-hand man and Gil Weiss his left hand.

In the course of their careers, Gil and George discovered that weight was a curtail factor in performance — founding a special society of weight engineers. At BuAer, Gil gradually took over responsibility for all naval aviation weight and balance matters. In 1941 he became the first head of the Bureau's newly-established Weight Control Branch — a position he would hold for 16 years that spanned the Second World War and the Korean War.

---

naval aviation from 1938 to 1973 can be accessed at Judith B. (Spangenberg) Currier's, "George Spangenberg Oral History", https://www.docdroid.com/x9czNLE/george-spangenberg-oral-history-pdf, or at aviation enthusiast Ron Downey's aviation history site, Aviation Archives, http://aviationarchives.blogspot.com/2018/02/george-spangenberg-oral-history.html.

8. Spangenberg said in the tapes: "By that time the situation in the country was that aeronautical job opportunities were available virtually everywhere and the companies were looking for people with a bit of experience so we all started getting job offers". ['We' apparently didn't include Jews... — DA] McDonnell Aircraft, to which Gil had sent an inquiry that remained unanswered, was a fledgling but growing manufacturer, and James McDonnell came to Philly personally to interview prospective employees such as George. McDonnell and Douglas only merged in 1967.

The May 1952 *Official Register of the Civil Service Commission* of "persons occupying administrative and supervisory positions in the legislative, executive, and judicial branches of the Federal Government, and in the District of Columbia Government" (archived online), duly noted the major players in the Navy's Evaluation Division and their salaries:

> William Z. Frisbie Director $12,200 (salary); George A. Spangenberg Assistant Director $10,800; Otto H. Lunde Head, Aircraft Proposals Branch $8,960; Charles S. Butt, Jr. Assistant Head, Aircraft Proposals Branch $7,440; Gilbert Weiss, Head Weight Control Division $9,600; and Keith Dentel Assistant Head, Weight Control Division $8,300.

The Society of Allied Weight Engineers' international journal *Weight Engineering*—published an unprecedented full-page *In Memoria* to

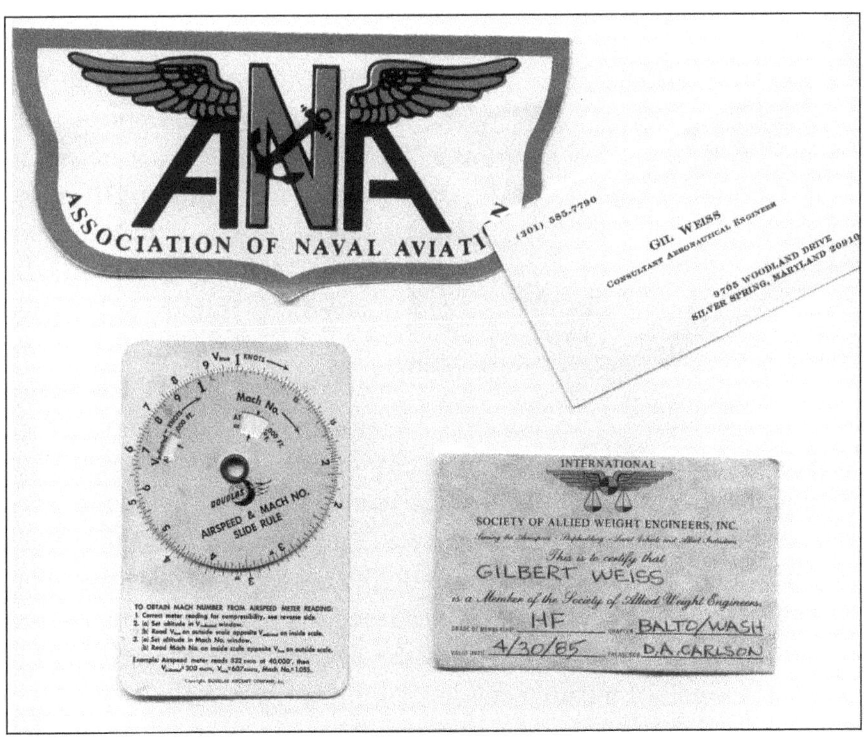

'Navy through and through'

Gil on the *opening page* of its Fall 1998 edition,[9] recapping milestones in his career:

> [...] During Gil's 16 years as Head of Weights at BuAer, he made major contributions to increasing the quality, standardization, engineering rigor and professionalism of the weight and balance discipline. He led the effort to standardize weight and balance forms, handbooks, and procedures for Naval aviation, and he was a firm advocate for establishing firm, but achievable, contract weight guarantees and explicit weight control requirements, including frequent periodic reporting to the customer.

~

Gil at the W building

Don't be misled by the professional jargon: In fact, the guys were a wacky group who in 1951 wrote a spoof marriage manual for one of the guy's wedding night written in BuAer or BuWeps jargon — which Gil naturally saved... ("You are authorized to utilize all tactical maneuvers necessary, within the structural limitations of equipment involved, for successful completion of this mission.") They conducted 10¢ betting pools on the date their wives would deliver — Gil having saved the one he won in 1946 — racking up $1.50 in profits. And they played practical jokes on one another, even on the boss, Bill Frisbie. According to Keith Dentel, Gil's engineers once laced his pipe tobacco with cut-up rubber bands...and Gil extended the suspense by pretending not to notice the smell of burning rubber that filled the room.

---

9. The full scanned article is among the obituaries in Chapter VI.

Gil wrote rhyming verse, oft with fractured cadence, for a host of occasions, personal and professional. One 'masterpiece' (the occasion remains shrouded in mystery) was an ode to a 1966 Vietnam-era troop-carrying helicopter that noted:

> The weight's too high! The ceiling's too low!
> The takeoff's too long! The hi-speed's too slow
> [...] The G's not there. Drag's gone to pot
> In South Viet Nam the cockpits too hot
>
> [...] No tread and bitty engine too.
> No weight, no cost — but there were damned few
> Who'd believe such a miracle could really be true.
> And 'twoud only be fantasy if it ever flew.

But working at the Navy Department had its moments. The Navy wasn't the Federal Bureau of Statistics where there were a slew of Jewish employees. Awareness of and sensitivity to antisemitism was a 'learning process' for George and the guys with whom Gil worked for 30 years — none of them Jewish. Jewish engineers in the Navy Yard were a rarity in those days (and may still be at a premium even today for all I know).[10] George Spangenberg would say in his eulogy (with gentlemanly delicacy) that there were "places Gil didn't go and places he avoided" suggesting there had been more than one antisemitic encounter — intended and unintentional — that muddied the atmosphere. George stressed that he himself hadn't been present at any of the incidents (plural). One particular painful one that Gil had shared with family was when the guys from the office reserved a place at a restaurant on the Eastern Shore of Maryland (sometime in the 1950s, since the Chesapeake Bay Bridge was only opened in 1951). When they got there, there was a sign at the entrance "No Jew Allowed". His office colleagues told Gil to just ignore it — shrugging it off as no big deal.

10. Gil noted to close family repeatedly with pride the presence of another Member of the Tribe in the Navy — Admiral Hyman Rickover, "Father of the Nuclear Navy".

But Gil refused to go in and they had to go look for another place to eat. George and Gil shared a passion not only for aviation but also gardening and woodworking, thus George felt comfortable enough to approach Gil to consult with him on a private 'non-work' matter—a quandary that Spangenberg chose to share in his eulogy at Gil's funeral:

> In the process of buying a house in an established area of Arlington I received a phone call from my wife Lillian, who had been called by someone involved in the mortgage process questioning whether 'we the Spangenbergs were, in fact, Jewish'. There were restrictions against Jews and other races in the deed. Could we prove our 'non-Jewish-ness'? I was abashed to say the least, and wanted to talk to Gil but didn't want to offend him in any way. I thought I knew him well enough that it wouldn't be a problem, so I turned the question around and asked Gil: "How did he prove he was Jewish?"[11] His reply, which didn't really solve 'my problem' was to say with a twinkle in his eye: "George, I've never had that problem".

It's amusing that in 1998 George had turned the question around in his mind (perhaps showing he *had* learned something) since he had, in fact, asked Gil "how can I prove I'm not Jewish?" and receiving the same cool reply. Little did he know, this incident and its details had become part of Weiss family lore... What's really interesting is, to his dying day in November 2000, Gil's boss and close colleague was completely oblivious that *choosing* to buy that house and *agreeing* to sign what in the 1950s and early 1960s was called a "restrictive covenant" that prohibited owners from selling their homes to 'Jews and Negros', said something about himself, nor could George fathom how such a choice on his part would go down with Gil...

There were other classic family stories about Gil's years with the Navy—years marked by our dad repeatedly calling home from the

11. In 1948 such racially restrictive contracts were ruled "unenforceable but legal" by the United States Supreme Court...whatever that says in the subtext.

office to say, excitedly, that there were people skating on the Reflecting Pool, and as we gathered our ice skates, Gil calling from the office to say the police were chasing people off the Reflecting Pool. If the ice was ever thick enough to make ice skating safe, *we* never got to ice skate on the Reflecting Pool even once... But there was the privilege of accompanying Gil to air shows at the Anacostia Air Base. Mementos of his travels for work included a small static-filled square cardboard 33 RPM phonograph recording mailed from post-war London that sounds like it was sent from Mars, and a long-lost glossy souvenir album from the aircraft carrier *USS Ticonderoga*.

In 1957, Gil was promoted to Assistant Director of the Bureau's Evaluation Division, when George Spangenberg became Director of the Evaluation Division with Frisbie's retirement.

Despite his herculean efforts, it seems weight was *still* a nagging problem a decade later, reflected in a memo written in January 1967 in which Gil Weiss suggested an "Incentive/Penalty Clause for Weight Empty and Vehicle Performance". Over a period of decades, the Evaluation Division developed guidelines and yardsticks for source selection in design competition to replace 1950-vintage procurement procedures that Gil labeled "over-optimism and 'brochuremanship', selling and buying on 'promises', poor checks and balances in the selection process, and unsophisticated evaluations" that Gil wrote, should be replaced by "procedural and decision-making controls, honesty on the part of the proposer coupled with higher-level controls over the buyer [...] and making the seller bear the responsibilities for his commitments".

'Source selection' — described in rough terms — was a process that spanned setting the proposed aircraft's mission capacities upon which the giant aircraft manufacturers such as Boeing, General Dynamics, McDonnell-Douglas, Grumman and so forth needed to base their designs; examining the blueprints and mockups of the proposals presented by the competing manufacturers (and independently evaluating their performance claims); and finally, deciding which bid (design submitted) was the best and would be awarded the lucrative multibillion-dollar Navy contract.

How many different submissions were they juggling in any one design competition? In a January 1962 memorandum Gil mentioned a design competition for a "carrier-based aircraft with sophisticated all-weather attack capability [and] a complex integrated attack-navigation system". Grumman won this competition, receiving $3.4 M — a standard fee believed to cover "preliminary engineering and design data, wind tunnel models and wind tunnel testing, and a wooden mock-up" for their winning design. In the above competition, Grumman was selected as the contractor after "a design competition in which proposals were solicited from 13 firms and received from 8". George and Gil's evaluation team had to examine all eight bids — including whether each proposal really did what it claimed to do.

Gil's career as a civilian engineer with the Navy spanned the Second World War to the Vietnam War, as he rose from the position of a junior engineer to become deputy director of the Evaluation Division.[12]

~

The history of naval aviation itself was registered in scores of official resin scale models bearing Navy insignias made by the companies of the bombers, fighter jets, helicopters and other aircraft manufactured for the Navy that decorated special shelves Gil built in the basement of the house in Silver Spring. He finally donated his collection that ranged from Second Word War bombers to modern jets like the Wildcat, the Hellcat and the Tomcat, to the Air & Space Museum in Washington, DC.

The only plane *not* on display in Gil's collection was General Dynamics' tactical fighter...the infamous F-111 — an inferior design chosen by Secretary of Defense Robert McNamara in 1962, over the heads of George and Gil (in fact, over the heads of the *entire* Pentagon Source Selection Board[13] of generals and admirals from the Army, Navy and Air Force) who had all chosen Boeing's submission as better designed, cheaper and more suitable for the multiple missions outlined in the

---

12. While George and Gil didn't always see eye-to-eye, anyone interested in a detailed history of the Evaluation Division can read relevant parts of transcripts of taped interviews with George Spangenberg (the man has a photographic memory for detail). See the URLs in note 7 of this chapter.

13. A joint Air Force-Navy undertaking, originally initiated by the Air Force.

design competition. McNamara overruled them, and at one point, when asked "why" he retorted, "*Because* [he could]!" with no logical explanation why he chose the design of General Dynamics — awarding the $6.5 B contract to the economically-troubled aircraft company in Texas — a decision that became known as the TFX Scandal (from the design model in the bid: Tactical Fighter, with 'X' standing for experimental rather than operational aircraft). The affair was investigated by Congress in 1963 on suspicion of serious conflicts of interest at the higher political echelons. In 1968, the Navy canceled its orders for the strange bird due to weight and performance issues.[14]

One of the two things[15] that could get our mild-mannered Dad agitated were certain things at work — and not just the TFX, but disagreements with George Spangenberg. While he considered his work challenging and fulfilling, there were far too many times that Gil would come home from work, put his briefcase on the sidewalk as soon as he walked up the driveway, and commence decapitating dandelions and yanking up crabgrass for a good hour before coming in for dinner — probably in lieu of tearing out the hair he didn't have or quitting his job.

Indeed, at one point in his professional life, Gil dreamed of a career change, fueled by aspirations to play a role in the space program. He

---

14. For an inside look, Gil's boss George Spangenberg discussed the F-111 at length in the transcripts of his memoirs, describing the three-ring circus of trying to design a one-design-fits-all plane with conflicting objectives and capabilities. See particularly pages 240-243 in Judith (Spangenberg) Currier, "George Spangenberg Oral History", https://www.docdroid.com/x9czNLE/george-spangenberg-oral-history-pdf or http://aviationarchives.blogspot.com/2018/02/george-spangenberg-oral-history.html. In addition, allegations were raised of possible political meddling based on vested interests behind the decision to award the contract to financially-troubled Texas-based General Dynamics. For an interesting 'period piece', see "The TFX Unveiled; McNamara Hails It", *The New York Times*, 16 October 1964, https://www.nytimes.com/1964/10/16/archives/the-tfx-unveiled-mcnamara-hails-it.html.

15. The other was my failure to fathom algebra.

approached NASA and was elated when they said they had a job for him.[16] He resigned from his senior civil service post with the Navy Department, and took his first extended vacation 'between jobs'...only to return to Washington to find out the job he was to begin, had somehow 'evaporated' into thin air! While his boss Spangenberg at the Navy Yard was thrilled to immediately reinstate him in his old position as deputy director of the Evaluation Division, the shock of 'finding himself without a job', even ever-so-briefly, left Gil — a Son of the Depression — shaken to the core. He never again so much as toyed with the thought of changing jobs and remained in his position with the Navy until retirement in 1970, after more than 30 years of service.

At his retirement party, the guys presented Gil with a humorous framed portrayal of the Source Selection Process as a memento (a process Gil had largely codified in writing since, unlike many engineers, he was skilled at writing coherently). The cartoon showed Gil and George determining the winner of the design competition by throwing darts at a target, blindfolded...a cartoon that hung in the basement office in Potomac for decades... His navy-blue front license plate with its signature golden wings saying "Fly Navy" sits on a high shelf to the right of my computer.

Gilbert Weiss' contributions to naval air power were recognized not only in membership in a host of professional organizations but also by the Distinguished Civilian Service Award[17] — the highest honorary

16. No one seems to know what the position was or what it entailed but any casual observer of the space program is aware of the sensitivity of weight as a crucial factor in payloads, reentry capsules, etc. Thus, I imagine (again, this is conjecture only) that this position was somehow connected to his expertise in management of design competitions or weight issues or precision in procurement. Some of the complexities of weight as a factor are reflected indirectly in the wonderful movie *Hidden Figures* about the role of African-American female mathematicians (called computers!) back in the days when complex calculations were based on pure brain power — using slide rules, not computers. Rafi still has Gil's slide rule... (One never knows when one will need a slide rule...)

17. Presented to Gil in May 1970 at his retirement ceremony, by Rear Admiral Tom Walker, Commander of the Naval Air Systems Command.

award the Secretary of the Navy can confer on a civilian employee of the Navy Department.

Going to Work for Grumman

Following his retirement in 1970, Gil was hired as a private consultant by Grumman Aircraft — using his expertise in source selection to critique Grumman's designs, and thus give them a better edge in winning Navy contracts. He did this by pointing out flaws in Grumman's designs and written proposals, accompanying them when they presented their proposal orally in person to Navy personnel. He worked in this capacity for a decade — flying up to Grumman on Long Island several times a month.

Dedicated Service Award

Did Grumman expect 'more' from him — a good word on the QT in 'the right places'? Fulfilling such a 'leveraging role' to influence the outcomes of a design competition never crossed his mind. Had he been asked he would not only have flatly refused but would have been devastated that anyone would think he would agree to such a thing or that the Evaluation Division with the objective procedures of source selection he himself had put in place, could be swayed in their decision not solely on the merits of design and performance. As the *Weight Engineering* journal noted — Gil Weiss was straight as an arrow:

> He was of the highest integrity, honest, dedicated, positive-minded, energetic, hard-and long-workings, thorough and tenacious (some would say stubborn!) for what he believed was right.
>
> [...] He was without any of the 'airs' that often

> accompany those in higher positions; he worked with everyone as an equal. He treated everyone with the greatest friendliness and respect and, more, always showed the greatest interest in and concern for others' personal lives and families.

An Unconsummated 'Courtship' with Israeli Aviation

No discussion of Gil's career would be complete without mentioning his unconsummated 'courtship' with Israel's aeronautical engineering community, which never took off.

After I spent a gap year in Israel, in 1963/4 with plans to immigrate to Israel, slyly and slowly I planted the notion in Gil's head that when he retired, he could go teach at the Technion, until my father began to repeat this mantra.

When the Six-Day War broke out, Gil took a reckless step that was totally out of character. Watching me drop everything[18] to fly to Israel

Distinguished Service Award, 1970

18. In the middle of final exams in my senior year at Temple University

on 30 May as one of the first Six-Day War volunteers, and shocked by Israel's isolation and the world's indifference to the fate of the Jewish state, despite his top security clearance and demanding job at the Navy Department and throwing caution to the wind, Gil marched into the Israeli Embassy and volunteered to go to Israel "to drive a tractor on a kibbutz". Taking one look at his CV, embassy staff chucked the 'tractor offer' and arranged a *shidduch* ('match') with the Technion (Israel's MIT)... Thus Gil was invited to spend a month in Israel in July–August 1967 'volunteering' at the Technion's Aeronautical Engineering Department.

The faculty asked Gil to give them a critique of their engineering curriculum. The curriculum, he quickly discovered, was highly theoretical, while in the same breath requiring each student in their last year of studies to 'design an airplane' as a final project. Gil explained to the professors that the program was too theoretical and lacked practical applied engineering skills and "nobody designs an airplane singlehanded these days — at most they design a wing strut". The advice fell on deaf ears. Feeling like a duck out of water, Gil banished any further thoughts of teaching at the Technion after he retired, although the visit did cement a lifelong friendship with the chief administrator of the Aero Engineering Department Moshe Nimrod and others he met while serving as one of the oldest and oddest Six-Day War volunteers.

Not one to give up, after Gil retired in 1970, I began brainwashing him to investigate coming to Israel to work for Israel Aircraft Industries where — conveniently — I was working in the human resources department.[19] I arranged an interview at IAI while the folks were visiting

---

although my professors passed me anyway on the basis of my work up until that point, and let me graduate *in absentia*. The only instructor who declined to waive the final was my statistics professor (Jewish) whom I'm convinced passed me for showing up for the exam hours before I left for the airport — an exam I took cold without even cracking the book.

19. In the office that orchestrated hiring engineers from abroad, then assisting the newly-recruited Jewish engineers get settled in Israel — personnel who had been enticed with attractive personal contracts to take jobs at IAI due to the economic slump in the American aircraft industry at the time — a brain drain in reverse.

Israel after Gil's retirement, but this never led to a job offer and he accepted a consultant position with Grumman. Objectively, his expertise in source selection has little relevance to IAI's operations.[20]

❧ *Afterhours with an Engineering Mindset*

Gil was an engineer no matter what he did. He filled the house with graphs and drafts and charts — whether he was concocting a graph to show how much of an audiotape was spent when recording operas on eight-inch reels; designing the mahogany buffet; laying out the floor plan and sketching the Cape Cod-style dormer (peak) of the house on Woodland Drive...or dreaming up a 'rod bender'.

He used spreadsheets for everything long before Excel became a modern management tool. Seasonal plantings were plotted on spreadsheets with placement, plant, type, height, germination, transplant height and remarks. Any actual purchase, be it a camera or a dishwasher or a car, was preceded by countless forays to examine all the options; all information was carefully laid out on graph paper prior to purchase, duly noting not only the features and cost of dozens of models and the location of the stores but also the name of the salesperson who helped him investigate this or that gadget or appliance at length, so he could both return to ask more questions...and make sure that particular sales associate would get the sales commission for their help

---

20. At the time, IAI was in the advanced stages of designing the Lavi (ultimately shot down in midflight when the United States ceased underwriting the aircraft's development — not only because the development costs were chronically beyond predictions, but also out of fear that the Lavi would complete with American warplanes in world markets). But the visit to IAI wasn't without reward. Gil ran into Gene Salvay (a senior Jewish engineer of his own generation in the aircraft design industry whom Gil knew professionally, for Salvay had been the first Jewish employee at North American Aviation). Gene had been cherry-picked ('headhunted') for a key position at IAI and the two reconnected after I began throwing out names of IAI 'acquisitions' perhaps he knew... Although Salvay returned to the States at the end of the his one-year contract, the 'flirt' with IAI, purely by coincidence, set in motion a lifetime friendship with Betty and Gene Salvay for both Pearl and Gil, and Rafi and myself.

and patience. Once chosen, instructions for every appliance ever purchased were archived permanently, most accompanied by the original warranty and sales slip attached. He fired off countless letters about appliances that went haywire or needed a replacement part — at times with some piquant details for the warehouse about the 'history' of the wayward device, why the malfunction was a safety issue, the identity of the owner and who would install the part.

Gil was 'wired' before computers became household items...that is, Democracy Lane revealed a labyrinth of stereo wires that ran along baseboards and under rugs, connecting dozens of speakers and VCRs scattered about the house that constantly played classical music — particularly opera. Although the year he died Gil was busy mastering the ins and outs of computers at age 83, sending long and detailed emails to mentors far and wide,[21] he never discarded his trusty Dalton Dead

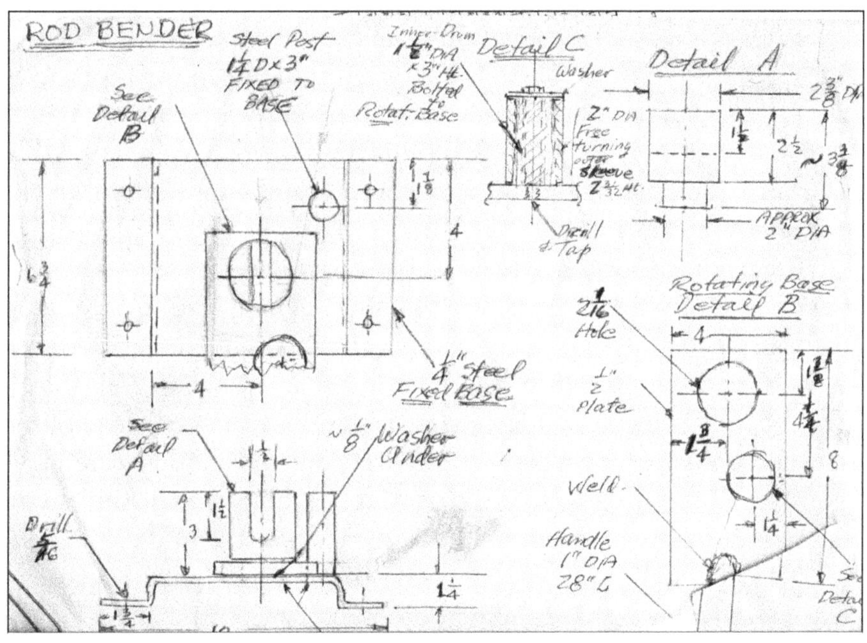

Rod bender

21. Don't miss David Platt's story at the back of the book about Matt from technical support at his Internet service provider...who came to Gil's funeral although he never met Gil face-to-face!

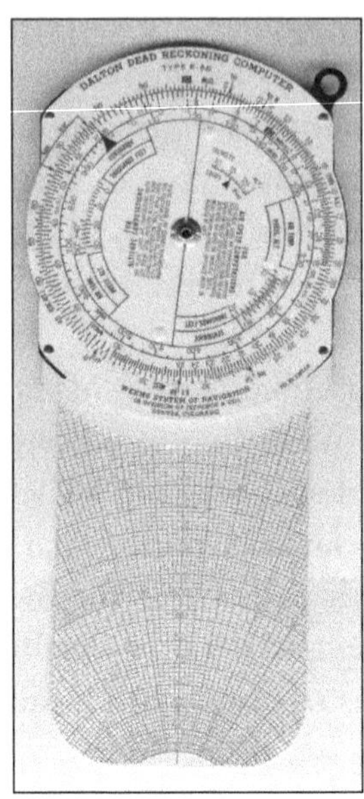

Dead reckoning computer

Reckoning Computer — a mechanical gadget that looks as sophisticated as a mariner's sextant, armed with turning wheels and graphs and used to compute airspeed and altitude. And he remained firmly attached to the world's first computer...or at least packaging — a flat, empty 10 x 2" cardboard box stamped "If in storage after 17 MAY 1953 the computer shall be tested and inspected before issue in accordance with T.C. 05-1-1".

~ *Recycling and Repurposing with Gil*

The Weisses, it should be noted for the record, were pioneers and paragons of recycling — collected coffee grinds well before it became fashionable to recycle garbage as a combustible, or turn it into mulch. As far back as the mid-1950s, every day Gil carried the basket of coffee grinds from the percolator out to the Blue Spruce at the back of the lot in Silver Spring, cupped in his hands as if it was the Holy Grail.

The truth is Gil believed *every* object would eventually find a new life. A worn-out wrench became a tool for roughing up a surface when one wanted to glue two pieces of smooth material together.[22] An old shower door, the spring from a screen door, an elastic bicycle strap, a piece of clothesline, discarded strips of aluminum and dozens of little nuts and bolts became a glass cutter. But some inventions were ingeniously simple. One classic was a contraption that hung behind an oil painting in the living room that kept the canvas at a 90-degree angle, parallel to the wall — made from a wire coat hanger taped to a piece of Styrofoam with duct tape. Some of these jerry-rigged gizmos looked

22. The fun part of cleaning out the basement with Asaf was my son holding up something saying — *Ima*, what in the world is *THIS*???? And by golly, much to his amazement, I would scrutinize the repurposed item and in most cases I knew instinctively, knowing my father, what it was used for.

downright hazardous, but a few remain an unsolved mystery as to their function. Readers of this memoir are invited to hazard a guess as to their use and send their submission to me.

Yet, along with Gil's fondness for turning old wooden coat hangers into notched push sticks for the table saw and using unused checks from closed bank accounts as scrap paper, the contraption that was the epitome of an unbridled desire to tinker and let nothing go to waste sat next to the stereo corner. Although equipped with giant state-of-the-art speakers in the living room to match an excellent ear for music, Gil had taken an old Nordstrom shoebox to serve as a 'housing' for an

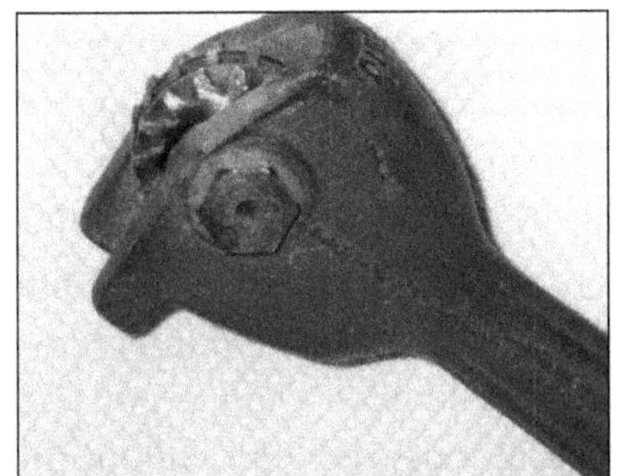

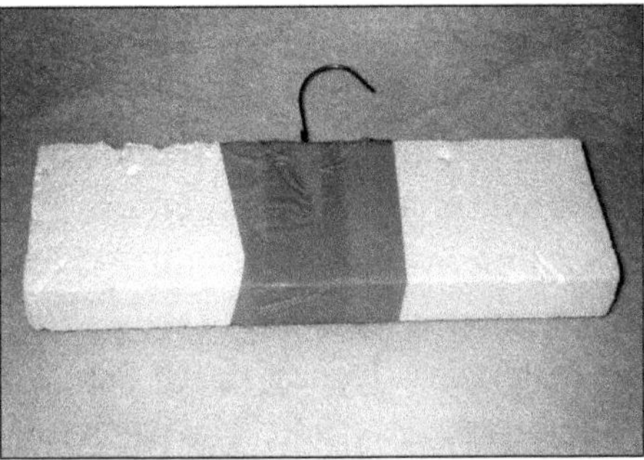

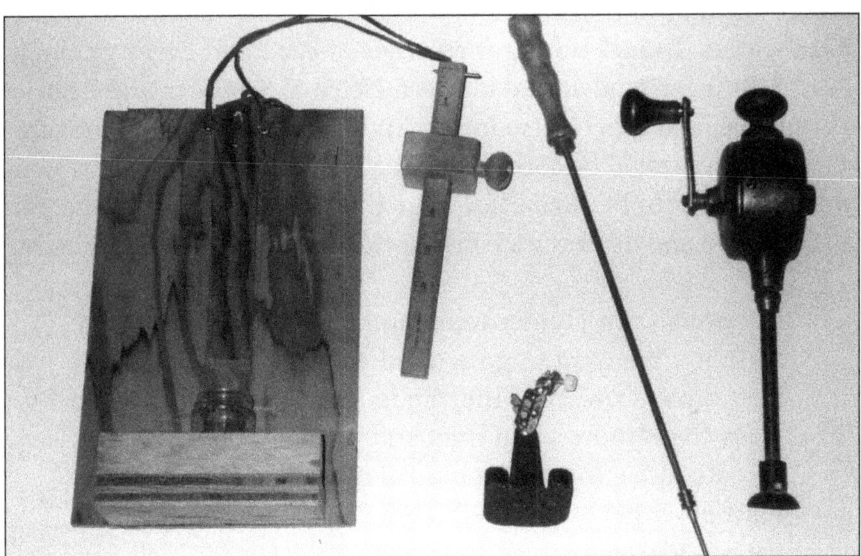

Top: Wrench turned 'rougher-upper' (L), Ultimate repurposing Good Junk (R)
Bottom: Gil's 'most mysterious' gizmos

old radio speaker which he backed with tissue paper from other shoeboxes that he hooked up to an old Walkman in order to create a radio. Among the items stashed in a back drawer of the bench, waiting to be resurrected, were used eyelash curlers with missing or deteriorating rubber and a handful of discarded garters. Go figure.

Pearl — The Ultimate Mentor

Graduation — Now What?

Although most women of her generation remained housewives, Pearl forged a career in education — first as a substitute elementary school teacher at Stanton Elementary School in southeast Washington and at Rollingwood Elementary in Maryland, then as a regular staff member at Arcola Elementary School. But at times, this took some prodding by women friends. There were only a few mementos of her career among the Memorabilia, but the contents of the taped interviews Pearl left as a legacy more than filled in the blanks. Pearl graduated Hunter in early 1936. The *New York Times* published a piece about the event — held in Carnegie Hall — with the headline "Hunter to Confer 472 Degrees Today" noting the names of each and every graduate. Pearl Schwarzer sandwiched between Helen S. Schwartz and Beatrice Vertheimer, and Ethel Netstein and Ruth Shanman. Most of the other 471 graduates would be competing for a handful of teaching jobs along with Pearl. But to be *eligible* for a teaching job, graduates had to pass an oral exam and demonstrate they spoke 'standard American English':

> My peers from Hunter were flunking the orals they were so strict. We used to go around college practicing 'How now, brown cow' and 'The rain in Spain falls mainly in the plain' to get our diction right and get rid of our New York accents...otherwise we would fail the oral exams. I passed, but I never got a job. There were no jobs for college graduates — few jobs and thousands of applicants for each one.

This was in early 1936 — when 16 percent of the veteran workforce was still unemployed and when, according to Pearl, "tall blue-eyed and blond-haired graduates of Ivy League colleges like Smith and Vassar were happy to get jobs as shop clerks at Bloomingdales and a short, dark-haired, buxom Jewish graduate from Hunter like herself couldn't even get a job as a shop clerk in a *schlock* shop[23] along 14th Street":

> I just couldn't get a job. I even gave up my pride and went to my relatives. [...] went to those Schwarzers begging them for a job (how much I hated doing that!). I knew I didn't have all the office skills but I told them I was a fast learner — and would they give me a job? All they had to pay me would be carfare and a couple of bucks a week so I could learn while working there — that I could answer the phone, keep ledgers, and so forth while learning some marketable business skills. Unfortunately, I had been in an academic program in high school and never learned to type, and definitely never learned stenography. I went there to ask the relatives for a job, and they turned me down.

This was the second and last time Pearl met the Other Schwarzers. The first time had been almost ten years earlier — at age ten:

> After my father died, I did meet one relative among the 'rich Schwarzers' (his name was Louie or Lee Schwarzer[24])

23. A Yiddish expression for shops selling cheap junky apparel along 14th Street, where the owners often stood outside cajoling passersby to come in and examine the merchandise. Pearl told me that she walked the entire length of 14th Street in high heels, going into every shop that looked promising, but no one was about to hire someone without business skills, if they were hiring at all. An April 1936 article in the *New York Times* about business practices during the Depression ("Business Leasing Covers Wide Area") cites La Mode Textiles — one of the businesses owned by the Other Shwarzers — was leasing 2,500 square feet (469 sq. meters) of warehousing in Manhattan.

24. The descendants of the Other Schwarzers have no recollection of a relative by the name Louis or Lee or Leo, and I found no such person online who would fit the profile.

who was very nice and kept in touch with us. One time he came and said this aunt [Dora Schwarzer — DA] "would really like to see the children". I remember my Uncle Abe made me a new coat for the occasion — a dark bottle green velvet coat with a leopard collar (My mother made sure we looked really nice because "they weren't gonna feel sorry for us!") [...] They lived on Riverside Drive in a very fancy elegant building and invited Ruth and me for lunch.

We sat down at this big dining room table with all this silverware at each plate — very formal with a maid serving the food. I kept watching my sister to see what she was doing. And I'm thinking "God know what kinda lunch we're gonna get" and believe it or not — we got eggs. Some kind of omelets, which was not what I thought I was going to get for lunch. [...] As we're leaving, this aunt presses something into my hand and says — "Buy yourself something! Whatever you want!" Outside my sister asks, "What did she give you?" and I open my hand and it's a small bill — something like $10 or $5 but definitely a miniscule amount even in those times. And we laughed and I said, "Well, it will buy me my gym suit..."[25] And we never heard from them again. The next time I saw the Schwarzers was when I finished college and couldn't find a job...

Teaching Homebound Children

Desperate, having exhausted all other avenues, in order to be eligible for a federally-funded WPA job designed to employ the homeless and unemployed, Pearl agreed to lie and swear under oath that she'd been kicked out of the house by her mother and had no way to support herself. Thus, in late 1936, she got her first teaching job — teaching homebound children. Pearl recalled those days:

Nobody was sent to teach them. and they weren't allowed

25. A gym uniform for physical education class consisting of a cotton shirt and bloomer shorts required for Physical Education class at school.

> in school because of their physical condition... I remember I had several epileptic kids, and a couple who were 'blue babies' — born with insufficient lung capacity so their skin has a bluish tint and they were not expected to live to maturity. [...] I can still picture the kids. [...] They were elementary school age — 2nd or 3rd graders. We taught them reading, writing and arithmetic. I went to each child three times a week, two children a day.
>
> They were so happy to see me and anxious to learn. [...] There was Frankie — about eight or nine years old, who would sit at the window and wait for me, and when he saw me he would get so excited that he would have an epileptic seizure and I couldn't teach him that day because after a seizure they usually slept. And I remember Rosa, whose parents owned a small dress shop where they sold housedresses and lived above the store. When she saw the teacher coming, she would bang her foot on the floor so they would hear her and come up [to unlock the door and let Pearl in].

Pearl, one should remember, was only 19 years old when she began teaching these children. She taught the homebound for about a year and a half, but the psychological burden became too much to bear:

> I found their condition so sad that I would come home and cry, and when I got assigned to the Lower East Side — 'that was it' (*sic* the straw that broke the camel's back) — really Crying Time. I would come home and simply lie down on the bed and cry. And my mother would try and console me, tell me I'm "doing good and think of that". But for me, working on the Lower East Side was personally traumatic because it reminded me how we used to live...and it was overwhelming.

~ *Designing Intelligence Tests with Dr. Pintner*

After she asked for a transfer[26] Pearl was assigned to a WPA project at Columbia University run by Professor Rudolf Pintner[27] designing intelligence tests[28] — work she described as "heavenly":

> This Dr. Pintner was interested in testing the intelligence of deaf children, and also designing tests for foreign-born children who didn't speak English. So he started with the deaf and he was devising an intelligence test.

Thus, Pearl had the privilege of working for one of the most illustrious pioneers and pillars of educational psychology at the pinnacle of Pintner's career (he died suddenly in November 1942). Pearl was not entirely cognizant in August 2009 when we made this particular tape, of how prestigious Pintner was and what a pivotal role he played in his field: Pintner's breakthrough research and design of non-verbal and picture-completion tests revolutionized the field of mental measurements

---

26. Pearl said she "got [the assignment] through connections" though she "did not remember if they told me about the job or I was sent there". Yet, it seems significant, in retrospect, that when Pearl asked for a transfer she had experience working with children with special needs, so the assignment was a good fit.

27. Pintner (1884–1942) was a professor of education at Columbia. See a piquant book review of some of Pintner's earlier work, Forrest A. Kingsbury, "Intelligence Testing: Methods and Results", *The Elementary School Journal* 24, no. 3 (1923), 230–1, https://www.journals.uchicago.edu/toc/esj/1923/24/3.

28. What was Pearl doing? For a general idea, see this 1937 publication, R. Pintner and D. G. Paterson, "Pintner-Paterson Performance Tests Short Scale — 1937", Randolph College Psychology Collection, https://ehive.com/collections/5889/objects/536101/pintnerpaterson-performance-tests-short-scale. For a description of test elements, see Rudolf Pintner, Jon Eisenson, and Mildred Stanton, "Tests Suitable for the Deaf", in *Psychology of the Physically Handicapped* (New York: F. S. Crofts, 1941), 76–87, https://archive.org/details/psychologyofphys00rudo/mode/2up. For Pintner's early non-verbal tests, see Rudolf Pintner and Donald G. Paterson, "A Scale of Performance Tests" (New York: D. Appleton and Co., 1917), 34–37, https://archive.org/details/scaleofperforman00pintuoft/page/38.

and intelligence tests for marginalized and special populations, who registered 'feeble-minded' using regular tests of the day:

> What I was doing? We[29] were devising the items for the intelligence tests and then Dr. Pintner would check it and if he thought it was a good idea he would have it built for us, and we would be sent out to test it on normal children. We made pegboards, shape and color selection games, and kids had to match the shape — like jigsaw puzzles. It was a wonderful job. This was in about 1939.

The Early Washington Years — Family First

Pearl only quit this job after Gil graduated and had landed a civil service job at the Naval Aircraft Factory in Philadelphia...which in less than a year led to their move to Washington, DC in December 1939. There were still no teaching jobs at the time in Washington, so they decided to start a family. Pearl found herself not only nurturing her toddler, Wendy — born in 1941 — but also her nephew during the early years of Michael Platt's life:

> The first time he was with me was when Michael was two months old because Ruth and Dan didn't have an apartment.[30] Then I gave the baby back to my sister and brother-in-law [Michael was left with a nanny — DA] but Michael was in and out of my house. Like during a polio epidemic.
>
> [...] I go up to visit them with Wendy... Now you have to know, we weren't going *anyplace* that there were other people, because of the epidemic — even to the corner drugstore

29. She describes her coworkers as "a wonderful group of people to work with — they were all great — a couple of City College guys, and girls from Hunter, like me".

30. The apartment over the store in northwest Washington that Pearl's sister Ruth and Dan had bought together with Nana was still occupied by the prior owners because completion of the house they were building was behind schedule — so, the three lived with the Cohen family while running the store from morning to late at night, while Pearl took care of Michael.

> to have a soda.[31] We were keeping our children away from crowds.[32] But Michael's nanny would take him out and let strangers lean over to say "*coochee coochee coo*" and "Isn't he cute!" That drove me nuts. Then I found out this caretaker had taken Michael to the *movies*...an infant to the movies. And I said—"That's it! I'm taking that child home!" So I took him back again. I don't remember how many times I took Michael back with me to my home. I really can't tell you.
>
> They would close the store at one o'clock [in the afternoon] on Sunday—open half the day, and they would come out to my house [in southeast Washington] and they would take us all out for a chicken dinner. That was my pay.

Pearl would only return to teaching more than a decade after they arrived in Washington, but she did occasionally try to find employment:

> Every so often I would look for a job. Julie (Schwartz)[33] got me a job at Lansburgh's department store as a salesperson but they fired me after one day.
>
> They had come out with a hat called a 'Turban'.[34] It was a piece of cloth gathered together in the front and you

31. Short for an ice cream soda—the beverage of the times, sometimes called an ice cream float which consisted of carbonated water and ice cream. The young man behind the lunch counter was called a soda jerk (honest!). See *Wikipedia*, s.v. "Ice cream float", https://en.wikipedia.org/wiki/Ice_cream_float.

32. To sense the terror these epidemics caused in the 1940s, see this late 1949 documentary "Epidemic's Children—1940s Polio Epidemic Fundraising Film with Iron Lungs 84610 HD", YouTube video, 10:00 minutes, 2014, https://www.youtube.com/watch?v=bws4KI2u6tk. The first polio vaccine only arrived in 1955.

33. Good friends who were as close as relatives—Leo and Julie Schwartz.

34. For a video clip on Turban hats and how to make them, don't miss this vintage footage, "How To Make Glamorous Turbans (1942)", YouTube video, 1:49 minutes, 2014, https://www.youtube.com/watch?v=8ymzUYtbKD8.

> wrapped it around your head and you made these lovely fancy arrangements with this long scarf. And Julie would stand there and demonstrate making these absolutely beautiful things...and I was a *klutz*[35] at this. I did the best I could, made $10 in one day (and felt good about it), but they didn't keep me.

During her 12-year hiatus from teaching, Pearl and Gil had two daughters. Wendy was born on 14 June 1941 — approximately six months before Pearl Harbor. I was born on 9 July 1945 — two months after VE Day (the day the war ended in Europe). Born very premature, in the seventh month of gestation — called in Yiddish a *zibelach* (from the number 7) — the fact that I'm sitting here writing this memoir boils down to blind luck, if you wish: A matter of 'location' so mammoth and scary and life-changing that at times I find it hard to wrap my head around it. I should have been blind from infanthood — perhaps the reason I wasn't totally devastated when I lost my sight in one eye in December 1987 to retinal detachment. (I had already beaten the odds with 42 years of full sightedness...and had no right to complain about fate.) Yes, I had the good fortune of 'only being born highly myopic'. Stevie Wonder, who was also born prematurely in 1950, was not so lucky...

The National Homeopathic Hospital in Washington where I came into the world was a facility that championed homeopathy — a medical approach that called for "stimulating the body's own healing forces to cure itself". Pearl ended up there because when she went into early labor, her obstetrician had hospital privileges at Homeopathic and could easily get Pearl a bed there.[36] Perhaps National Homeopathic's conservative corporate culture was in my favor: Whether a budgetary choice or a philosophical-ideological one, or both, the facility had few incubators. And all were taken. So I was placed in a 'heated crib' where

35. Yiddish for 'all thumbs'.

36. Pearl once told me how she was hospitalized, ordered to remain on complete bed rest (crying and eating an entire box of chocolates for consolation) in the hopes her early labor pains would dissipate, to no avail.

private nurses my parents hired fed me with an eyedropper around the clock for weeks on end. That I survived at all was somewhat of a miracle.

In the 1940s, infant mortality was a leading cause of death, and one in five preterm infants died, and almost all those as premature as I was — weighing less than two pounds at birth — didn't survive. Introduction of intensive neonatal care in incubators with supplementary oxygen piped in to assist breathing and allow time for premature lungs to mature — a recent introduction in the 1940s — had enabled many more preemies to survive.

Only in 1950/1951 — five years after I was born — did a smattering of articles begin to appear in the professional literature postulating "intensive oxygen therapy as a possible cause" of some 7,000 preemies by 1953 having lost their sight in the post-war Baby Boom. Nailing down the culprit behind the 'blindness epidemic' — that irreversible damage to such infants' retinas was being caused by totally unregulated use of high doses of oxygen for prolonged periods — took *years* to pin down because no one believed something as beneficial and innocent as oxygen could do harm![37] NIH even turned down funding for the first request for a clinical study grant submitted in 1950... Until the results of the first studies came in showing the culprit was indeed oxygen, the air mix was being jacked up or turned down on the basis of "guesswork" by staff on duty, ranging from 85–95 percent pure oxygen.

---

37. Read this fascinating article that recaps the 1940s "blindness epidemic", written by a former preemie, Michael Millenson, who lost sight in one eye. Michael Millenson, "For Tiny Infants, Too Much Oxygen Can Mean Blindness. Too Little Means Death", *Washington Post*, 16 November 2015, http://wapo.st/1SxbLYc?tid=ss_mail&utm_term=.82fa5b4afc16. And see this short University of Pennsylvania School of Nursing article, Elizabeth A. Reedy, "Care of Premature Infants", https://www.nursing.upenn.edu/nhhc/nurses-institutions-caring/care-of-premature-infants/, relating about the introduction of the first incubators and how it was finally discovered that oxygen was the culprit behind so many blind infants. To this day, oxygen management for preemies — the level of oxygen in the 'air mix' in incubators — is a delicate life-or-death balancing act between survival and blindness, how to keep preemies with underdeveloped lungs alive, breathing and without brain damage with oxygen supplements, while preventing permanent damage to their eyesight.

Wendy's baby scrapbook was filled with greeting cards with congratulations on the birth of Pearl and Gil's first child, where Gil occasionally preserved 'pearls of wisdom', one that became a classic of family lore, in light of Pearl's lifelong weakness never to pass up a good cup of coffee:

> Having observed Leah Abbott nursing Glenda [in 1946], Wendy asked her mother why she didn't nurse her infant sister like Leah did. When Pearl replied — "Because I have no milk there", Wendy inquired, "Not even water?" "No" she replied. "Not even coffee?" asked Wendy, incredulous. "No" replied mother. By this point, totally baffled, Wendy blurted out: "Then what are they for???"

As for my baby scrapbook — my parents didn't know if I would even survive — and if I remember correctly there weren't any cards of congratulations while everyone held their breath. The scrapbook was, however, filled with receipts for private nursing bills that testify to my survival against all odds, blissfully unaware for years of the close call with an entirely different destiny I had been spared.

I wore Coke-bottle thick glasses from the age of two but I wasn't blind. There were some liabilities, however. Alas, classrooms in the 1950s were arranged alphabetically, with the Ws always at the back where I couldn't see the blackboard if my life depended on it. Special permission to 'break the rules' and seat me in the first row had to be obtained at the start of every school year, a process that could take a week or more in limbo. I will remain forever indebted to my parents for going to the expense of pricy new contact lenses[38] — just on the market in 1958 when I was in 7th grade — a liberating experience in an age and at an age when a combination of eyeglasses and curly hair was a walking disaster. The myopic in subsequent generations will

---

38. Perhaps the contacts were a silent apology for forcing me to go to exceedingly awkward weekly dance classes with 'Groggy' as a 6th grader to learn to jitterbug and cha-cha-cha, where being a *klutz* as well, I was always chosen last as the children paired up.

always be indebted to John Lennon for making eyeglasses 'cool', but this only began in late 1966.[39]

Restarting a Career

In 1951, with both kids finally enrolled in school, Pearl began to think about returning to teaching. She once told me that I had trouble adjusting to kindergarten, crying bitterly, and she ended up staying (and helping the teacher out, for weeks) until Mrs. Croskrey gently suggested it was time to cut the apron strings...saying ruefully: "Pearl, if you want to teach, you'll have to get your own classroom". Pearl began substituting at the local school where her own children were enrolled — Stanton Elementary School. The pay for substitutes was $10 to $12 dollars a day:

> I started substituting when you were a kid. [...] We both remember how once I substituted in your class [in 3rd grade — DA], and you giggled and were embarrassed and didn't know what to call me — Mommy or Mrs. Weiss... By that time the entire economy had changed.

However, it was only after the family moved to Maryland in mid-March 1955, after building a house in Silver Spring Maryland, that Pearl began teaching full time. Although initially she was seeking to substitute off-and-on, she was offered a 'permanent' substituting position, replacing a pregnant teacher:

> The supervisor [at the Board of Education in Rockville] offered me a full time job filling-in for a teacher who was five or six months pregnant and past the time she was allowed to work. Teachers weren't allowed to work once they were 'showing' — that is, had any sign of a belly!

39. See "John Lennon's Iconic Glasses", YouTube video, 0:57 minutes, 2010, https://www.youtube.com/watch?v=S30dv5OsK0Y. For a short article on the story behind Lennon's glasses, see "John Lennon Begins Wearing 'Granny' Glasses", The Beatles Bible, https://www.beatlesbible.com/1966/09/06/john-lennon-begins-wearing-granny-glasses/.

> I said, "Gosh, I don't know..." She said, "Look, it's almost spring break time. School ends in the middle of June. It's not a lot of weeks and we need you". [...] I decided to take the job [at Rollingwood Elementary adjacent to Rock Creek Park in Chevy Chase] teaching a combined 1st and 2nd grade. The room was a huge room that had been divided into two classrooms, which was very hard, but somehow I got through to the end of the year with flying colors. By then, I was told that there was a 2nd grade position open [for the next year], and by then I was 'hooked'.
>
> I liked it there. The school was lovely, and it had a very large Jewish population of well-educated parents who were wonderful. I was enjoying it and we were enjoying the money.

Building the house on Woodland Drive in Silver Spring had run $25,000, not the $18,000 to $20,000 they had estimated and the family had moved in with $100 in the bank and a mortgage to pay...at which point their '48 Dodge died within weeks and had to be replaced with a new 1955 Chevy... A second income was a blessing.

The requirement that pregnant teachers who began to 'show' had to leave the classroom that triggered the job opening that placed Pearl back on track career-wise is a phenomenon that deserves a bit of context. In today's day and age where pregnant women unapologetically share their growing bellies in the public space, no longer camouflaged under loose-fitting maternity garb, it is hard to even begin to fathom attitudes and norms surrounding pregnancy only a few decades ago. No, it was not that school boards across America were being overprotective of the welfare of the growing fetus or the expectant mother. Nor was it an 'aesthetic matter' (claims such a sight was 'a distraction'). The truth is, educators viewed a belly as an 'elephant in the room'. That kids would ask 'questions' about where babies come from that teachers didn't want to answer and that school boards thought had no place in the classroom. Even the slightest intimation there was a sexual realm to life, even married life, was taboo in those days; there weren't even double beds in the staging of the bedrooms[40] of married couples featured on American TV sitcoms in the 1950s. And, of course, there were no books for tots explaining unspoken truths like *Everybody Poops*, not to mention unmentionables like how babies are made. In fact, fear of bellies was across the board. Up until the early 1970s public school districts in the United States forcibly banned pregnant girls from attending their regular high school, as well. In many cases where teachers were forced to take maternity leave at five months, this was leave-without-pay, a double-whammy since accumulated sick leave couldn't even be used during a teacher's absence because "pregnancy was not a disease"...[41] Only in 1974 did the United States Supreme Court declare that mandatory unpaid leave policies were unconstitutional and it was illegal to force pregnant women to take maternity leave on the assumption they are incapable of working in their physical condition. But only in 1978 was federal legislation passed — an amendment to the Civil Rights Act of 1964 called the Pregnancy Discrimination Act of 1978 — that called a spade a spade, defining mandatory maternity leave a discriminatory practice 'because of sex' or 'on the basis of sex' — abolishing the practice. Following two years at Rollingwood, Pearl began teaching at Arcola Elementary after a clerical glitch on her record led the Rollingwood principal to fire her for 'lack of certification'. Pearl almost quit her teaching career as a result:

> I wasn't willing to go back to school to get certification... I didn't mind going back to school, but I didn't want to take any more stupid education classes! I was ready to give it up.
>
> I called Alice Jaffe — my friend who was also a Hunter grad and a teacher, and I told her what had happened. She

40. At the most, the protagonist was putting on makeup or vacillating what to wear, never in bed.

41. For more background, see, for example, Laurie Levy, "Pregnant Teachers", *Huffington Post*, 6 January 2015, https://www.huffpost.com/entry/pregnant-teachers_b_6424210 and Warren Weaver Jr., "Supreme Court Rules Pregnant Teachers Cannot Be Forced to Take Long Leaves", *The New York Times*, 22 January 1974, https://nyti.ms/1XVugsR.

> told me "that's ridiculous". And she wasn't about to let me simply throw in the towel. When she called me back, Alice told me — "Call Baltimore [where the headquarters of the State Board of Education were located — DA]. I've arranged for you to have your credits reviewed. Someone has made a terrible mistake!" I went to Baltimore and there was no problem. It was a clerical error and I was completely certified from my courses at Hunter.

But by the time things were straightened out, Pearl's 2nd grade position for the 1956/7 school year had been filled by someone else. The new job offer she received from the Board of Education was a 3rd grade in a new school:

> I say [to the supervisor in Rockville, the Montgomery Country Board of Education] "but I just mastered the 2nd grade curriculum!" and he replies: "So, you'll learn 3rd grade... You'll just be taking the kids from where you left

Pearl's 1963 Arcola class

> them, to a little higher level. We really want you to take it". That was Arcola in Silver Spring — close to home.
>
> I taught at Arcola Elementary — at first in 3rd grade for many years, then 5th and 6th grade in a team teaching situation.

Pearl was the kind of genuine educator who loves kids and knew how to nurture the individual child — each in his or her own way, leaving an indelible impression on her pupils' lives. Indeed, when sitting *shivah* in Washington in January 2014 after Pearl's death, a stranger walked in, a woman in her mid-sixties whom no one recognized. She turned out to be Dr. Wendy Garson, who explained her presence: "Mrs. Weiss was my 3rd-grade teacher". Garson, an ophthalmologist, had come especially to Gaithersburg, Maryland from Vienna, Virginia that winter evening to make a condolence call after she saw the death announcement in the paper!

Two other former 3rd graders left their recollections in the comments of the *Washington Post* obituary and on Legacy.com. One — a cantor by profession — volunteered to sing at the funeral service as a gesture to an unforgettable teacher. Pearl also bonded with and mentored new teachers such as Mary Williams Betters[42] and Phoebe Bauman. Both became lifelong friends. Pearl even proofed Phoebe's doctoral thesis for spelling errors.

~ *Team Teaching Modeling*

The early 1960s were years of innovation in education, particularly in wealthy Montgomery County.[43] Pearl would play a role in two pilots,

---

42. Mary Williams, an African-American (a rarity in the Montgomery County school system in those days) whom Pearl mentored as a fledgling teacher and who became a lifelong friend.

43. I myself was one of the guinea pigs in two innovative-but-harebrained schemes that failed completely: One, mastering French quote 'naturally' — orally with headphones and a tape recorder with no written material whatsoever for the entire first year of French. Not only was there no way of knowing the difference between 'we' and '*oui*', the method was a disaster for anyone who was visually minded and needed a written text to memorize best. The

developing forward-looking curriculums — the first, the concept of team teaching in elementary schools; the second, special needs curriculums for high school age at-risk youth.

Under a federally-funded pilot, Pearl together with fellow teachers Phoebe Goodwin and Joseph Cerwonka developed a team-teaching model[44] for elementary schools at Arcola — three classes of 5th and 6th graders operating out of a small auditorium with flexible accordion dividers. The model they developed optimized the learning experience for their pupils by allowing team teachers to complement and utilize one another's individual strengths — ironically, particularly Joseph Cerwonka's background.

Male teachers were a rarity to begin with, but there was such a shortage of teachers they were hiring people with no educational background whatsoever — any college graduate willing to promise they'd get certified by taking the requisite education courses at night. Cerwonka was an interior decorator with a classical education who applied for a teaching job after a friend dared him to 'walk-the-talk' after he complained about 'the dreadful state of education'. Pearl recalled how their team teaching setup operated:

> Cerwonka had a marvelous education in the classics, architecture, music, history. An all-around Renaissance Man.

---

concept of different learning styles simply didn't exist. The second fiasco was a Pavlov-based learning system for mastering plane geometry based on encyclopedic-size loose-leaf workbooks — built entirely on filling-in-the-blanks over-and-over *ad nauseam* (1. A=B 2. B=__). We guinea pigs completed only 15 of the 98 theorems by the end of the school year. Parents were up in arms when school officials said the participants would have to repeat the course thus credit was given, but only those strong in math went on to study solid geometry. However, there were also wildly successful groundbreaking programs I had the luck to participate in. One, called American Civilization, a team teaching setup with half a dozen teachers, coupled American history studies with period literature in lieu of English. The word 'interdisciplinary' wasn't even in the dictionary then. Even fellow student, pollster Stanley Greenberg, recalled this unique program in his writings about his growing-up years.

44. Today, team teaching is an integral part of teaching at all levels.

> As soon as we [Phoebe and Pearl] met him we 'knew' he was gay.[45]
>
> We used a regular curriculum, but it was an enriched curriculum — most of this Joseph's doing because he had a wider background than we did. The kids in the three 30-pupil classes rotated. I taught mostly language arts. Sometimes we would combine all three classes — like a movie about Roman architecture and I don't remember about what subject. It was a wonderful experience.

As far as his teaching career was concerned, Joseph Cerwonka was 'in the closet'. In those days, not only were teachers and other government officeholders forced to take a Loyalty Oath swearing they were not 'subversive persons' — a document in which one "certified they were not engaged in an attempt to overthrow the Governments of Maryland or the United States". Discovering a man was gay was grounds for dismissal as a "poor role model for students".[46] Gays and communists (past and current) were barred from teaching in the public-school system.

That was back in the late 1950s and early 1960s. And today? Yes, there are openly-gay teachers and, generally, boards of education cannot fire such individuals without 'good cause' and must tread carefully due to current interpretation of the 14th Amendment (equal protection

---

45. Cerwonka's 'secret' was safe with them and they had opportunities to meet Joseph's partner...and covered for their colleague when Cerwonka failed to get to work on time due to a drinking problem.

46. For some input on gays in the classroom, see Todd A. DeMitchell, Suzanne Eckes, and Richard Fossey, "Sexual Orientation and the Public School Teacher", *Public Interest Law Journal* 19, vol. 65 (2009): 65–105, https://www.bu.edu/pilj/files/2015/09/19-1DeMitchellEckesandFosseyArticle.pdf and Anthony E. Varona, "Setting the Record Straight: The Effects of the Employment Non-Discrimination Act of 1997 on the First and Fourteenth Amendment Rights of Gay and Lesbian Public Schoolteachers", *Commlaw Conspectus* 6, vol. 1 (1998): 25-49, https://repository.law.miami.edu/cgi/viewcontent.cgi?article=1650&context=fac_articles. See also a discussion of ENDA at *Wikipedia*, s.v. "Employment Non-Discrimination Act", https://en.wikipedia.org/wiki/Employment_Non-Discrimination_Act.

of the law and due process). Yet, in many cases when authorities seek to withdraw the teaching certificates or fire a teacher with an alternative lifestyle, what can possibly constitute 'good cause' is long and varies greatly by the levels of tolerance of the surrounding community and what is viewed as unacceptable conduct — in and outside the classroom. Perceived reasons for dismissal have ranged from LGBT teachers whose private lives are an open book[47] to a single mom with a child conceived with the assistance of a sperm bank. Observers say even today, many gays prefer to resign rather than fight and face their private lives becoming the talk of the town in local media, even if they are out-of-the-closet and totally within their legal rights, say observers. To date, the Employment Non-Discrimination Act (ENDA) that seeks to add a prohibition to discriminate in hiring and employment on the basis of sexual orientation or gender identity, not just race, religion and gender has been before the Congress since 1997, yet has failed to pass year after year.

Meeting Special Needs of Youth-at-Risk

Following the success of the program, Pearl Weiss was again tapped to develop another pedagogic model, a federally-funded three-year pilot program at Northwood High School — two teachers, with 16 mentally or emotionally-challenged youth at risk of dropping out of school — who were slated to be placed in a work-oriented curriculum. Pearl described her first meeting with the Northwood principal:

> He goes and shows me this room. It's filled with old washing machines and spare parts...part of the [current] 'non-academic track' and he told me this was a repair shop. I said, "Not where *I'm* gonna teach. These kids sound like they have been cast off already and what you are telling them is that they are garbage". I told them I'm not coming.

47. See Amanda Machado, "The Plight of Being a Gay Teacher: LGBT Educators Walk a Fine Line between Keeping Their Jobs and Being Honest with Their Students", *Atlantic Magazine*, 16 December 2014, https://www.theatlantic.com/education/archive/2014/12/the-plight-of-being-a-lgbt-teacher/383619/.

> He said, "Well, we do have one room...but you would have to work with someone else — two teachers together". So I said, "Oh. Do you have the other teacher already?" It turned out she was a former special education teacher — Francis Jordan...and we hit it off on the phone. Attached to the room was a small conference room, and a storage room — and I thought to myself — this is perfect for team teaching! And it worked out perfectly.
>
> Francis Jordan had a science and math background and I had the history and language arts background. Basically, we didn't do a lot of that — but rather basic education of reading skills, work skills, 'attitude'. It was a good match. [...] When we began, there was no curriculum. The kids were at various levels, with different abilities. We had borderline retarded. One kid who was very very bright, but was a behavior problem. Another was autistic.

Their mandate was to design a framework that would keep such potential dropouts within a school system that was at a loss how to deal with their special needs. The Work Orientation Curriculum (WOC) model Francis and Pearl designed from scratch — 'hit and miss' based largely on intuition — integrated half-days in the classroom spent learning marketable job skills (from job-oriented reading comprehension and arithmetic, to work ethics and etiquette) with half-days in the workplace. The team placed pupils in salaried employment in genuine jobs in the afternoon that were tailored to the abilities and interests of each student,[48] monitoring and counseling students and working with their employers to ensure a successful work experience.[49] The experience of one of their 16 pupils reflects Pearl's magic touch — a student Pearl spoke of in the tapes:

---

48. For example, a bright-but-troubled kid who loved movies was set up as a projectionist's assistant at a movie theatre.

49. Principles that are still cogent today as America grapples with the challenge of an ongoing high school 'dropout epidemic' (the situation has improved since 2000 but still exists).

> She was sent to us as an autistic student — although there was no word for this at the time. Alice could read and loved reading. She was a quiet and sweet girl. She didn't have social skills... We got her a job in a library, and eventually she got a job at NIH[50] delivering mail and other material to different departments. The last I heard from her (she would call me) Alice told me she was still at NIH. This was perhaps 20 years ago [1989 — DA] and I used to hear from her every year. She would call me up and tell me what she was doing. Alice must have been in her 40s by then, and she told me she eventually would be retiring from this job and she sounded wonderful.
>
> Why was she in the program? What made her 'at-risk'? I'm not sure they knew what they were talking about... Autism was a new word in those days. I think she was high-functioning, and had this been today, she might have been diagnosed as Asperger's.

~ *Becoming a School Counselor*

Gaining a Master's in counseling was set in motion by the requirement that teachers keep abreast of developments in education to renew their certification to teach in Montgomery County. Here again, her friend Alice Jaffe was a moving force urging Pearl to apply such courses towards a Masters by enrolling in a graduate program at George Washington University. It took Pearl five or six years to complete her Master's degree:

> I was teaching at Arcola. I went down to George Washington University in the District to check it out, but I didn't know that I had to tell them what I wanted to specialize in...that's how much I knew about graduate school.
>
> I'm looking over the list and I say to myself, "Well, I

---

50. National Institutes of Health in Bethesda, Maryland, the world-renowned primary medical research agency of the federal government of the United States.

> don't want to be a reading teacher, I know how to teach reading...but to do this all day long?!" Looking it over, one of the choices was counseling. Alice was a counselor and I knew she liked it, so I picked counseling as my specialty.

Some of the coursework was fascinating — marked by reading breakthrough books that subsequently became cornerstones of the professional literature, such as Paul Goodman's *Growing Up Absurd* (1960) and Eric Berne's *Games People Play* (1964), which Pearl read, then passed on and shared with her youngest daughter whose reading tastes were and still are exceedingly eclectic...

After completing her Master's degree in counseling in 1967 Pearl served as a 9th-grade school counselor at Parkland Junior High School until her retirement in 1971. She recalled her work at Parkland:

> I became a 9th grade counselor at Parkland Junior High. Of course, every counselor has her own way of working. But the first thing I did was to get to know each kid — 400 of them. And I remember an awful lot of them. [...] I would try and find out if they had any problems — say, with a particular teacher, and I'd talk to the teacher to try and resolve things or ask for the child to be transferred to another teacher because I felt this particular teacher was not right for this particular kid. Or problems at home.
>
> Once I called a mother in for a conference. I had gotten to known her daughter (who had sort of attached herself to me) and I told her, "Your daughter craves attention, she's really starved for attention and while I know you have a large family, can you give her 15 minutes before bedtime — just for her?" And she looked at me and said "Mrs. Weiss, do you have any idea what it is like to make dinner for 12 every night?" And I said "No, I don't. I'm having trouble imaging it". So you have incidents like this you remember, too.

~ *Retirement — Now What?*

What's rather startling, looking back, is Pearl's teaching career spanned 20-something years, while her retirement spanned (gulp!) 43 years. In one of the taped interviews Pearl talked about retiring when she did, saying that in retrospect it was a mistake and left her at a loose end:

> When I retired, I was a counselor [...] What happened was Gil retired because he had 31 years in government service, and he would get up and make me breakfast and pack me my lunch. He only worked four or five days a month as a consultant for Grumman...and only when they needed him. It was a year or possibly two [that I was working and he was semi-retired], and I got jealous. ("Why am I working??? He's free. We can go on vacation whenever we want!")[51] So I retired. [...] And we were at a point financially where we didn't need my income—although I was slated to become the head of the counseling department.
>
> In retrospect, I was sorry I retired. I missed it, so I would take myself to museums, but when I would see a teacher with her class visiting a museum I would ask myself—"What am I doing here? Why aren't I with *my* kids?!"
>
> So, what did I do with my time? I started taking free classes at GW. They allowed alumni to sit in on any class for free—audit the class, without taking the class for credit or paying tuition. I took courses in subjects I never had a chance to study such as art courses—art appreciation or art history [...] I enjoyed my retirement, but shortly after I retired I had a very hard time adjusting. I didn't spend much time with Gil; I spent it taking courses and got very involved in those [the lecturers always encouraged her to participate fully in class discussion, not merely audit silently—DA]. And we had an active social life with our own friends.

---

51. In the subtext, this meant they could come to Israel (tickets were expensive) for leisurely month-long visits...and do so in the spring and fall, when the weather is nicest.

~

There was a lot left unsaid in Pearl recollecting how she expected once she retired that she and Gil would do more things together, and the reality of adjusting to retirement that wasn't quite as she envisioned it. She only said, with candor, without expanding on it: "I didn't spend much time with Gil".

Gil was probably either working in the garden, puttering about in the basement, out playing tennis or researching the purchase of some appliance. The fact is, Gil had never been an intellectual companion for Pearl, although he was the Love of Her Life (and vise-versa). As a couple, however, "having an active social life with their own friends" — going to plays, concerts and museums and going out to restaurants with friends — were activities that Pearl (or the other women) arranged. The men went along. Emblematic of this 'arrangement' when an art exhibit didn't interest Gil, he could always be found examining how the museum display cases were put together.

Pearl and Gil have often been described as the ultimate couple. They earned this accolade honestly — in the genuine mutual admiration and respect they exhibited and the 'space' they gave one another to 'do their own thing' and permission to grow. But the harmonious relationship that worked for them was problematic when emulated too much as the model for a perfect marriage. Oedipus aside, my sister and I as young women always declared we wanted to marry a man like our father. For me,[52] it wasn't just a matter of impossible standards or too high a bar. It was clearly a 'model' ill-suited to my temperament. I almost married a man who was the sweetest human being one can imagine who simply adored me. I broke off the relationship (and broke his heart) not only because I needed an intellectual partner — a need he couldn't fulfill, but also because I have an ornery adversarial streak. I realized, like my father, Aaron would *never* fight; every argument or point of tension in our relationship would be my doing, and he would look at me with a bewildered 'what did I do wrong' look and I'd hate myself

---

52. Did this 'unrealistic' picture of a good marriage play a role in my sister's three marriages? Perhaps.

for it. Wendy and I never saw our parents fight. Not even raise their voices. Not once. And they didn't fight behind closed doors either. Gil, coming from a household of constantly bickering parents, absolutely refused to fight and held harmony up, above all other considerations. So he accommodated. Or he withdrew to the Shop or the garden. I wanted-needed a spouse who was my intellectual equal and companion, intimately involved in my world. He had to be first and foremost a person who shared my passions for politics, history, art — an intellectual soul mate, not just my husband and helpmate — someone with whom I could discuss and argue for hours. When Rafi walked into my apartment — a blind date — and immediately went to peruse the books and examine the art on the walls, it was love at first sight. Indeed, we talked for hours on end...daily, for decades. He would not only be 'the wind beneath my wings' in launching a career as a journalist — very much an enabler in a host of ways; during 48 years together there was never even the slightest risk I would be the only one picking a fight.

~ *Pearl as In-House Mentor and Enabler*

Pearl's students — in the classroom and as a counselor — were not the only kids for whom she served as a mentor. Even when she was home, Pearl — no one called the folks Mr. or Mrs. Weiss — was always 'on duty' in the eating alcove in the kitchen — our cramped informal classroom and a second home for countless conversations about everything from the agonies of adolescence to controversial political issues and books, discussed over coffee and Nana's *rugelach*.

One needs to keep in mind, that in the 1950s and 1960s women were not supposed to be intellectual or strong figures. Pearl was a powerful positive female role model in an era awash in "I Love Lucy"[53]

53. A television program — one of many of the era — where the woman is a homemaker waiting for breadwinner hubby to come home from work and jobs and roles were strictly gendered. See Morganne Mallon, "Women in Media: 1950s Television", Morganne's Civic Issues Blog, 19 February 2014, http://sites.psu.edu/civicissuesmallon/2014/02/19/women-in-media-1950s-television/. For a glimpse, see as an example, the sitcom "Leave It To Beaver: Cooking and Woman Talk", YouTube video, 1:15 minutes, 2016, https://www.youtube.com/watch?v=aPAQZigokTc.

figures. If today we all know the future belongs to the nerds and knowledge is power, back in the 1950s and early 1960s kids (especially girls) interested in politics rather than parties were — ahem — exceedingly uncool. Beyond the books and ideas shared, Pearl assured me and my friends on the margins in school[54] that while one might be a social misfit in the heyday of proms and beehive hairdos, one was definitely not a creep for thinking. Yes, intellectualism might turn one into a wallflower, but it was no malady. In the subtext, she gave 'permission' to girls to develop their voice and to be their own person and gave the 'outsiders' — the Heidis, the Elinores, the Daniellas — dignity.

This wasn't always easy.

❧ *'Walking-the-Talk' at Home*

Among the Miscellaneous that Gil saved was a lengthy paper Pearl wrote for a Master's course in social psychology at George Washington University (GW) in DC, which I discovered in cleaning up the house in 1998 — devoted to working through her relationship with her then 17-year-old daughter (me) and my choices (aided with insights in the margin in red from the professor). The objective of the paper was, or so it appears, to use principles of social psychology in the course syllabus to solve a problem — hers as she put it: "How can I recognize and accept that her activities are meeting her needs? (my goals for her are not her goals)" — to which the professor wrote in the margins: "They never will be".

Pearl complained that I was so involved in my own interests that I

---

54. This requires a bit of qualification: While definitely on the social margins, besides finding a place in a Zionist youth movement outside the mainstream, in typical in-your-face fashion, I had already carved out my own space at Montgomery Blair High School — establishing a monthly parliament called the Blair Forum that discussed controversial political and social issues, and the Blair Book Club that read and discussed *Catch-22* before it became a cult classic or was heralded a prophetic seismograph of things to come. Each club attracted a turnout of about two dozen participants on a good day, out of a student body of over 2,000... In the school cafeteria there was a table where such students who didn't fit the mold habitually congregated at lunchtime (some tablemates were members of Habonim).

ignored the family. Indeed, I still remember the time — I believe I was in 8th grade — that I came home from hours 'out and about' and my mother met me at the front door as I was heading straight for my room and told me evenly but exasperated, "If you walked in the door and I was lying on the floor out cold, you would simply step over me and go to your room". I was so chagrined that I tried to be more sociable and less adversarial, at least for several weeks. Seriously conflicted (she described herself as "ambivalent"), Pearl said she admired my "independence of thought" but almost in the same breath felt I had "tunnel vision". Intellectually, she recognized that my group of friends in the youth movement fulfilled a host of needs, providing companionship and "opportunities to use my talents [...] and to stretch and grow to keep up with this bright and capable group" but she viewed us as "conformists within our own circle". She charged that I was "carrying my non-conformity to an extreme".

She was particularly bothered by our rejection of American aesthetics (no makeup, untamed hairstyles, jeans and sandals[55]) that Pearl viewed as unkempt and a conscious in-your-face drive to be quote "unattractive", stemming, she reasoned, from "low self-esteem". But in writing the paper, Pearl came, with difficulty, to recognize the importance of me finding a compatible peer group in the Habonim Labor Zionist Movement — a whole group of nonconformist kids who shared my tastes and interests and outlook on Jewishness and American norms and consumer culture.

But in working through her problem, Pearl concluded she had to pick her battles, saying she hoped in lieu of ultimatums (i.e., a confrontational solution), if she and Gil invited me to accompany them to the theatre enough times — knowing I loved good theatre — perhaps

---

55. An aesthetic that within a few short years came into full bloom in a much more radical form with the Flower Children... On the last bastion in need of liberation — embracing kinky Jewfro hair — a more recent phenomenon, read these two wonderful essays: Samantha Shokin, "When I Found a Place Where I Belonged, I Finally Came to Love My Jewish Hair", *Tablet*, 30 January 2014, https://www.tabletmag.com/jewish-life-and-religion/159313/love-my-jewish-hair, and Netana Markovitz:, "Big Hair, Don't Care", *Tablet*, 22 August 2016, https://www.tabletmag.com/sections/news/articles/big-hair-dont-care.

I would begin to enjoy getting dressed up, writing that "change has to come from within". Of course, this was a lost cause, but in the meantime I got to see a lot of plays in my last two years of high school and subsequent periods living at home, unaware of the ulterior motive. It should be noted that years prior to this, Pearl had already gone to bat to mitigate the agony of shopping for clothes — or shopping for anything for that matter — saving me the 'torture of the racks': Shopping *for* me, bringing home clothes I could try on and choose what I wanted, without having to be dragged to the store. If I hated being forced to wear dresses when the family went out[56] Pearl had always reduced the discomfort by letting me choose which one I *had* to wear...despite the fact that I was in the habit of latching on to one dress I disliked the least and wearing it to death — until others, no doubt, thought I only possessed one 'very worn' dress.

Nevertheless, in the course of reexamining her feelings, Pearl concluded that perhaps many of the things she saw as "compensation" for weaknesses were actually the signs of a quote "actualized person" and "adequate personality" and the problem was largely her own perceptions and projections. Pearl never said this in regard to projection, but in retrospect I suspect that my being 'unpopular' with one or two friends in elementary school and middle school and being 'on the sidelines' of *conventional* adolescent social life in high school[57]...and Pearl's desire

56. I believe the last time I wore a dress or a skirt was 1969, with one exception: My wedding dress in 1972 — a hand-me-down. My longtime friend Elinore Liebersohn Koenigsfeld offered me hers when she asked what I was going to wear, and I told her I dreaded shopping for a wedding dress. This instantly solved 50 percent of the need for the proverbial 'something old, something new, something borrowed, something blue'. My Great Aunt Estelle supplied the rest, making me a lovely veil with a blue ribbon...LOL. Rafi — a neatness freak — unknowingly threw the veil out with the garbage hours before the wedding, but luckily the trash collectors realized this must be a mistake and left the boxed veil on top of the emptied trash cans in the apartment building's garbage room.

57. In sharp contrast, in 10th grade I had already become a valued and core member of a close-knit peer group within Habonim, invited into the inner circle that planned and led weekly programs for the entire Washington contingent,

to 'correct this', was at least partially the product of her own marginalized status as a kid due to a combination of economic circumstances and age gaps with her classroom peers — having been, to quote the tapes, "a lonely kid", who in her own words was "not very assertive". Was this a misplaced desire to 'save me the grief' she experienced in her own childhood? To mold me in the image of my popular older sister fueled by the same inner needs, assuming I must be "unhappy" and feel "inadequate" for not being like my "most attractive older sister" [whom Pearl said was] "very successful socially"... (Rest assured, as an adolescent and young adult Wendy caused our parents grief in other areas that could fill a book...but she will have to write that one.)

It took a lot of 'working through' for Pearl to realize her needs and my needs were not the same. She closed her paper saying that she needed to:

> [...] transfer to my home and my relationship with my daughter the atmosphere I try to have in my classroom, the acceptance I try to give each of my pupils, and the support I try to give them to help them towards growth and maturity.

Did Pearl ever really fathom that despite being an American history buff, by nature I had always been 'out of synch' with the *zeitgeist* of the country where I was born long before I joined Habonim — uncomfortable with its values and cultural norms — thus, beyond questions of Jewish identity and continuity, America 'was a bad fit' for me. Probably she never got it.

Legacies are not a last-minute affair. They are something each one of us 'works on' — for better or for worse, throughout our lives. Core messages

---

which in every sense had become my center-of-gravity. Pearl noted parenthetically that I had chosen to assume a Hebrew name four years earlier, but in silent protest insisted on calling me 'Diana' throughout the paper...

we consciously or unwittingly shared. Special moments we may have forgotten but others cherish or recall cringing. Indelible episodes and special attributes — good and bad. Likewise, I think every person has a special room or virtual space where that person 'resides' in our gray matter. You say a name, and — bingo! — that's how you see the person. Not just a face, grinning or scowling as the case may be, but the whole person instantaneously pops up in your mind's eye. Gil's space is surely the Shop or the garden, pushing a piece of mahogany through the table saw or pulling up weeds in the garden, some grass clippings stuck to his hairy chest and beads of sweat on his brow, a glass of cold Nana Water™ in his hand. Nana's room is surely the kitchen — cutting raisins for *rugelach* or making a Nana Egg™. And Pearl? Her space is unquestionably around the family 'conference table' in the eating alcove adorned by a unique permanent centerpiece — the pile of bills, coupons, unopened mail and little notes and To Do lists — reading the newspaper, a mug of fresh perked coffee by her side.

While the eating alcove was always everyone's most popular gathering spot by choice, there were many homes in the 1960s where the living room was exclusively reserved for grownups. The living room furniture in the Weiss household was made to be sat on by everyone, including the kids and their friends (and not just because Gil never finished the recreation room).

Pearl and Gil had a gravitational pull on anyone who entered their orbit.[58] Despite Pearl's misgivings expressed in the term paper, the Weisses' legendary hospitality never faltered throughout my high school years, hosting countless late-night *kumzitzes* (Habonim sing-alongs) around a candle in the basement, cementing a warm lifetime relationship with the *shaliach* (Israeli emissary) to the youth movement and giving me unfettered use of the family car on weekends, including driving friends home from activities who lived miles and miles away whose parents were less supportive of their children's choices. And, for decades after, Pearl walked-the-talk of what she said in the conclusion of that paper.

58. Wendy once quipped that when she split with the man in her life, the ex-boyfriend or ex-spouse was always more distraught about losing her parents than losing her...

Pearl and Gil never attempted to leverage the difficulties (some shared in The Lost Art of Letter Writing) to try and lure me back to the States, having recognized my happiness lay in Israel.

The relationship was very close and supportive in a myriad of ways, not only on letting me be my own person; the 'vow' Pearl took when I was 17 in that course paper was best reflected in a tribute I wrote to Pearl on her 90th birthday *in absentia* about her response when being with my mother in America and being with my family in Israel left me painfully conflicted when the Second Lebanon War broke out on 12 July 2006, days before Pearl's 90th birthday. At 2:00 AM, very distraught, less than 24 hours before I was to leave for the States and just after Hezbollah began pounding the north of Israel from Lebanon, threatening to also target Tel Aviv with missiles, I called wailing–"Mom, what should I do?!" Pearl replied: "Listen, you have to be close to your family now. And remember, I'll be 90 all year long".

That kind of pillar of support wasn't a one-time deal. It was a constant. Another example is typical: When Gil had a massive heart attack in 1984. After four weeks of touch and go, Pearl almost collapsed on the floor assuming the worst, when we walked into the cardiology ward at Washington Hospital Center at visitor hours to find an empty stripped bed and the nurse holding out a plastic bag, saying "Here's his stuff" thinking we knew he had been sent back to the ICU (due to a defective pacemaker that indeed almost killed him). This setback occurred just as my husband Rafi was about to collapse under the combined weight of the farm at the height of the summer growing season, and three young children (ten, eight and three years old). Here as well, I was torn between 'here' and 'there'. Pearl looked me in the eye and said: "I think it's time for you to go back to your family because they need you more now. I want you to remember — whatever happens with your father — if he survives or he doesn't, you were here when I needed you the most".

After a miraculous recovery (despite losing 25 percent of his heart muscle and suffering a stroke to boot) Gil would enjoy another 15 years of good health, what Pearl labeled "his bonus years". Suffice it to say, when the roles were reversed and Pearl needed someone to drop everything to become her Rock of Gibraltar in medical emergencies in her declining years or to meet other burning needs,[59] a safety net of strong lifetime relationships within the family was already in place, woven over time.

~

Growing up with an in-house teacher had its moments, of course — some rather humorous in retrospect.

Pearl's faith in my potential was extraordinary, in fact amazing, all things considered. If she had any thoughts that I might be brain damaged from lack of enough oxygen, being so premature, or suspected I was 'slow' ('borderline retard' in the parlance of the day) or at least on the autistic scale...she never let on. I'm convinced I would probably have been placed in special ed, had there been the same sensitivity then as there is today to 'special needs' children; I test badly and scored 65 in standard IQ tests even in junior high school. So, am I the epitome of an over-achiever? Or the ultimate late late late bloomer? The fact is, Pearl always made me feel wonderful — that I was tops, even when I was bringing home Cs and Ds in elementary school and junior high, and mostly Cs in high school in every subject but English and history. This was no mean feat for a professional educator in the Dark Ages prior to 'multiple intelligences' or 'individual learning styles'.

Of course, this didn't stop Pearl from doggedly trying to correct two scholastic flaws — my penmanship and my spelling. There were endless but fruitless attempts to tutor me in cursive writing. After giving up trying to get me to make 's's that look like sailboats, I found

---

59. Spending six weeks putting the house in order back in 1998. Or in November 2004, after Asaf called Israel (during a short stop, on his way to report to Fort Jackson in North Carolina for an international course in military economics) to say "something is terribly wrong with *Savta*..." Pearl was taken to the hospital with pneumonia, and I jumped on a plane to take care of her for a month. Then in 2006, a three-and-a-half-month sojourn in Washington during the cascading health crisis that climaxed in Pearl moving to Minnesota. Many other times over the years, living a tad closer, Wendy was the frequent flyer and fixer, not to mention seven years in Minnesota about which my sister has reminisced at the back of the book.

I'd been enrolled in a summer school typing course after graduating middle school (which I failed due to lack of coordination and had to repeat at the beginning of 9th grade as an elective). A top-of-the-line mechanical portable typewriter followed. It was only when I heard from a prospective employer in the mid-1990s that a graphologist reported I was an astounding person the likes of which she had never encountered—'warm', 'industrious', 'honest to a fault', 'quick to learn', 'exceedingly bright' and 'creative' to boot—that I stopped hiding my handwriting as if it were a harelip and began to feel at home with my own particular free-for-all style where print and script run hand-in-hand and no two letters look the same.

The other blight no elementary school teacher could let pass was spelling. Thus, efforts to improve my spelling were far more persistent—almost a lifelong pursuit: As a child, each summer was marked by a renewed crusade to teach me phonics for a language that has more exceptions than rules. Summer exercise workbooks were optimistically 'planted' in my trunk on the way to sleepover camp, tucked under the flashlight, pens and pencils and a supply of 3¢ stamps. I never opened them. Pearl never stopped buying them. But talk of tenacity! For the first two decades I lived in Israel (up to age 40 plus) I wrote long letters home once a week, and Pearl faithfully *returned* some of the pages with the worst errors circled with a red pencil and the correct spelling in the margins. It was only when I threatened to stop writing that she stopped nagging.[60] But as soon as PCs appeared on the market in the mid-1980s, a check arrived...to purchase a computer with spell-check software, a new invention.

Nevertheless, there were some lasting legacies of a resident teacher on the home front: Pearl was the wellspring of both her daughters' rich vocabularies and almost impeccable grammar and she continued to correct others' grammar literally to her dying day, a moment shared at Pearl's funeral:

60. I am thoroughly convinced that poor spelling is a built-in handicap like dyslexia—in my case, lack of pattern recognition somehow linked to a similar inability to identify faces and a loss at figures.

> Fair warning to all: Wendy has already assumed the role of the Weiss family grammar police. On Monday evening—already quite reticent as she withdrew from life—Mom broke the silence in a half-whisper: "Better than I" she said, then retreated back into silence. Yes, those were some of her 'dying words'—correcting a good friend, Norma, who had come to visit, pointing out that it was incorrect to say "Pearl, you're better than me"...

There was more. Pearl nurtured a love affair with literature and ideas that lasted a lifetime (and together with the rich vocabulary and good grammar, was the foundation for my instant success as a writer). Her love of books was marked by the ecstasy of going to the library together, browsing leisurely through book stores, sharing articles and dissecting movies or just talking or exploring ideas that continued well into her nineties. When I was still in high school, Pearl allowed me to 'steal-adopt' any books in her library I wanted to supplement my own growing personal library—including all her hardback Hemingways, John Steinbecks and Thomas Wolfes, all of which I took with me to Israel, with her blessings.

This became a family legacy of sorts on my part: Several years ago I invited my kids to do the same—to 'go shopping' in my library. Albeit there were a few books I was not yet ready to part with that I bought Efrat copies of instead, such as *Games People Play* (that *I* had 'inherited' from Pearl). My daughter went home ecstatic with two running meters of philosophy books and some poetry volumes to compliment *her* huge library—a windfall for both of us since in a phone call several days later she shared her astonishment and new-gained respect: "*Ima!*" she exclaimed, "You actually *read* all these philosophy books. I see all the notations in the margins". One of my most memorable moments with Pearl, was the delight of touring London together[61] in 1999 when

61. When it became difficult for Gil and Pearl to travel to Israel (on their last trip, *both* were escorted from the plane to baggage claim in DC in wheelchairs to be picked up by their nephew David—Gil with water retention in his legs and Pearl having tripped over the dog the last night and limping), I began going annually to the States for a month to five weeks every year and

she was already in her eighties — just the two of us, so much in synch that we spent six hours in the Museum of the Moving Image[62] — unplanned and without so much as looking at our watches.

Nevertheless, a reflection of her childhood experiences, Pearl found it exceedingly hard to accept that I, her younger daughter would, quote, "willingly choose to become an immigrant" as Pearl told me once in early 1968 with anguish, as I prepared to leave for Israel for good.[63] Yes, Pearl passionately wanted her children to enjoy all the fruits of 'being third-generation Americans' — a status she and Gil had worked so hard for.

---

the grandkids took turns going, too. Pearl had come to visit the grandkids in Israel on her own in the fall of 1999 — the first time in years (i.e., following Gil's death). I took her half-way home — the two of us spending almost a week in London, going to museums and plays and concerts — before escorting Pearl to the airport to board a plane directly from London to Washington.

62. This lovely museum closed in 1999 and was never reopened on the same massive scale — a genuine loss. For a peek of what it contained, see Jo Brodie, "Much Missed — MOMI, London's Museum of the Moving Image", Stuff That Occurs To Me, 2 January 2014, https://brodiesnotes.blogspot.com/2014/01/much-missed-momi-londons-museum-of.html.

63. The running argument whether one could have it both ways — whether Jewish life in America was sustainable for those who were non-observant but wanted their grandchildren to be Jewish — or whether the only place this was possible was Israel, hung in the air when Pearl shared ruefully decades after I made *aliyah*: "I attended a funeral in New York and I looked around and there were almost no Jews left..." (The statement reflected the fact that some of my close cousins had completely assimilated, intermarried and were not raising Jewish children, if they were having children at all. — DA) A broader look at the family tree as a result of this memoir is a tad more optimistic, but on the whole, the family follows trends of massive intermarriage (71 percent among non-Orthodox Jews) and weakening commitment to invest in Jewish continuity, characteristic of American Jewry today. See this thoughtful 2009 op-ed by academic Jack Wertheimer, "Time for Straight-Talk about Assimilation", *Forward*, 23 September 2009, https://forward.com/opinion/114911/time-for-straight-talk-about-assimilation/.

The decision 'to become an immigrant' would not pose a problem for me. I easily immersed myself in Hebrew culture and never felt marginalized.[64] But, irony of ironies, I found myself reliving the nightmares of her poverty-stricken childhood for a good number of years, barely eking out a living under the shadow of economic uncertainty, a struggle to put food on the table and many sleepless nights fearing we would lose our home and our farm[65] — to debts that were overwhelmingly the product of a broken, overbearing and fundamentally untenable socialist system Pearl once thought was the solution. Doubly ironic: Financial hardships have not been absent from the lives of many of my third-generation American counterparts who remained in the States, and it seems the unprecedented social mobility, economic comfort and job security our parents' generation came to enjoy was a one-generation phenomenon.

Supporting Roles with Others

The 'supporting role' in the lives of others described in this chapter continued to be played out in Pearl and Gil's home long after Wendy moved to Minnesota and I moved to Israel in the late 1960s.

Over the years Pearl had an equally decisive impact on the lives of friends, relatives and anyone who happened to wander into the Weisses' unique household after they were empty nesters — including a family of youngsters who had fled Vietnam and arrived in the United States in 1980 in their teens, without their parents (read Lydia Trang's recollections at the back of the book), first-generation American immigrants

64. My Hebrew was so good that when I became a journalist, some of my highly stylized features in *Davar HaShavuah* (the weekend magazine of Israel's oldest Hebrew daily) were cited and quoted on the Friday morning roundup on the radio among the 'best reads for *Shabbat*' (the equivalent of the Sunday paper).

65. During this time, more than five families that had bought farms in Kfar Warburg more or less during the same time period we did were forced to sell their farms — bankrupt, some leaving homeless and almost penniless, having lost their investments, for several leading to divorce in the process. A joke circulating in those troubled times: 'How can a newcomer to Israel become a millionaire? Come to the country with two million'.

who were in need of not only practical assistance like income-generating work and help with their English but also American role models and warm hugs, which Pearl and Gil spontaneously provided.

For a good number of years after becoming 'empty nesters' Pearl and Gil had both felt rejuvenated by the presence of their dynamo granddaughter Lisa Bard who came to live with them while studying social work at the University of Maryland. But their years of unflagging support and attention through thick and thin came at a cost. Pearl reveled in sharing her granddaughter's studies at the University of Maryland. But there's something called 'too much of a good thing': Over-involvement to a fault on a host of levels ultimately left Gil 'odd man out'. Pearl — despite her background as a counselor — was unable to see there was a problem there or to set boundaries during the years Lisa lived with them or near them, as their granddaughter's needs-demands increased beyond reason as she worked through her problems, exacerbated by growing medical problems — at times aggravated by a tendency to test herself to the breaking point, leaving her grandparents to pick up the pieces. Pearl's symbiotic relationship with Lisa would remain a constant through Pearl's life,[66] but Gil and Pearl were only able to reestablish equilibrium in their couplehood after Lisa moved out for the last time.

During the same time frame in Pearl and Gil's retirement years, Gil went to bat with well-penned arguments on a host of public and private peeves. They ranged from demands that Montgomery County makes Democracy Lane safer (think 'speed bumps' or enforcing the speed limit) after Gil almost got run down *inside his own yard*, to fruitless attempts to sing the praises of a sacked synagogue cantor by

---

66. While Pearl came to recognize that some aspects of their overly-intertwined relationship were not healthy, Lisa's presence, Pearl told me at one point, alleviated her loneliness (that growing isolation/'invisible' status old age and widowhood all too often carry) — particularly when Pearl found that after Gil's departure, the Quartet didn't *always* include her when they went out together (then the integrity and intensity of this social safety net slowly wilted of natural causes in any case, as deaths and health issues intervened). In this sense, for Pearl, Lisa was a lifesaver and fulfilled an existential need for companionship.

an "Ad Hoc Committee of Concerned Congregants" he organized. But the folks — both Pearl and Gil — being 'people persons' to the core was epitomized by a 'thank you letter' Gil got from the gal *he* ran into in 1998, almost killing her and totaling her car. She wrote:

> Dear Mr. Weiss,
>
> I want to thank you so very much for your wonderful attitude and your care and concern for my well-being after our collision. Your actions were so admirable and I want you to know that my husband and I really appreciated your phone calls, too,
>
> Sincerely Gail Lanier

Another incredible sign of the same way Pearl and Gil affected people they encountered — everyone they met, no matter how briefly: In 1998 when Gil died "even Gil's oncologist from the hospital sent Pearl a long condolence letter".[67]

67. Noted in an email I sent to my family in Israel on 17 July — a week after the funeral — "the mailbox is filled with [condolence] cards".

Chapter V

Of People, Times and Places

What was life like in the Weiss household and what was it like to grow up in Washington in those times–during the Second World War and through the height of the Cold War?

Memories of Skyland and Silver Spring

Growing Up in Southeast Washington

Skyland, with its garden-style apartments, where the Pearl and Gil rented an apartment in late 1939, was another planet from New York and heaven-on-earth in Washington's looming housing shortage. They were lucky to have been among the 'early arrivals' in the massive influx: The job market exploded during the Second World War, quadrupling the number of civilians employed by the government between 1940 and 1945 — peaking at 10,000 new arrivals a month...*after* Pearl and Gil had procured living accommodations in Skyland. But Skyland, and Southeast Washington in general as a place to settle-in had not been their first choice:

Skyland in SE Washington, 2018

> A friend told us the only place for a Jewish person to live and feel comfortable was in Northwest Washington, but every apartment we could afford was below par — dirty and

> run-down. A friend of my stepsister Pauline[1] said 'why don't you come out here — to Southeast Washington?' She said there was a new development being built right near where she lived — and we got a [two-bedroom] garden apartment for $40 a month — with trees and grass all taken care of by the management. That was Skyland.

In reading about Washington in the 1940s, I was rather surprised to discover that Fred Kogod, the self-made Washington businessman who financed Nana and the Platt's deli/grocery in Northeast Washington in 1944 was also the real estate developer who had built Skyland Apartments in 1939. Today, Skyland is a 'gated community' with the same squat two-story redbrick 'townhouse'-like duplex apartments, an oasis in a largely run-down area.

The word 'Skyland' immediately conjures up the distinctive scent of 1940 vintage apartments with their polished hardwood floors and bathrooms with a can't-quite-describe stamp of 'stoniness' always hanging in the air, given off by the small geometric unglazed bathroom tiles of the era. And seasonal sounds and smells — of wet woolen socks from sledding drying on steam radiators in winter, and the call of the crickets — and the cicadas once every seven years — through open windows in summer, above the jingle of the Good Humor man in his ice cream truck. The tactile delight of playing with the suds that spilled out onto the polished concrete floor of the public laundry room located on the corner of the ground floor of the adjacent apartment building, with its bank of industrial size washing machines. Flashbacks of a small galley-like kitchen off the dining room, and a living room dominated by Gil's self-crafted bookcase; an overstuffed green velvet sofa flanked by dark-stained end tables embellished with a lace-like lip around the edge. And in the middle of the room, parked in front of the television, an unvarnished child-size chair with a woven straw seat identical to the one in Van Gogh's famous oils,[2] which as a child I would 'ride'

1. Pauline was one of Dave Lefkowitz's daughters.

2. The most iconic of the artist's numerous oils and sketches on this topic, see The National Gallery in London, https://www.nationalgallery.org.uk/paintings/

backward as if it was a horse, while watching “The Lone Ranger”.[3]

A hideous trap or an innocent railing?

My most vivid (and earliest) memories are of Raymond the gardener with his monstrous black lawnmower that looked like the Grim Reaper from the perspective of a toddler locked in a playpen in the front yard as Raymond came closer and closer... The second most vivid memory was the time I poked my head through the iron railing of the banister to the second story of our Skyland apartment and got stuck. In the middle of soaping my head to free me, Gil quipped in jest that they just might have to cut off my head to get me out... For the future, I kept my poking around to climbing in and out of the big rectangular plywood dustbin on wheels for discarded paper smelling faintly of cigarette butts that sat near the public laundry room, where my best friend Nancy Gatzke and I searched for foreign stamps.

At the height of McCarthyism, with the hearings being beamed across the nation on television,[4] the atmosphere was contagious: We were sure the stamps we found — some with portraits of Hitler, some with portraits of the Queen of England — belonged to a Skyland spy.

---

vincent-van-gogh-van-goghs-chair.

3. To view some of the first of the 1952 television series *The Lone Ranger*, go to “The Lone Ranger | Season 1 | Full Episodes”, YouTube video, https://youtu.be/putXSdjlztE?list=PLjkUwl9vY2dx-8Qpn4w3CWFLKyu0dY-NtE. Snippets from the 1933 to 1954 radio show can be heard at, “The Lone Ranger”, Old Time Radio Westerns, https://www.otrwesterns.com/westerns/the-lone-ranger/.

4. For a short documentary on McCarthyism, see “McCarthyism in America”, YouTube video, 10:30 minutes, 2014, https://www.youtube.com/watch?v=iFHhqlfypOo.

Anything not American was suspect. Likewise, the looming German Orphanage on the hill overlooking Skyland, half-concealed among the trees on Good Hope Road, looked sinister with its round Romanesque-style medieval keep and conical roof, and as a child—keep in mind, this is only a few scant years after the Holocaust—I was convinced it must surely harbor escaped Nazis.

Family rituals? We knew summer was at hand when Gil began hooking up his miraculous window-fan circulation system in the days prior to air-conditioning, designed to 'make the air go around corners'—a gallant but hopeless engineering feat devised to beat Washington's horrendous summers into submission.[5] In fact, in the 1950s, Great Britain classified Washington as a hardship post for British diplomats due to the city's heat and humidity. As a child, I thought my father was surely defying the laws of physics with this cooling system. The other sources of respite from Washington's 90-degree heat and 99-percent humidity were going for rides in the car after dusk with all the windows open, along the Anacostia River where a huge concrete tunnel ran parallel to the road and the river for a long stretch that I was sure must conceal an atom bomb factory (also a reflection of the times). Actually, it was the original Model Basin in the old Navy Yard for testing the hydrodynamics of ship hull design.

Part of growing up in the Nation's Capital was knowing our father had a special pass to whisk him out of Washington in the event of a Soviet ballistic missile attack on Washington. We were supposed to rendezvous in the aftermath of World War III at the Schwartz family's home in Aberdeen, Maryland. I often wonder if the Duck 'n Cover drills[6] that sent schoolchildren scurrying to kneel in a fetal position under their desks with their hands over their heads as an appropriate response to being nuked by a hydrogen bomb weren't the root of so many of my contemporaries becoming Flower Children.

---

5. One window fan pulling the hot air inside the house outside, a second window fan around the corner blowing the 'cooled' air back into the room...

6. See vintage footage of Duck 'n Cover drills at "Duck and Cover clipped", YouTube video, 2:51 minutes, 2008, https://www.youtube.com/watch?v=89od_W8lMtA.

There were other iconic images of summer: Collecting thousands of Japanese beetles in mason jars, a scourge that literally covered the bushes in the 1950s, creating grape-like undulating clusters that covered the bushes, weighing down the boughs and skeletonizing the leaves. Authorities requested children collect as many as possible in killing jars in a pathetic attempt to address the crisis. And at dusk, the universal children's delight of the times, collecting zillions of fireflies that were in abundance — taken home to illuminate the children's bedrooms with their soft greenish glow. And speaking of summers, there were Victory Gardens at the bottom of Skyland Place — kitchen plots, initially in response to wartime shortages and rationing[7] that Skyland continued to rent out for a nominal fee in the 1950s. Every summer we watched Gil hammer in his tomato stakes while a congressman from Texas with a five-gallon watering can and a ten-gallon hat tended his cucumber plants 'next-door'. In fact, one of my first memories as a child was crouching in the gutter looking for 'treasures' where the curb let off and the gardens began. Metal nuts washed down the street in the rain, worn out washers, tiny springs — minus an occasional slightly corroded penny fished out of the pools of oily water in the ruts, were always proudly presented to my father for his "Good Junk box". In fact, once Wendy and I gave Gil a box of Good Junk for his birthday.

There was the wrath of Skyland's gardener Raymond, complaining I was 'ruining the grass' from repeatedly playing in the dirt with my plastic Fort Apache playset[8] on the same packed spot in front of the house[9] humming to myself "Mares eat oats and does eat oats and

---

7. See this 1942 government film encouraging the planting of Victory Gardens "Victory Gardens in World War II", YouTube video, 1:37 minutes, https://www.youtube.com/watch?v=Lnwle4dsEgc.

8. See the original 1951 Marx "Fort Apache" play set here: http://marxwildwest.com/Wonderland.html#fort_apache. I was never enthusiastic about dressing up 'paper dolls' though we did that too...

9. Google Earth testifies that to this day, grass still doesn't grow in that spot to the left of the sidewalk... It was there in 1951 I suspect that my older sister — not much of an enabler — decided to call me Pig Pen behind my back. On *Peanut*'s Pig Pen persona, see *Wikipedia*, s.v. "Pig-Pen", https://en.wikipedia.org/wiki/Pig-Pen, and "Pig-Pen", Peanuts Wiki, https://peanuts.fandom.

little lambs eat ivy".[10] Bought in 1951 for $5 with my Hanukah *gelt*,[11] the tableau's snap-lock stockade and guard towers and molded rubber Cavalry and Indians (a forerunner of Playmobil) were always augmented by Indian 'encampments' with tepees and campfires made of twigs.

At the corner near the entrance to Skyland was a deli with dill pickles in a barrel. And just up the street, the Naylor Theatre where kids went to the movies on Saturdays. The stage curtain once caught fire from a spotlight in a theatre packed with kids; luckily, before we could panic, the flames were put out with a fire extinguisher by a children's performer named Hop-Along Cassidy who was entertaining the audience between double-features. (Incidentally, nobody called the fire department or thought to evacuate the theater.) And there was a Five and Dime (the precursor of today's Dollar Store) just across the street from the Naylor Theatre that sold not only crayons and erasers but also a rainbow assortment of live day-old baby chicks for a dime at Easter, alongside the chocolate-covered marshmallow bunnies. (I believe my cousin David Platt is the only kid whose chick grew to maturity and for a time the Platt's had a full-grown rooster that sat in the branches of a small tree in the back yard and made a racket.)

In those days, kids not only walked to school (unescorted); the majority went home for lunch since most mothers in those days were housewives. Between nine and three there was 'recess' — when all the children were forced outside into the playground for some 'fresh air', including in the dead of winter, provided it was not raining or snowing. I hated recess with a passion and not only because it was a hopeless exercise trying to cover our bare legs from the cold: Girls had to wear dresses to school and there were no tights. The best we could do was assume a crouching position, which didn't prevent our legs from taking on a reddish-blue paisley hue under knee-length coats. Nancy and I and Judy Thurm would position ourselves for the duration on

---

com/wiki/%22Pig-Pen%22.

10. Up until not so many years ago, I thought this ditty was a nonsense rhyme — "Marsey dotes and dosey dotes and little lamsy ivy, a kiddle eat ivy too wouldn't you" — until the actual lyrics dawned on me.

11. Money in Yiddish.

the edge of the raised delivery ramp next to the back entrance facing the schoolyard that always smelled of slightly sour milk — served with a graham cracker as a mid-morning snack underwritten by the Congress to ensure every American child would get a glass of milk daily.[12] From a safe distance, we would eye the boys playing dodge ball and the girls playing hopscotch against the backdrop of a cacophony of shrieks as other kids ran helter-skelter around the playground chasing one another (even recalling watching this activity is still anxiety-producing) as we waited for the teacher on 'playground duty' to blow her whistle signaling that the 20-minute recess was over and we could line up to go back inside.

One of the perks of living in Washington, DC was the city's free museums that were like a second home for the children of the metropolitan area. Countless Saturdays were spent on the Mall viewing — wide-eyed — the Smithsonian Institute's massive collection of vintage Iron Horse locomotives, dinosaurs and life-size three-dimensional portrayals in huge glass display cases of the life of this or that decimated Indian tribe. For years, I dreamt of becoming a diorama designer when I grew up. One can't help but note that more than half a century later, the Smithsonian's National Museum of the American Indian (opened in 2004) is still solely devoted to the "culture, traditional values, and transitions in contemporary Native life" — glorifying the same folklore of yore (they added Indian code-talkers and code breakers in the World Wars) while delicately skipping over the less photogenic aspects of Native American history... The Trail of Tears isn't even mentioned, while the Holocaust Museum — devoted to making consciousness of the Holocaust an integral part of the American Experience, not just the Jewish Experience — sits just off the Mall. Parallel to the Smithsonian there were numerous visits to Washington's art museums[13] including

12. Schools received federal assistance — reimbursement for operating School Milk Programs that began in 1940 in poor neighborhoods and were virtually universal throughout America by the 1950s.

13. Where we bought reproductions of our favorite paintings on display, to frame and hang on the wall above our beds — mine (how could it be otherwise) was a Van Gough chair just like my television chair.

attending children's art classes on the weekend at the Corcoran Gallery.

What were the neighborhood and the neighbors like?[14] There were only three or four Jewish families in the entire Skyland complex — including Pearl and Gil's best friends the Abbotts. The neighbors' kids in our row of eight apartments included Dickey Jones, the 'blind kid' who used to barrel down the sidewalk on his tricycle based on 'feel' alone, and Patty Pitts — the obese 'retarded girl' with bad breath and her two siblings, and us. Just down the street opposite the gardens lived my best (and lifelong) friend Nancy Gatzke — who was also a tomboy and loved to climb trees and play in the woods. The Gatzke's Christmas tree with its exquisite glass antique decorations from Europe was a source of secret envy every December — while Nancy once got her mouth washed out with soap by her strict Minnesota-born Lutheran mother after I taught Nancy the word 'damn'.[15] There were the Bad Boys from the Judge family down the street who terrorized all the other kids in the neighborhood, and Rusty — the red-headed kid who got whipped with a belt by his father, an Irish policeman, for calling us "Dirty Jews". Grouchy Mr. Baron lived next door and sweet Marie lived across the street next-door to the Abbotts — a spinster who always put out a marvelous bowl of shiny new pennies in a crystal bowl at Halloween with instructions to children that they could grab 'a whole fist full' for their trick 'r treat bags of goodies. Even after we moved to

---

14. Incredibly, Google Earth shows 2354 Skyland Place hasn't changed *at all* in 80 years, except for a window air conditioner in the living room in lieu of Gil's miraculous cooling system that went around corners. It is as if time has stood still — the same row of eight red brick townhouse apartments with white mantels above the front door (maybe the shutters are new). The public laundry room entrance is still there just to the left, with the complex's steam heating power plant chimney. Only the playground 'up the steps' behind our house is now a parking lot. Take a tour of Skyland with Google Earth at https://goo.gl/maps/vG5MdUwMgCs. Imagine with your mind's eye, victory gardens and the woods at the end of Skyland Place, today replaced by a row of single dwelling houses.

15. This was after both the Gatzkes and the Weisses had moved to Silver Spring. Nancy and I dreamed as kids of having a horse farm. As adults she bought three horses — one of them a retired race horse — while I bought a farm...

Maryland, we continued to periodically visit the elderly childless Swiss couple Mr. and Mrs. Bissell and their parakeet Billy, not only to savor again Mrs. Bassell's incredible chocolate-cream pie but also to reminisce how Mrs. Bassell would soothe Wendy when she was cranky as a baby with the magic of a Talking Medicine Cabinet: The Weiss and the Bessell apartments[16] had a common wall including two recessed medicine cabinets back-to-back in the bathrooms with no insulation in between...thus the Talking Medicine Cabinet was born.

One of the highlights of childhood was watching Norman Abbott's tiny 8-inch black and white TV.[17] Sitting in a semi-circle on the floor watching the "Howdy Doody Show",[18] all the kids wore eyeglasses for myopia or eye patches for a 'lazy eye'...all except Myrna who had perfect vision but put on an eye patch so as not to feel left out. And speaking of eyes, life in Skyland was marked not only by 'going down to the lines' at the end of the street once a week to hang wet laundry on pulley-rigged clotheslines in the woods; twice a week we also traipsed down into Washington after school for what were heralded as 'eye exercises'—promising to improve our eyesight. We were a carload of kids—Wendy and I, David Lesser and Glenda Abbott—with her sister Myrna going along for the ride and keeping us entertained with the 'Mary Sidewalk' stories she made up.[19] Dr.

16. Pearl and Gil's original two-bedroom apartment in Skyland, prior to Nana joining them.

17. Which either Norman built—he was an electronics engineer (the story I got), or was given to him by a friend in manufacturing (according to Myrna). In any case, there was no case—just the screen mounted on a base where exposed wires and vacuum tubes could be seen at the back.

18. For a taste of children's television in the late 1940s and 1950s (actually the show ran until 1960!), see the "*Howdy Doody Show*, The (Intro) S1 (1947)", YouTube video, 2:21 minutes, https://www.youtube.com/watch?v=pnUGAe0yqz4. The wooden marionette Howdy Doody had 48 freckles (one for each state in the Union)...

19. The fact that Myrna became a computer person rather than a children's book author is everyone's loss.

Kraskin[20] not only claimed he could strengthen eye coordination by tracing stereoscopic drawings of houses and horses, and improve acuity or focusing by watching numbers flashed on a screen with a projector in a darkened room, with instructions to write down the sequences. He also claimed he could improve nearsightedness by staring at a kaleidoscope in a darkened room for an insufferable length of time (something like twenty minutes at a go, which was an eternity for a 1st or 2nd grader like myself). But who complained? At the end of each session, we children were rewarded — allowed to choose a whole candy bar out of a huge glass jar next to the receptionist's desk at the door. (This medical practice still exists — only today it's labeled 'vision therapy' or 'vision training' and they no longer claim to cure myopia.) And after eye exercises, just around the corner as we headed for the car, we would give pennies to 'the legless beggar with the monkey and a cup' propped up against the side of a building on F Street, a Washington icon of the 1950s. Four decades later Pearl found Gypsy, the monkey, in the Aspin Animal Cemetery[21] along with Edgar Hoover's dog, when she accompanied me to gather material for a story for *Davar*'s weekend magazine on dog cemeteries during one of my annual visits[22] — Pearl scouting out the most interesting gravestones to photograph, including the ones with a Jewish Star, while I interviewed the proprietor.

It is hard to fathom the freedom kids enjoyed in those days — playing in the woods for hours — making and shooting bows and arrows, building forts and just exploring, totally unsupervised by adults, without

20. Were all our doctors Jewish? I know there was Katz (the optometrist), Katzen (the dentist) and Kraskin (the...oh well, — forget it).

21. For the incredible story of the F Street beggar of our childhood — Eddie Bernstein, actually a rags-to-riches saga, and his monkey, see "Eddie 'The Monkey Man' Bernstein: A Rags To Riches Story", Pet Cemetery Stories, https://petcemeterystories.net/2018/08/13/eddie-the-monkey-man-bernstein-a-rags-to-riches-story/#more-383.

22. Another memorable joint jaunt during my annual visits — the hours Pearl and I spent at the Newseum in Alexandria, Virginia as I gathered material to write a profile for the Israeli newspapers on this unique museum of the media and news-making. See https://www.newseum.org/.

fear of pedophiles molesting, kidnapping or murdering them. Flashbacks of landmark events during the Weiss family's 16 years in Skyland include integration of the schools in 1954 when Pearl had to drive Wendy to Kramer Junior High though a crowd of white supremacists and protesting parents yelling obscenities, but those years were mostly marked by the prestige of having a mom who worked at the same elementary school her kids attended.

Babysitting 'Annie Oakley'

If one runs out of flashbacks of the times, Gil's Memorabilia contains additional prompts: There were the periodic visits from FBI agents scrutinizing the titles in the bookcase.[23] And, of course, mementos Gil saved from the Second World War — such as an "Application for Supplemental and Occupational Mileage" dated July 1945, requesting more than five gallons of gas a month because four other Navy employees from Skyland were using Gil's 1948 Dodge to carpool to work. He even saved leftover gas ration stamps, just in case... Also among the personal family mementos is a 1949 note from eight-year-old Wendy, having been pressed into service as a babysitter for her four-year-old sister.

> Mommy–
>
> Diana was talking-Shooting her guns–and she didn't Stop TaLKING UntIL 11: O'CLOCK AND SHE WAS jumping on and off her bed. And She was borthering Me so much until I Read her Two Comic Book and here They are. And She was running around The room and Making Lots of Noise. <u>She</u> <u>was</u> <u>very</u> <u>Bad</u>.
>
> Sincerely
> Wendy

23. For more on this, see the section Letters from Spain.

The Dream House in Silver Spring

Pearl and Gil moved to the suburbs in 1955 when their children were in 4th and 8th grade—to a house designed by Gil—his dream house with a Cape Cod-style dormer in the front, just as he wanted it. Built by a private contractor in Silver Spring, it had four bedrooms, allowing the kids to have separate rooms. The Shop became Gil's haven; the eating alcove with its facing benches—the nook where Pearl 'held court'. The house and garden, together with the Shop was the culmination of a dream for Gil.

The word 'Woodland Drive' conjures up flashbacks of the hum of lawnmowers and the sweet aroma of fresh-cut grass in the summer and the smell and the crackle of a fire in the fireplace in winter (especially the time Wendy and I decided to make a fire for our father when he came home from work, and forgot to open the chimney damper...). The aroma of chicken soup on the stove or *rugelach* in the oven filling the house. The smell of sawdust and turpentine as one descended the gray wooden steps into the basement. Images of the Baldwin baby grand piano (there must be a story behind this—how Pearl and Gil came to acquire a baby grand...) that dominated the space between the living room and the dining room.[24] Recollections of the slightly sour smell of the gray insulated box at the back door entrance in the 1950s where several times a week the milkman delivered non-homogenized milk under aluminum foil caps and sour cream in glass returnable bottles. Homemade bird feeders on a pole in the back yard (my

Woodland Drive in Silver Spring

24. Where everyone took piano lessons although I never even got past the first grade book of the *John Thompson Modern Course for Piano*, mostly playing *underneath* the piano with the dog or my toys. For all those who took piano lessons in the 1950s, savor those iconic bars, "John Thompson Modern Course for Piano First Grade All", YouTube video, 31:47 minutes, https://www.youtube.com/watch?v=QB8Y_96By9E.

most 'sophisticated' woodworking projects), stocked in winter with a transparent Plexiglas seed dispenser and frozen peanut butter and suet on a spike. Gil's vegetable garden with its tomatoes and cucumbers and green beans at the back of the lot, mixed with the unmistakable whiff of marigolds. A bug collection in glass display cases with mahogany trimming. Raising live praying mantis pairs in a screen cage, fed dead flies impaled on thin strands of screening wire waved back and forth until the mantis pounced, watching mesmerized as the female ate the male after mating, then spun a cocoon on a small branch — taken out and placed close to the site of the summer vegetable garden as a natural biological insecticide. And the dogs: Perky, the scrappy wire-haired terrier, then Black Knight, a cowardly and timid Sheltie.

Perky was a frisky and unruly adopted 'rescue dog' whose prior young companion had thrown down a flight of steps and broken his hip, which Perky always favored and lifted when the barometer was falling, thus serving as a reliable in-house weather forecaster. Dog obedience classes under the tutelage of Miss Clancy — after a battle of iron wills between the two transformed Perky into a model house dog. But when left to his own devices, being high strung (perhaps the reason this breed is called a wire-haired terrier) Perky would occasionally pick fights with neighborhood dogs three-times his size, including Big Boy — a mild-mannered Dalmatian next door. It took several years, but two full-size Boxers up the street eventually cornered Perky in the stairwell to the basement entrance when no one was home, and literally tore Perky to shreds, breaking my heart in the process.

The Weisses fenced-in the yard and got Black Knight — a misnomer for an excruciatingly timid young adult miniature Shetland Sheepdog from a puppy mill. Having been traumatized as a puppy by his mother and grandmother and made the outcast of the litter, Black Knight came with a long illustrious pedigree and a considerable discount. And being criminally inbred to produce a perfect black Sheltie, Black Knight suffered from seasonal eczema that kept the local vet, Dr. Roeder, in business for almost two decades. But Black Knight became an affectionate dog and we loved him back, although he continued to turn tail and run to hide under Nana's bed whenever the doorbell rang.

Woodland Drive was a 'United Nations'. The Weiss house was

flanked on one side by Jewish business people — the Weiners with their two mousey daughters (rarely seen). On the other side lived a large 'All American' Catholic family — the Romeros, a lawyer with five children and a huge train set that occupied most of their basement while several jalopies decorated their back yard which father Bob and his boys tinkered with every weekend. Across the street were two Greek immigrant families — the Bouis brothers — also business people. And down the street resided two spinster sisters — the Yudoffs. There was a significant Jewish component to the neighborhood which was a mixture of business people and professionals.[25] It was a fairly typical suburb for its times *a la* Montgomery County (not counting certain neighborhoods that had restrictive covenants excluding Jews and non-Caucasians).[26] Membership in the new 'Jewish' Indian Springs Country Club which opened in 1958 didn't last long. Indian Springs had been formed because all the other country clubs in DC didn't accept Jews, so the Jews formed their own country club. Gil and his girls, however, were 'ducks out of water' because most of the Jewish men were off on the golf course, and most of the Jewish women came to play mahjong or bake themselves bronze in the sun along with their JAP daughters. *No one*

25. As a result, a good proportion of the school body was Jewish. As for the 'neighborhood girls' the majority were the archetype upon which the term JAP (Jewish American Princess) took root in the 1950s. For a profile of the JAP, see Jamie Lauren Keiles, "Reconsidering the Jewish American Princess", https://www.vox.com/the-goods/2018/12/5/18119890/jewish-american-princess-jap-stereotype. My best friend in the neighborhood was Lynn Clement from my Girl Scout troop (mostly JAPs) who was also a tomboy who liked mastering knots and hiking in the woods — an army brat with a basketball hoop in the driveway, whose brothers were forced to call their dad 'sir'... In middle school I met Elinore Leibersohn — a year younger than I, who had moved into the neighborhood, and we became close friends.

26. For more on the racists and the antisemitic undercurrent that permeated Washington in the 1950s and early 1960s — including the restrictive housing covenants and White-Christians-Only men's clubs and country clubs — read the 2019 profile by economist/commentator and TV personality Ben Stein (a contemporary and fellow classmate), Ben Stein, "Growing Up Jewish in D.C.", *The American Spectator*, https://spectator.org/growing-up-jewish-in-d-c/.

was swimming and the family had the Olympic size pool almost exclusively to themselves. The next year the Weisses joined the Jaffes and a host of other Jewish families at the YMCA's pool and tennis courts (the 'old' Indian Spring in Silver Spring). Yes, we signed cards that we believed Jesus Christ was our Savior, but the milieu was far more *heimish* (Jewishly 'homey') than Indian Springs.

A Watershed Event Seldom Shared

In the mid-1970s, Pearl and Gil suddenly chose to sell the house and move to Potomac. Officially, they claimed knowledge of plans for a subway station just up the street was the catalyst, and that from a tax and home equity standpoint, it would be a good move. The Metro station was slated to be built literally just up the block (it only opened in 1990) and they had apprehensions such proximity would clog street parking with commuters' vehicles, and impact negatively on the safety of the neighborhood by offering 'easy access and a swift exit' for unsavory dudes who could work under the cover of unfamiliar commuters who would be traversing the neighborhood to reach their cars. As it was, some 5,000 homes adjacent to Washington's rim road interchanges (that included the Georgia Avenue exit from the beltway, right near the house) had already been targeted in the 1960s by a gang of robbers dubbed 'the [Capital] Beltway bandits' who used the Beltway for a quick getaway after burglarizing nearby homes.

But there was another reason they rarely mentioned (perhaps tied to the Beltway bandits) that was a catalyst for abandoning their dream house: Upon returning to the house in Silver Spring from a trip out of town[27] Pearl and Gil found the house had been broken into. There were swastikas on the doors, women's undergarments spread out on the bed in a suggestive manner with a message in lipstick on the mirror threatening rape next time (i.e., besides the *mezuzah* on the door, the house had Judaica prominently displayed and was clearly a 'Jewish home'). The incident left them shaken to the core. They no longer felt safe and Pearl did not want to stay in this house alone when Gil

27. This incident was also mentioned by Gil's boss George Spangenberg in his 1998 eulogy.

traveled for work (he was going up to Grumman regularly). This antisemitic incident and fears the perpetrators might return to make good on their threat was a major catalyst in selling their dream house, and in 1975, they moved from Silver Spring to Potomac — to the house on Democracy Lane.

Gibby's green thumb had begun to germinate in Silver Spring — fighting dandelions and crabgrass, rooting *ligustrum* cuttings in coffee cans in the basement every winter to extend the hedge with the Romeros, planting zinnias and marigolds in the spring and nurturing dwarf fruit trees and two blueberry bushes...and the famous *photinia* bush on the side of the house that Nana was supposed to jump into to break her fall when escaping from her ground-floor bedroom, in the event of a fire. But the true masterpiece was the landscaping of the house in Potomac, Maryland — planned in detail and equipped with the latest state-of-the-art drip irrigation equipment, different texture beds with shrubs and groundcover, and brick and slate walkways, patios and edging. It was truly a *magnum opus.* As luck would have it, Gil had completed this massive landscaping project just before he had that massive heart attack in the summer of 1984 and his cardiologist said to a large extent he could chalk up his miraculous survival on having been in top physical condition — in part from *schlepping* around literally tons of slate and brick — before this medical emergency struck.

A quarter of an acre of azaleas

Both Woodland Drive and Democracy Lane were studded with Gil's favorite shrub — azaleas. And both yards reserved a place at the back of the lot for his beloved cucumbers and home-grown vine tomatoes... and, of course, a compost pile. Little did I know, the green thumb gene I inherited (I also had my own small garden in the back lot in Silver Spring) would germinate into a yen for a full-blown farm — foolishly ignoring the Hebrew adage: "You don't have to buy the whole cow to drink a cup of milk".

Travels with the Weisses

In the course of his pioneering work standardizing design specifications for the Navy, Gil Weiss traveled to post-war London in 1953 in a cavernous prop-driven troop carrier with canvas seats along the walls that make today's cramped cabins in tourist class look like the lap of luxury. Somehow he succeeded in bringing back as a souvenir a fragile circular pendulum clock under a glass dome–all in one piece, along with a ballet program from the Royal Ballet signed by Margot Fonteyn for his 12-year-old daughter Wendy...which Wendy still has among *her* Miscellaneous more than 67 years later... One of the classic stories about his travels was the time Gil went to the West Coast for an aeronautics conference, ended up living in the same clothes for several days due to lost luggage woes, and on his way *back* to Washington, spotting his lost bag sitting patiently on a cart in the Detroit airport which hadn't been on his itinerary on the trip West.

~

And there were family vacations. Vacationing with Nana and Grandma Weiss at a dumpy 'resort' near Niagara Falls in 1950 where hearing a commotion below, Gil ran out to cut the head off a huge blacksnake dangling above the heads of the grandmothers sitting on a bench in the garden under a leafy decorative trellis. (Why Gil went on vacation with an ax in his bags remains an enigma.) There was also that definitive week at the Bushes' farm in Stroudsburg, Pennsylvania in the summer of 1952 where Wendy caught a rainbow trout, Nana fell through a rotten board on the pier ending up with a badly lacerated leg, and I got badly bitten by the farming bug. There were unforgettable family vacations at the Abbotts in Asbury Park building dikes in the sand as the tide came in that conjure up flashbacks of sand underfoot, the arid smell of creosol from the boardwalk quaffing over the dominant tang of salt in the air, mixed with the unmistakable trademark smell of black inflated inner tubes baking in the sun.

Yes, Asbury Park! I almost forgot! We almost lost Gil twice. Once when he had a massive heart attack at age 69 in 1984, the other back in 1954 when he was 39–the fault of 'Loona the Tuna'. Loona the

Vacations at the Abbotts—Asbury Park, NJ

Tuna–that we got in the mail for a dollar and a Star-Kist tuna label — almost cost him his life. Gil swam right out into the Atlantic Ocean after that dumb 4-foot long red and yellow inflatable plastic fish and almost didn't make it back.

There was a month-long cross-country journey by car to the West Coast in 1960[28] with a borrowed wheezing window-mounted 'desert cooler' that smelled like a damp sleeping bag (no AC in those days) and a mysterious clickety-clack sound under the hood of our '55 Chevy that accompanied us from somewhere in the Midwest heading west, appearing and disappearing, but always vanishing within sight of a service station. We visited all the major state parks in the west. We water skied on Lake Mead (after gregarious Gil struck up a conversation with a family towing a speed boat, and Wendy taught me to use Tampax® when I got my period the day before we reached Lake Mead). We saw our first palm tree ('hairy lollypops') in LA, and — Innocents Abroad — traipsed off the highway to visit the Petrified Forest in Arizona at high noon in open tops and no sunscreen or hats (that's how much we knew about deserts).

Much later Pearl and Gil took countless trips to Israel, for several years staying in places in Kfar Warburg that would rival Tobacco Road, one such place describe optimistically in a 1978 letter from Israel saying:

---

28. Pearl could painlessly and 'automatically' renew her certification as a teacher without taking the "additional dumb pedagogy course" she detested, by horizon-widening travel. No doubt she had to keep a journal and submit it, but strangely enough, no such record emerged among the Miscellaneous, although there were enough 'travel documents' among trip mementos 30 years later to substantiate she'd taken the trip.

> [...] It's old, like ours more or less—but has a bathtub (with tile) [...] The only place that's bad is between the eating alcove and the kitchen the floors are different levels and the floor tiles are cracked, but after all you are not living there permanently. [...] Some problems with the electricity but they expect to have it fixed in several weeks once the walls dry out from the winter.

The new house with a guest bedroom—today my office—was only completed nine years after buying the farm in July 1973 and half a year before Nadav was born in April 1981. During that period, the farm only had a tiny three-room 72 square meter (775 sq. foot) house and close-by accommodations needed to be found. But later, the 'little house' was renovated and transformed into Pearl and Gil's own personal one-bedroom vacation house with a large fully-equipped kitchen and living room—private accommodations where they spend a month to six weeks a year....and where the grandkids could stop for popsicles after school, visit and do stuff with their grandparents and 'sleep over' in turn.

Gil and Pearl had no less adventurous times in Europe—Greece, Italy, Spain, Ireland, Switzerland and other destinations on the way back from Israel—once, arriving in England when the entire country was closed down for three days for Boxing Day, another time oversleeping and missing their plane. Gil saved every airline stub and boarding pass they ever used—not only 'memorable flights' on Air India and Iberia Airlines (one where Pearl passed out due to faulty air circulation). Among a carton filled to the gills with travel mementos were: old insurance claims; museum entrance tickets; old tourist brochures of places visited and places missed; countless maps, Trip Tiks[29] and AAA books

29. In the days before GPS, narrow spiral-bound flip charts published print-on-demand for a fee by the American Automobile Association or AAA that mapped one's route from point A to B (even cross-country)—marking the highway one should take, and all intersections, towns, etc. on the route; the 'navigator' in the front passenger seat would flip to a new page every 10 or 15 miles. See Carol Margolis, "Remember TripTik?" Pearls of Travel Wisdom, https://pearlsoftravelwisdom.boardingarea.com/2014/01/remember-triptix/.

Travel souvenirs

on tourist attractions and accommodations dating back to the 1950s; a longhand list of expressions in Greek and shorthand list of expenses in Italy in a small spiral notebook; invoices for car rentals, dollar exchange rates, hotel bills including a meal at the *Singing Bird Restaurant* in London (soup, stew, lemon soda and coffee) totaling £7.35; unused Kodak home movie film with a 1981 and 1984 expiration date and used handmade titles for editing movies for every trip every taken together ("Daniella Efrat and Asaf visit USA, April 1977") with a mini studio of cutouts of buses, airplanes and cardboard letters for enhancements. Also in this 'time capsule' was a packet of *Souvenir Views from the Adirondack Mountains* stipulating "1½ cents postage without message" on the cover; a $3.00 child's all-day pass to Colonial Williamsburg good for 5 August 1955 and a July 1950 postcard to Wendy at Camp Louise from Niagara Falls with a picture of an "aero cable car" bearing a message from Pearl clarifying the car "wasn't closed in" and noting that "Diana was a little afraid at first and worried that Suzie would fall into the river. But by the time the ride was over she wanted to go again".[30]

Undoubtedly, one of the *strangest* mementos Gil chose to keep was a comic book of *Ricky and Debbie in Sardineland* from a trip to Maine, although a 1984 *Peter Pan Peanut Butter Activity Calendar* studded with coupons was a close runner-up.

The closest to home in the 'must save' pile of places visited was a National Park Service flier explaining what to do if you fall into fast rushing water at Great Falls — the series of rapids and falls 14 miles upstream from Washington DC on the Potomac River — with a table of the number of drownings annually between 1975 and 1986 case-by-case noting under what circumstances they occurred. Not only were the victims fishing, canoeing, hiking, swimming, boating or rafting — but also "sunbathing" (two cases) and "rock hopping" (seven cases). Most important — if *you* fall into the river at Great Falls, remember: "Float through the rapids on your back with toes up and pointing downstream".

~

While not exactly a vacation, there were frequent trips to Virginia on Sundays to visit Pearl's sister Ruth — a larger than life figure in every

30. I haven't the foggiest idea who Suzie was — perhaps a doll, but having been five at the time, I still remember the trip across Niagara Falls as a terribly frightening affair and am still afraid of heights.

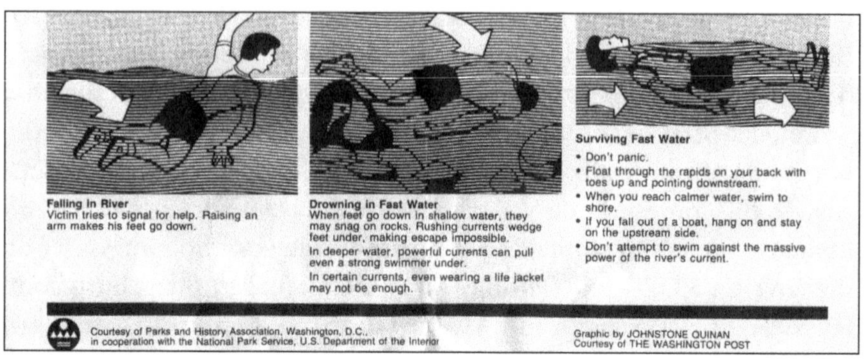

Great Falls—National Park Service visitor flyer

sense of the word. It was not only her intimidating size (a dearth that put Ella Fitzgerald and Mercedes Sosa to shame), but her demeanor—both scary and fascinating, and mesmerizing and liberating all mixed together. Ruth followed no social conventions—be it word or deed. And being a redhead, she had a hot temper to match, so God help anyone who crossed her, from restaurant service vendors to Fidel Castro. I can still hear our Aunt Ruth's harangue on one such visit. Having become accustomed to vacationing in Cuba under Batista, Ruth described in intimate detail peppered with four-letter words, "a body search of her pussy" in search of money or valuables, that she was forced to undergo upon arrival in Cuba after Castro took power in 1959.

Nine out of ten times, such family gatherings took place in the Shirlington Delicatessen and Restaurant—opened in 1946 after the Platts sold Max's Deli in Northeast Washington. It was situated in a shopping center where, except for the restaurant, all the stores were always closed when we visited due to Sunday blue laws.[31] The submarine-shaped Shirlington Deli with its line of dark red Naugahyde upholstered booths along one wall and a deli section along the other where fancy cold cuts for parties were prepared by Bill the 'platter man' (where we knew the tangy dill pickles in a barrel were stashed) was undeniably our aunt's

31. Blue Laws (the original one in 1781 was printed on blue paper) restricted shopping or banned sale of certain items such as alcohol on Sunday on religious grounds.

dominion. Such visits were timed for a Sunday mid-day fried chicken dinner or steak served on sizzling-hot oval metal platters.[32] The front booth would always be reserved for us in advance — within earshot of

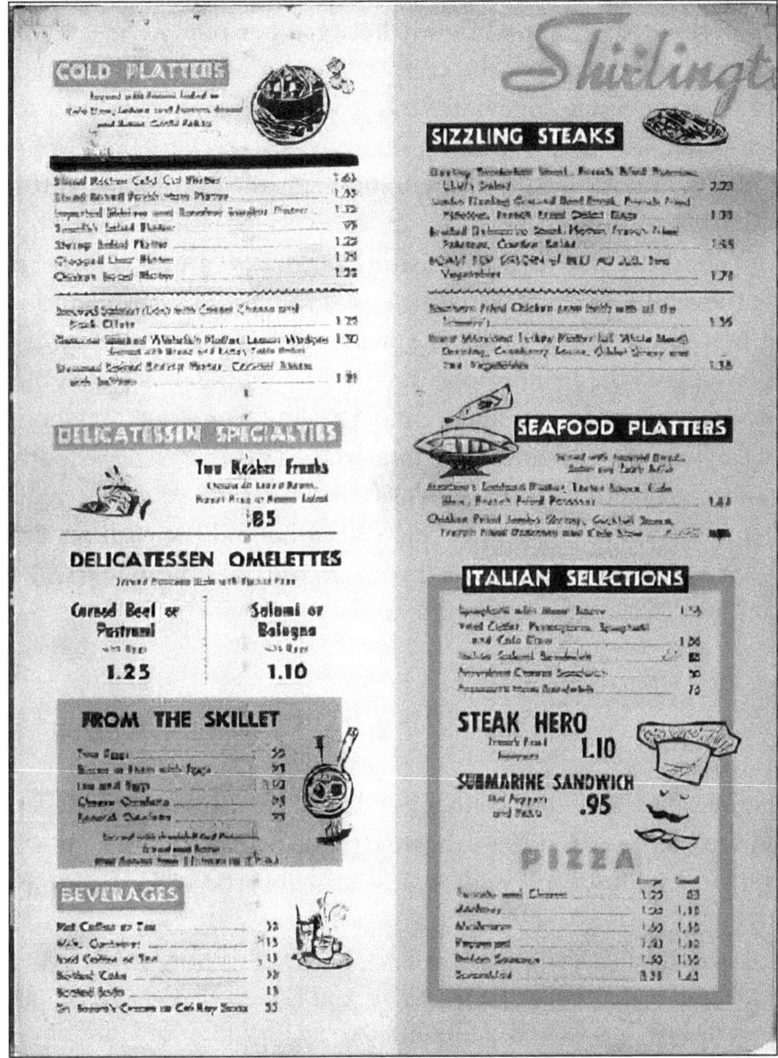

Aunt Ruth's Shirlington menu

32. To savor the yummy food not to mention the prices, see the entire 1960 menu on David Platt's website: http://www.davidplatt.com/shirlingtondelicatessen.html.

Aunt Ruth, who most of the time remained perched on her high stool, manning the mammoth black gold-trimmed cash register on the counter to the right of the door, sporting different color hair in ridiculous hairdos that varied from visit to visit, an unfiltered Chesterfield cigarette perpetually clamped tightly between her pursed lips. Habitually, Ruth would dominate the conversation, mostly to share her complaints—grumblings punctuated by a combination of 'dears' and strings of four-letter words *no one* in the 1950s used—certainly not in public. Not just God damn, shit and hell but also son-of-a-bitch...and the 'f word' that left us awed with her audacity.

As children, our favorite pastime—once we'd finished our meal, while the adults continued to visit—was to stand transfixed and wide-eyed before the exotic delicacies in the glass display case under the counter next to the Prince Edward cigars[33]—ogling in disbelief the tins of chocolate-covered ants and bumblebees in syrup, fried grasshoppers, smoked clams and other bizarre fare, to the left strange paper currency from foreign lands and two-dollar bills pasted with peeling yellowed and stained Scotch-tape to the plate glass behind the cash register. In every sense of the word, such travels across the Potomac River were paramount to a visit to a foreign land.

Jewish in the 1950s

As noted, there were less than a handful of Jewish families in Skyland when the Weisses lived there, however, nearby Naylor Gardens—a co-operative neighborhood built in 1943[34]—absorbed a large number of

---

33. The source of Gil's legendary wooden cigar box collection for Good Junk. All kids in the 1950s kept their pencils and erasers in a cigar box in their desks at school. Thanks to Aunt Ruth, we could have three or four or five mellow-smelling cigar boxes—the deep ones, the shallow ones, the tiny square ones—just for the asking.

34. Naylor Gardens was built by the Defense Housing Corporation, a federal agency that constructed housing for those pouring into Washington during the Second World War. (There were two more similar housing developments in Virginia.) The 748-unit complex was run by its residents, as a coop—including

Jewish professionals who, like Gil, came to Washington to work for the federal government during the war. So many people were streaming in that in 1941 alone the local Jewish Community Center assisted some 4,000 Jews in finding housing.[35] And, by 1945, the Jewish population had risen to 20,000. By the 1950s, Greater Washington's Jewish community numbered 81,000 people—the sixth-largest Jewish community in America. By then, almost half already lived outside the city, mostly in Montgomery County.

Even Jews who were not at all observant gravitated toward friendships with other Jews. All the young Jewish couples arriving in Washington and starting a family had left family behind, and they became substitute kin for one another—friendships that lasted a lifetime. Pearl recalled:

> [With the war] suddenly we had an influx of Jews. Naylor Gardens, where the Lessers and the Goldsteins lived, had that little wooden community center,[36] and they started a nursery school there. It was a coop, and we decided to join. They had square dancing, so we started going to learn square dancing and met the Jaffes there. And then a bunch of us women had gotten together. Edith Lesser had talked about being bored (although that was an intimate revelation women generally didn't share in those days). And I said there are so many things to do. We called the League of Women Voters [and got involved] but there were a whole bunch of us.

As for Pearl's women friends, among the family lore is the time Pearl escalated the fight for women's rights beyond membership in the League

---

the 'community center'—a postage-stamp size affair. Today, Naylor Gardens is resident-owned apartments, but it is still managed as a coop. It constitutes an 'oasis' of tranquility in a depressed area of Washington.

35. Cited by the Diaspora Museum in its profile of the Washington Metro Area's Jewish community, "Washington D.C.", Beit Hatefutsot: The Museum of the Jewish People, https://dbs.bh.org.il/place/washington-d-c.

36. Which could perhaps accommodate two squares of four couples each...

of Women Voters and Hunter Alumni. I believe Pearl was in her eighties when this incident occurred — a move taken in the spirit of liberation from social conventions that all too often comes only with age, reflected in the poem by Jenny Joseph, "When I Am Old I Will Wear Purple".[37] But it was equally the epitome of Jewish *chutzpah*: A group of women — I believe they were all alumnae of Hunter, most of whom were Jewish in any case,[38] who had gone out together. As usual (and little has changed even today in this department), the line for the 'powder room' was long while the men's room had no line whatsoever. Pearl announced to the women waiting in line — her group and perfect strangers — that they all were going to "liberate the men's john" and she marched right in...with a trail of women behind her, to the astonishment of the one or two men washing their hands at the sinks.

While Pearl and Gil viewed themselves as very cosmopolitan — and were even founding members of an interracial social group called The Clams — in fact, 95 percent of their friends were Jewish... The Weisses, the Jaffes, the Silvermans and the Summers became inseparable, closer than family. They not only belonged to the same synagogue and lived within walking distance of one another. The relationship was so tight between the Weisses and the Jaffes that they even had a legal agreement that if something happened to one couple, the other couple would raise their children. And there was a wider circle of dozens of other families in their social circle — also Jewish and with children more or less the same age.[39]

As already noted, Gil had no Jewish education whatsoever and his parents were totally non-observant. Nana had grown up in a very Orthodox household, but she had other priorities as a young widow struggling to support her kids. Pearl said in retrospect:

> I don't remember if we had a Passover *seder*. I remember

---

37. Read the full poem, Jenny Joseph, "When I am Old", Barbados — Poems and Poetry, https://barbados.org/poetry/wheniam.htm.

38. A glance at the 472 names in Pearl's graduating class in early 1935 published in *The New York Times* confirms this.

39. Including the Rossoffs, the Bergs, the Millers (2), and countless others.

> some very memorable traditional meals. One holiday with what was called a *tzimmis* — a carrot dish made with dumplings and dry fruit and carrots.

Thus, Pearl and Gil were totally unobservant as a young couple. I don't remember them even having a real Passover *seder* until the mid-1950s after we moved to Silver Spring:

> We knew we were supposed to go to a synagogue [on the High Holidays] but neither of us had any experience with synagogues. We went to one — the B'nai Jacob Synagogue — but they didn't let us in. So we went to another and that's where we learned that you needed *tickets* to get in[40] and you had to be a member. We didn't know this. We felt very rejected.

The wake-up call — realization despite being totally unaffiliated and non-observant, that 'the kids needed a Jewish education' — came after Wendy came home from school asking, "What am I?" Another kid had said she was Catholic. Apparently the last straw was an incident that entered family oral history that occurred about the same time: how Myrna burst into song in a department store elevator singing — "Jesus loves me, this I know"[41] with Wendy chiming-in — to the approving nods and smiles of the gentile women in the elevator. They were little kids, perhaps first graders, but Leah and Pearl were mortified.

As a result, in 1951 Gil and Pearl became founding members of Temple Sinai,[42] along with the Jaffes, the Lessers and many others among

---

40. To be a dues-paying member of the congregation (or buy a pricy seat for the High Holidays if they had room). No free 'walk-ins'...

41. To hear this song, see "'Jesus Loves Me' by Listener Kids", YouTube video, 2:49 minutes, https://www.youtube.com/watch?v=owx3ao42kwI.

42. For years, the congregation held Shabbat services in the Bethlehem Chapel of Washington's mammoth Gothic-style National Cathedral on Friday nights (with the crosses on the altar covered up) until Temple Sinai's iconic Pagoda-shaped synagogue on Military Road in Northwest Washington (officially

their circle of Jewish friends — but not before a short-lived attempt to enroll Wendy in an educational program at the only synagogue they knew about:

> There was a little synagogue down Naylor Road. The same B'nai Jacob Synagogue where we tried to go on the High Holidays [after we arrived in Washington]. We didn't know the difference between Reform and Orthodox. It was a tiny little Orthodox *shul*. So we enrolled Wendy in their Sunday School. It was so awful — the instruction — that she didn't last long. We agreed with her.

Up until they joined a synagogue, there was a small honest-to-goodness Christmas tree in the Weiss household in Skyland complete with tinsel and ornaments and Christmas stockings on the railing where Gil hung all the holiday greetings cards received in the mail in December. This practice stopped abruptly in 1951, but not before their two girls, in protest, scotch-taped a poster-size sheet of paper in the shape of a green Christmas tree to the wall of the dining room (that I brought home from kindergarten specifically for that purpose), concocted ornaments and our own wrapped 'presents' to put under the 'tree'. But that would be the last celebration of Christmas in the Weiss household. It was replaced by eight days of nightly presents in an attempt to ameliorate the uncomfortable sense of Otherness mixed with envy that the Christmas season brings. In fact, I came to look forward to Yom Kippur as a small kid: For some reason, Pearl and Gil felt their daughters should be kept out of school on Yom Kippur (perhaps because

Christmas cards on the railing, 1947

---

supposed to symbolize 'a tent in the wilderness') was built.

they joined Temple Sinai in 1951 when I was six). I distinctly remember Yom Kippur being so special because it was the only day of the year when my sister — who was four years older — played with me since almost everyone else in Skyland was at school.

Jewish children in the 1950s found their own ways of dealing with the presence of Christmas — thus in an era when Christmas carols — not *Jingle Bells* and *Rudolf the Red Nose Reindeer*, but *real* Christmas carols such as *Silent Night, Go Tell It on the Mountain*! and *Hark! The Herald Angels Sing* — were taught in music lessons at school and sung at festive public schools celebrations, with each child contributing a tree decoration for the school tree, I found equilibrium in the lower grades at Stanton Elementary by singing the songs along with all the other children, but only mouthed silently the loaded word 'Jesus' and 'Christ' and 'our Lord'... By high school, I had 'graduated' to demonstratively reading a well-thumbed copy of Henry David Thoreau's *Walden* in homeroom while my classmates said the Lord's Prayer (a public-school practice only banned in June 1963 as I was graduating high school).

When we were already living in Silver Spring (with a *mezuzah* on the door and where schools had a large contingent of Jewish kids), as a preteen I had gone one Friday night for dinner at the Jaffe's and came home impressed with the white tablecloth and the candles. I asked my mother why don't we do the same. Pearl's reply: "OK, you want to light candles? You're in charge to remember!" Of course, this slowly grew into the full *megillah* with Pearl lighting the candles and Gil singing a full *kiddush* over the wine every Friday night. Likewise, their knowledge of and involvement in Jewish ritual and synagogue life — particularly Gil's,[43] grew. After joining the synagogue, Gil held his first Passover *seder* after attending a synagogue 'How-to' class...and the rest is history. Many holidays were a collective affair shared by the Jaffe, Silverman, Summers and Weiss families — particularly memorable, breaking the Yom Kippur fast, always held at Funny and Jack Jaffe's.

---

43. He and Jack Jaffe sang in the choir for years, and Gil headed a committee of DIYers who volunteered when the synagogue needed help with an enhancement requiring woodworking tools and skills, and Gil even served as a funeral usher.

We all attended Sunday School held in the Jewish Community Center on 16th Street in downtown Washington until a synagogue was built — the reason our parents joined Temple Sinai in the first place. So we'd know we were Jewish. I remember absolutely nothing of the instruction save building *sukkah* booths in shoeboxes and the rabbi's riveting children's sermons on holidays, particularly the one about how "the Egyptians turned on their water faucets and blood came out". The rest remains a complete blur up until my Sunday School teacher in 7th grade (Shirley Ulman) gave me all A's on my report card[44] (keep in mind I was consistently bringing home poor grades in public school). Stunned — in fact ecstatic — overnight I became fascinated with what seemed to be the catalyst behind this marvel. Judaism. However, Israel and Zionism were not part of our education, nor was it part of the Jewish awakening in the Weiss household. At most I associated Israel with ugly thick orange candles at Hanukah that dripped all over the place and yucky *buckser* (dry carob pods in Yiddish) at Purim, both of which our Sunday School teachers told us "came all the way from Israel". At age 11, I clearly remember the 1956 Hungarian Revolution, vaguely aware something was going on in the Middle East at the same time.[45] The Sinai Campaign didn't resonate at all, certainly not as a 'Jewish' event that ought to spark interest. Israel would only enter my Jewish consciousness in December 1959 in 9th grade when Phyllis Tittelbaum — a school chum from middle school — invited me to a meeting of Habonim.

Pearl and Gil developed a close relationship with Temple Sinai's rabbis–Balfour Brickner (who left in 1961) and Eugene Lipman (who replaced him, retiring only in 1985). Both became pillars of Reform Judaism in America. In my teens, both Brickner and Lipman served as mentors and were 'responsible' for my strong Jewish identity. It was

---

44. I suspect everyone got high grades...after all, this was not public school. The whole objective of Sunday School was to make Judaism something likeable and positive in our minds, how much knowledge was imparted was secondary.

45. I vividly remember the photos of Soviet tanks on 24 October 1956 in front of the Hungarian parliament; I do not remember the Sinai Campaign that began on 29 October 1956.

'Brick' who recommended I read the seminal work by Mordecai Kaplan *Judaism as a Civilization*[46] that shaped and affirmed my worldview of what being Jewish meant. As an adult I remained in contact with both men for decades — despite a parting of the ways ideologically with 'Brick' who — disenchanted with Zionism and the Jewish state — became one of the ideologues behind a *Tikkun Olam* ('repairing the world') Judaism. Already in 1964 — *before* the Six-Day War, Balfour Brickner had urged me to "go found a kibbutz in the South" rather than immigrate to Israel. But we kept up the dialogue for decades in sporadic correspondence, and my mastery of Hebrew and successes as a writer were a source of pride for both these early mentors.

As part of this process of a growing Jewish identity and commitment (together with the impact of historical events such as the Six-Day War and other experiences, some covered elsewhere in this book), Pearl and Gil came to respect and support in every sense (although not totally understand) their youngest daughter's decision to live in Israel. Their support was not limited to material assistance for their two daughters in 'hard times', but also unflagging moral support sorting out conflicting allegiances and priorities.[47] What Pearl and Gil never forgave was

46. 'Brick' would quip that Kaplan's emphasis on a cultural Judaism rather than a theological one could be summed up as: "There is no God and Mordecai Kaplan is His Prophet". For me, another watershed event in shaping my worldview was the 1961 Eichmann Trial. The dissonance between what I read in *The Washington Post* every day, and the one almost parenthetical sentence in my 10th grade *World History* textbook ("Six million Jews were killed in what is called the Holocaust") — a textbook that dedicated two thick chapters to the Second World War, brought the realization that the Holocaust was not central to the American Experience — only the Jewish Experience. I was an avid American history buff but this was a rude awakening to the fact that my ancestors were not at the Alamo, and the Eichmann Trial changed my center of equilibrium.

47. What this meant and how it was played out is discussed earlier in the section 'Walking-the-Talk' at Home.

my decision not to speak English with my kids, forcing them for years to use their limited Hebrew and accept running translations by others to communicate with their Israeli grandkids, until the three began studying English in school.

Relics of such difficult times could be found among the Memorabilia, including a letter in Hebrew (with my English translation below) from 2nd grader Asaf in 1984 that he asked to write on his own initiative when he was eight years old accompanied by a picture of his garden with drip irrigation and a fence around it:

> To Pearl and Gil shalom,
>
> I received your greeting card for my 8th birthday. You wrote my name with a ץ not a ף so I'm correcting you. Thank you very much for the money for the birthday. Daddy will order me citrus saplings and I'll plant them in my garden.[48] School is nice to learn in and in the Kfar I go to an art *chug*.[49] In the 1st *chug* we draw a rainbow and clouds.
>
> Many kisses, Asaf

A newsy 1985 aerogramme to Pearl and Gil from 11-year-old Efrat, (at the beginning of her second or third year studying English) was a gem, written at the tipping point when having to have an intermediary to interact with their grandchildren became a thing of the past:

> Dear Gil and Parle. Hellow. How are you? I'm fine. Today at morning I don't had something to do so now I make kookis and now a ½ from their are in the oven. Nadav is tray to make shape and he is stand on the chair and tell me (I wite at Hibroo): Efrat, *ze lo hitkalkel ly–hasevivon*"* Jest a menet—I got to see if the kookis good. No they are not.
>
> So, how are Lisa Ben, Wendy and Bil[50] fil? And what

48. Thirty-six years later there is still a lemon tree and a red grapefruit tree where Asaf's garden used to be.

49. *Kfar*—a village, in Hebrew. *Chug*—extracurricular class.

50. Wendy's 'significant other' at the time—Bill. Rachel was my cousin Toni's

Asaf's aerogrammes bridged the language gap.
Note the flowers at the bottom of the page.

about Sum? When he is sail? And what about Bil? And Rachel? And Dawn? And Ann? And Tony? And how about Nanna? How she is fil? Tomora I wil have a test about all what we lorn at classes 4, 5 and 6, and at Monday I wil have a test about Jopan. It's a hard wik, with many tests. When we had 4 testes at English — 100. Yesterday we had show of Jopan and my teacher tel me to give my noat-book to the show. So Good Buy from Efrat Ashkenazy

* The *dreidel* didn't get messed up.

The bond with Wendy and her family was established not only in face-to-face encounters where body language worked splendidly in the near

---

daughter who is the same age as Efrat, and some of the Platts (Sam, Dawn, Ann) all of whom Efrat had met on visits to the States.

absence of Hebrew;[51] it was cemented by the huge carton from Dodah[52] Wendy that arrived every year like clockwork bearing 'the distinct smell of America' (it's a product of the 'American detergent'). The box was filled with practically new 'used' clothes (no import tariff) from Ben and Lisa that Wendy faithfully saved for a full decade until they were the right size for her niece and nephew — including much-coveted genuine Levi's jeans and Gap T-shirts and sweatshirts (that cost a small fortune in Israel). Of course, there were certain items no Israeli kid would be caught dead in, such as a bright tangerine pair of shorts. Such content went into a 'dress-up suitcase' that got plenty of use in play and at Purim — the above 'no way' item pressed into service along with a matching tangerine jersey from America in one of Asaf's most original Purim costumes: Dressed up as a Raw Carrot complete with a pointed orange crepe hat and green fringed tights...

Despite the geographical distance and 'mediated' communication for so many years, the bond was incredibly strong. As Efrat (24) and Asaf (22) wrote Gil in 1998 when it was clear the end was near:

> We had thought today, how odd it is that we have seen you for only about 15 times in all our lives, sometimes for only a short period, and still got so attached to you. We do have relatives closer than 6,000 miles. But we don't feel so close to them than to you. We guess the reason is [...] that you are such a special person. We got so excited each time you came to Israel, not just because of the M&Ms that you brought, but also because of the special relationship we always had. In the beginning, we could not understand a word you were saying, in light of your lousy Hebrew. What we did not have a problem with was understanding your love and care. [...]

---

51. When I arrived with Efrat and Asaf at National Airport the first time — they were ages one and three — Wendy plopped down on the floor next to the baggage carrousel, cross-legged and with the only Hebrew she knew introduced herself "*Ani Wendy!*" — spread her hands for a hug and instantly broke the ice.

52. Aunt in Hebrew.

The fact that Gil and Pearl had forged such a very strong bond with their Israeli grandkids despite the language barrier never erased this issue from the slate.

Leaving aside my own love affair with Hebrew and my husband's very limited English and other factors behind this decision, the difficulties and frustration Pearl and Gil faced made it impossible for them to even begin to get a handle on the fact that speaking English with my children in the home for the sake of my parents would have thrust me into the position with my own children of an Other looking in. LOL: When the folks appeared in my dreams, Pearl and Gil spoke perfect Hebrew.

Pearl and Gil and the path their lives took — professionally and personally — are emblematic of those whose parents left Eastern Europe in search of a better life in America. They epitomize the quantum leap many of their generation of American Jews made as second-generation Americans[53] — from poverty in an era of gaslighting and tenement life to comfortable middle class living in the space age and the computer revolution, from marginalized status in times when a Jew could not get a job as an engineer, to a time when all the Chairs of the Federal Reserve since 1987 to very recently (2018) have been Jews, as I noted in the Preface. But for Jews, historically such prominence in the political, economic and cultural realms has always carried its own risks — irrelevant only if one passionately believes in American Exceptionalism.

While this work focuses on their generation's achievements, there are incidents in the narrative that suggest the presence of unsavory undercurrents that spoil what appears to be a unique Jewish success story of 'and they lived happily ever after'. Rattled by growing antisemitism, the response has oft been self-delusionary, preferring to ignore the enduring nature of antisemitism[54] and how it operates:

53. The term used by demographers for American-born children of foreign-born parents.

54. Zionism was also overly-optimistic in this respect: Assumption that the

> [...] Antisemites have always focused on whatever constituted the core of Jewish existence – that is, the content that at any given time is the wellspring of Jewish vitality and unity. Until two generations ago, Jewish life's core was Jewish religious beliefs and cohesion as a religious community, and therefore 'heretic' doctrine and rituals and 'clannishness' were the prime charges in the antisemite's arsenal. Since the early 1950s, Jews have become increasingly secular and integrated into non-Jewish society. Especially in North America, two abiding themes have emerged as dominant binding forces for Jews, parallel to nominal religious affiliation: Jewishness had focused on the Holocaust – its memory and its meaning, and Zionism – identification with and support for the Jewish state. [...] Therefore, attacks on the traditional theological-cultural orientation of Judaism have been replaced by a form of political antisemitism that centers on Israel bashing [...] vilify[ing] and delegitimiz[ing] the State of Israel.[55]

---

root of antisemitism was the abnormal state of Jews as a dispersed minority or a 'ghost people' as Leon Pinsker termed it, expecting that a process of 'auto-emancipation' (being a sovereign nation like all other nations) would solve the problem of antisemitism. Instead, irony of ironies, the Jewish state is branded an abnormal construct, even an "affront to the natural order..." See Eylon Aslan-Levy, "Anti-Zionism and the Fear of Jewish Ghosts", *Tablet*, 13 December 2016, https://www.tabletmag.com/sections/israel-middle-east/articles/anti-zionism-leon-pinsker.

55. Excerpt from the seminal monograph that I wrote in 2004 on the nature of the 'New Antisemitism' for the think tank and Israel advocacy entity Myths and Facts, and how one can separate Israel Bashing from legitimate criticism of Israel. To read the full piece, see Eli E. Hertz, "Poisonous Antisemitism", Myths and Facts, http://www.mythsandfacts.org/Conflict/poisonous-antisemitism.pdf.
NOTE: This piece was part of a mammoth research and writing project on the Israeli-Arab conflict (books, white papers and op-eds) conducted between 2003-2006, work-for-hire that was ghost-written for the founder and president of *Myths and Facts* Eli E. Hertz, and published exclusively under his byline.

Thus, the resurgence of antisemitism in its current forms is not the fault of the failings or shortcomings of Zionism and the Jewish state — real and imagined. The 'timing' is not coincidental, but attributing mounting antisemitism in America to the divisive political climate, amplified by the negative side of the Internet, or thinking Jew-hatred is merely collateral damage from anti-immigration sentiment or laying the blame at the door of the Trump Administration is at best myopic: 70-plus years after the Holocaust, 'shame' as a restraint has simply worn thin.[56] Antisemitism is no longer considered impolite or poor form and today, Jews everywhere — including America, find themselves to one degree or another sandwiched in a crossfire of antisemitic rhetoric that is no longer an undercurrent. It's open, unapologetic and even fashionable on *both* sides of the Atlantic and *both* sides of the political spectrum, even among the political elites in the American Democratic and British Labour parties. This is a global phenomenon, not an American one, but it casts a shadow over the American Dream and the foundational myth of American Exceptionalism that Pearl and Gil's generation seemed to affirm.

Among the omens that undermine the belief that America is different from England or France or Israel is the climate at Gil's *alma mater* NYU. Once a game-changing entrance pass for the sons of European

---

56. Despite the best efforts of American Jewry to erase the dissonance felt by Jews between the American Experience and the Jewish Experience (very palpable in the 1960s, see note 46 on World History studies and the Eichmann Trial) by initiating a United States Holocaust Museum just off the Mall coupled with promoting Holocaust curriculums in the schools, for most Americans the Holocaust remains a distant impersonal event about someone else's tragedy that on a time scale is about as immediate to Millennials as the American Civil War was for Baby Boomers. According to a 2019 study by the Claims Conference ("The Holocaust Knowledge and Awareness Study"), 31 percent of all Americans and over 41 percent of American Millennials don't know six million Jews were murdered in the Holocaust; 49 percent of Millennials have never heard of Auschwitz and can't name a single concentration camp or ghetto (not even the Warsaw Ghetto); and 22 percent haven't heard or are not sure if they have heard of the Holocaust at all. See http://www.claimscon.org/wp-content/uploads/2018/04/Holocaust-Knowledge-Awareness-Study_Executive-Summary-2018.pdf.

Jewish immigrants to becoming Americans, NYU recently awarded the university's 2019 Presidential Service Award for "extraordinary and positive impact on the university community" to Students for Justice in Palestine. (Yes, the dudes that organize Israel Apartheid Week on campuses accompanied by the genocidal chant 'From the [Jordan] River to the [Mediterranean] Sea Palestine shall be free').[57]

The Holy of Holies — the Shop

A 2006 survey conducted on behalf of *Wood* magazine found that approximately 5.5 million Americans actively participate in woodworking as a hobby, but I believe the Shop (with a capital S) was unique. So did some of Gil's fellow woodworkers who found the sheer volume and diversity of 'stuff' at his disposal mindboggling As Jack Wessel — a fellow engineer and hobbyist — would say in the tributes at the back of the book:

> After being given a tour of his basement workshop with its many small, labeled drawers, I think I'll make one drawer of my own [in my own shop] and mark it "String — too short to save". We always claimed that Gil surely had such a drawer in his shop. Mine will have a sub-heading: In memory of Gil Weiss — Boss Mentor Friend.

Where did a love of woodworking begin?

Skyland Apartments was special not only because they were garden apartments surrounded by bushes, trees and grass, but because of the rent-free windowless basement space under one of the rows of apartments where half-a-dozen hobbyists had workbenches and woodworking tools. One of the men even built a small sailboat there (with hand tools, mind you), made piece-by-piece and assembled elsewhere.

---

57. Meaning a '*judenrein* Israel' if you missed the subtext. On NYU, see the article Liel Leibovitz, "Get Out", *Tablet*, 7 May 2019, https://www.tabletmag.com/sections/news/articles/get-out.

As his letters to Pearl testified, Gil was planning and executing small or fairly simple projects — from a step-stool to a pipe rack — while still in Skyland. The hand tools from Skyland days — the coping saw and two hand-held drills with their signature dark purple handles, and a small vintage planer — now rest mutely on a bookshelf in my office for posterity.

Once in Silver Spring, Craftsman™ industrial quality power tools were purchased one-by-one and augmented by home-concocted grinders, sharpeners and polishers powered by repurposed household appliance motors. A loose-leaf notebook documented projects completed, going as far back as the 1941 pipe rack, the 1942 bookcase and circa 1945 wooden cornices around the windows in Skyland and a merry-go-round lamp. In addition, the 'archive' included plans for Gil's master cabinetmaker projects in solid mahogany. Gil also had a file of contemplated but undone carpentry projects that were only rivaled in volume by the number of photos, certificates and art waiting in the Shop to be framed — enough for a lifetime or two. As Gil's favorite quote (from cartoonist Bill Watterson) tacked to the wall just inside the door declared: "God put me on this earth to accomplish a certain number of things. Right now, I am so behind, I will never die".

I'm probably the only adolescent girl who ever asked for a power jigsaw for her sixteenth birthday. But that isn't surprising: I spent hours in the garden and in the Shop with my father beginning with Skyland days — although the only artifact of my hours in the Shop is a pair of solid mahogany maple leaf trivets for hot pots cut out on my jigsaw as a Mother's Day gift.[58] To get me past high school algebra and chemistry, Gil devoted endless hours upstairs trying to share with me (without success) the beauty of mathematics, but he also spent countless hours downstairs in the Shop helping me pass 8th-grade geography in middle school with "extra-credit projects" — large plywood maps the teacher wanted that lit up when you found the Belgium Congo. As much as I loved the Shop, Gil — fearing for my fingers — never let

58. And some hearing issues that I suspect are related to many hours of exposure to the roar of an industrial strength power saw (and a tractor) in days when no one wore protective ear gear.

his myopic younger daughter use the power saw (or the power mower, for that matter). After I joined Habonim and my interests shifted, my beige bench became a shelf for rooting *forsythia* cuttings and parking paintbrushes in turpentine, but being a Weiss daughter, I still wield a mean hammer and am not about to give up my screwdriver. Likewise, my sister Wendy.

Once Gibby graduated to solid mahogany, over the years, parallel to unending home improvement projects such as screening-in the porch or finishing the basement rec room (only completed after his kids were grown) Gil first crafted a nest of tables to get a feel for the material. Then he embarked on three masterpieces: the buffet followed by the custom-designed stereo cabinet and the breakfront—all still in the family and in fairly good condition thanks to seven coats of varnish, each rubbed down with wet steel wool to a fine finish.

I don't think Gil ever touched another piece of mahogany or embarked on another master project with wood after that. It was as if with those three works of perfection he had conquered his own Mount Everest. I know he never touched that black walnut in the rough he had been aging for decades.[59] He puttered around in the Shop a lot, but the projects were practical things he or someone else needed, or projects with grandkids and other young people—although in his later years he did succeed in cutting off the tip of a finger on the table saw. Gil's focus as a craftsman to the core seems to have shifted to other materials after the breakfront was completed. The landscaping of the Potomac garden in the early 1980s was a project of equal magnitude and equal perfection–a crowning achievement in aesthetics that embodied the same qualities behind those mahogany masterpieces, only in another language.

---

59. See note 1 in the Preface about the black walnut, a gift from a friend who cut down a massive walnut tree. In 1984, after a close brush with death and a four-way bypass, Gil told me, overcome with emotion, that he wanted to turn that black walnut into a large polished three-dimensional heart and donate it to Washington Medical Center for the foyer...but I imagine once he was home and over a slow recovery, looking back made it too traumatic to embark on such a project.

Gil's masterpieces in mahogany

~

For the extended Weiss family, the Downstairs — be it on Woodland Drive or Democracy Lane — provided an endless supply of 'neat stuff' children thrive on, just waiting to be discovered, examined, explored and used to make neat things with their dad/granddad/uncle to take

Relics of Gil's shop 'projects' with grandkids

home or just hold, touch, finger, play with and covet for a minute and put back for next time.

No one has captured better the sheer magic of Downstairs for two generations of children and grandchildren well into adulthood than grandson Ben Bard—and the pain of having to part with it all.[60] And at its heart, the 'Holy of Holies' with its mahogany sign in relief at the entrance: SHOP.

60. The Snubbers & Grommets remain in Ben's possession.

The iconic SHOP sign (in pure mahogany) at the entrance to Gil's woodworking shop

"Downstairs"
by Ben Bard

Once I've entered 10500[61] and hugs are complete, I sit down at the white kitchen table for a snack and some catching up. We chat for a while, GrandMom doing most of the talking, GrandDad with only occasional comments; he's listening. After some time we disperse. I put away my bags and take off my shoes, GrandMom visible at the sink, GrandDad invisible but noisy now, somewhere sawing or drilling or sanding, wood his willing victim. I can't wait long, and step quietly to the basement, feeling the drop in temperature as I descend.

As I walk down the wood-paneled hall toward his workshop I pass the ping-pong table folded up, leaning against

61. 10500 Democracy Lane — his grandparent's house in Potomac, Maryland from the time Ben was a preschooler, well into adulthood.

the wall. I was no older than nine when it broke. The crowd was upstairs and my cousin Dawn and I were in the basement as she crawled up on top of the table. She started jumping up and down, laughing, swinging her arms. I told her not to but my cute older cousin charmed me into joining her in the romp. We jumped with great delight until the table collapsed under us with a thump and we slid down to the carpeted basement floor. Previously in my childhood, I had stolen my sister's candy from her room, at the coercion of my best friend. The ping-pong table was only the second time I had ever broken the rules. The noise of the collapsing table brought adults from upstairs down. And GrandDad yelled. In my whole life, this was the only time I ever saw him get mad. And as best as I can recall, it was the last naughty deed of my childhood.

Beyond the table and a quick left brings me into the basement storage room, "the middle room". It's chilly, but strips of velvety cherry-red carpet laid along the cold concrete floor keep my bare feet warm as I peruse the aisles of this junkyard candy store. On the right are shelves holding empty cardboard boxes, old luggage and wrapping paper. Behind the door live the games: Clue, Yahtzee, Rummikub, and the old air-driven organ with keys too small for adult fingers.

To the left, my favorite nook of the entire house: King Edward Imperial cigar boxes colored yellow with red, white, and blue writing, stacked in columns, resting in rows, neat rectangular labeled order. The realization of GrandDad's favorite adage, "Never throw away Good Junk". I examine the collection of boxes, each with its own masking tape label, as I have countless times before: Doorstops. Chain. Fuses. Drip irrigation. Kitchen cabinet latches. Corks. Furniture BRG pads. Shell cases. Coat hangers. Puzzles. Furniture glides. Spools. Pulleys & glide mechanisms, small. Mechanisms (this box is tilted open as if the sequestered colony of gizmos is attempting escape). 602 cyl. Insulating fiber/leather/plastic. Misc. fittings. Carry handles. Ubrascope rods/gears/bellcranks/racks/pinions. (A fascinating box — what, after all, is an ubrascope? The pieces inside resemble drawing compasses with springs and gears and turns, some rusted, pointy, intertwined with neighbors. I picture all of the ubra-amputees salvaged for these gems.)

In the middle of the cigar boxes are balanced two Amphora pipe tobacco cans labeled 'bearings' and then the yellow, blue, red, and white cigar boxes begin again. Paper fasteners — metal/plastic. Curtain rod fittings, shades. Curtain/drape brass rings. Shower curtain plastic hangers. Drape rod plastic slides. Hanger hooks. Drape rod cords and pulls. Locks. Leather laces. Piano weights. Knobs. Hose clamps. Locks/keys latches (with a lone metal key on a large paperclip peeking out). Casters. Small casters. Watches/straps. Plastic rings and plugs. Clothes pins-springs. Plastic strap fasteners. Steel angles corners. Threaded fittings and ferrules. Steel angles-misc. Snubbers & grommets (my favorite). Small rods/solid. Steel corners. Metal-flats. Steel flat

The Good Junk

straps. Aluminum hook with screws. Metal rods-cups-flat. Galvanized tin, flat (with small penciled drawings of a circle with a dot in its center, a square, and a rectangle, all in parentheses). Three more tobacco cans fit below the counter, one of Venetian blind fittings, and two marked Pleated drape hooks. Likely 50 years of Good Junk, and just the small pieces at that.

GrandDad is in the garden now as I exit the storage room and approach his personal sanctuary. A wooden sign hanging over the doorway reads, simply, "SHOP". As I enter, my eyes adjust to its density. I smell GrandDad: Old Spice and Sawdust.

I breathe the wood and feel it on my bare feet. The power tools, their figures seen through the darkness, stand watch. Clockwise from the entrance, I recognize the 12-inch band saw, radial saw, small jigsaw, table saw, bench grinder, two polishers, drill press, belt sander, lathe, joiner. Only one tool, the second polisher, is not a Craftsman; it's homemade from a leftover washing machine motor. The grinder has a pair of plastic goggles slung over a handle. The small jigsaw was my tool of choice as a child when I

Gil's Shop 1

cut out shapes of bunnies, ducks, and frogs out of eighth-inch boards. GrandDad would trace out the pattern and I would follow along the lines. I stood on a stool to reach.

I search for the light switch between empty picture frames hanging on the wall. The illuminated scene overwhelms and delights. To my left, the old green file cabinet has its top metal drawer partially open, exposing dozens of little glass jars filled with screws, nails, brads, nuts, bolts, washers. Eight other drawers follow suit, each with a collection of strong magnets — mined from the backside of decrepit speakers — clinging to its face.

Neighboring the file cabinet is the workbench. I pull the drawstring of the fluorescent lamp above, illuminating after several flashes the bench's landscape. To the west are Elmer's glue, two red plastic darts, black electrical tape, and a bottle of Liquid Nails propped against the wall-mounted pencil sharpener. A tool for attaching snaps partially covers a package of oak dowel buttons, 100 count, $3.50. A metal Band-Aid box houses 14 pieces of chalk. A spool of wire sits in an old ashtray along with several AC adapters that spill onto the benchtop. Four clothespins sit beside them. To the east, a bottle of turpentine, a black and silver Texas Instruments calculator, a plastic jar of toothpicks, and three large round beige rocks. Three razor-sharp planes sit in a row, one made of all metal, two with dark brown wooden handles. In the central lands of the benchtop is an old black rotary dial phone covered with sawdust and specks of paste or spackle. Right next to it sits a white Sony digital clock radio and an analog voltmeter. In front, a blue plastic mug displaying Josie and the Pussycats houses a fine collection of worn-down pencil stubs. Contents of the five wooden drawers built below the bench each have a specific assigned category. Chopsticks & small plastic cups. Soldering irons (at least ten). Metal reels from clotheslines. Socket sets. Utility knives and broken steak knives (I call this the 'sharp things' drawer).

At the rear of the bench are thin wooden rails, one on top of the other, with holes drilled through the top rail at even spaces. Tools stand vertically, one in each hole, lined up in neat rows. Scissors, screwdrivers, drill bits, funnel, emery board, red rubber bulb siphon. Eight shoehorns. The holes continue around the corner, past the edge of the workbench. Tape measures, pipe cleaners, bottle opener, dentist's mirror, scribes, awls, punches. The holes blend seamlessly into the pegboard that covers the perimeter of the shop. It strains under the weight of additional screwdrivers, hammers, wrenches, pliers, awls, and rules of every shape and size. At least two dozen C-clamps straddle the metal hooks on the board — small, medium, large, extra-large — looking like a wall of a torture chamber. Wire has been bent into crude hooks supporting Kleenex, light bulbs, and three flashlights (including one that straps around your head). More hooks for a thermometer, micrometer, wire cutter, horseshoe magnet, pipe cutter, military compass, Chalk-o-Matic. A hatchet and several small saws — coping saw, ripsaw, crosscut saw, back saw — rest against a crowbar that is itself used as a hook. Seven huge steel clamps used in cabinetry work, each between three and four feet long and supported by extra-large metal hooks, fill the remainder of the wall.

At the horizon of the pegboard sits another bench[62] covered with two sets of tiny clear plastic drawers in blue metal housings. One set has twelve rows and the other ten, each row with five drawers. One hundred and ten drawers, filled. Above are shelves of drill bits, organized in clear glass jars with masking tape labels. 9/32, 7/32, 3/16, 5/16, broken. 'Broken' — a jar just for the broken bits! Bits of bits. Skinny shelves hold sandpaper purchased by the ream and a shoebox of steel wool. Four yardsticks lean against the shelves' edges.

62. Built for me, his ten-year-old daughter, when the family moved to Silver Spring.

A long shelf above, mounted on the wall, is dedicated solely to drills. Heavy silver electric hand drills from Sears with thick black power cords; the chuck key is held to each by an aging snippet of frayed tan twine. A history of power drills, from left to right, where no old tool ever dies but merely rusts in peace. More long shelves protrude from those few walls not covered in pegboard. Paint, spray paint, paint thinner, varnish, polyurethane. Metal boxes on the shelves give shelter to chisel sets, hand router, blow torch, propane torch, and a Dremel tool. Beneath one shelf sits a wicker chair, partway through its Dremel renovation.

On the final piece of wall next to the doorway, along a skinny vertical strip of its own protected territory, is the glass cutter, craftily constructed from brass springs, stainless steel razor blades, and a portion of an old shower door frame. GrandDad saw a similar glass cutter slice gracefully through picture glass in a framing shop. It would make his work much easier, he thought, as he penciled careful diagrams on an envelope and later went to work *building* his own. (Yes, they could be purchased.) The result, used proudly for his framing jobs, hangs at eye level next to me.

Gil's Shop 2

> The centerpiece of the workshop is The Table. The Table contains all of The Projects in progress. The Table's surface is a smooth-rolling hilltop of piles with a roll of masking tape balanced at its summit. Piles masking piles of unframed art, certificates, magazine clippings, pictures from calendars, diplomas, unopened packs of drill bits, rotary saw blades, Dremel tool bits, gadgets to be fixed, gadgets to be played with, lists of projects, lists of lists. The Table is where some things have been kept for a week, others for a decade. GrandDad often says, "I think it's on The Table, somewhere". And, little by little, GrandDad finishes projects on The Table, but never at a rate faster than new ones are added to the top. Which is good, because I'd worry if the table were ever empty. And I think he would, too.

Thank goodness Ben didn't show this to us when Asaf and I were separating family Memorabilia from the Good Junk back in 1998, otherwise I would have been transfixed and never been able to touch a single furniture glide, spool pulley or carry handle, not to mention ubrascope. By capturing the inventory on paper, everything has been saved 'as is' for posterity, compressed like a computer file or high-definition photo image—reducing two tons of bulk to manageable size—a few thin pages, without losing any of its dearth.

Gil's Shop 3: The 'Table'

Life with Nana

Tribute to an Exceptional Caregiver

No memoir of the Weiss family would be complete without dedicating a special section to recollections of Nana. Pearl's mother lived with Pearl and Gil through a good part of their early marital years[63] — from the mid-1940s in Skyland in Southeast Washington until the late 1960s in Silver Spring on Woodland Drive. While there are bits and pieces throughout this work[64] including quotes from the tapes about Pearl's upbringing, Nana was a mammoth presence in the Weiss household that deserves her own 'space' in *Playing Detective with Family Lore.*

A word of context: Our contact with our New York grandparents — Gil's parents, Ben and Hannah Weiss — was brief and infrequent: Trips to New York were often timed to coincide with unforgettable 'fancy New York weddings' marked by cocktail dresses and platters with caviar. New York was a grueling ten-hour drive from Washington — some 386 km (240 miles) linked by two-to-three lane highways shared by cars and truck traffic going through the jam-packed center of Baltimore and Philadelphia. Eventually one reached the New Jersey Turnpike (opened in November 1951) and its Howard Johnson's rest stops with the promise of clean bathrooms and "28 flavors" of ice cream in crisp sugar cones. We knew we were close to our destination when the nauseating smell of New Jersey's oil refineries penetrated the windows. As children, New York was associated with wind-swept

Nana (Anna Lefkowitz)
1890/1893–1986

63. They had only lived in their own place with privacy as a couple for a little over four years before Nana joined them in 1944.

64. There may be some redundancy here, so bear with me...

streets with newspapers flying like urban tumbleweed, a creaking scary elevator in our grandparents' building (we didn't have elevators in Skyland), the dark almost windowless interior of our grandparents' one-bedroom apartment at 1990 Ellis Avenue in the Bronx and Pop Weiss' grimy tire and battery garage. In the apartment, the aroma of sunny-side-up eggs swimming in sweet butter always seemed to hang in the air along with the faint hint of mothballs — against a backdrop of the occupants' constant bickering. Such impressions[65] were mitigated by the delight of cookies from the iconic black-and-white checkered New York bakery *Stevenson's* and marzipan acorns from *Barton's Candy*, picked up just before leaving New York — to be taken back to Washington. Nana's presence, by contrast, was constant.

☙ *Nana™ as a House Brand*

Nana was, as the title suggests, a nurturer by nature — ensuring there was always Nana Water™ — cold water in a tall jar in the frig, in the days before air conditioning when kids played for hours outside in the heat and walked up to two miles to school (regardless of the weather). She was the one who took care of the children in the Weiss household when they were sick[66] — this in a time of limited antibiotics and before the arrival of vaccinations for childhood diseases such as chicken pox, mumps and German measles, when polio epidemics still gave parents nightmares. Thus, the children in the Weiss household were nursed back to health from bad colds and the flu and the above on crushed aspirin in applesauce and Nana Eggs™ — soft boiled eggs that only Nana knew how to make just right — soft enough to be swallowed with a strep throat but without the yucky 'slippery' as we called it. Her tender loving care was always augmented with Jewish

65. Truly at the last minute, this impression was balanced by the addition of an entire section on the Avenel period of Gil's upbringing that paints a more complex and dynamic picture of Ben and Hannah when they were in their late twenties and thirties and of Avenel, thanks to input found in the *Avenel Bulletin* from 1922 and 1923. See Gil's childhood in the section Growing Up as Second-Generation Americans.

66. Which also allowed Pearl to begin substitute teaching, then fulltime teaching.

Penicillin — home-made chicken soup.[67]

Yes, Nana reigned over the kitchen — baked or broiled chicken almost every night, complemented with a starch and a cooked vegetable. The only time I remember someone else in the kitchen was the time Gil brought home live lobsters to Skyland, where much to my horror, I swear I can still hear those lobsters trying to climb out of the pot as they were steamed alive! Nana never cooked by recipes — she cooked by hand — literally and figuratively[68] using her hand as a measuring cup and 'feeling the dough' to determine if it was the right consistency. Consequently, when like most girls, Nana's granddaughters asked her to teach them to cook, she would say "I'll show you..." deflating our initial enthusiasm by making the entire dish while we passively looked on. I only learned to boil an egg at Temple University, at age 20.

Pearl was able to extract the recipe for Nana's jumbo-size feather-light *kneidelach* for posterity by measuring the ingredients as Nana made them, but for almost a generation, it seemed that her *rugelach* recipe had been lost forever, 50 years after we savored the last cookie...until I was struck by a sudden flash of recognition. I realized my mother-in-law Aviva's cookie dough (from Europe) has more or less the same ingredients that I remembered from watching Nana bake cookies (flour, butter, sugar, cream cheese) and Aviva's cookies had the same crisp texture as Nana's *rugelach*. I realized Aviva's recipe was 'the one' when I had this flashback of Nana brushing her cookies with egg whites to make the nuts and cinnamon and sugar stick...leading by a process of elimination to the realization that the egg *yolks* were in the dough, just like in my mother-in-law's recipe. Thus, with a few adjustments, Nana's signature horseshoe-shaped *rugelach* sprang to life!

Of course, reconstruction of her *rugelach* conjures up images of what we Weisses label Nana Jobs™ — any tedious sitting-down jobs Nana always had the incredible patience to do — from snapping the ends off a pot of fresh string beans from Gil's garden or pairing socks,

---

67. There was always a struggle over who would get the cockscomb swimming in the soup...

68. Apparently passed on in the DNA I also do most cooking by handfuls rather than cupfuls and mix stuff with my hand rather than a spoon.

to cutting up the raisins into tiny pieces[69] and fine-chopping the walnuts[70] for her *rugelach.*

But from time to time, Nana disappeared from our lives for weeks on end. When she felt she needed a break from the family, or that Pearl and Gil needed a break from her, Nana would announce she was "going out on a 'case'" — once going to New Jersey to take care of Leah Abbott[71] who had been incapacitated by glaucoma. Most of the time she went to stay with this or that new mother of family or friends, serving as a practical nurse, caring for the newborn and the household, until the mother had regained her strength.

Nana's rugalach

69. One can use currants...

70. One can use a food processer...

71. Leah, as a token of thanks, gave Nana the silver Russian-style samovar that now sits on the buffet in my living room. The Abbotts were Pearl's and Gil's best friends. As noted, their two children — Myrna (Kasser) and Glenda (Lush) — were the same age as their own kids. The Abbotts had moved to New Jersey in the early 1950s where Norman was working on what were then top-secret radar projects.

~ *Fleeting Fragments of Life with Nana*

There are countless moments and images that epitomize life with Nana and 'flesh out' the picture:

- Nana's bedroom with her huge cherry wood dresser and high matching double bed with 20 cm (8 inch) diameter 'cannon-balls' at the corners, with enough space underneath for an 11-year-old to crawl and fall asleep hugging the family dog after downing four full cups of wine *and* the Cup of Elijah at the Passover *seder*.
- Nana in her mammoth silky soft black seal coat in a cold car in winter, where a grandchild could snuggle against her ample bosom until the heat kicked in. Nana all dressed up on the way to synagogue on *yuntif*[72], sporting her cameo brooch[73] to match the tiny diamond studs she'd worn for as long as we could remember her. Nana going out or coming back from 'a case' dressed in white from tip-to-toe. And the most authentic and indelible image: Nana 'on duty' in the kitchen, girded by a full-length faded apron that she only took off in the evening before retiring to bed.
- Nana's gasps and 'oys' that punctuated every punch delivered in fistfights in the Westerns aired on television, no matter how many times the family assured her the movie actors were only pretending to hit one another, no one was hurt and the sound of the blows were sound effects created by smashing two cabbages together.
- Nana always telling people 'she came from Austria'...what turned out to be a stretch of the imagination[74] although perhaps she

72. The Yiddish term she used for Jewish holidays.

73. I inherited her dearth but not her cameo complexion.

74. A reminder: 'Austria' meaning part of the Austrian-Hungarian Empire — which for most East Europeans was what was registered on ship manifests and 'place of origin' in American census data. Today the area she came from is part of Ukraine.

never knew.[75] What's for sure: 'Austria' sounded better than saying she came from Poland, and the most backward part of Poland at that — Galicia.[76]

- Going out on walks with Nana as small children to pick wild strawberries on the edge of the woods that lined Good Hope Road leading to downtown Washington. And Nana's strawberry patch with a dozen strawberry plants (under square plastic mesh 'cages' that didn't always keep out the wild turtles) — an enterprise that was part of the family's gardening plot[77] at the bottom of our street which Gil filled with stake[78] tomato plants.
- Nana, taming my unruly curly mop into submission when I was small, by twisting my hair into long corkscrews on holidays. Nana, when I was much older, trying to rein in my rebellious streak, admonishing me repeatedly for outspokenness during a 'radical socialist' phase in late adolescence warning: "*Shah*, your father will lose his job!"
- Nana baking once or twice a year — making quantities of her signature *rugelach*, packed away in round Maxwell House Coffee™ tins and stashed in the 18 cubic-foot freezer in the basement. And stealing down to raid the freezer, opening the cans of Nana's cookies — one-by-one on different occasions — to eat one cookie that surely wouldn't be missed...
- Nana and Pearl conversing in Yiddish when they "didn't want the children to understand". (Of course, Gil was left equally

---

75. Nana entered the United States at age nine and never attended school where she might have studied geography and perhaps known about the Division of Poland. What she did remember vividly was Emperor Franz Joseph had passed through her village as a child.

76. Pearl related how as a kid she would tell other kids (whose parents apparently hailed from the more cultured part of eastern Poland — Lithuania or *Lita* in Yiddish/Hebrew: "I'm a *Galitzianer* (from Galicia) and I'm proud of it!"

77. The entire garden was perhaps two-by-four meters, including Nana's strawberry patch at the back.

78. For most of my life I thought these were a 'steak tomato' variety, huge tomatoes to be cut in thick slices, not a climbing trellis variety.

clueless, since he didn't understand Yiddish either.). And the way Nana used '*mamaleh*' as a term of endearment for anyone and everyone she encountered.

- And speaking of speaking Yiddish, how when about the age of 12 when I said I wanted to learn Yiddish, Pearl was fit to be tied after her mother chose as Lesson One to teach me by rote the East European ditty: *Shikker iz der Goy* (the Goy is drunk)/ *Shikker iz er* (a drunk is he)/ *Trinken miz er* (he must drink)/ *Vayl er iz a goy* (because he's a Goy). I was left to learn the rest of my non-existent Yiddish from the 1958 phonograph record *Theodore Bikel Sings Jewish Folk Songs.*
- The way Nana could always elicit a smile from infants — even the crankiest baby — by rapidly clicking the tip of her tongue against the inside of her upper lip: *lubeh-lubeh-lubeh-lubeh lubeh-lubeh-lubeh-lubeh* (eight times)...followed the surprise pursed-lip...'*poop*' that triggered a smile. And Nana's special fluttering birdcall — whistling *ah-tu-tu-tu-tu-tu-tu--tu-tu-tu* (nine times), insisting she could talk to the birds and that they would answer her.
- Nana reading a newspaper or book, her lips slowly and silently moving across the page — with reading skills only mastered as an adult on her own. Nana signing documents, carefully forming each letter of her signature one at a time in cursive writing–A-n-n-a L-e-f-k-o-w-i-t-z. Of course, she ate corn-on-the-cob in the same methodical manner: one row at a time. But that was not the only thing Nana 'did her own way and at her own tempo'...
- Nana wouldn't have been Nana if after dinner, she didn't insist on going through all the leftovers from everyone's plates (even if there were guests at the table, much to Pearl's and Gil's embarrassment) meticulously picking the bones after lamb chops or a chicken dinner, to salvage every scrap of meat and every piece of gristle — collected in a small pile in a used napkin as an after-dinner treat for the family dog.[79]

79. Black Knight lived a happy and full life and died of old age in his sleep,

~ *Nana's Most Outstanding Attribute*

Nana was a 'survivor' who through sheer determination and an indomitable constitution never let circumstances — and crises came fast and furious — overwhelm her. One is left truly awed by her survival skills, and how she "make a go of it" as she put it. It is impossible, even today in retrospect, to fathom the strength of character and determination Nana was able to muster during the countless crises in her life, and one can only admire her disposition. Despite all the troubles and obstacles she faced — born in a tiny poverty-stricken *shtetl* in Galicia; orphaned at a tender age — left to fend for her younger siblings, including the hardships of the journey to America in steerage, unescorted; life in America with a terrible stepmother who never let her go to school, assigning her to take care of her stepsiblings; marriage at a young age while still mothering her two sisters under the same roof; losing a child, then being widowed from her husband within the short space of two years[80] and left to support her remaining two children without any real assets or job skills, Nana never lashed out at others and never turned bitter about the cards she was dealt in life — the tragedies, the missed opportunities, and hardships she faced. And she kept her warmth and sunny disposition even into her declining years at the Hebrew Home in Rockville.

But Nana definitely wasn't a wimp, and couldn't be pushed around. She had a stubborn streak epitomized in family lore in the saga of 'Nana lowering the broom on Mr. Barrett': The time when Mr. Barrett — our irritable next-door neighbor in Skyland — began banging on the ceiling one evening, at perhaps eight or nine PM, because Nana was sewing in her bedroom...situated over the Barrett's living room. Much to Pearl's embarrassment, Nana, hopping mad, grabbed a broom and began banging on the floor in response.

Life with three generations under one roof had its moments: Nana

---

Nana having faithfully fed him his after-dinner treat to his dying day.

80. To reiterate: First losing her son Joni who died four months before his fifth birthday in the summer of 1916 polio epidemic — two months after Pearl was born. Then two years later in autumn 1918 losing her husband Michael during the influenza epidemic (together with Nana's stepbrother).

was part of the family, but not without points of friction. Vivid memories surface of her response to young whining children saying 'I'm bored', with: *Nemes kepeleh und klap en venteleh* ('Knock your head against the wall') which, inevitably, was met by even louder kvetching, even howls of protest. Nana had a stubborn 'Do It My Way' streak that went beyond complaints about her 'I'll Show You' method of teaching her granddaughters to cook. This was best reflected in the way Nana would insist on taking the plates off the table and putting them in the dishwasher herself immediately after dinner — a chore assigned to the children. Wendy and I would (how could it be otherwise) *purposely* procrastinate by drawing out conversation at the dinner table until an impatient Nana got up and did the dishes herself, frustrating Pearl and Gil who never realized the kids had 'set her up'...

Nana was not a demanding person and her wants and needs were very modest — thus, she surprised everyone when after I came back from a gap year in Israel in 1963/4, she turned to Pearl out-of-the-blue and shared a dream: "Pearly", she said. "I want to go to Israel!" Thus, in 1965 at age 76 Nana did so, spending five weeks in the country on her own, not on a tour. The trip was handled by a cousin of the Jaffes who was an Israeli travel agent. He arranged accommodations and her getting 'ferried' from place-to-place during the time she spent in Israel (Tel Aviv, Jerusalem and the Gesher Haziv[81] guest house). Her only other trip abroad was also to Israel: After I moved to Israel in 1968, Nana repeatedly declared — "When Daniella gets married, I'm going to the wedding" — a wish that was granted in 1972, despite the complex logistics, since by then, over 80 years old, she walked with difficulty, but she walked up the four-and-a-half flights to our apartment in Ramat Gan to attend the wedding. Literally step-by-step.[82]

---

81. The kibbutz where I had spent my gap year in 1963/4.

82. A small affair held in the living room of our 84 square-meter (904 square feet) apartment, with approximately two dozen guests in attendance though it *was* 'a catered affair' with a 'waiter' and a cocktail-style buffet of canapés in the eating alcove. Two weeks later, an article appeared in the Hebrew daily that hung on the frig for years: "Only snobs have apartment weddings".

The Rugelach and Kneidelach Recipes

As already noted, once or twice a year, Nana would bake up a storm — making *rugelach* in quantity, baking sprees that included making round cookies from the same dough, cut out with a spent *yahrtzeit* candle holder-turned-drinking glass.

Here is the reconstructed recipe for Nana's *rugelach*, for future generations. Measurements are a bit weird, due to conversion from European measurements:

8⅓ cups self-rising flour[83]
1¾ cups of butter[84]
1½ cups sugar
⅔ cup and 4 T of thick sour cream or Philadelphia cream cheese[85]
6 large egg yolks (don't throw away the egg whites!)
a pinch of salt
1½ cups of chopped walnuts
1½ cups of currants (or cut-up regular raisins)
½ cup of cinnamon and sugar

Cream butter and sugar in a mixer. Add egg yolks one at a time and mix at high speed to form a fluffy mixture. Add a pinch of salt and the sour cream and continue to beat until well blended. Add the flour and beat until the flour is well mixed in. The dough will leave the sides of the bowl. Put the dough in a plastic bag in the frig for several hours, or overnight (if you get distracted, you can even leave it there for several days).

Divide the dough into four balls. Roll out one ball on a lightly floured flat surface — thinner than piecrust dough but not

83. 1 kg and 1/3 cup per 50 g = 3 x 350g packages of Osem self-rising flour.

84. Or mostly butter, making up the rest with butter-flavored margarine = total, 400 g.

85. 200ml of 15-percent-fat sour cream in Israel.

as thin as noodles. Sprinkle currants and chopped nuts on the dough and lightly press them into the dough. Sprinkle lightly with cinnamon and sugar. Cut out triangles with a knife. Roll up from the broad end to the point and bend into a horseshoe shape (you may have to 'squish' them after rolling them up, to get the right shape). Place on a cookie sheet covered with parchment paper ('baking sheets'). Repeat with the rest of the dough. Bake at 180°C (350°F) until the cookies turn golden brown (not pale). Move around in the oven — front-back, up-down... The recipe makes four large cookie sheets — baked two at a time. Enjoy.

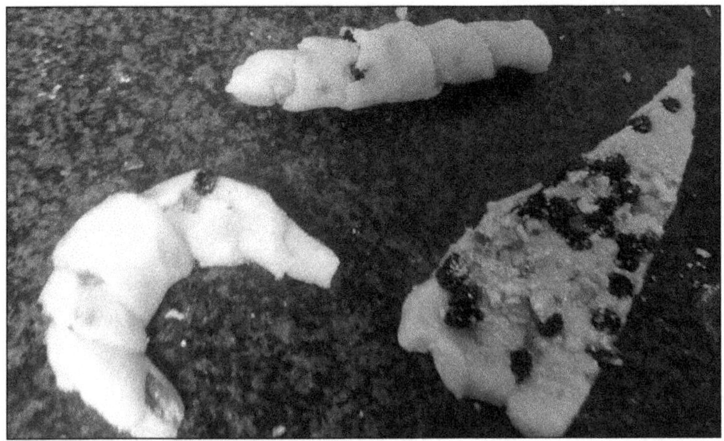

Nana's rugalach

To make Nana's signature cookies: Cut out rounds with a wide-lipped glass if you don't have an empty *yahrtzeit* glass. Brush the rounds with egg white leftover from making the dough and sprinkle lightly with cinnamon and sugar, and some finely chopped walnuts. Bake until golden brown.

And the *kneidelach*? There is a funny story in Sara Kasdan's Jewish recipe book *Love and Knishes* about the husband who complains his wife's featherweight *kneidelach* (matzo balls) "were all right, but they're not

Nana's signature 'featherlight' kneidalach

like Mama used to make". One day, the bottom fell out of the matzo meal box and all the matzo meal fell into the *kneidelach*, but no longer a newlywed, his wife went right ahead and made the *kneidelach*, figuring "he'd eat 'em anyway" even if they came out "hard like rocks and heavy like lead"... "Ahhhh, this is a *mechi'eh*",[86] exclaimed her husband after one bite: "Now *this* is the way Momma used to make *kneidelach*!"

Here is the original recipe for Nana's feather-light *kneidelach*:

6 eggs, separated
1 teaspoon salt
1 cup matzo meal
2 tablespoons melted schmaltz (chicken fat)
2 tablespoons of soup

---

86. 'Literally 'life-reviving' in Yiddish — a rejuvenator, a genuine pick-up.

Beat the egg whites until stiff with a hand mixer. In a separate bowl, combine the yolks, salt, melted schmaltz and soup. Quickly pour the yolk mixture into the egg whites with the mixer—a few seconds for it to turn light yellow. Sprinkle the cup of matzo meal into the bowl and stir vigorously with a fork—just enough to blend the two, and put the *kneidelach* mixture in the frig for five minutes to 'rest'. With wet hands, drop walnut-size balls into a large pot of rapidly boiling water, and cook for 30 minutes. Enjoy!

Others Speak of Nana 1986

Pearl described memories of her childhood with Nana in a poem she once wrote, read at Nana's funeral on 11 October 1986:

Was it only yesterday
that you banished my midnight terrors,
near your warm and ample bosom,
brushed my long straight hair
and plaited it into tight braids,
band-aided and kissed a scraped bleeding knee,
made the hurt disappear.

I watched with awe,
as you expertly stretched the dough
to the far ends of the dining room table,
nimbly filled it with goodies,
and rolled it into long thin strips,
as the delectable strudel came
piping hot out of the oven.

I was there saying
"Can I eat the candy?" that oozed out.
"Of course", you'd say.
"I purposefully made it that way".

You were always in the kitchen,
big apron covering your dress,
presiding over huge batches of *rugelach*,
cookies hot from the oven,
or big pots of *kreplach* and *pierogi*.

Years later, with a family of my own,
I wanted to reproduce that wonderful aroma.
I asked you for the recipe
...and you'd say: "I'll show you"...
and precede to put it all together
without a measuring spoon or cup.

"How much of this or that, Momma?"
And you would answer: "Feel it until it feels just right".
I've tried, Mamma...
but it never tastes or smells like yours.

Wendy shared her memories of her grandmother Nana in a funeral eulogy (excerpts):

> [...] Most of my memories of you are warm fuzzy ones. Skin so soft to touch, a black seal coat to cuddle up to, a little tin voice singing to the birds and me — the same tunes over and over. But I never got tired of them. They were always sung with love and sincerity that you could give them. The smells of cooking chicken, *rugelach* and gefilte fish filled my olfactory senses in turn — depending on the occasion. How sad and frustrating it was the day you no longer had your own kitchen in which to work. It was one of your happiest places. You were so at home there. [...] I want to thank you for being there for me, for accepting me through all my stages of discovering and growing. I want to thank you for my youthful skin and my ability to survive — both of which I attribute to you.

Chapter VI

Profiles and Tributes to Two Special People

Here at the back of the book is the place promised in 1998 for anyone who wanted to add their two cents to this work — now in a much-expanded form than the 'modest memorial booklet' I initially envisioned and promised to put together two decades ago. It brings together words written about Pearl and Gil on various occasions — past and present, thoughts by people for whom the folks were special.

It opens with Newspaper Profiles. This section contains the expanded news obituaries published by the *Washington Post* and *Washington Jewish Week* — in the space on the obit page reserved for and written by the editor of the section about outstanding ('newsworthy') longtime residents of the Washington Metropolitan Area and prominent national figures. Pearl and Gil's professional achievements brought them this honor. There are also other pieces published in other media.

Last but not least — the much-promised section Parting Words, Eulogies, and Reminiscences from Others, including anecdotes, defining qualities or parting words from grandchildren, other family members, friends, work colleagues, mentees and a slew of others who knew Gil or Pearl or both — delivered or written at one time or another over the past two decades, many especially for this work.

Newspaper Profiles

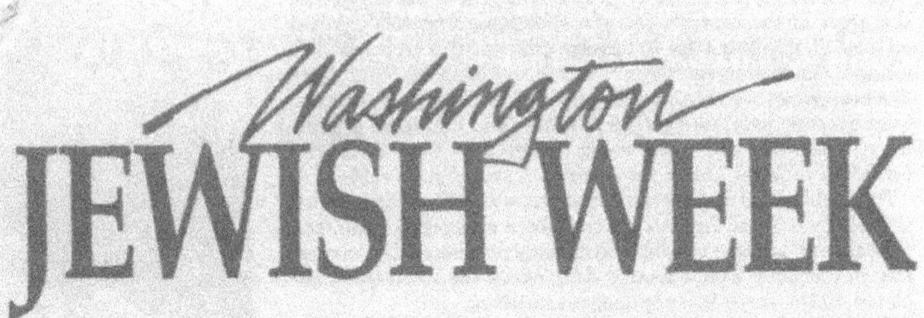

Gilbert Weiss, 83

Gilbert "Gil" Weiss, 83, a leading aeronautical engineer and longtime Washington resident died of cancer on July 8 in Rockville.

Weiss was born in Perth Amboy, N.J., and grew up in New York City, graduating *magna cum laude* from New York University in 1938. He began working for the Navy in 1939 — joining the Bureau of Aeronautics in Washington, D.C., where he became a key figure in the development of naval air power.

He was the founder and director of the Navy's Weight Control Branch of the Engineering Division from 1941 to 1957 and assistant director of the Evaluation Division of the Naval Air Systems Command from 1958 until his retirement from the civil service in 1970 — playing a pivotal role in the development of more than 100 naval aircraft of all types — from the World War II Corsairs to the F-14 Tomcat.

His expertise and outstanding contribution to aviation and the Navy was marked in particular by receipt of the Navy's Meritorious Civilian Service Award in 1965. Following his retirement from the Navy, Weiss worked for over a decade as a private consultant in the aircraft industry.

Weiss was a resident of the Washington area for 49 years. In addition to professional organizations such as his leadership role in the foundation of the Society of Aeronautical Weight Engineers, he was a member and supporter of various interracial frameworks throughout his lifetime — including life membership in the NAACP, and CLAMS — the latter a local interracial social and action group. He was also a 40-year member of Temple Sinai and a member of PNAI— Parents of North American Israelis.

Weiss' primary contribution to the community went beyond professional or organizational frameworks. A master carpenter and expert gardener by avocation, his true lifetime "hobby" was people — helping others he encountered, hundreds of people of all backgrounds and all ages with whom he bonded with ease and aided in a myriad of small but significant ways.

Weiss — "Gil" to all those whom he encountered — is survived by his wife of 62 years Pearl Weiss and his two daughters: Wendy Weiss Bard of Minneapolis and Daniella Ashkenazy of Kfar Warburg, Israel; his brother Bernard Weiss and sister Mildred Swiss of Florida; and five grandchildren — two in the United States and three in Israel.

Services were held on July 12 at Temple Sinai. The family sat *shiva* in Potomac. ■

In Memoria — Gilbert Weiss

Gilbert Weiss, former Head of the Weights Branch of the Bureau of Aeronautics and Honorary Fellow of our Society, died on Wednesday, July 8, 1998, after a brief illness.

Gil was born in 1915 in Perth Amboy, N.J. and grew up in New York City. He got an early exposure to things mechanical through helping out in his father's auto repair shop. Like so many others, he was captivated by Charles Lindbergh's solo flight from Long Island to Paris in 1927. It set his heart on a career in aviation. He attended the Guggenheim School of Aeronautics at New York University and graduated near the top of his class in 1938. He started his career at Burnelli Aircraft on Long Island and then joined the Naval Aircraft Factory in Philadelphia, Pa. In 1939 he transferred to the Bureau of Aeronautics in Washington, D.C., where he spent the remaining 31 years of his very distinguished full-time professional career.

At BuAer, Gil gradually took over responsibility for all Naval aviation weight and balance matters. In 1941 he became the first head of the Bureau's newly-established Weight Control Branch, in which position he served until his promotion to Assistant Director of the Bureau's Evaluation Division in 1957.

During Gil's 16 years as Head of Weights at BuAer he made major contributions to increasing the quality, standardization, engineering rigor and professionalism of the weight and balance discipline. He led the effort to standardize weight and balance forms, handbooks, and procedures for Naval aviation, and he was a firm advocate for establishing firm, but achievable, contract weight guarantees and explicit weight control requirements, including frequent periodic reporting to the customer. He also played a significant role in the founding and start-up of the SAWE, and in establishing Government-Industry coordination as a major function of the Society and a major feature of the annual conferences. As the first Navy representative to the G-I Committee, he headed the effort to develop the first interservice coordinated weight specification, AN-W-11, the predecessor to MIL-W-25140 and SAWE R.P. 7. His many significant contributions to our field were recognized in his being named an Honorary Fellow of the Society in 1956.

As Assistant Director of the Evaluation Division, Gil became an unsurpassed expert on all aspects of BuAer's aircraft design requirements and its acquisition, specification and contracting policies, practices, and procedures. Moreover, because of his dedication and his superlative ability to work with others, he was very effective at applying this general knowledge to the specific needs of individual programs. Gil's expertise in this arena is particularly impressive when one realizes the tremendous changes in the technical state of the art that occurred during his career (not least of which was the successful marriage of jet aircraft and the aircraft carrier), as exemplified by the fact that his career began with the F4U Corsair and ended with the F-14 Tomcat.

Despite the outstanding accomplishments of the second part of Gil's career, his former colleague, George Spangenberg, for many years Head of the BuAer/BuWeps/NAVAIR Evaluation Division, has said, "To me, Gil's greatest contribution was his successful effort in raising the status of the weight control function in airplane design to its present acceptance as perhaps the most important single element involved in achieving a successful outcome." In 1965, Gil's leadership in both weight engineering and aircraft acquisition were recognized by his being awarded the Navy's Meritorious Civilian Service Award.

After retirement in 1970, Gil continued to lead a very active life, which included service as a private consultant on aviation matters and pursuit of his many other interests, among which were tennis, woodworking, gardening, general "handymanning," mentoring young people, involvement with numerous organizations (including his church, the NAACP, and Parents of North American Israelis), and, greatest of all, his family. He is survived by his wife Pearl, one brother, one sister, two daughters, and five grandchildren.

As all who knew him would attest, Gil was a superlative human being. He was of the highest integrity, honest, dedicated, positive-minded, energetic, hard- and long-working, thorough, and tenacious (some would say stubborn!) for what he believed was right. Most importantly, he was a true gentleman. He was without any of the "airs" that often accompany those in higher positions; he worked with everyone as an equal. He treated everyone with the greatest friendliness and respect and, more, always

showed the greatest interest in and concern for others' personal lives and families. He was a "class act." To again quote George Spangenberg, "Gil is the clear winner of any and all 'good guy' contests."

Gil Weiss was one of the small core of creative pioneers of the Weight Engineering profession and our Society. His will always be an integral part of the heritage we all share.

One of Gil's colleagues, Roy Welson, wrote to Pearl following the publication of the piece above in the *International Journal of the Society of Allied Weight Engineers*: "I've never seen such a tribute in SAWE publication before! And to one who's been retired from Weights for almost 30 years! I cannot add a thing!!"

The Washington Post

Gilbert 'Gil' Weiss

Aeronautical Engineer

Gilbert "Gil" Weiss, 83, a retired aeronautical engineer who was involved in the development of more than 100 Naval aircraft—from the World War II Corsairs to the F-14 Tomcat—died of cancer July 8 at Shady Grove Hospital.

He was an expert on the Department of the Navy's aircraft weight-control function in the cost and performance of military aircraft and one of the architects of the Navy's acquisition, specifications and contracting systems.

Mr. Weiss began his career in 1939 with the Department of the Navy's Bureau of Aeronautics. He then founded the Navy's Weight Control Branch of the Engineering Division in 1941 and served as its director for the next 16 years.

He was assistant director of the evaluation division of the Naval Air Systems Command from 1958 until his retirement in 1970. In 1965, he received the Navy Department's Meritorious Civilian Service Award. In retirement, he worked for more than a decade as a private consultant in the aircraft industry.

He was born in Perth Amboy, N.J., and grew up in New York City, where he graduated from New York University. He had lived in Washington and then Silver Spring before moving to Potomac about five years ago.

Mr. Weiss was a founding member of the Society of Aeronautical Weight Engineers and a life member of the NAACP and CLAMS, a Washington area interracial social and action group. He was also a member of Temple Sinai in Washington and PNAI, Parents of North American Israelis. His avocations included carpentry, gardening and mentoring young people.

Survivors include his wife of 62 years, Pearl Weiss of Potomac; two daughters, Wendy Weiss Bard of Minneapolis and Daniella Ashkenazy of Kfar Warburg, Israel; a brother; a sister; and five grandchildren.

Pearl Weiss, 97, pioneering educator
By Ian Zelaya
10 January 2014

Pearl Weiss, 97-and-a-half, a veteran of the Washington Metropolitan Area for 67 years, died on Monday, Dec. 23.

Mrs. Weiss was a retired educator whose professional life reflects an entire generation of college-educated women for whom teaching blazed a trail for the unlimited career opportunities women now have in society.

In addition to years in the classroom as an elementary school teacher who left an indelible mark on many of her students, Pearl Weiss played a key role in two forward-looking curriculums – the first, the concept of team teaching in elementary schools; the second, special needs curriculums for high school youth-at-risk.

Born on the Lower East Side of New York in 1916, Pearl (née Schwarzer) Weiss was raised by her mother after her father died in the 1918 influenza epidemic. Completing high school in 1932 at age sixteen, she went to Hunter College, graduating in early 1936 with a bachelor's of arts in education.

During the Depression she worked as a WPA employee teaching homebound students. After moving to Washington, D.C., in 1939 with her husband Gilbert Weiss (an aeronautical engineer with the Navy Department who became one of the architects of naval air power), Pearl Weiss began substituting then teaching at Stanton Elementary School in Southeast Washington, a career she continued in Montgomery County after the family moved to Silver Spring, Maryland in 1955.

The early 1960s were years of innovation in education, particularly in Montgomery County. Under a federally-funded pilot, Pearl Weiss developed (together with fellow teachers Phoebe Goodman and Josef Cerwonka) a team-teaching model for elementary schools. Operating out of a small auditorium with flexible dividers at Arcola Elementary School, they developed a model allowing team teachers to complement and utilize one another's individual strengths, thus optimizing the learning experience for their pupils. Today, team teaching is an integral part of teaching at all levels.

Following the success of the program, Pearl Weiss was again tapped to develop another model – a federally-funded three-year pilot program at Northwood High School (developed together with fellow teacher Francis Jordan) that sought ways to keep potential dropouts within the school system, which was not equipped to deal with their special needs. The Work Orientation Curriculum (WOC) model they designed integrated half-days in the classroom – inculcating marketable job skills (from job-oriented reading comprehension and arithmetic to work ethics and etiquette) with half-days in the workplace. The team placed pupils in salaried employment in genuine jobs in the afternoon that were tailored to the abilities and interests of each student, monitoring and counseling students and working with their employers to ensure a successful work experience – principles that are still cogent today as America grapples with the challenge of a "dropout epidemic" of mammoth proportions. After earning a master's degree in counseling in 1967 from George Washington University, Pearl Weiss served as a school counselor at Parkland Junior High School until her retirement in 1971.

Pearl and Gil Weiss were founding members of Temple Sinai in Washington, D.C., and Pearl was active in the League of Women Voters and Hunter College Alumni. During the last seven years of her life, Pearl Weiss was a resident of a senior housing project in Minneapolis, Minnesota.

She is survived by two daughters, Wendy Weiss Ackerman of St. Louis Park, Minn., and Daniella Ashkenazy of Kfar Warburg, Israel; five grandchildren – Lisa Markland (Dave) and Ben Bard, Efrat Kaplan, Asaf Ashkenazy and Nadav Ashkenazy (Eti); and three great-grandchildren Itamar and Yoav Kaplan and Rotem Ashkenazy.[1]

---

1. Ian Zelaya, "Pearl Weiss, 97, Pioneering Educator", *Washington Jewish Week*, 10 January 2014, http://washingtonjewishweek.com/pearl-weiss-97-pioneering-educator/.

The Washington Post

Pearl Weiss, educator in D.C., Montgomery

By Bart Barnes

Saturday, January 11, 2014

Pearl Weiss, an educator with the Washington and Montgomery County public school systems who helped develop a team teaching model for elementary schools and a special-needs curriculum for high-risk students in high school, died Dec. 23 at a senior care community in St. Louis Park, Minn. She was 97.

She died of natural causes, according to the death certificate.

Mrs. Weiss retired in 1971 after having served as a school counselor at Parkland Junior High School in Rockville.

Pearl Schwarzer was born in New York City, where she graduated from Hunter College in 1936. She settled in the Washington area in 1939 and taught at Stanton Elementary School in the District before working for the Montgomery school system in 1955.

She helped develop a team teaching model at Arcola Elementary School in Wheaton on a federal grant in the 1960s. Later, at Northwood High School in Silver Spring, she helped devise a work-orientation curriculum for at-risk students. In this program, students spent half a day in school and half a day in the workplace outside school.

In 1967, Mrs. Weiss received a master's degree in counseling at George Washington University.

With her husband, Gilbert Weiss, Mrs. Weiss was a founding member of Temple Sinai in Washington. He died in 1998 after 65 years of marriage.

A former resident of Silver Spring, Mrs. Weiss lived in Minnesota for the last seven years of her life.

Survivors include two daughters, Wendy Weiss Ackerman of St. Louis Park and Daniella Ashkenazy of Kfar Warburg, Israel; five grandchildren; and three great-grandchildren.[2]

---

2. http://www.washingtonpost.com/local/obituaries/pearl-weiss-educator-in-dc-montgomery/2014/01/11/b9d5d158-7a28-11e3-b1c5-739e63e9c9a7_story.html.

AMERICAN JEWISH WORLD

Pearl Weiss

age 97, the most wonderful mother, grandmother, friend and mentor imaginable and a resident of Sholom Home West in St. Louis Park, died peacefully in the arms of her daughters on Dec. 23. A veteran resident of the nation's capital, Pearl was buried in the Washington, D.C., area next to the love of her life, her husband of 65 years, Gilbert (Gibby) Weiss and mother Anna Lefkowitz. Pearl is survived by her daughters, Wendy Weiss Ackerman (Allan) of St. Louis Park and Daniella Ashkenazy (Rafi) of Kfar Warburg, Israel (and their spouses); grandchildren, Lisa Markland (Dave), Efrat Kaplan (Ziv Rubinstein), Ben Bard, Asaf Ashkenazy (Yossi Shushan) and Nadav Ashkenazy (Eti); and great-grandchildren, Itamar, Yoav and Rotem. Pearl was an outstanding educator and school counselor, who left her mark on countless students — so much so, that a former third-grader, now 63, came to pay her respects! Among her accomplishments, she pioneered team teaching in elementary school and a groundbreaking work-oriented curriculum in high school for youth at risk. A 'people person,' in her seven years at Sholom, Pearl — with her infectious smile and interest in others' lives — left an indelible impact on residents and staff alike. Pearl would have been honored to have memorial contributions in her memory dedicated to Hunter College Alumni, or Sholom Home West. To celebrate Pearl's memory, a get-together for family and friends, residents and staff, will be held on Monday, Jan. 6 from 4 to 5:30 p.m. at Sholom Home West, 3620 Phillips Parkway, St. Louis Park.

Parting Words, Eulogies and Reminiscences from Others

A Father's Day Letter
Written by Daniella to Gil
after a Massive Heart Attack
August 1984

NOTE: A word about role reversals: I'm now 75 and Gil would have been 105 if he'd lived forever as his favorite cartoon quipped. But back in 1984, on Father's Day, when I, his youngest daughter, was turning 40 and Gil was turning 70, I appended a message to a Father's Day card which I read to him in the hospital on 16 June 1984 — miraculously still alive but facing (hopefully) a slow recovery following a four-way bypass and complications galore. Gil — how could it be otherwise — saved the card.[3] The content[4] seems an apt place to start this section of family tributes, because it captures a few priceless Gil Legacies passed on but overlooked elsewhere in this work.

I always feel like you're looking over my shoulder when I concocting some

3. Gil also saved one of the daily menus, a user's manual called "Living with your pacemaker"— *the one that almost killed him* when it malfunctioned and had to be removed — and all the handwritten drafts of the messages we left for well-wishers in July 1984 on a newfangled device, an answering machine, which we hastily purchased. Among them, the unforgettable pivotal outgoing message saying: "This is the Weisses. It's later Thursday evening. Gil's condition at the Washington Hospital Center worsened today and we almost lost him. He was rushed into surgery and had a quadruple bypass. One-fourth of his heart has been totally destroyed. He also has other extremely serious complications. For right now, his condition is critical. For his wellbeing, no phone calls, visitors or flowers are allowed. Thanks for caring. Please let us know you called". A flood of calls and cards followed from across the nation and around the world.

4. Even then (a few scant years before I became a writer) greeting cards were not my communications channel of choice.

Daniella and Gil, 1993

sort of gadget for the house, or as if I'm inside your skin as well as mine when I'm mowing the grass or fixing a shorted electric wire or when I'm helping Asaf with his homework and he's doing everything in his power to make me explode saying "But I don't understand..."

Although we live far apart — when I'm with the kids, especially with Asaf, sometimes I get this funny feeling that I'm you, and Asaf is me — doing things with his hands all the time, with wood, making a garden, helping in the yard...and he even hums to himself like I did (rather than whistling) whenever he's concentrating on something.

Not everybody has a special Dad like you and there are a least a half a dozen people who have called this week who are sort of half-brothers and sisters, because you were their Dad, too and that is how they felt about you when things looked bad.

Rafi Ashkenazy[5]
Parting Words to Gil
July 1998

I'm writing again because I have a lot to say. I am fully informed by Daniella. Gil — you don't know how much I want to be with you. I am going everywhere and think about your rough times. I went to your carpentry tools which are waiting for you in our yard. I imagine how you blow life into them, and I hear the hammer and saw, the clamps and the nails. How you play with them like they were an orchestra and you are the best conductor. I remember your high skill in all you touch. I don't forget the Wildcat, the Hellcat and the Tomcat, which you gave your 'touch' to them. Your good spirit that you spread to everybody and everything and everywhere. I am standing near your tools and think about all my feelings for you through them and I feel I am very close to you even although the ocean is between us. Dear

5. Sent to Gil in his final days from Gil's son-in-law, Daniella's husband.

Gil, you are very dear to me, and to all of us, and we are very close to you in this difficult time. I look on your grandkids and my wife that you gave me personally and I know we all are with you. We give you the great love back, the same love that we get from you through all the years. Be strong, dear Gil. Love, Rafi.

EXCERPT FROM OCTOBER 2004 AT GIL'S GRAVESITE

We all have special memories of Gil who was a unique person. Some remember him primarily for his impressive career [...] Gil was a person who always gave the person he was talking to, no matter who it was — at work, or at home, the feeling that he was an equal, no less intelligent or worthy than he. [...] You, Gil, accepted me immediately as a member of the family — 'as is' with a lot of warmth and affection although I am not an easy-going person, all the more so in my younger years...

You followed our agricultural saga from the start with a lot of empathy and sense of involvement. You sought in your own mild-mannered way to suggest ways of improving the looks of the farm — but at the time we didn't have the energy to deal with such 'minor issues'. I am happy to let you know, Gil, that your recommendations have finally borne fruit — and in the last year we finally took your advice and painted the farm buildings white as you suggested decades ago. I gaze at the buildings enjoying the 'new look' and kick myself for not having done it earlier so that you could see the improvement with your own eyes — the open spaces from tearing down part of the poultry run, the landscaping, the gravel and brickwork, and last but not least, the whitewashed siding. And your son-in-law as the gardener — a new role for me...

EFRAT AND ASAF ASHKENAZY[6]
PARTING WORDS TO GIL
JULY 1998

We had thought today, how odd it is that we have seen you for only about 15 times in all our lives, sometimes for only a short period, and

6. Sent to Gil in his final days from his three Israeli grandchildren — Rafi and Daniella's children.

still got so attached to you. We do have relatives closer than 6,000 miles. But we don't feel so close to them than to you. We guess the reason that we got so attached to someone in such short visits is that you are such a special person. We got so excited each time you came to Israel, not just because of the M&Ms that you brought, but also because of the special relationship we always had. In the beginning, we could not understand a word you were saying, in light of your lousy Hebrew. What we did not have a problem with was understanding your love and caring.

Asaf: I have to think about you every day when I lose another hair. It's good to have someone to blame... The best compensation is that I also got your smart brain, so I forgive you.

Efrat: I can't forget how both of you helped me with my decision to study law. Asaf and you were born to be engineers. For me it was a little, just a little more complicated. I always thought that ∞[7] is an 8 that fell down on its face... What I promise is to be a successful lawyer.

Nadav, who is not here at the moment,[8] is the inheritor of your love of airplanes. It doesn't seem that he is going to be a pilot, but, for sure, he'll be 'in the business'. Nevertheless, all our photo albums are filled with pictures of us in the Air & Space Museum at ages 10, 12, 13, 14, 17, 18 and 23... It seems like we have grown up inside Lindbergh's plane.

You can be sure that we will all find our perfect spouses, have lots of kids, a dog, a big yard and a huge barbecue. We will always try to follow your perfect relationship with Savta Pearl but you know no one can compete with you.

Well, this is starting to look like a farewell letter, when all we meant was to cheer you up and let you know how much we love you. We really do.

Asaf and Efrat (also for Nadav)

7. The symbol for 'infinity' (for the math-challenged).

8. Nadav was out of contact when penned, in the midst of a *Gadna Avir* air cadets' drone course in the north (completing his 'solo' with flying colors, although having recently discovered he was color-blind, his dreams of becoming an IDF pilot had to be scratched).

Rabbi Mindy Portnoy[9]
Building Relationships — Not Just Things
July 1998

Coming to Temple Sinai in 1985, I first met Gil during what Pearl and Gil called "his bonus years" — after a near brush with death that I didn't know about: Gil was so energetic and vibrant and so caring, so full of life and passion and spirit, that it was difficult for me to even imagine him any other way.

Gil was a man who appreciated his life while he lived it and had few regrets and was surrounded by loving family members. His main concern in the days before he died was making sure Pearl would be able to manage — an attribute not surprising to those who knew him.

A creator and builder he added substance and beauty to the world he inhabited — from airplane design to furniture and landscaping. Gil blessed the world with his mind, his hands and his spirit...designing their home in Silver Spring, doing all the home repairs (while helping out at the homes of friends and neighbors, as well), creating beauty in nature as an expert landscaper and gardener. But Gil was first and foremost a builder of relationships as well as things.

As a couple, Gil and Pearl were best friends, lovers, confidants and companions of the highest order — the kind of marriage that our Sages spoke of when the rabbis talked about 'matches made in Heaven'. Gil loved his family. He was thrilled about Wendy's upcoming marriage to Allan. He read every word of Ben's PhD thesis. He forged a special relationship with Lisa who lived with Pearl and Gil at various periods of time. And although part of his family lived in Israel, he managed to establish a unique and individual relationship with each of his Israeli grandchildren.

Gil considered his career the best career anyone could have and made exceptional contributions to his field, but that's only one piece of the person Gil Weiss was. With his busy vocation and avocations, how did Gil find time for anything else?! He was actively involved in interracial organizations such as the Clams and the NAACP and for 40

---

9. A rabbi at Temple Sinai in 1985. Excerpts from her eulogy delivered at Gil's funeral.

years volunteered at Temple Sinai — organizing a committee of Do-It-Yourselfers who built things needed by the synagogue; he was a veteran member of the choir; and chair of the ushers' committee for funerals. And he also participated in PNAI — the organization of Parents of North American-Israelis. But his greatest contribution to other's lives was his love of people and his active caring for them.

Gil was a person who looked for the good in other human beings and usually found it. Probably every person present here today could tell some story about a favor, a kindness, a *mitzvah* Gil did for them. Gil was sensitive to the needs of others — and actively helpful to them and on their behalf, whether you were an old friend, or a newcomer to America or a neighbor around the block, Gil always had a smile, a warm word and often a real deed he would do for you.

He loved people and they loved him back.

George Spangenberg[10]
My Professional and Personal Relationship with Gil
July 1998

My association with Gil goes back to 1939 when we were both working in the design group of the Naval Aircraft Factory. I had been at NAF for about four years. Gil had only been there about six months. After interviewing people in Philly, Mr. Frisbie — then the senior design engineer at the Bureau of Aeronautics in Washington — selected the two of us for a grade promotion and a transfer to what was his two-man section in the Engineering Branch of BuAer in late 1939. At the time — despite goings-on in Europe and the build-up in the United States in anticipation of war, the Bureau of Aeronautics was a small organization responsible for the entire field of naval aviation, from writing of requirements, to design and development of the aircraft, as well as what is now the off-Nav part of planning, budgeting, building and training. We occupied merely two floors of the old Navy Building. The size of the Bureau at the time is reflected in the fact that Mr. Frisbie took us for a tour of the entire operation when we arrived — right

10. Gil's boss at BuAer for more than three decades — head of the Evaluation Division, from a eulogy at the funeral in July 1998.

up to meeting with Admiral John Tower. It's inconceivable today that two P-2 and P-3 grade employees would be asked to see the Chief of the Bureau upon arrival.

Our little group was responsible for "design coordination and contract airplane design" — making sure the structural requirements didn't overpower power plant requirements and so forth, as well as running competitions and proposal evaluations. [...] To me, Gil's greatest contribution was his successful effort in raising the status of the weight control function in airplane design to its present acceptance as perhaps the most important single element involved in achieving a successful outcome. Thus, we now hear, not always correctly, program managers reporting that their particular development is "on weight, on schedule, on cost". Gil led the Navy effort in standardizing weight forms, handbooks and procedures, as well as starting the industry's professional Society of Aeronautical Weight Engineers — an organization that made him an Honorary Fellow, its highest award, in 1956.

[...] Slowly the names [of the Bureau of Aeronautics] changed–from BuAer to BuWeps and then Systems Command but it remained, in its essence, BuAer. For the first 17 years, Mr. Frisbie was our immediate boss. After his retirement, I became Gil's boss on paper at that point, and he became my assistant of the Evaluation Division and relinquished his title as head of Weight Control to Keith Dentel — although there was no change in the nature of our collaborative relationship.

Before closing, I feel I must remark on what was rank discrimination against those of Gil's ethnicity in this region of the country that probably exists to this day. Gil's house in Silver Spring was vandalized when he was on vacation[11] and we all sympathized with him but we didn't do a heck of a lot. I was never involved [sic. present] in any of the [antisemitic] incidents directly, but I would later learn directly from him that there were places he didn't go and places that he avoided. Only one incident touched me — a very minor one — but disturbing

11. Spangenberg was referring to the swastikas and antisemitic messages during a 1970 break-in that apparently took place in the six months before Gil retired in May 1970. See the second half of the section Memories of Skyland and Silver Spring in Chapter IV about the incident which prompted Pearl and Gil to sell their 'dream house'.

at the time. In the process of buying a house in an established area of Arlington I received a phone call from my wife Lillian, who had been called by someone involved in the mortgage process questioning whether 'we the Spangenbergs were, in fact, Jewish'. There were restrictions against Jews and other races in the deed. Could we prove our 'non-Jewishness'? I was abashed to say the least, and wanted to talk to Gil but didn't want to offend him in any way. I thought I knew him well enough that it wouldn't be a problem, so I turned the question around and asked Gil: "How did he prove he was Jewish?" His reply, which didn't really solve 'my problem' was to say with a twinkle in his eye: "George, I've never had that problem".

[...] Describing what a truly 'good guy' Gil Weiss was, is difficult. A final thought came to mind. Handle the problem as some handle evaluations with numerical rating systems. What would be the factors? Why not the Boy Scout Laws? They impressed me when I was a Scout and I still remember them. "A Scout is: Trustworthy, Loyal, Helpful, Friendly, Courteous, Kind, Obedient, Cheerful, Thrifty, Brave, Clean and Reverent". In my evaluation, Gil would win any such competition hands down. With somewhat less facility on my part, I bet that he would also win a Ten Commandments contest...

Jack Jaffe
A Forty-Seven-Year Friendship[12]
July 1998

Pearl and Gil and Funny and I go back a long time. We actually met in about 1951 [when living in Southeast Washington — DA], and none of us were particularly interested in religion at the time. We all became interested for one reason or another, but the Weisses joined us as founding members of Temple Sinai from the beginning in 1952. One of the reasons was we had invited them over for several Friday night dinners and Daniella was 'taken' with the Friday night ritual at our house — lighting the candles, a *challah*, white tablecloth — and when she came home she told her parents "It would be nice if we had that at home". And that was when we all joined Temple Sinai. Gil and

12. Delivered at the funeral.

I were both about the same size, both sang in the Temple choir and were often mistaken for one another by others.

He wasn't only an aeronautical engineer. He was a cabinetmaker and an electrician and an all-around Fix-it Man. If you need an appliance repaired or a leg glued to a piece of furniture or a lighting fixture hung, he was always available with his toolbox; his basement workshop was legendary. Gil was a man who couldn't say no. Once Funny and I ordered a new garbage disposal. Although we'd arranged for its installation, Gil heard about it and said "Why pay an installer? I can do that..." and insisted on installing it himself. Not that he didn't have a long list of projects waiting at home for him.

Oh yes, Gil was a List Maker supreme. Mainly he made a list of 'things to be done' but he was also a great planner: Every project had its plans and design and drawings and charts. And when it came to a major purchase he would spend hours, sometimes days, researching the product, comparing prices and features to come up with the best deal.

[...] Gil was a great tennis player...and therein lays a tale: We were four families living in Silver Spring — the Weisses, the Silvermans, the Summers and the Jaffes. One summer when our children were young, we decided to spend a week at Watoga State Park in West Virginia. Somehow we found some old wooden tennis rackets lying around and brought them along. That was the beginning of a wonderful tennis foursome among the four of us men. Gil was a natural athlete and picked up the game very quickly and developed great form and whoever was his partner knew he'd be on the winning side. Only after his almost fatal heart attack in 1984 did Gil stop playing tennis — saying his coordination was off.[13]

[...] Above all Gil was a gentle man and a loving man. Rarely did he raise his voice in anger. Yet, if he latched on to a cause, he held on tenaciously until he felt it had been resolved — one way or another.

---

13. Largely due to a stroke when inserting a pacemaker — that left him with permanent impaired peripheral vision on one side.

Tony Robinson[14]
Speaking for the 'Extended Family'
July 1998

I've had the wonderful fortune to live near Uncle Gibby and Aunt Pearl for 28 years, which has given me the distinct honor of spending hours and hours with two of the most wonderful human beings I have ever, and probably will ever, know.

Most people when asked about their family usually respond telling about their husbands or wives, parents, children and grandchildren. For Gil Weiss — who happens to be Uncle Gibby to me — family had an entirely different definition: He never drew boundaries. No matter how one entered the family — by birth, marriage or adoption. No matter how many generations were spanned, each of us knew we were completely loved and accepted. Over the years, I don't know how many conversations he and I have had when he talked with incredible pride about 'our wonderful family'. Not so very long ago we were sitting and talking about the family...and he began drawing a family tree. Sheet after sheet of paper which he spread across the table until five or six pages of fairly small print captured the names of the people whom he thought 'reasonably' captured The Family.

I sometimes marvel how one human being could stay in contact with so many others in a meaningful and powerful way. In a world where so many people use geographical distance for an excuse for not being in communication, Uncle Gibby found the time for 4th cousins, great-great-nephews, parents of in-laws, and more, as well as his own immediate family.

I learned about relatives from a man who spoke of each and every one of them as if they were the most special person alive. And that is the essence of the man [...] Unlike me, so many of the other family members did not have the honor of spending thousands of hours with Uncle Gibby. But that has not diminished the impact he has had on them. [...] He was creative and inquisitive. I always thought of my uncle as 'a Renaissance man'. His interests ranged from art to engineering,

14. Gil's niece (Bernie and Sylvia Weiss' daughter), excerpts from her eulogy at the funeral.

from gardening to tennis, opera to junk collecting...and boy could he give a great hug and kiss! It seemed that whatever other people in his life were interested in or concerned about — became an interest or concern of his.

When he and Aunt Pearl decided that so many of their younger family members were involved in computers, they decided to take a basic computer course. I remember sitting at the kitchen table drawing pictures of how the disks and the printers and the CPUs and modems all hung together. [...] In his indomitable style, Uncle Gibby dove into it with the zest he tackled everything. And it was no surprise that in short order, he had collected email addresses from distant family members, to facilitate them being in touch with one another.

Gil Weiss is a hard, even impossible act to follow...to pass on in our lives the values he stood for: To love those who pass into and through our lives, family or friends. To honor and respect individualisms and differences. To strive to be the best at whatever we choose to take on. To live every day in our lives fully, as if it could be our last.

Lisa Bard[15]
To My GrandDad
July 1998

GrandDad. [...] Your harmonious voice will echo forever in my memory. You have filled me with words of wisdom, praise and love. You have inspired my talents. You have influenced my dreams and aspirations. You are my determination and my achievements. You are my role model and have shown me that the sky is truly the only limit. You have left me the gift of patience, loyalty and giving. You have passed on so much to so many. With you in my life from my earliest days, taking care of me like your own child, I was never alone, I was never incapable and I was always important. You made me soar above the clouds. You are the garden's stormless rose. You are the wind supporting the plane's wing. You are the art of the crafter. You are the thoughtfulness of the intellect. You are the world's peace. You are the heart's love. [...] You are my example. You are my hero. You are my GrandDad forever.

---

15. Gil's American granddaughter (Wendy's daughter), delivered at the funeral.

Dan Weiss[16]
Remembers Uncle Gibby
July 1998

[...] I recall the conversations we had throughout the years, the pride in your voice when you spoke of family accomplishments. Uncle Gibby [was] always such a positive influence and inspirational figure — a great example of how one should conduct oneself — both personally and professionally. Always a gentleman. These ideals have become a part of me, and will always be with me.

Jack Wessel[17]
Gil Weiss: Boss. Mentor. Friend.
July 1998

It was probably within a year after Gil retired from NavAer. He had accepted a consulting position with Grumman Aircraft and had come into the office with a contingent of the Corporation's engineers and contracts people to discuss certain facets of the detail specifications for a contract, as yet unsigned. After much discussion we finally reached an impasse — Gil and I were arguing some point and the discussion became rather heated. Finally Gil said to me, "Jack you are not willing to compromise on any part of this". I replied, "You're right Gil, and you are the one who taught me to insist on no compromise on these aspects of the detail spec". Gil came back with "Gee, I didn't realize I was that bad". I answered, "I prefer to think it was one of the reasons you were so damn good". We left the problem for discussion at a later time. Gil and the Grumman people left. Five or ten minutes later, Gil came hurrying back into the office alone, threw his arm around my shoulder and said, "Thanks, Jack!", and then was gone. I didn't know then, nor do I know now, what he meant, but I do know that I was on Cloud 9 every time I thought about it.

I had been at NavAer for about a week or ten days...when Gil came out to my desk, sat down and without any preamble said "Jack, I'm

16. Gil's great nephew (Bobby Weiss' son), written the day before Gil died.

17. The Navy employee who replaced Gil as deputy director of the Evaluation Division when Gil retired.

going to retire in three years, so you have that long to learn everything I know about this job". Learning everything that Gil knew was Mission Impossible. As George Spangenberg once said, "No one in the Navy knows as much about the Navy procurement system as Gil Weiss".

In trying to put these things that I remember about Gil on paper, everything comes back in such profusion that it is hard to pick and choose. After being given a tour of his basement workshop with its many small, labeled drawers, I think I'll make one drawer of my own [in my own workshop] and mark it "String — too short to save". We always claimed that Gil surely had such a drawer in his shop. Mine will have a sub-heading: In memory of Gil Weiss — Boss Mentor Friend.

Dudley Cate[18]
Reminiscences — Personal and Professional
July 1998

I joined the Weights Branch of the Evaluation Division in 1963 — a young and impressionable engineer, and Gil was the sort of person who would make a lasting impression on even the very unimpressionable!

Gil treated everyone as a fellow-worker. I never had the sense that he was holding his superior rank over me or anyone else. Notice that I said "worked with Gil" — not "worked for Gil". That was really how I always felt it was.

Gil was a bundle of energy who always moved at full throttle. He worked hard — and long. I used to hear through the grapevine about his long-suffering carpool who often sat for a long time after 4:30 waiting for Gil to arrive. From what I also heard, the fact that Gil had one of the very few inside parking passes had a lot to do with why his carpool was so long-suffering!

[...] Gil was thorough — working every aspect of a task to its full completion. Gil was tenacious for what he believed was right. I never experienced this, but I heard much about the specification negotiations meetings at SAWE[19] conferences that would go on and on, and

18. A member of Gil Weiss' engineering team in Weights Control at the Evaluation Division.

19. Society of Aeronautical Weight Engineers.

on — sometimes until after midnight — until Gil had 'outlasted' everyone else on the points he felt were important.

[...] Gil had the highest integrity and the strongest dedication to naval aviation. It was always very clear that all his work and actions and decisions and recommendation were done and made solely in the best interests of the Fleet, the Navy and his Country.

[...] While I was very impressed with Gil from the start, only as the years passed did I come to fully realize what a powerful combination of wonderful qualities he possessed, and how amazingly fortunate I was to have had the opportunity, the privilege and the job of working with him.

Keith Dentel[20]
A Down-to-Earth Boss
July 1998

I first met Gil in the early 1940s at one of the first national meetings of the Society of Aeronautical Weight Engineers. At that time I was an aircraft engineer with Glenn Martin [aircraft company] and Gil was the Head of the Weights Branch at the Bureau of Aeronautics. In short order, Gil facilitated my entry into the Navy in uniform and assignment to his engineering group in Washington [...] As a leader Gil was a very caring person, not only proficient in his engineering, but with a knack for integrating, in his own quiet way, the best capabilities of his staff in their work in weight analysis and performance analyses... The world will miss a wonderful guy, but I'm sure the Great Power of our Universe will welcome Gil into this new dominion as one of His best engineers.

Following Pearl's passing in December 2013 and *15 years after Gil's funeral* Keith's wife Marcene Dentel wrote an online condolence note to the Weiss Family speaking of "the vitality, humor, and love that Pearl and Gil brought to this world".

20. Gil's work colleague for three decades and Deputy Head of Weights Control under Gil.

Bill Crenshaw[21]
Friend and Gentleman
July 1998

Gil did much in elevating the status of the Weight Branch. He was very supporting of SAWE — the Society of Aeronautical Weight Engineers. He was always willing to do a job well and take on another. He was always concerned with the welfare of others. He was a respected engineer and dedicated family man. I am privileged to have known him. He was a friend. He was a gentleman.

Remembering Pearl and Gil: 2013–2018

There are pros and cons to longevity. Pearl left us in late December 2013 at age 97½ with no outstanding illnesses...dying of old age.[22] No heart disease. No diabetes. No Parkinson's. No dementia. She ate lunch — with no restrictions on salt or sugar intake. She took a walk down the corridor with her walker. She got into bed for a nap...and never got out again. She died a week later.

Pearl was almost the last to go from her generation: Only Judy Summers from the inseparable Washington crowd (the Weiss-Jaffe-Silverman-Summers Quartet), and her sister-in-law Millie Swiss among the relatives — both of whom were younger — outlived her by a few years.

In late 2016, two years after Pearl died, I sat down determined this time to finish *Playing Detective with Family Lore* (far too long on my own bucket list). I had finally completed transcriptions of hours of taped interviews, and inserted choice passages with anecdotes and insights into the body of the text, to dovetail Gil's Memorabilia that

21. A friend and colleague of Gil's from industry, who joined the Weight Division in 1967.

22. The *Washington Post* demanded the obituary editor receive a scanned copy of the death certificate to *prove* this was so, before he could run a news obit in the paper.

Pearl in her mid-90s

originally served as the scaffolding for *Playing Detective with Family Lore.*

Adding a 'Pearl section' to the tributes presented a challenge: There are almost no contemporaries to speak of — relatives, close friends or work companions more or less from 'her generation' — to write about 'the Pearl I knew'... Among the handful left, some eluded attempts to find them. Others are burdened by dementia or computer illiteracy. Among younger 'candidates', some are occupied with grandkids or health issues or other more burning concerns. Nevertheless, the input received with or since Pearl's passing was impressive — perhaps the most incredible in my mind, memories from three former 3rd grade students.[23]

This closing chapter at the back of the book opens with excerpts of words spoken in Washington at Pearl's funeral in late December 2013 — including my eulogy on behalf of the family — *A Tribute to Our Mom's Jeans.* It is followed by Wendy's wonderful piece — *My Seven Years with Mom*, written in late 2018, that not only captures in Wendy's words and a few choice photos, the last seven years of Pearl's life in Minnesota, but also a deepening one-on-one relationship that deserves a special place in this book. It closes with the words of others.

Some are one sentence. Some are a full page. Some are tributes written for an occasion (noted where pertinent) — excerpts and abridged parting words and funerals eulogies. Many were written especially for this book. There are words from sons-in-law. From grandkids. From

23. Rochelle Helzner, Myra Hofberg Cohen and Wendy Gerson — the last, a former *chanichah* (protégé) of mine in Habonim when Gerson was ten years old, who was also Pearl's third grade pupil in elementary school at the time. Dr. Gerson's actions in making a *shivah* call, spoke louder than words.

other members of the extended family in the widest sense: Family not only by virtue of birth. Words from work colleagues and from personal friends and protégés. All testify how Pearl and Gil touched countless people due to the way they would embrace the people who came into their lives, with their warmth, their empathy and nonjudgmental respect for others, always ready to help or just to be there for anyone in need — ranging from a friend to a neighbor or a perfect stranger in need of practical gardening advice, a spell-checker or a table saw, to marginalized, stressed-out or troubled young people at this or that stage in their lives, in need of an ear or a shoulder, a job or a tuna sandwich, or a roof over their heads during the summer, for a few weeks or a few months...or several years. Or just a hug.

We continue to 'celebrate Gil's life' every time one of us bends down to grab a weed or a hammer, solve a tough math problem, deliver a mean tennis serve, mentor a green immigrant or do something nice for someone else 'just because'. Likewise, we 'celebrate Pearl's life' every time the kids pile into their parent's bed to read the weekend papers (or just for the closeness), discuss books or politics around a kitchen table or Shabbat dinner, and every time we take the time to lend an empathetic ear (I mean *really* listen) to another person over a cup of coffee, or reach out and embrace someone.

Left: Asaf, Nadav and Pearl, 2004
Right: Daniella and Rafi 'taking the newspaper to bed', circa 1980

A Tribute to Our Mom's Jeans
Eulogy written by Daniella on behalf of the family at the funeral service for Pearl Weiss in the Washington Metro Area
26 December 2013

In praise of Pearl's jeans/genes

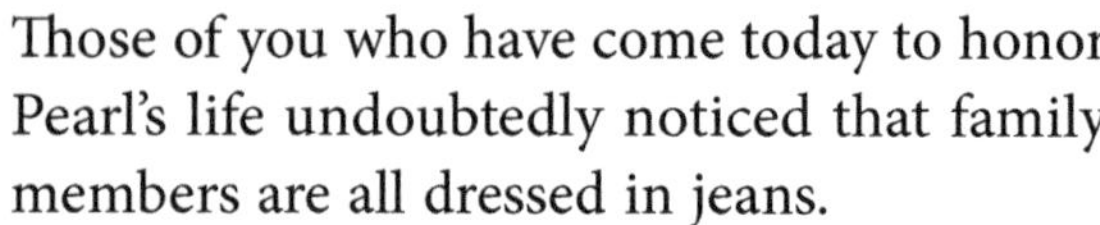

Those of you who have come today to honor Pearl's life undoubtedly noticed that family members are all dressed in jeans.

When I told Wendy I only had the jeans I'd come with, she said 'I never liked black at funerals—I'm going in jeans, too'. And the Israeli family, unaware of American dress codes, only arrived with jeans. Only Ben brought a suit. We only got Mom into her first pair of jeans at age 70, but from that point forward, she refused to part with her jeans to her dying day... Thus—fittingly—we stand here in our jeans in tribute to the legacy of Mom's jeans/genes, in every sense of the word.

~

I'm speaking on behalf of Wendy and myself.[24]

Mom—your most indelible and telling attribute was your accessibility as a 'people person' and as an enabler. You left your mark on so many people, at every stage of your life!

You were and remain our mom and our mentor. Nurturing wasn't

24. The rabbi from Temple Sinai spoke of Pearl's life and accomplishments; son-in-law Allan Ackerman spoke about how Pearl was like a 'second mom' (his own mother having died when he was a young teen); granddaughter Efrat chose a poem by Dahlia Ravikovich in Hebrew and English on behalf of the Israeli clan, and granddaughter Lisa added some words for herself and her brother Ben. I (Daniella) read tributes from Pearl's son-in-law Rafi about Pearl and Gil, and parting words from grandkids Nadav and Eti who remained in Israel with Pearl's great-granddaughter three-week old Rotem. Unfortunately, no tape was made by the funeral home that could be transcribed.

by *shtupping* us chicken soup—that was Nana's job. You set an example for us as an unapologetically strong intelligent woman...the kind of women both Wendy and I became—each in her own way, each at her own pace. I'm so glad that besides protecting you like a she-lion during your seven years in Minnesota, Wendy had the privilege of experiencing that close mother-daughter camaraderie I had—the two of you discussing books and doing crossword puzzles and watching political debates on TV.

In your career, you left an indelible impact far beyond the family—touching countless school kids you taught or counseled—who years later would come up to you, saying "Mrs. Weiss, Mrs. Weiss—do you remember me???" And by golly you always did, and you always had something to say about each that made them feel special.

That same quality—the empathy and compassion and interest in others from all stations in life continued—even in your nineties in Minnesota. To be adversarial or cynical, to be mean or demeaning wasn't in your vocabulary.

Thus, during the week-long period we spent with you as your body shut down, Wendy and I witnessed an amazing phenomenon: The extraordinary sense of loss that enveloped staff at all levels—from Frio the cleaning lady to Sophia the receptionist to Edwin the head nurse, and countless others—exemplified by Doris the RN on duty at 4:00 AM who confirmed your death, stethoscope in hand with tears running down her cheeks. You knew everyone's name—from the people who changed the towels to the nurses. You knew whether they hailed from Nigeria or Ethiopia, the Midwest or the Mideast—and asked about *their* lives, and you always said thanks.

Is it any wonder that we, in turn, were literally embraced by hugs every time a staff member entered the room to change your position, administer morphine or sedatives, or just ask how you were? They showered us with food...even inviting us to take a shower in the residents' bathroom—providing towels and shampoo. In a facility where death is a constant companion or just around the corner—oft met with a shrug of the shoulders by other residents, defense mechanisms simply collapsed: Countless residents asked permission to enter your room to say their goodbyes—to thank you for being part of their lives, saying things like "Pearl was the first person I met. She was my first friend here when I was at a loss". Devastated, many broke down as they left the room, leading us to comfort the comforters.

It's hard for us to follow your example, Mom — to be a little less critical and cynical, a little bit more compassionate and sensitive to others and less self-centered and selfish — but we know this is one of your strongest legacies for us.

Of course, there are other legacies, and if we are here to 'celebrate your life' — not just mourn you, this includes a host of humorous traits and life lessons we can learn.

- Let's note for the record and for all fitness freaks among us: The *modus operandi* for longevity should be Read More — Exercise Less. For eight decades, Mom never engaged in sports whatsoever — beyond mental gymnastics, but she lived to the ripe old age of 97½, departing without any debilitating illnesses — truly dying of 'old age'.
- Having said that, at 97 she astounded the physiotherapists by setting a record on the NuStep machine — pulling on those levers at Level 5 difficulty for up to 25 minutes at a time — as if they were the handle on a casino slot machine. Mom, in tribute, the staff plans to hang a photo of you on the wall 'working' that NuStep — citing your age...to encourage other patients.

Pearl with the Nustep machine

- Secondly, I must issue fair warning to all: Wendy has already assumed the role of the Weiss family grammar police. Indeed, on Monday evening — already quite reticent as she withdrew from life — Mom broke the silence in a half-whisper: "Better than I" she said, then retreated back into silence. Yes, those were some of her 'dying words' — correcting a good friend, Norma, who had come to visit, pointing out that it was incorrect to say

"Pearl, you're better than me"...

- Lastly, rest in peace, Mom. Wendy can assure you that she will continue to nag me about my fashion tastes on your behalf — and that's why — having arrived in Minnesota with a carry-on holding a laptop, two pair of blue jeans and these corduroy jeans — I'm wearing this white sweater of hers that Wendy picked out, instead of the earth-colored one I would have preferred.

My Seven Years with Mom
Wendy Weiss Ackerman
December 2018

When we celebrated Mom's ninetieth birthday in Maryland in July 2006, she gave us the keys to her car and I said "Thank you!" She may have been small in stature but she made up for it with independence and self-confidence. In July 1998 when Dad was dying, his biggest concern was his 'Pearly' and how she would manage. My promise to him was that he could 'take that one off his list' — whichever list she was on... We would take good care of her. Little did I know what that entailed!

Nearing the end of 2006 there was a noticeable decline in Mom's ability to live alone and her health was beginning to fail. It was at that time that Daniella and I, along with others, made the difficult decision that she could no longer live independently. As there wasn't anyone in Maryland who could advocate for her, we offered two choices: Minnesota or Israel. She chose Minnesota. We began the task of putting her condo on the market, setting aside items that would be coming to our house and selling or giving away the things she would not need in her new surroundings. We packed up the rest and on 2 February 2007 Mom and I flew 'home' to her new life in assisted living. It was the coldest day of that Minnesota winter: Below zero and minus 50°F with wind-chill factored in, it was the worst, but there would be plenty of what we call in Minnesota 'layered days'!

My life with Mom began as I slept with her for the first few nights in her new 'double' bed. She then kicked me out saying that I needed to 'go sleep with my husband'! So typical! When her furniture and other belongings arrived, her surroundings began to feel familiar. In our house we removed a lot of 'our stuff' to make room for Dad's made-with-love furniture, their collection of art and other worldly possessions. We had previously installed the Murano chandelier that had graced the dining room of the places they'd called home in Maryland. Whenever Mom was at our house, she was surrounded by her life, from art on the walls to placemats and napkins.

I guess it was about three months after the move, while I was 'still' attempting to sell her condo, getting insurances to pay up, finding new doctors, closing accounts, opening others and spending many hours almost every day with her that she announced: "I never realized how much work was involved managing my affairs and what you and Daniella meant by 'needing someone to advocate for me'. Thank you for 'making' me move". I was rewarded with the impish smile that I got to know quite well. At age 90 she'd finally realized I was a capable adult.

Within the first year in assisted-living, there were some mishaps that took away more of her confidence (illnesses, falls, ambulance rides and hospital stays) so she decided to permanently move next door to the nursing home at Shalom where she would have 24/7 care. It was still only 900 steps from my house, door-to-door. I can't count how many times there were emergencies but I do remember that often it was I who sensed something was wrong, rather than a staff person telling

Pearl in Minnesota, 2007–2013

me so. Yes, there was stress but at least I was in charge.

When the weather was nice we went for walks with me pushing the wheelchair. Invariably, at some point Mom would tell me we should turn around because 'I' was getting tired. We loved to sit outside and just enjoy the sunshine. In bad weather we would slowly meander the halls. She always enjoyed the exercise with her walker. When I volunteered at Shalom, Mom took part in the weekly art projects. She had never held a paintbrush before but was totally involved. I also took her for her first ever pedicure. We attended all kinds of concerts. Ate in or out (she loved good food). And we worked on crossword puzzles; when she began to cheat I would hand her the eraser. We listened to music, watched movies, news, political debates and Obama's inauguration which was a highlight of her fight for equality. Her memory never ceased to amaze me.

When she started having trouble with her eyes, she began picking out a book, and I would read it to her. When we were shopping I would often hang my purse over the handles of her wheelchair. Without failure, if I turned away, Mom would disappear. Without footrests she would swiftly scurry around, her head way below the merchandise, and I would run around the aisles yelling "Mom! Mom!" — because at this point she couldn't hear the 'family whistle'.

We would go for long rides with the sunroof open and I would point out anything that I thought would interest her, but she rarely responded. What I never realized was that she was so short her line of vision was barely above the bottom of the window. She had never seen the sights! All she saw were the incredible cloud formations in Minnesota that never ceased to amaze her. After this dawned on me, she explained: 'She just enjoyed being with me and nothing else mattered'. But I bought seat cushions!

One highlight during our seven years together: Every Mother's Day Allan and I would pick her up in the car, go for a long ride and stop someplace to pick up lunch for our annual picnic. Never one to stay home, she was included in all gatherings and holidays. It was heartwarming to watch her delight and involvement. At such gatherings, there was an unmistakable tone of contentment in her voice, and it was clear how much being included meant to her — a source of joy for both of us!

I have to credit my loving husband Allan who understood my stress and often helped me in more ways than I can count. His love for Mom and her love back were beyond words. There would be phone calls or a voice message that things weren't good. That she needed me immediately. Other times her messages were so upbeat I couldn't stop laughing. OK, so there were ups and downs but that could be expected. Cousin Jodi and friends Norma, Meir and Estelle were constant visitors at Shalom, while Valerie's twice-a-week massages were an ongoing pleasure. Everyone loved our mom.

I will be forever grateful to my sister Daniella for making the long trek from Israel as often as she could. She made me feel like a guest by taking over my kitchen and spending long days with Mom.

As the years went by, Mom often told me that I was what kept her alive. I believe that. Every year we celebrated her birthday in July. She rarely asked for much, so when she requested that for her 94th the only gift she wanted was for her children and grandchildren to all be together to celebrate I made preparations. Unfortunately, a war in Israel interrupted those plans. But considering how many times over the years she said her goodbyes to whoever happened to be with her visiting, I was determined to make that wish a reality. And so, in July/August 2011 — for her 95th birthday — I did it! There were plenty of details getting the Israeli clan and Ben to Minnesota but it was a blast. There were eight of us sleeping in the house. It was a fantastic chaotic extended slumber party lasting many days. Unfortunately, Lisa, Dave, Nadav, Eti and Rafi could not join us, though most visited later. Taking their place were some special Minnesotans. It was a time we will always cherish. At the 95th celebration, many of us reminisced about special times.

One more thing that I must share: Mom, the English teacher, almost always corrected the grammar of anyone around her. In fact, Daniella once said to Mom that she would be on her death bed and still correcting someone's grammar. Sure enough, she did!!! I had a sign in my kitchen that said "I am silently correcting your grammar!" Unfortunately, Mom willed me her verbal trait... Those who knew her only have to imagine and everyone else will understand.

Looking back over those seven years, I want to close by sharing what Mom and I shared during these seven years: Mom and I developed an unbelievable attachment during the years that she was here. I always thought of us as a mother and daughter with a very healthy relationship, however, when she moved here, we immediately started to bond in a way that we hadn't for 39 years living twelve hundred miles apart. When I'd voice this thought, saying 'how cool it's been' and 'how strong our bond has become' she replied: "It has been absolutely wonderful. Wendy, you've been beyond what any parent could expect or even hope for and Allan has been like a son to me. My heart is simply overflowing with love for everyone". She'd look around the room, and turn to me, and say: "You have fulfilled my dream!"

Because I had always believed that my connection with my parents was healthy and close, it never occurred to me that there was yet another level to loving and caring. Over the seven years until her death in late December 2013 at the ripe young age of 97½, our bond and our love continued to grow. Prior to this, I never knew what we had been missing. She was one beautiful and incredible little woman whom I think about daily. She'll always remain close to my heart, and I can still feel her soft gentle hands in mine. Never for a moment did I regret that she came to Minnesota.

Allan Ackerman[25]
Son-in-Law
2018

My mother-in-law Pearl and I had the opportunity to develop a unique relationship in our years together, right from the beginning of my marriage to Wendy. In fact, from the standpoint of time, she was a mother in my life nearly as long as my own mother, who passed away when I was 13 years old.

Pearl shared a wonderful Alaskan cruise with Wendy and me, a trip that marked our first wedding anniversary. It was there that I discovered her skill at playing table tennis (and got to see Pearl demolish the table, diving forward to return a serve). The ship had a computer room where I taught her how to play Solitaire when we were at sea. I

25. Wendy's husband.

have fun videos of her trying to negotiate the ship's hallways during rough weather, as she listed from side-to-side, even when she was sober. Pearl accused me of trying to get her drunk and fast asleep, so that I could fool around with my wife (the three of us shared a cabin) and it was only years later I learned the truth...after Pearl told Wendy she only *pretended* to be sleeping at the time, and knew what was going on, perhaps the reason she chose to sleep in the bunk bed and we got the queen size bed... And speaking of sobriety, I was the person who turned her on to Bailey's Irish Cream liqueur as a nightcap—which Pearl said "worked *so much better* than Tylenol PM"...

The day Pearl moved to Minnesota, we showed her that we lived very close to her new residence, literally 900 steps from our door to hers. As we approached our home, she commented about how amazing our Midwest skies were, and she knew she would be comfortable living here. As her legs became weaker, and she started using a walker and wheelchair, we installed ramps in our house to make it easier for her when visiting, and we kept a stepstool in my minivan, as well. After a while, she became physically unable to enter and exit our vehicles by herself; I would lift her and help her in. Pearl had a wonderful sense of humor and the lighthearted repartee the two of us oft engaged in was epitomized the time I was lifting her into the passenger seat and I apologized, saying—"I almost grabbed your butt in the process, Pearl"...to which Pearl responded with a laugh, saying—"I wish you would have!"

Pearl became part of my own family, too. My relatives loved her, and were always certain to include her for holidays, dinners and all *simchas*. Pearl was especially close with my cousin Jodi Gordon, and was almost like a grandmother to her. Jodi visited her frequently, many times bringing along Lexi, her tiny Chihuahua. Lexi knew her own way to Pearl's room on the second floor at Sholom. She would run to the elevator, and when the doors opened, Lexi would run down the halls to Pearl's room and jump up into her lap. Pearl really loved Lexi, too.

Pearl had a special love of Chinese cuisine, and we had two Chinese restaurants we used to take her to—one very close to Sholom, the other about three miles away. One day, while Wendy was out-of-town, I went to visit Pearl. As I arrived, Jodi was also there visiting. Pearl announced she'd like to go out for dinner. I asked her what she would like; she said she wanted the Chinese buffet. We invited Jodi to join us, so we all got into the car, and I drove over to the restaurant close to Sholom. As I parked the car and turned off the engine, Pearl said—"Not *here*!" I said—"What do you mean 'not here'???" No, she wanted me to start the car and take her to the *other* restaurant, three miles away. There was no arguing with her...so off we went.

December 2013: A parting shot

The last time we took Pearl to *Kol Nidrei* services, I got her in the car, stuck her wheelchair in the trunk, and since we were running a little late, I was speeding to make it to *shul* in time. As I'm approaching the synagogue, a squad car behind me turns on their lights and siren to make me stop and ticket me. I continue into the synagogue parking lot, the cops right behind me, lights flashing. Everyone watches as I exited the car, open the trunk, and take out the wheelchair to help this frail, little woman out of the car and into her chair. By this time the police were watching what I was doing (along with the rest of the congregation) and were kind of embarrassed. They turned off their flashing lights and merely asked me to drive slower. I told Pearl afterwards that I should take her with me whenever I need to get somewhere in a hurry...

Pearl was an amazing lady, a wonderful and significant part of my life. We developed a very loving relationship and I cherish these years we had together very much and the memories I carry with me.

I can't resist one last and unforgettable anecdote in closing. Given her sense of humor, no doubt Pearl would have risen to the occasion with an apt retort, had she been with us, but this happened hours after she passed: Sholom required that we vacate all her belongings from the room within 24 hours, so the next person on the waiting list could move in...and due to 'liability issues' they couldn't store anything on the premises even for a few days. Thus the next morning, I found myself loading her dresser on a rolling gurney cart and pushing it all 900 steps between Shalom and our house across the highway in the middle of a snowstorm. I don't have to tell you what this six-foot-long dresser looked like, covered with a blanket against the elements, as I exited Sholom... Suffice it to say I received the strangest looks from people at the entrance and in the parking lot — not to mention passing motorists, at the sight of this surreal exit... A unique sendoff, for sure.[26]

Rafi Ashkenazy[27]
Son-in-Law
Excerpts — Tribute to Pearl on her 85th Birthday
July 2001

[...] You and Gil have been a part of us at every step and word in our house — in bad times as in good. I always said to myself that I would never go near a girl until I saw her mother. The first time I broke my resolution — I found my wife. It may have been a long shot in the dark, Grandma, but I hit the bull's eye with my mother-in-law...and I hope my wife Daniella will be just like you at every age. In good spirits and in good shape...and, always with a word of encouragement when things get tough. I hope you will never change and will remain the fantastic person you are and have always been.

Excerpts — Farewell (from Israel) Read at the Funeral
December 2013

[...] I met Pearl in 1972, just before Daniella and I were married. Dear Gil Weiss quipped to me — saying, that 'he and Pearl had been married

26. When Allan placed the dresser in the basement guest room, in putting the drawers back in, he spied a ring — barely visible — wedged tightly in the joint of one of the dresser drawers. Gil must have lost it who-knows-when because no one remembers him wearing this silver ring with wings and the initials GW on the face. It had hidden and survived multiple moves and movers...from Silver Spring to Potomac, from Potomac to Leisure World and from Maryland to Minnesota. No one in Gil's professional circles has a clue what it signifies (I inquired — from NYU and NavAer to every professional organization Gil ever belonged to...) but I now wear it in his memory.

27. Pearl's Israeli son-in-law.

for 37 years, and he hoped we would reach that milestone...and more'. I quipped back that 'I couldn't imagine being married to the same women for 37 years'... Well, 42 years later, I'm still with the same woman — his dear daughter Daniella. Gil's good wishes have become a reality. In the ups and downs of marriage, I have always viewed the two of you as a source of wisdom, guidance and admiration, to get over the bumps of couplehood — a legacy we carry with us.

When our children were born (Pearl and Gil's three Israeli grandchildren), their behavior as grandparents — the warmth, the goodwill and knowledge they shared, and the relationships they built that bridged distance and language gaps — are a legacy that all three of our kids Efrat, Asaf and Nadav carry with them. Likewise, Pearl's great-grandchildren — Itamar, Yoav and little three-week-old Rotem — inherit this 'Weiss legacy': Pearl and Gil remain pillars of guidance for all, of the importance of building deep and honest relationships, for their modesty, showing us all how to be mensches to one another — that is, to be good human beings.

Dear Pearl, how blessed we are to have had you in our lives, as our mother, mother-in-law, *savta* and great-grandmother.

[...] I want to thank Wendy on behalf of all of us, for her loving devotion all these years — that undoubtedly contributed not only to dear Pearl's longevity but also [to] her quality of life. Thank you, Wendy. *Todah. Todah raba.*

Lisa Bard[28]
Granddaughter
Excerpts — Read at the Funeral
December 2013

Your life was amazing and filled with laughter and love, wisdom and intelligence, experience and wonder. You learned and taught every day. You knew how to give and to receive. You were gentle and loving and the best example the world will ever know of being a truly wonderful and incredible person. [...] I remember catching fireflies as night, lights to keep bedtime less scary and knowing that I was loved when you'd

28. Wendy's daughter and Pearl's eldest granddaughter.

hold a buttercup under my chin (others thought this was to see if they liked butter). That yellow dust was everywhere. Ladybugs made wishes come true as did eyelashes blown off a fingertip. We picked apples and berries and flowers from the backyard. You pushed me on the swing set, kissed my bumps and bruises, and made the big world less ominous to a then little girl. You helped me through every phase of life, from birth through today. You were my encouragement, my example, my unconditional love, my everything. [...]

You're the melody in the song. You're the meaning in the words. You're the movement in the dance. You're the love of my life and the center of my universe.

Nadav Ashkenazy and Family[29]
Grandson
Excerpts — Read at the Funeral (in Nadav's Absence)[30]
December 2013

Still sharing stories from the past and present and always interested in our lives and of those around you at the Shalom Home, you reached a ripe old age still clear of mind to the end. [...] Full of life, with a winning smile, poised but down-to-earth, within minutes you conquered the hearts of everyone you encountered, with your gentleness and your interest and concern for others. [...]

Three weeks ago your third great-grandchild[31] was born — this time, a girl. [...] You were able to watch Eti's pregnancy online, and see little Rotem via Skype video and hear her voice. [...] No matter how brief this meeting was, you'll leave your stamp on Rotem, just as you have on others before her. It's as if you refused to go before you could conquer her with your winning smile and warmth — passing on all those positive attributes of yours to her, as a life legacy. [...] We know, wherever you are, that the harmony with others that characterized your life

29. Pearl's Israeli grandson Nadav and his wife Eti.

30. Eti had just given birth to their first child, a girl: two-week-old Rotem (who would be followed three years later by a boy, Nitzan).

31. Pearl's older great-grandchildren being Efrat's sons: Itamar and Yoav Kaplan.

will continue to shine down on our lives, protecting us from discord.

Nadav Ashkenazy
Grandson
December 2018

One of my sharpest memories from childhood was the yearly visits of Saba and Savta[32] in the summers. The warmth of those visits, with Savta Pearl going out of her way to embrace me and the interest she always showed in me is still palpable, while Saba Gil was exemplified by two dominant traits that I seek to emulate in my own private and professional life. First of all — *derech eretz* (good manners or 'to be a *mensch*'), patience and serene temperament. I have always thought of him as the epitome of kindness towards others — his respect for their person and sensitivities, whoever they be. This was all the more prominent in Gil's desire to make others he encountered always come away feeling good, no matter whether it was a nameless person he encountered in the grocery, or a grandchild with endless questions.

The second trait was his technical professionalism. As an aeronautical engineer, Saba's perspective and grasp spanned the overall system down to the last screw or bolt. Their yearly visits in Israel endowed me — as a child with technical potential — with an opportunity to learn from a master engineer, to internalize a technological approach. Whatever the task that Saba Gil took upon himself, he would define the need, set forth alternative solutions, then plan the best solution — with patience, dedication to the smallest details and uncompromising quality throughout.

To have had these two special people in my life, without a doubt played an important role in shaping me as I matured and reached adulthood, in my military service and as I advanced professionally as an engineer and as a manager.

I chose my professional path early, at age 16 — when I became cognizant of the pleasure I derive from technical challenges and finding technical solutions. Today I'm the owner of an engineering firm and an entrepreneur — a career that focuses on finding solutions to technical

32. Grandfather and grandmother in Hebrew.

and technological problems. In doing so I carry with me the legacy of my grandparents—both in my devotion to professional standards while daring to think out-of-the-box, and in my determination when getting the job done, to conduct myself with *derech eretz* and honesty, to maintain good interpersonal relations as much as attention to detail. I also strive for the same milieu of *derech eretz*, patience and tranquility that exemplified Gil and Pearl as people and as a couple, in my own family life.

Eti Ashkenazy[33]
Granddaughter-in-Law
January 2018

I met Savta Pearl during a trip to the States in the fall of 2011 with Nadav, whom I had been going with for a year. We arrived in Minnesota exhausted after a long flight (that including our luggage not arriving, stuck somewhere in Europe with no idea when it would arrive). We arrived at Doda[34] Wendy's and she greeted me warmly with a hug that within minutes made me feel part of the family. Despite our fatigue, we went straight to Savta Pearl's place at the seniors' complex where she lived.

It didn't take any time to grasp what a special person I had the honor of meeting. Within minutes I fell in love with Pearl and her captivating personality. I found myself engaged in a lovely and lively discussion with a 95-year-old woman who seemed to grow younger from minute-to-minute the more we talked. She would say what was on her mind but didn't try to fill in the moments of silence with small talk; when we asked 'why are you silent?' she answered honestly and straight-to-the-point with a sentence I'll never forget: "I just don't have anything else to say". Her ability to take interest in people she encountered and find something of interest for those she met, her ability to remember stories in detail as if they occurred yesterday—not 70 years ago...made us forgot our fatigue, thirsty and curious to hear more.

During our stay in Minnesota we spent a lot of time with Savta

33. Nadav's wife.

34. *Doda*: Aunt in Hebrew.

Pearl — going on trips to the falls and the forests, going out to eat hamburgers and other places, sharing Wendy's hospitality, and getting to know other residents at Shalom. In introducing me to her friends at Shalom, Savta Pearl 'upgraded' me, saying: "This is my grandson and his fiancée"...even before Nadav popped the question. She said repeatedly "I used to have a sharp mind" but her sixth sense and emotional intelligence were very sharp: Even I wasn't aware that in the wayward suitcases was an engagement ring that Nadav planned to pull out at a romance spot on one of Minnesota's lakes...

Counter to the plans, we suddenly found out we had lost track of time, and we were scheduled to leave early the next morning and hadn't even said goodbye to Savta Pearl... (And Nadav had not yet proposed!) We managed to delay our departure and reschedule a few days later, and things went forward as planned (the lake, the ring, etc.): We were able to share with Savta Pearl the exciting news that we were getting married, and to receive her blessings. Pearl shared with us two little secrets she had for her long and happy marriage to Gil (whom unfortunately I never met firsthand). I'll always keep her two secrets for couples in mind: One — don't go to sleep angry. Two — love your spouse more than yourself.

This meeting with Savta Pearl left a deep impression on me, and it was very important to me to go again to visit her. In the meantime, we had gotten married, and I had a growing tummy (a fetus we dubbed 'Cashew'). We sensed time was at a premium and while I was still pregnant was the best time to go back to the States, before we were tied down with a family — that way we could symbolically share with Pearl first-hand the 'continuity of generations'. We enjoyed an additional week with Pearl and Wendy in 2013 — one filled with warmth, love, doing things, sharing stories — just like the first visit. In retrospect it provided us with a unique opportunity to part with Savta Pearl a few months before she passed away. She died two weeks after the birth of our first child — our daughter Rotem.

I only met Savta Pearl twice in my life — a sum total of two weeks, but I feel like I've known her much longer, She left a tremendous impression with her special personality and the stories she told us, and I can feel her love embracing me.

Asaf Ashkenazy[35]
Grandson
January 2019

To grow up in a small village in the south of Israel at the end of the 1970s and 1980s, before Internet and accelerated Americanization, was very different from the way children grow up today. The differences between Israel and the States were vast. As a child with grandparents from America, I felt like I was very lucky.

We looked forward to the thrill of their periodic visits. Impatiently, Efrat and I waited to discover what surprises from across the ocean their heavy suitcases contained. Communication between visits was primarily via audiotapes and letters — mostly one-page aerogrammes. Mom would read us the letters from Saba and Savta in translation and we would dictate our replies of what we were up to for translation. Later, for many years, every year Mom would disappear for a time to visit her parents in the States, almost as a matter of routine, while we were left to ensure everything went like clockwork at home, a catalyst for early maturation and taking responsibility.

But earlier, I remember going to visit when I was in third grade (1986) when Saba had just recovered from a heart attack. It was an enchanting trip during which we meet a slew of American relatives, visited countless museums, marveled at television with multiple channels (compared to one station back home), ate in restaurants (what I don't remember doing at home except when Saba and Savta came to visit), and of course visited the gigantic toy store Toys R Us. The Passover *seder* that year was huge, very special and memorable. The contrast of all this with daily life on a little moshav was hard to absorb.

That year Saba and Savta began to visit us in Israel again, more frequently — living in the little house next-door on our farm which became a hub of activity in their presence. Each year, Saba continued a never-ending list of repairs and enhancements in their house while Savta cooked up a storm and gave mom a run for her money in the culinary realm.

During subsequent visits to the States, I spent a lot of time with

35. Rafi and Daniella's 'sandwich' son.

Saba in the garden and in the Shop. He — a pencil always balanced behind his ear — helping me plan and build all sorts of things. Accompanying Savta to supermarkets (with coupons in hand, of course — a practice that didn't exist in Israel) — these food stores' size was hard to comprehend. We enjoyed endless conversations on the sofa in the living room and in the kitchen, watched movies together, and took trips to local attractions (from Great Falls to the various malls) and farther afield to Annapolis, Baltimore and New York.

The language barrier with them was quickly broken, and we began to communicate more, and as the years passed the number of meetings grew and the tie became much more 'personal' and less and less about 'stuff'. Israel was becoming more American. The arrival of Toys R Us in Israel came at a time when we were already grown, and that couldn't change anything, but the Toys R Us sign will always engender a visceral response, remembering good times with them in America.

Although Saba passed away in 1998 and Savta in 2013, each left an indelible stamp on me. The same precise and analytical thinking I share with Saba Gil, from the lists I make — just like him, to reading the instruction manual of every new device cover-to-cover — reflect traits and interests that led me to study engineering (at the Technion, as expected). But parallel to this, I also carry a legacy from Savta Pearl — curiosity and a thirst for knowledge, along with the ability to relax for a moment to watch a movie, to take in an art exhibit or to read something interesting.

Last but not least, Pearl and Gil's relationship with one another was something to admire. Although it was clear to everyone that Pearl was the boss and Gil sort of went along, something in the bond between them simply worked. They appeared very much in love even after 50 years of marriage. This unique form of couplehood is something I admire and seek to emulate today in my longtime relationship with my partner Yossi — balancing the methodical exacting mind of an engineer, with a free spirit of an architect, firmly planted in the humanities who sometimes forgets to close the refrigerator door... I think that's one of the most important things, and the essence of their legacy which I hope will guide me in my life.

Yossi Shushan[36]
Grandson-in-Law
Off-the-Cuff — at Pearl's 95th Birthday 'Reunion'[37]
18 July 2011

This is an opportunity to say thank you, Pearl, for the opportunity to meet you. I heard about you from Asaf for the past seven years. I'm sorry that I didn't have the chance to meet you before but I'm glad I got to meet you now [...] My grandmother died at age 65 of cancer, and I never got to know such an old person like you. And I'm here talking with you — and you are clear, and you are clever and you have knowledge that no one can have because of your age. It's a wonderful experience for me. I never met anyone your age who can manage [sic. get along] like you. What I mean to say is 'you're one of a kind'.

Efrat Kaplan[38]
Granddaughter
April 2019

My mother has done an impressive job in what she labels 'filling the holes' in the Weiss family saga; I'm simply amazed by this incredible writing project that seeks to preserve in words the history-biography of my 'American Saba and Savta'.[39] Despite meeting them in person only a limited number of times for short periods (as much as one can 'measure' such a thing), these encounters left a stamp that I want to

---

36. Asaf's life partner.

37. Pearl made it clear, she didn't want a 'gathering of the tribe' when she died. She said she wanted a reunion of the family while she was still kicking — helping to pay for the air tickets from Israel to make it happen. Thus, most of us gathered at Wendy's in July 2011 — many sleeping on couches and even mattresses on the floor — for a week-long celebration with Pearl...which didn't prevent a *second* reunion in Washington of the Israeli and American branches of the family two and a half years later, when Pearl died. To return to 2011, we sat down to 'officially' celebrate her 95th birthday in the den over a strawberry-topped ice cream cake.

38. Pearl and Gil's Israeli granddaughter (Rafi and Daniella's daughter).

39. Grandmother and grandfather in Hebrew.

try and share here. Their seal is not biographical or historical, nor is it genetic; rather, it's the upshot of a question...an enigma I encountered as a child and teenager that I'll try now — in midlife — to put in words in the form of a question that in itself is an answer.

Since I find myself almost speechless facing the sheer breadth of this family saga project, I decided to skip the nostalgia and memories of Pearl and Gil's visits that my parents and my brothers described so well; rather, I will try to describe the way Saba Gil and Savta Pearl left their stamp on me and the eternal enigmas they envelop that affect my being and who I am. Three fundamental questions — similar to the one's Emanuel Kant asked if you wish (What can I know? What ought I do? What may I hope for?). In examining my own life, I see them as questions passed on to me by Saba and Savta.

The fundamental questions about love (analogous to the Kantian one — What can I know?): As a child and young woman, I saw their couplehood as perfect. This perception also drew on the way they were described by others — my parents, other family members and friends. One couldn't miss the love that existed between them, particularly the respect they had for one another and the manner in which they talked to one another. But on a deeper level, beyond appearances, I saw an ability of each to exist as an individual alongside the other, to have separate lives with different interests, and at the same time to share their lives and their love. The family myth holds Savta was the one who made the decisions epitomized by Saba always saying to Savta (only half in jest) "Your wish is my command". But such a perception misses what made the relationship between them so special — and it resides, I believe, in the way this couplehood of theirs, filled with differences, rested on neither of them trying to cancel or erase the other's uniqueness. Thus, Saba took special interest in the garden, the Shop, music and craftsmanship; Savta's were in the realm of art and reading. Neither tried to transform or remold the other in their own image. Each recognized the other's loves and interests and knowledge — thus allowing each to exist as a separate individual without trying to erase the differences, without seeking absolute symmetry, in essence, enabling the two of them to maintain such a harmonic relationship over so many years together.

As for the fundamental question of desires (analogous to the Kantian questions — What ought I do?): I saw from an early age how Saba Gil and Savta Pearl lived lives full of desire that never left them bored or stuck in a rut. Each of them found purpose in their work, as well as their daily routine. I watched Savta make the orange juice in the morning, perk the coffee and bake fish with the same seriousness-purposefulness with which she read books or looked at a painting in a museum. Saba was the same, in the way he took care of the garden with the same dedication and precision with which he filed his unending notations on yellow legal pads or fixed a broken appliance. Everything they did in life was done with love and dedication. I would call this 'a life lived with passion'.

The third fundamental question-the How (analogous to Kant's — What can I hope for?). It's the oldest question, the Taoist riddle of Lao Tzu: Is the path wiser than the one taking it? Both Saba Gil and Savta Pearl paved their respective paths in a way that left room for a lifelong shared path, as well. One could view their life story as simply one of social mobility but this doesn't explain the sheer sense of joy they manifested in their lives. I believe this zest emanated from the way each in their own way invented themselves along unmarked paths. From an early age, Savta was determined to pursue a degree in the humanities and become a teacher, Saba to study aeronautical engineering. Each was a path-maker on unpaved ground in their respective field. Savta Pearl designed special programs to counter school dropout, and saw herself not only as a regular teacher but also as a mentor for each of her students. I strive to carry on this social legacy at the Psychoanalytic Center I and others established in Tel Aviv for treatment of youth-at-risk. Saba Gil was ahead of his times in recognizing that choosing the best airplane design lacked the discipline of a professional practice, and he went about giving this its missing structure. Likewise he was determined to find a place as a Jew in unchartered waters within the Navy. In my various roles in public commissions in Israel on key issues of governance, I believe I follow their tradition of finding my mission in the public sector, rather than the private sector. Saba Gil and Savta Pearl each sought a unique endeavor that would enable them to live lives filled with passion and substance, rather than 'going with the flow'.

These three components together — love, desire and innovation are fundamental elements I feel they have passed on to me, and I try to embody all three in my own actions and endeavors. Thus, in my professional life — my positions in the public sector and my social volunteer projects, Saba Gil and Savta Pearl remain a constant presence as I also explore and beat a unique path through uncharted territory in my own endeavors.

Ben Bard
Grandson
At Pearl's 85th Birthday
July 2001

I present not a story nor a poem, but a list: Top 85 GrandMom-isms (purely from her grandson's perspective, of course):

1. A glass of orange juice in the morning — Whether you are thirsty or not. 2. Grandma sitting with bent leg tucked under *tush*, hand on foot, surrounded by *Washington Post*s. 3. Sitting with bent leg tucked under *tush*, hand on foot, napping on pile of *Washington Post*s. 4. At the oven, peeking inside, saying — "Ooooh...that looks gooooood"... 5. Standing at the counter slicing and layering *mandel* bread, *en masse*. 6. Packing a 'GrandMom lunch' for my road trip back to school: sandwich (w/ lettuce to keep the bread from getting soggy), small bag of veggies, piece of fruit, dessert treat, drink, napkins. 7. At the sewing machine taking up pants, letting down pants, letting out pants. 8. Kugel: one to eat now, one wrapped in foil for the trip home. 9. Sitting at the kitchen table (in *her* chair), early morning before anyone else is up, with coffee, telling stories from long ago (like the one about the trip down South when Mom was conceived). 10. A big hug when I first enter the house, her head on my chest, my chin on her head (and I must still be growing because my chin seems to be getting a little higher each year...) 11. Sending me to fetch something from the basement freezer, wrapped in foil and labeled on masking tape with a date (from the days before cordless phones were invented). 12. Knitting at the speed of light, sweaters produced before the eye, while never looking down and while easily holding a conversation with you. 13. Slicing tomatoes downward, towards her hand, the way you're never supposed to do it.

14. Telling me she found yet another cousin my age who lives nearby and giving me little slips of paper with all the necessary info to make contact. 15. Torn-out newspaper articles with my name written at the top, sent in the mail. 16. Picking a piece from the just-cooked turkey, eating it, saying 'mmmmmmm' while we all stare and drool. 17. Buying a coat on sale, seeing it advertised at a better price, driving back to the mall and returning it to the store to rebuy it at a better price. 8. A grandmother with a 500 MHZ Pentium, 20 Gb hard drive, two printers, scanners, video camera, six VCRS, five televisions, separate phone and fax lines, and a cell phone. 19. A grandmother who taught her engineer grandson how to change the fax paper when it ran out. 20. A good deal on toilet paper results in three basement shelves of 84 rolls ("well, it won't spoil"...). 21. Eyeglasses on top of her head, searching every corner of the house for her eyeglasses. 22. The ability to create a seven-course dinner, last minute...from leftovers! 23. Handing me the phone to talk to a cousin who I've never heard of. 24. "Gibby...dinner!" 25. Splitting the shopping cart into three loads so each of us can use a one-coupon-per-customer coupon. 26. More coupons than people? Leave a partial cart of unpurchased goods in the aisle, go out to the car, come back in, get in line again with the new coupon (note: wear hat and dark sunglasses second time around). 27. Getting more mileage out of half a glass of wine than we do on the rest of the bottle. 28. Bottle: b-o-t-t-l-e — pronounced "bah-ul". 29. A busier social schedule at 85 than I have at 32. 30. Using the stovetop as a perfect place to stack newspapers. 31. Me opening the plastic container in the car and eating all 52 *mandel* bread cookies on the road trip back to school. 82. (See 52 cookies, that's like 52 things... You didn't think I was going to 85?). 83. "To whom" — "To WHOOOOOO-MUH". 84. Buying a coat on sale, seeing it advertised at a better price, driving back to the mall and returning it to the store to rebuy it not only at a better price, but *with a new coupon* she found, as well! And finally.... 85. Being remembered by students she had 60 years ago, which comes as no surprise, since she has always been as much an inspiration to me as she has to anyone who gets to know her.

Rhea Goodman[40]
Cousin and 'Almost Contemporary'
December 2018

I have delightful memories of Pearl and Gil coming to Santa Fe to visit me in the mid-1980s [when Pearl and Gil were in their seventies — DA]. I had moved from New York (forever!) to Santa Fe in November 1982, and Pearl and Gil chose to visit me and Santa Fe a few years after I had settled in.

Ten Thousand Waves — a world-class outdoor hot tub and spa in Santa Fe that is now internationally known and always makes the list of the 'Five or Ten Best Spas in the World' — was new. The spa is done in the Japanese style, exquisitely and authentically, and even then, back in the mid-1980s when it began with four or five outdoor hot tubs on the mountain, going there was a very special event. So I suggested that Pearl and Gil and I take a 15-minute drive up the mountain and take a hot tub together. And to further enhance the experience, I suggested that they indulge in a "toke" of cannabis with me before we go. I remember that they were skeptical at first, but game to do it, until push came to shove, or mouth came to joint, that I seem to remember they declined.[41] Knowing my own penchant for being a rule-breaker,[42] I liked the idea

---

40. Pearl's first cousin (daughter of Nana's sister Aunt Yetta/Pearl Cantor and the youngest of the five Cantor children (born 1932). Rhea, at 87, was still hosting a unique radio talk show called "Living Juicy!" http://www.livingjuicy.org/about-rhea-goodman/ before she died in the fall of 2019 of brain cancer. Luckily I had shared the part on the Reiter's roots with her in late 2018.

41. DA: According to Wendy, years later Pearl and Gil shared the story about the joint and the jaunt to the mountains with Wendy, whose response was: "You did WHAT?!" (incredulous they would do something so out-of-character as getting into a Japanese moon-shaped hot tub stark naked with other people). As for the joint, Pearl told Wendy they had taken a few puffs but "nothing happened". (They'd compared notes: "Gil, do you feel anything?" "How about you, Pearly?"). Wendy discovered — close to two decades later — that they didn't know they had to inhale the smoke!

42. Rhea's motto: Life is short. Break the rules, forgive quickly, kiss slowly, love truly, laugh uncontrollably, and never regret anything that made you smile. Life may not be the party we hoped for, but while we are here we should

of suggesting to my sweet, straight-laced, but game cousins that we should break the law a little. I loved the idea of getting them a bit high in Santa Fe...as though 7,000 feet [2100 meters — DA] is not enough.

Phoebe Bauman
Fellow Teacher and Friend
2018

Pearl was ageless, one of the youngest people I ever knew. She was always with it, sharp as a tack, knowledgeable about current events and a source of sage advice.

While I was at Arcola Elementary, I enlisted Pearl as my 'spell-check'. I am a miserable speller and I could always count on her to look at my room boards and my correspondence to correct the inevitable spelling errors. As a relatively new teacher, and certainly new to Montgomery County, she took me under her wing. And not only at school! Al and I soon became part of the Weiss family, and they became part of ours. (Somewhere in our house is a picture of Pearl and Nana with Deborah on her first birthday...and Deborah will be 47 in August!)

Al still talks about how much he learned about gardening from Gil, who gave us so much help when we were having our house built. Most of all though, we were blessed with Pearl and Gil's unlimited practical and moral support when we were in the process of adopting David. He is now almost 52 years old, and the proud father of two gorgeous and accomplished daughters, ages 21 and 23.

Lydia Trang[43]
Mentee and 'Adopted' Family Member
January 2014

I feel very fortunate that Pearl was a big part of my life and my siblings'. Pearl and Gil provided all of us with care, guidance and love when we were newcomers and just regarded us as family members.

---

dance. [Good advice for all of us — DA.]

43. Written also on behalf of her brother Danny Trang (and her other siblings) — tracing an evolving relationship that spans 25 years and more — including some role reversals.

November 2018

My three siblings and I escaped South Vietnam by boat in November 1979 without our parents and other siblings. After staying on a refugee island in Malaysia for one year and a refugee center in the Philippines for another six months, we were finally eligible to settle in the United States in July 1980. As newcomers to America, my brother Danny and I were students at Kennedy High School in Francis Jordan's ESOL class.[44] One day we shared with our teacher that we desperately needed to earn some cash and Mrs. Jordan introduced us to Mr. and Mrs. Weiss.

Danny and I then started to work for them every other Saturday. I cleaned their house while Danny worked on their yard. Pearl Weiss taught me English and a lot about American culture during these times. She also taught me how to be strong and confident, how to be the best person I can be, and how to work hard to obtain an education in the United States. While working with Mr. Weiss, Danny learned a lot about horticulture, and woodworking because Gil had an amazing workshop in the basement. Shortly after we got to know each other, the Weisses introduced us to their friends. Before we knew it, we were busy every weekend cleaning houses and doing chores for their friends, the nicest and most caring people. They were the Abbotts, the Betters, the Neustadters, and the Warshaws. They treated us amazingly well and cared a lot about our wellbeing.

We also became part of their families — especially the Weisses who became our friends, parents, grandparents and confidants. They often regarded us as their 'adoptive children' and introduced us to their friends and family as such. Pearl and Gil had a heart of gold and were the most loving, caring and generous people we had ever met. They provided us with an abundance of guidance and resources to function well in our everyday living. Whenever we had a question, we never hesitated to ask them. Although our English was limited, they found different strategies to communicate with us. Such limitations never stood in the way. They always had the time and patience in matters

---

44. English Speakers of Other Languages. Francis Jordan had team-taught with Pearl at Northwood High School, establishing a program for potential dropouts together. See the section Pearl — the Ultimate Mentor.

that concerned us. Nothing was ever too much to ask!

As newcomers living here without our parents, we craved parental support and Gil and Pearl Weiss filled those shoes. Not only were they the nicest and kindest individuals, their children and grandchildren also accepted us and regarded us as members of their family. Whenever we saw them at the Weisses' house, they embraced us with open arms. They also understood the difficulties we were experiencing with English and adjusting to our new life in the United States.

Danny and I continued to work for the Weisses and their friends for many years. Even while I was attending college, I would help Pearl out whenever I was available. Sometimes I would just stop by for a visit so that they could catch up on my life — over tuna fish sandwiches that Pearl would make me almost every time I came to clean or visit (and a treat I always looked forward to). Later on in life, when Pearl lived at Leisure World, I'd stop by her lovely apartment to sit on her balcony to chat, to listen to Josh Groban CDs together, to cook for her, to take her out to lunch or to take her to her doctor's appointments.

My siblings and I considered ourselves the most fortunate people that we met the Weisses and their friends. Our lives would have been much more challenging if it weren't for their support and love, for which we will forever be grateful.

Edwin Mandieka
Chief Nurse on the 2-West Wing[45]
In the Sholom Home — Minnesota
January 2014

Reading your eulogy in Washington, Pearl's presence was palpable — with my eyes watery trying my best to hold back the tears from running down my cheeks despite the jeans. [...] The staff and I were honored to work with Pearl. Words can't underscore enough Pearl as a whole. She was patient, always smiling and loved humor. Her demeanor was contagious and I could only hope that when I get old, I can continue to be polite, thankful, find humor and be patient even

45. A certified nurse who mid-career chose to enroll in med school, and today is a physician doing his residency.

during distressing times, as she was.

Meir Bargeron
Volunteer at Sholom Home — Minnesota
January 2018

The first time I came to visit Pearl Weiss at Sholom Home a number of years ago I was struck by a small poster on her door that established her no-nonsense manner, tempered with just a bit of wit: "Getting Old Isn't for Sissies".[46] When I opened the door, I saw that her walls were graced with family photographs taken over nine-plus decades. And sitting in a chair by the window was Pearl herself. She invited me in, even though she had no idea who I was, or why I was coming to see her. That afternoon began a simple and beautiful friendship.

I was a "volunteer visitor" — approved by the facility to spend time with residents, who spent many more days inside than outside, and for whom one day may not have looked much different from another, were it not for enrichment programs like the one I was a part of. The coordinator who interviewed me and matched me with Pearl told me, "I think you'll really like her. She likes to talk about things".

The volunteer coordinator was right indeed. Pearl was friendly and outgoing and told me many stories about her fascinating life. During our visits in her room, or our strolls around the campus (Pearl by wheelchair and I by foot), she talked about her childhood, about her teen and young adult years, and about the family she and her husband Gil created. Pearl would often point to a photo on a wall or on a table, sometimes asking me to bring it to her, and then she would tell me a story about whoever was featured in the image. I heard about her husband, her daughters and their husbands, her grandchildren and her great-grandchildren. Pearl's command of the details of her family's history was amazing, and her love of every member of the family was boundless.

While Pearl told wonderful, heartwarming stories from her considerable history, she existed very much in the present moment. During

46. A quote from American actress of film, television and theater Bette Davis (1908-1989): "Old age ain't no place for sissies".

our visits, we had many discussions about current events, social trends and of special interest to me — Judaism and Jewish life. We discovered common interests and I learned much from our visits. Pearl had a strong intellect, abundant wisdom and a delightful wit.

As I got to know Pearl, and later her daughters and their husbands, I was treated to profound generosity. Our relationship started as the result of an "enrichment program" and I have, indeed, been enriched by knowing Pearl and her family. As the poster on her door indicated to me on my first visit, Pearl faced aging with grace, tenacity and humor. The photo gallery of memories was a testament to the love and joy of family life. Pearl's stories were the embodiment of wisdom and illustrated an amazing life of a loving and accomplished daughter, student, wife, mother, teacher, counselor and beautiful human. Pearl Weiss' life was a blessing to her family, friends, students, caregivers and everyone else she encountered. It was an amazing privilege to know her.

Norma Shpayher
Volunteer at Sholom Home — Minnesota
January 2018

Pearly became my friend the very moment I met her. Polite. Enchanting. Active. Responsive. Loving. Intelligent. Everlasting.

Estelle Fox
Volunteer at Sholom Home — Minnesota
January 2014

Pearl was a blessing every day that I knew her. She lit up my life and I'll be forever grateful for the hours we spent together at Sholom.

Patti Freeman
Volunteer at Sholom Home — Minnesota
January 2014

I got to know Pearl when I visited the Sholom Home with my dog Coco. She was one of my favorite persons to visit. Always reading a good book and so positive. She was a wonderful woman who inspired me.

Toni Robinson[47]
Niece
January 2014

Aunt Pearl was the ultimate matriarch and 'social director' for the Washington, DC family (blood and assimilated). The many wonderful hours spent enjoying her and Uncle Gil's hospitality are a treasure.

Mike Platt[48]
Nephew
November 2018

Uncle Gibby and Aunt Pearl were my alternate parents in many ways. Uncle Gil went to my various sports banquets since my Dad showed no interest in attending with me. I spent many pleasant vacations during the summers at their house in Silver Spring while in high school. And it was Uncle Gil who was at the hospital waiting with me when Sam was born, always there for me when I needed advice, and a good shoulder to cry on when I needed that (bear in mind I was all of 19 when Sam was born). The years after Sam was born included many wonderful dinners at Uncle Gil and Aunt Pearl's house for various holidays and they were more family to me, Ann, Sam and Dawn than my own family.

David Platt[49]
Nephew
January 2019

My earliest recollection of visiting Aunt Pearl and Uncle Gil was my parents and brother and me driving to visit them when they lived in Skyland in Southeast Washington. I must have been less than five years old at the time (since I know when I was born, and they moved to Silver Spring in 1955). I certainly remember spending countless hours at their house during my childhood.

I had an affinity for math and science and since my father was not well educated, I leaned on my Uncle Gil a lot when I needed help with

47. Daughter of Gil's brother Bernie and Sylvia Weiss.

48. Eldest son of Pearl's sister Ruth and Dan Platt.

49. Youngest son of Pearl's sister Ruth and Dan Platt.

those subjects...and even more so when I got to middle school and high school. I even remember him attending a 'father/son dinner' with me after I won an engineering award at the regional science fair. This ceremonial dinner came at a particularly rough time for me since my father had passed away when I was in my senior year of high school, and my mother had been hospitalized with phlebitis. But my Uncle stepped in and substituted for my father, and Aunt Pearl substituted for my mother while she was in the hospital.

They were always there to help when called on and they never expected anything in return. When I had an emergency appendectomy when I was 11 years old, I still remember how after surgery at Doctor's Hospital, as I was being wheeled out of the recovery room they were there. (I heard Aunt Pearl saying to Uncle Gil — "He won't recognize us" but when as I passed them I said — "Hello Aunt Pearl, Uncle Gil"...)

After my mother moved to Florida halfway through my freshman year of college at William & Mary,[50] my new home base became 9705 Woodland Drive, until my mother moved back to Virginia 18 months later. I remember coming up to the DC area every month or so to visit (and there was a standing invitation to stay with Funny and Jack Jaffe, if Aunt Pearl and Uncle Gil were out-of-town). The Jaffes, who were renowned for their hospitality, lived a few blocks away on Tilton Drive — affectionately dubbed by all the 'Tilton Hilton'.

In 1975 Aunt Pearl decided she had lived through the Capital Beltway construction mess for years and she was not going to live through the extension of the Washington Metro's Red Line and construction of the Forest Glen Station a mere two-tenths of a mile from their home. So the house hunt began... (1975 was a big year for real estate, since there was a federal tax credit of five percent on the purchase price of a new home — up to $2,000.) So, I bought a condo, my brother bought a townhouse and even though Aunt Pearl and Uncle Gil did not purchase a new home (so no tax credit), they did buy their home in Potomac — on Democracy Lane.

At some point Uncle Gil decided he needed to find out about "these personal computers". My Cousin Toni Robinson's tech company

50. In Williamsburg, Virginia — 240 km (150 ml) south of Washington, DC.

was selling their surplus computers that had become outdated, and Uncle Gil decided to buy one. He asked me to come help him with it as he wanted to find out about this "Internet thing" and learn to use email. However, the new 'acquisition' needed serious upgrades; with spare parts that I had from upgrading my own PC. 'Pick and choose', I replaced components in his system with better parts replaced in my own computer, purchasing a few items that I didn't have spares for — like a decent dial-up modem, and got him set-up with my own Internet provider for just $10 a month for dial-up access and an email account.

In typical fashion, my Uncle Gil became fast friends with Matt — one of the high school students handing technical support for this private Internet provider–and Matt helped Uncle Gil whenever he got stuck. But the more Uncle Gil got comfortable with what he labeled the "black magic" of the Internet, his need for support became much more infrequent. But a friendship had been cemented, and Matt would call Gil to make sure he didn't need anything if he didn't hear from him for several weeks...

When Uncle Gil passed away, I called Matt to let him know (requesting he leave the Internet service in place and I would pay the bill if Aunt Pearl or my cousins forgot to, aware that they would be relying on Internet access after the funeral). Matt made me promise to let him know when and where the funeral service would be. As we were carrying Uncle Gil's casket out of the synagogue, I saw Matt in the crowd — a person who had never met Uncle Gil face-to-face. I went over and he shook my hand, hugged me and told me, "I'm really going to miss my talks with Gil". I think Matt epitomized the feeling that almost everyone who met or spoke to Uncle Gil had: Everyone cherished their contact and time with him.

I know I did and the last time I spent with Uncle Gil — in 1998, was truly precious to me. On the morning of 5 July — a Sunday, a few days before he died — I left my house at 7:15 AM to arrive at the hospital at 8:00 AM, parked my car and went up to my uncle's room. My 'cousin' Maggie Morin[51] had arrived an hour earlier, fed him his breakfast,

51. Leo and Julie Schwartz's daughter.

shaved him and was waiting for me to arrive before she went home. Uncle Gil perked up in his bed and asked me what I was doing there. I told him it was time for "Breakfast at Wimbledon" on television... where his favorite (and my favorite) player Pete Sampras was in the final against Goran Ivanisevic. Of course, Pete Sampras won, and at the end of the match Uncle Gil told me he loved being able to talk tennis during the Wimbledon Men's Final with someone who knew the game. After the awards ceremony, Aunt Pearl and my Cousin Daniella came into the room and asked — "What are you doing here David?" I didn't have to answer. Uncle Gil announced: "We're watching the Wimbledon Final and talking tennis".

Several years later, I spent nine days in London and one of the excursions I knew I had to take was to the All England Lawn Tennis Club at Wimbledon. I remember going through the museum and found out that I could go out into the top section of the stands to see Centre Court. I knew Uncle Gil was standing beside me as I recalled our last morning together back in 1998. He was more than an uncle and he treated me like more than a nephew. We were more like father and son.

Aviva (Ann Platt) Bruyer
Sam and Dawn's Mother and Michael's First Wife
November 2018

I can remember so well many Passover celebrations held at the Weiss home in Silver Spring, with Nana making all the special dishes. On festive occasions — holidays and birthdays — Aunt Pearl *always* asked me to wash her precious crystal, because she *knew* I would be very careful.

When I first met Mike back in 1960, one of the first places he drove me to was that home in Silver Spring. So much happened and changed over those first years of Sam and Dawn's life.

Anecdotes? I can remember in particular one Sunday afternoon when the kids got into Aunt Pearl's undergarments and they were very funny showing off and parading around for all of us. I also remember when Daniella visited in the States and Asaf (a baby at the time) cried and cried, and I was able to hold him and get him to stop.

In the home in Potomac, among my fondest memories is all the beautiful landscaping that Uncle Gibby created, and his fantastic vegetable garden.

Sam Platt[52]
Great Nephew
November 2018

Aunt Pearl was such a special person. I will always be grateful for the caring that she and Uncle Gibby gave Dawn and I during some tough times. I also think back on their visit with us in Virginia Beach, and what fun we had.

Myrna Abbott Kasser[53]
Lifetime Friend of Best Friends
December 2014

I've had a love affair with Pearl since I was about three months old.

Steven Vozenilek[54]
Longtime Financial/Retirement Advisor
January 2014

When I think of Pearl, I can hear the laughter and spunkiness in her voice, and the genuine interest in me and my family. It's not something you feel from many people, especially in today's world. But by her demeanor and approach toward others and life, she was one who deservedly helped define her generation. She was one of the greatest of the Greatest Generation.

Elinore Liebersohn Koenigsfeld
Close Neighbor and Lifetime Friend

52. Mike and Ann (Aviva) Platt's son.

53. Eldest daughter of Pearl and Gil's best friends — Leah and Norman Abbott who were "as close as even closer" than relatives.

54. Who once told me that throughout his long association with Pearl as her financial advisor handling her stock portfolio, over the years he came to feel like he was a member of the family and Pearl was like a grandmother, not a client.

Comment — Response to a *Washington Jewish Week* Obituary, January 2014

It is wonderful to read this well-written, thoughtful and informative article about a woman I admired and loved. As a friend of her daughter, I was often in her home in my teen years, always made to feel so welcomed by Pearl and Gil. I often talked to Pearl about my teen problems, and she always provided warm moral support and a wider perspective: a wise and kind person.

Later in life, Pearl and Gil would often spend a few days with our family near Tel Aviv when they came to Israel, and we made several lovely trips together. This article is a comfort to me, as it gives the larger picture of the meaning of her life.

"Eli" (as only Pearl and Gil called me)

Marta Wassertzug
Hebrew Teacher and Friend
January 2018

Pearl and Gil and I go back maybe 30 years. They both came to my Hebrew class for adults to improve their language skills in preparation for their visits with Daniella and her Hebrew-speaking grandkids who still didn't know English. Thus, I learned a lot about Daniella's family, her work and so forth in the process.

Then Pearl volunteered to serve as my in-laws' first English teacher, which added a lot to our friendship from the Hebrew class. My mother-in-law took very well to English as Pearl taught her, quickly adjusting to a new language...the last language she learned, alongside the five or so other languages she had learned since infancy in Europe. But Pearl couldn't get my father-in-law to write a straight sentence... He had been a writer and a journalist in Argentina and couldn't complete a simple assignment, relying heavily on the dictionary to construct sentences — some of which were pure 'gems'...with which your mom had to put up in helping him!

Our growing friendship tightened once my husband Bernie got to see Gil's workshop. Bernie had similar interests. Upon Gil's death, Bernie tried to find an institution to take the entire workshop for a good cause — as a donation, but he was unsuccessful. Consequently, many tools ended up in *my* house, (and now my apartment) and I now have the same problem of disposing of them (!)...although one of our sons has — thankfully — taken some off my hands.

While I continued to visit Pearl in Leisure World after she moved out of the house in Potomac, when Wendy moved Pearl to Minnesota in 2007 (for me, the boondocks and beyond reach) — it was a good move for Pearl, but bad for our friendship that simply couldn't survive the long distance...except for occasional phone conversations.

Ronit Klomek Ratner[55]
Part of the 'Extended Ashkenazy Clan'
December 2018

I first met Pearl and Gil when I was in my late teens.[56] There was immediately a special click of 'chemistry' and a sense of mutual affection. The age gap between us was immaterial, because Pearl and Gil possessed a youthful spirit and it was clear that every tie with young people in Israel filled them with joy.

It was almost a matter of course that upon completing high school I went out to 'conquer' America, and Pearl and Gil's home constituted a very significant stopping point in my travels. Gil immediately mobilized himself for the task at hand, and energetically set forth to show me the wonders of Washington — the capital. With a sparkle in his eye and his own special brand of American pride, we didn't miss a single museum or one historical monument — from science to art. To this day, Washington remains in my memories as a 'gift'...as Gil and Pearl presented it to me, and there is this warm place in my heart for this special couple–so overflowing with love for others.

Miri and Josef Rosen
Longtime Friends of Pearl and Gil in Israel
from Israel Aircraft Industries

55. Ronit's mother — Rachela (née Ashkenazi) Klomek — is Rafi's first cousin from moshav Orot, situated just a few kilometers from our village, Kfar Warburg, both east of Ashdod.

56. In the mid-1970s.

January 2014

Somehow we felt that Pearl was eternal, a person without age.

Heidi Steffens[57]
Great Niece
January 2016

Gil was a delight — warm and caring and open, Pearl — also fun. I remember most walking into the Weiss house and Aunt Annie in the kitchen cooking something delicious. I've never been able to eat anyone else's *rugelach*, hers were so incredible.

Bruce Swiss[58]
Nephew
2014

Living in New York all my life I didn't have the luxury of visiting my Aunt Pearl and Uncle Gibby but they always visited us here in New York. Their patience and wisdom were there whenever we needed it, greatly admired and appreciated. I can't count how many times I had spoken with them on the phone seeking advice, and their warm support is a legacy.

Myra Hofberg Cohen
Former 3rd Grade Student
January 2014 at Legacy.com

Pearl Weiss touched my life as my 3rd grade teacher at Arcola Elementary in Silver Spring over 50 years ago. She was a special teacher who really cared about her kids and went that 'extra mile' to make sure every day was special for us. More than once she had to correct me when I would accidentally start a sentence with, "Mom"... not "Mrs. Weiss"... I'll always remember her with a smile.

Cantor Rochelle Helzner
Former 3rd Grade Student
In a *Washington Post* Obituary Talkback

57. The daughter of Dorothy (née Cantor) Steffens — Pearl's first cousin.

58. Younger son of Gil's sister Millie (née Weiss) Swiss.

As a nurturing teacher of mine at Arcola Elementary School about 50 years ago, Mrs. Weiss introduced me to Pearl Buck as well as other wonderful authors. Our paths crossed occasionally over the years and she was always interested and delighted with my successes. She is an inspiration.

Appendix A
The 'Other Schwarzers'

I was able to piece together a picture of the Other Schwarzers and trace their descendants — an objective that escaped Pearl and me back in 2003.

This 'journey' began when in early 2017 I decided — out of curiosity and all the more so in hopes of finding a photo of Pearl's father Michael — to systematically go through all the Schwarzers in scanned raw data of the 1910 and 1920 US Census (and a 1915 New York State Census), courtesy of the Mormon database.[1] Yes, we all know *why* the Mormons compiled it,[2] but it was a 'priceless' source of information in every sense, accessible to the public for free, and at times offered scanned copies that even the Ancestry.org website (that hides part of its materials behind a subscriber paywall) lacks...

On such genealogy websites, census forms that offer scanned copies of the forms filled out in longhand by census-takers record the names of the head of the household and all members and their relationship to the head of the household (wife, daughter, mother-in-law, boarder, servant, cook), each person's age or year of birth, immigration year or number of years in America, whether literate or not, in some cases — years of schooling, country of origin if foreign-born, occupation and more.

It was in this online expedition that I stumbled upon an Esriel

1. At http://familysearch.com.

2. There was a scandal that they were extracting information on deceased Jews to 'convert them after their deaths' so the poor souls wouldn't burn in hell... See one of the latest celebrity cases that took place in 2012 reported in the *Times of Israel*: Nathan Burstein, "Murdered Jewish Journalist Daniel Pearl Converted by Mormon Church", *Times of Israel*, 29 February 2012, https://www.timesofisrael.com/murdered-jewish-journalist-daniel-pearl-converted-by-mormon-church/.

Schwarzer. I stopped to take a look. There — off-screen to the right — was the column with Esriel Schwarzer's occupation, listed as 'silk jobber'. I googled 'jobber'. It's a term for a manufacturer, tradesman, or wholesaler who deals in small lots of goods or 'jobs', or acts as an agent, middleman (intermediary), or a sub-contractor, and usually does not deal directly with the principal customer. By 1925 the New York State census listed this Esriel and his son Nat as "silk merchants" — suggesting the business had expanded significantly.

What made me stop scrolling at Esriel Schwarzer in the 1920 Census? His unusual Hebrew first name. Most Jews named Schwarzer in the Ellis Island records came over with European names such as Herman, Bernard, Oscar or Edmund, or had common Jewish names such as Abraham or Josef. Not Esriel. In census data even those with familiar biblical names like Jacob or Moses often Americanized their names to Jake or Moe. (This same tendency even led my father Gil's parents Ben and Hannah Weiss to briefly adopt the names 'Benny' and 'Annie' on their marriage certificate before they went back to Ben and Hannah.) However, Esriel stuck with Esriel his entire life[3] and it stood out.

NYC's Historic Records (even online copies) authenticated Esriel's tie to 'our Schwarzers' via their shared father Jonas, as he appears in various American artifacts. There was Michael's 1918 death certificate, his son Joni's nickname "John David" and little Joni's tombstone "Yonah David". They matched Esriel's 1928 death certificate that lists his father also as "Jonas David". The ship manifest when Esriel arrived in America 1891 with his wife Dora clinched things: It stated Esriel originated in Jaroslaw. Bingo!

Esriel's mother is listed on his death certificate as Blooma Greenberg; Michael's as Pearl Waldman (and Perli Waldman in Polish archives), establishing a paper trail that certified my mother Pearl Schwarzer's father Michael (Menasche) Schwarzer, born in 1877, was indeed the product of a *second* marriage by Jonas Schwarzer. Esriel, born on 15 November 1862 — to Jonas and his former wife Blooma Greenberg — was definitely the 'lost half-brother' spoken about hazily in oral family lore.

However, because the Polish registry of births, marriages and deaths

3. His descendants at times called him 'Eli' for short.

translated into English only begins in 1877, there is no record so far of Jonas' previous marriage, nor the birth of Esriel. Nevertheless, a Jonas Schwarzer was found, who was born in 1836 and died in 1902 at the age of 66; he probably was Esriel and Michael's biological father. The parents of this Jonas were listed as Isak Nota Schwarzer and Bluma Weichholz — taking Michael and Esriel's progenitors back another generation, as well. In this exercise, I felt like I was scripting a personal revised rendition of the Book of Genesis.

New York Historical Records of births, marriages and deaths subsequently revealed Esriel's entire family tree, or at least most of it. Stage-by-stage through census data, marriage licenses and other archival documents, I was able to update descendants all the way to living kin. Surviving kin noted in online newspaper obituaries, followed by Google searches, enabled me to contact three living 'fourth generation' Schwarzer descendants by email and two by phone. Like us, no one carries on the Schwarzer name except Ed Schwarzer who in 2017 had no offspring, was in his eighties and was in frail health. Their input, together with further Internet sleuthing, shed light on these biological cousins' lives, occupations and lifestyles — reflected in vintage newspaper archives including the society page and period periodicals, alongside the census data.

Esriel and Dora had four children — two girls (Gussie and Lillian) and two boys (Nathan also recorded in census data as 'Nat' and 'Nate', and Max).

A key juncture was the discovery of digitized First World War draft cards that not only reveal how Michael 'looked' (his stature); his draft registration record substantiated that the two Schwarzer branches, despite the socioeconomic and age gap, were close prior to Michael's untimely death: 41-year-old Michael had gone down together to register for the draft with his 19-year-old nephew Nathan Irvine Schwarzer.[4]

---

4. Nat Schwarzer married Selma in 1931 and had one son — Edward Schwarzer (born *circa* 1934) who never married and, as noted, was not available to query.

Their cards bear the same date and sequel registration numbers.[5] The real surprise, however, was the identity of the nephew's employer where Nate told army officials he was a "stock clerk"—the Schwarzer's silk importing firm that had eluded us when Pearl and I first keyed in 'Schwarzer' and 'silk' back in 2003: I learned later that La Mode Textile Company at 461 4th Avenue New York had prospered up until the outbreak of the Second World War which devastated silk imports from France, according to Dale Laszig—the parallel 'family archivist' among the Other Schwarzers.[6]

Another document—the 1940 census—shows both Nathan and Max were by then working at Solomon [Textiles]. The two Schwarzer brothers were at the same plush Manhattan address (327 Central Park West). All the neighbors had live-in maids according to the 1940 country-wide federal census and the 1925 New York state census. Nathan was living at his brother Max Schwarzer's place along with their respective wives and kids: Max's four older children ages 13 to 19 (Lenore, Gene, Peggy and Babbitt) and Nat's only one-year-old child (Edward). The census was taken on 6 April 1940 a mere month before Germany invaded France; by June the Nazis had completed their conquest and all exports from France to the United States most probably were cut off.

It would appear that this half-brother of Michael's came to America with assets. Even when Esriel and Dora arrived in America from Hamburg in 1891, the ship manifest shows the couple, in their twenties, were assigned a shared cabin (2-4)—that is, they were definitely not traveling in gender-separated steerage dormitories. Moreover, the ship - the *Augusta Victoria*, was brand-new—launched in 1889 after a major refitting. It was one of the world's first "express steamers" that made the Atlantic crossing in less than seven days, with accommodations for 400 first-class passengers, 120 second-class, and only 580 steerage passengers. The ship was advertised as a "floating hotel" which served as a cruise ship on the Mediterranean in winter (in fact

5. 12 September 1918 (12 31-9-13-c and 12-31-9.14-c).

6. But in his 1942 Second World War registration, Max Henry Schwarzer—by then in his fifties— reported he was a "private broker of textiles".

the first cruise ship ever).[7] Esriel and Dora's children grew up in the lap of luxury — with a live-in maid-cook and a chauffeur among the household in census data. Male grandkids went to school in places like Yale. For the most part, like Dora, the girls didn't work once they had families, because 'they didn't have to'. The Schwarzer children, as well were well off — reflected in a 1930 census which shows not long after the 1929 stock market crash, Lillian and her first husband Benjamin Landay (who were still together) resided in Lawrence, Long Island (a plush neighborhood of bankers and wealthy merchants and so forth). They had a live-in maid and live-in nanny under the same roof to take care of the household and their two small children — an infant and a three-year-old toddler.

After the silk business became a casualty of the Second World War,[8] among the Schwarzers' business enterprises was a publishing company of miniature volumes of the works of famous authors — especially Shakespeare sets, very popular at the time.[9] The business in Amherst, Massachusetts was called Knickerbocker Leather and Novelty Co. What about the green set of miniatures Pearl and Gil had? No connection. It was published by *another* company in this lucrative publishing niche — a fad worldwide — and was *not* a gift from the 'nice cousin' Lee or Louie Schwarzer mentioned by Pearl in the tapes, as I first surmised... The

---

7. The ship's name is sometimes spelled *Augusta Victoria*, sometimes *Auguste Victoria*. Originally it was registered with an 'a'– a misspelling of the Empress' name only discovered after the ship was launched. This was rectified in 1897 (to *Auguste Victoria*) after Esriel and Dora sailed to America in 1891. But use of an 'a' is very common–for instance, the historical "Augusta Victoria Hospital in Jerusalem". For photos of the luxurious interior of the *Augusta Victoria*, see the vintage footage "S.S. Kaiserin Auguste Viktoria, Hapag, Interior, Chopin Waltz 64, No. 2", YouTube video, 4:29 minutes, https://youtu.be/qqWlvErKl1A.

8. Esriel's children may have remained in other kinds of textiles, having dealt in "cotton goods" in 1915, although already by 1920 Gussie was doing the bookkeeping and Nate was in sales in their silk business.

9. For more about miniature books, see "Antique Shakespeare 24 volume set Knickerbocker Leather Miniature Books in the original case", YouTube video, 0:54 minutes, 2015, https://www.youtube.com/watch?v=sW4suu99PEA.

family remained well-padded despite the Depression, and at one point, according to one of his descendants, Esriel even looked into buying the Grand Concourse Hotel...

Money can be a blessing,[10] however, it doesn't shield families from *tzuros*[11] and the Other Schwarzers had their share of difficulties.

For example, the marriage in 1925 of Esriel's daughter Lillian to another 'moneyed Jewish family' — from Great Britain was not a happy one: Benjamin Landay — a family that pioneered the phonograph and record business — was a womanizer, walked out of the marriage without paying a cent of support for his two children, and the Landay Brothers music chain that sold musical instruments, sheet music, gramophones and records went bankrupt in 1931[12] during the Depression. After her husband left her, Lillie lived for several years with her two small kids in the home of her older sister Gussie, until several years later she remarried a wealthy owner of a clothing factory in Richmond, Virginia. Despite being a Wharton graduate, her second husband Irving Friedman was a poor businessman himself, including starting a

10. Both Nana and her cousin Lillian were left without a breadwinner — Lillian when her husband deserted her with two small children. Nana was left with two small children when her husband died. However, Lillian had a family safety net that picked up the slack.

11. *Tzuros* — Yiddish for troubles.

12. There are hundreds of articles about Landay's in the *Music Trade Review* that can be searched on the online Arcade Museum's "Jukebox and Music History Project", https://www.arcade-museum.com/library/search-music/. See, for example, 1912, 1923 and 1925 profiles in *Music Trade Review*: "Landay Bros. Player and Music Roll Parlor", 1912, https://mtr.arcade-museum.com/MTR-1912-55-20/37/; "Good Advertising for the Small Goods Department", 1923, https://mtr.arcade-museum.com/MTR-1923-76-23/115/; "New Landay Store Opens in New York", 1925, https://mtr.arcade-museum.com/MTR-1925-80-19/33/, and "Progressive Musical Instrument Corp. Reports 300 Per Cent Business Increase", 1925, https://mtr.arcade-museum.com/MTR-1925-81-14/49/. The Landay's chain had ten stores in New York in 1925. About the February 1931 bankruptcy of the Landay's chain, see "Schedules Of Landay Bros.", *Presto Times*, February 1931, 14, https://presto.arcade-museum.com/PRESTO-1931-2255/14/. They had $574,752 in liabilities and $1.9 M in assets.

flying cargo business that only after he bought his first cargo plane, failed to attract the clientele needed to actually take off. I exchanged emails and talked briefly to Lillian's grandson Robert Landay Friedman of New York, who became Orthodox as an adult,[13] was active in pro-Israel endeavors, and his kids visit Israel often, although due to deteriorating health, he himself no longer traveled. Unfortunately, Robert knew nothing about Michael, although Friedman was able to add some details of the Other Schwarzer family's saga.

Landay store, circa 1915

Uncovering the Other Schwarzer branch of the family tree as I searched for more information about Pearl's father Michael sometimes left me breathless, and in at least one case, with a sense that this search for the Other Schwarzers had come 'too late':[14] Discovery that the grandsons of Pearl's Aunt Dora — all three sons of Esriel's daughter Gussie Schwarzer and Moe Leipzig (Jay,[15]

---

13. The Schwarzer family had been members of the plush Reform synagogue Rodef Shalom in Upper Manhattan.

14. Mitigated only by the fact that none of these online archives existed when Gil died in 1998.

15. Jay was attending Yale when the Japanese hit Pearl Harbor. After the war, he became a journalist and established a successful music agency in Los Angeles — had three children: 1. Carol Chaves (also in the creative arts) who has one son, Gilbert Chaves. 2. Mathew (also an artist, who lived off-grid in the New Mexico desert). 3. Dale Laszig (a payments industry journalist) who lives in NJ, married late in life and has stepchildren. Dale provided most of the input on the Other Schwarzers, and told me that it 'seems to be in the DNA' that there are those in each generation of the Other Schwarzers who remain single (or marry late, like herself) and never had kids. The family call it the 'Uncle Lloyd gene'.

Lloyd[16] and Stanley Leipzig[17]) were aviators. Two served as pilots and the third as an aircrewman in the Second World War. Surely Gil would have had a ball meeting them and gabbing about the aircraft they flew and aviation in general. Afterwards the three got involved in the entertainment business: Jay founded a music talent agency and was a writer and journalist who published novels and plays; Lloyd was a VP of Advertising and Publicity at United Artists and elsewhere. But the significance of the data gathered about the Other Schwarzers was often in the subtext, where my journalistic skills kicked in, filling in the blanks and at times telling a far more complex story than the Weiss family oral history tells.

Besides adding a generation to the family tree, the most important piece of information gathered from various sources is the age gap between Michael and his half-brother: Esriel became a wealthy silk merchant well before Michael or Nana arrived in America and met on the Lower East Side. Esriel was much, much older — 12 to 15 years older (born 1861 to 1864) than Michael (born 1877).[18] Because of the age gap between the two half-brothers, they were in the same generation *genealogically*, but a generation apart *chronologically* in years. The huge age gap in their births and Michael marrying relatively late widen the gap for future generations even further. Michael was only 13 or 14 when his brother left for America in 1891, and they only met again eight or

16. After the war, Lloyd Leipzig entered the entertainment business in LA and rose to the position of VP of Advertising and Publicity at United Artists and never married. See *New York Times* obituary, 1 December 2010, https://query.nytimes.com/gst/fullpage.html?res=9806E0D7143AF932A35751C1A9669D8B63.

17. Stanley was a 'serial entrepreneur' who went from the restaurant trade to selling air time, had two sons — Greg who has two children, and Rickie Leipzig who never married. See the *New York Times* obituary in previous note.

18. Esriel's date of birth varies in documents: Age 29 according to the ship manifest upon arrival in America in 1891 (born in 1862), on American census data (varying from 1861 to 1864), age on naturalization papers (born 15 November 1862), and date on his gravestone (born 6 December 1863). Michael was definitely born in 1877 according to Polish records; despite his age varying in America documents such as his marriage certificate, the most detailed document is Michael's draft registration (born 18 August 1877).

nine years later when Michael arrived in America in 1899/1900. Furthermore, Nana was much, much younger than her husband.

This is significant in trying to understand the dynamics of family relations, the break in communications and what triggered it: The sister-in-law whom Nana (just widowed with two children under the age of ten) told with blunt and wounded pride in 1918 after Michael died in the flu epidemic that 'she [Nana] didn't need her help and she'd take care of her own' was Dora Schwarzer. Her maiden name was Dora Rettich and she was born in 1866.[19] In other words, the age gap was tremendous. Nana's sister-in-law was approximately 27(!) years *older* than Nana who was born in about 1893. Moreover, besides the economic gap that left them worlds apart, the situation would have been intimidating. Here was Anna Reiter Schwarzer — from a tiny *shtetl*, without any formal education and even lacking basic reading skills at this point in her life, and here was Dora Schwarzer who was not only much older but also literate with an 8th grade education[20] and quite 'worldly' — living among the upper crust, holding lavish weddings (one held at the Astor Hotel), traveling abroad.

I suspect there was another, no less significant, gap — in personality and upbringing. I couldn't help but notice that in one census, Dora Schwarzer said she also knew German — not just Yiddish and English, suggesting she came from a German-Jewish ('*Yekke*') background. But when it turned out that Dora was born in Galicia (not in East Prussia as I expected) I thought this disproved any such conjecture on my part that she might have received a *Yekke* upbringing, but I was wrong. Against all odds, it turned out that the family of the Geshergalicia.org board member Mark Jacobson (whom I'd queried about the illegible name of Dora's birthplace on Esriel's citizenship application)...also

19. As noted elsewhere in the research, ages and so forth vary. Although census data says Dora was born in 1865, when she sailed for America with 29 year old Esriel, she is listed on the 1891 ship manuscript as age 24 (thus born in 1867). But 1866 seems most probable, for that is the year of birth, in fact her exact birthday — 21 July 1866 — engraved on Dora Schwarzer's tombstone.

20. Recorded in the 1925 New York Census that Dora could read and write, and in the 1940 census (when she was living with daughter Lillian) that she had an 8th grade education.

hailed from Stryj! He explained:

> I know a lot about Stryj, it was the town where my grandmother was born in 1902 and where she grew up before coming to America. [...] Before 1919 this was Austrian territory. School was taught in Polish and German, my grandmother spoke German fluently and was never in Germany. The Austrians required Jews to adopt fixed, hereditary surnames in the 1780s [perhaps the source of the Rettich surname which would have been spelled Riddisch in German — DA] and required they be Germanic to assimilate into the Austrian German culture.

It is probable that Dora Rettich — like my mother-in-law who was born and grew up in the town Eydtkuhnen on the German-Russian border[21] — carried to one degree or another the stamp of eight years of German schooling–not only well-schooled and highly cultured, but polite and respectful; methodic and orderly, diligent, trustworthy and punctual; straightforward to a fault while at the same time undemonstrative and somewhat distant (traits that fueled the derogative expression *Yekke potz* due to rigid expectations of the same behavior from others, a personality type capsulated in a more recent quip that 'a *Yekke* is someone who dreams in Excel'...

Thus, as a community German Jews were perhaps cultured, but

---

21. In fact, this small town where Aviva's family (Hoffman/Mannheim) lived, was one of the nine border crossings for the massive exodus (a million Russian Jewish émigrés between 1899 and 1913) headed for the port of Hamburg, where German authorities and shipping lines weeded out those who it was clear couldn't pass inspection at Ellis Island. An eye-witness wrote: "every Russian emigrant is compelled, before crossing the border of his country, to submit to a physical examination, to take a bath, and to have his baggage disinfected at one of the following inspection stations: Memel, Tilsit, Eydtkuhnen, Prostken, Posen, Ottlotschin, Interburg, and Illowo". See American consul's report: O. W. Hellmrich, "Inspection of Emigrants by the Hamburg America Line (1903): Mr. Hellmrich to Mr. Peirce", Gjenvick-Gjønvik Archives, https://www.gjenvick.com/Immigration/Inspection/.

definitely not renowned for their warmth; Nana, by contrast, was the archetype of a natural-born nurturer whose warmth and outgoingness was one of her most outstanding attributes. Objectively, *all* these factors — from the age and education gap, socioeconomic circumstances and life experiences, and differences in personality — would be an intimidating combination for Nana that would hardly induce good vibes and bonding between the two women, all the more so in Michael's absence. This lack of common ground would be amplified in terms of incompatibility if Dora was *not* an approachable and accepting 'people person' to begin with. Input from descendants of the Other Schwarzers suggests Dora's relationships with others — including her own close kin[22] lacked warmth and intimacy. Thus, it would not be out of character that the same Dora suddenly two years after her own husband Esriel dies, out of the blue asks to see her two nieces when Ruth was around 19 years old and Pearl was around ten or eleven...after which they never heard from her again, although Dora Schwarzer only died in 1941.

The data about the Other Schwarzers also explains the puzzling setting of that 'invitation to lunch' as recalled several times in the tapes by Pearl: A kid at the time, Pearl expected to 'meet her cousins' there. But the ages of Dora's four children in digitized census data show Dora Schwarzer and Esriel (the latter already deceased) were for all intents and purposes 'empty nesters' when this visit took place around 1926 or 1927 — the reason Pearl doesn't remember any children at the lunch table, only Dora and an "older relative"...and a servant serving lunch. That other person was probably Nathan Schwarzer, the youngest of Pearl's four first cousins who was still single and well into his twenties (since when the census-taker called in April 1930 he was listed as 27 years old and living under the same roof as his widowed mother). Dora didn't give Pearl a hug or squeeze her hand as they were leaving...only pressed a small bill into Pearl's hand as they departed.

---

22. Illustrated in the closing paragraph to this section regarding Dora Schwarzer's relationship with her grandchildren that strongly suggests Nana's sister-in-law was not a warm *persona* with anyone (not the kind of person who would invite her grandchildren to snuggle up to her black seal coat in the backseat of a cold car). Going out of her way to make Nana feel accepted or comfortable would not be part of her makeup.

Were there other living siblings? It is very likely not only from the number of Schwarzers without a 't' in surrounding towns in the regional Lvov registry. According to ship passenger manifests of those arriving back in New York after traveling abroad, Esriel and his wife Dora were in France in 1925, returning via Cherbourg to their 135 Madison Avenue home. One of their sons also traveled to Europe arriving back via a French port in 1931.[23] Furthermore, Nana had told Pearl that Michael stayed for a period in Paris on the way to America from Jaroslaw. No one knows the identity of these Paris relatives. Or any others.

Unfortunately, this laborious search for a picture or mention of Michael in oral or written family history among the Other Schwarzers came to naught. The only 'relevant' photos the Other Schwarzers' memoirist Dale could find and send me were studio photos of Esriel and Dora Schwarzer.[24]

Dora's grandchildren were, apparently, not close to her as we were with Nana, although Dora also lived under the same roof as her daughter Gussie for a time after she was widowed and in her declining years[25]—just as Nana had lived with Pearl and Gil. But apparently it is there that the similarity ends. According to the Other Schwarzer's family lore, Dora would cuss at the grandchildren in Yiddish when they got rambunctious playing in the house and one the boys (among the threesome who all became pilots or aircrew in Second World War), would "tell her to shut up and call her 'an old douche bag'".

23. In 1931 from Le Havre, Nathan Schwarzer and his wife Selma. This was apparently a honeymoon voyage judging from the proximity to announcement of their wedding two months earlier on the *New York Times* society page.

24. Esriel (6 December 1863–18 January 1928) and Dora (21 July 1866–20 September 1941) Schwarzer.

25. In 1940 Dora was listed as residing with her divorced daughter Lillian Landay, and her two grandchildren Beverly (13) and Edward (10) but the family archivist Dale Laszig said for many years she was living with her other daughter, Gussie and Moe Leipzig and their three boys.

Dora, who suffered from diabetes, died in 1941 at age 75—her residence listed as 393 West End Avenue in Manhattan, a block from Riverside Drive and the Hudson River (just as Pearl remembered it). She was buried in Union Field—the posh cemetery[26] of the upscale Reform synagogue Rodeph Shalom (founded 1842), alongside Esriel who died in January 1928, at 65 years of age.

Left: Dora Schwarzer, 1865–1941
Right: Esriel Schwarzer, 1862–1928

26. Union Field is a forested 63-acre enclave of NYC purchased in Queens in 1878, marked by manicured bushes, lawns and trees, studded with many ornate gravestones and huge family mausoleums, whose 'ambience' is a far cry from the unadorned rows of crowded tombstones typical of Jewish cemeteries. See: http://www.unionfieldcemetery.org/ufc_about_us.html... or just google "Union Field Cemetery" for a tour-like peek by brochure.

Appendix B
The Family Tree

Clearly, it was far too complex to enter a family tree within this book but there is an online family tree that can be accessed and viewed on the book website at www.playing detective.com.

Anyone who has additional information — dates and places of birth, marriage, death, maiden names of spouses, occupations or other missing siblings or children that can add to this family tree (or finds an error in the data) is encouraged to contact the tree manager — Wendy Weiss Ackerman — via the book website with "WWA Family Tree" in the subject line.

~

In closing, it should be noted: This tree was a collective endeavor compiled over several decades. Special thanks are due to a number of kin who made the construction of an online family tree possible.

First and foremost to Gil Weiss himself. Two decades ago, Gil struggled to compile a family tree using snail mail and long-distance telephone calls, only later accelerated by email (but when online archives were in their infancy) — a project started by his brother Bernie before him. For several years in the 1990s he gathered much of the raw material for the Ehrlich tree in schematics drawn longhand on yellow legal pads — including links to the Israeli branch of the family he gave me when I left for Israel in 1968. No less essential, throughout the audiotapes made between 1997 and 2012, Pearl traced the history of her branch of the family — the Reiter clan and the Schwarzers (also recorded by Gil in some form on yellow legal pads). In the late 1990s computer-literate kin — grandson Ben Bard and niece Toni Robinson — took over, digitizing the data Gil provided with now-antiquated genealogy software. But they had the foresight to preserve the data in pdf form that can be read today.

My sister Wendy Weiss Ackerman took this material and other sources and built the online family tree on Ancestry.com cited above — now expanded with information on lost branches of the family — including the Other Schwarzers that I compiled from online archives in the course of researching this memoir (even Esriel's descendants don't have one, though Nisana Gross of the 'Israeli Ehrlichs' has a partial family tree on another website — Myheritage.com). Lastly, a special thanks is due to Gina Ehrlich Burrell — a descendant of Gil's Uncle Izzy Ehrlich — who updated her extensive branch of the tree and painstakingly gathered data that fleshes out the lives of Ehrlich descendants living and dead.

Appendix C

Photo and Publishing Credits and Permissions

"Gil's Favorite Comic Strip" — *Sally Forth* by Greg Howard-King Features Syndicate.

"Radikhiv Marketplace" — courtesy of the Archives of the YIVO Institute for Jewish Research, New York.

"Radekhiv marketplace 1900" — courtesy of the Archives of the YIVO Institute for Jewish Research, New York.

"Market Square 1900" — photographer unknown, *circa* 1900, in the public domain.

"Radekhiv Market Square today" — courtesy of the *Encyclopedia of Ukraine*, Vol. 4, 1993, Canadian Institute of Ukrainian Studies.

"Radekhiv" (in Hebrew), courtesy of the Center for Jewish Heritage in Poland.

"*Furst Bismarck*" — vintage Hamburg-Amerika Line poster-Gjenvick-Gjønvik Archives, in the public domain.

"Unescorted children, Ellis Island Museum Exhibit", photographer Daniella Ashkenazy.

"Joni's Gravestone" — courtesy of Mt. Zion Cemetery, photographer Monica Ortiz.

"Michael's Gravestone" — courtesy of Washington Cemetery, photographer Mike Ciamaga.

"Nikolayev shipyard *circa* 1900" — photographer unknown, Wikimedia Commons.

"Downtown Nikolayev 1900" — photographer unknown, in the public domain.

"Podolia Province 1917" — map, Wikipedia Commons.

"Belz Great Synagogue *circa* 1905" — photographer unknown, Wikipedia Commons ('Sholom Rokeach').

"Belz" *circa* 1930 — courtesy of the Polish National Library.

"Downtown Jassy-Streda Lapusneanu *circa* 1900"—screenshot from documentary, *Iasi 1860-1973*, Laur Montza (Youtube.com).
"Ben Katine (R) Dave Lipton (L)" and "Dave Lipton Memorial Poster", courtesy of Eunice Lipton.
"Hunter College *circa* 1930"—photographer George G. Rockwood, courtesy of Hunter Alumni Association.
"Skyland in SE Washington 2018"—Wendy Ackerman screenshot, Google Street View.
"Landay Store, *circa* 1915"—*Talking Machine World* magazine, 1915.
"Esriel Schwarzer" and "Dora Schwarzer"—courtesy of the Other Schwarzer family archivist Dale Laszig.
All other photographs are from the Weiss family archives and photos of family Miscellaneous taken by the author.
Quotes on Jaroslaw fairs and antisemitism in Jassy from the Databases of the Museum of the Jewish People reprinted with the permission of the Museum.
Quotes from the *American Jewish Yearbook 1901–2*, reprinted with permission of the AJC Archives.
Quotes from the *Avenel Bulletin* reprinted with permission of the Woodbridge Library and Woodbridge Historical Society.
Quotes from "A Death on the Ebro" by Bill Wheeler in *The Volunteer*, March 2015/1996, reprinted with permission of the Abraham Lincoln Brigade Archives (Albavolunteer.org).
Quote from "Poisonous Antisemitism" by Eli E. Hertz, reprinted with permission of the author and *Myths and Facts*.

A special thanks to the New York City Historical Records Department staff that provided photocopies of a host of family documents requested from marriage certificates to death certificates, literally within hours and free of cost.

About the Author

Daniella (née Weiss) Ashkenazy was born and raised in the Washington, DC Metropolitan Area and immigrated to Israel more than 50 years ago (in 1968 in her early twenties). She is a well-published bilingual Israeli freelance journalist.

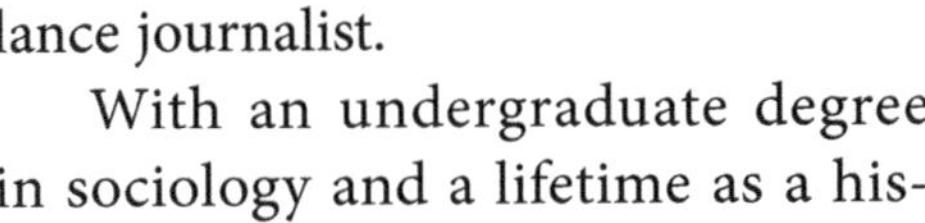

With an undergraduate degree in sociology and a lifetime as a history buff with far-ranging reading tastes, since 1985 Ashkenazy's works — commentary, political analysis, humor and satire columns and major features — have appeared in Hebrew and English in Israel's leading papers and periodicals, from the *Jerusalem Post* and *Israel Scene* to *Davar*, *HaOlam HaZeh* and *Yediot*. Her highly stylized features in Hebrew were often quoted on Israeli radio among the 'best reads' of the weekend papers.

Parallel to journalism, Ashkenazy freelances as a translator and developmental editor for Israeli academics. As a pen-for-hire, she researched and ghostwrote two books and countless white papers and op-eds for *Myths and Facts* (www.mythsandfacts.org) about the Israeli-Arab conflict. Ashkenazy also served as editor-contributor to a well-received academic volume published in 1994 by Greenwood Press about the IDF's non-military facets and the *Challenge of the Dual-Role Military*.

She lives with her husband Rafi in Kfar Warburg — a rural village south of Tel Aviv, and has three adult children and four grandchildren. More information about the author on the book website: www.playingdetective.com.

Daniella Weiss Ashkenazy can be reached at daniella@playingdetective.com.

www.ingramcontent.com/pod-product-compliance
Ingram Content Group UK Ltd.
Pitfield, Milton Keynes, MK11 3LW, UK
UKHW021711190726
13853UKWH00001B/488